# The Scholar's Guide to Arithmetic: Or, a Complete Exercise-Book

## John Bonnycastle

# BONNYCASTLE'S
# SCHOLAR'S GUIDE
## TO
# ARITHMETIC;

### OR,

## A COMPLETE EXERCISE BOOK FOR THE USE OF SCHOOLS.

## WITH NOTES,

#### CONTAINING

### THE REASON OF EVERY RULE, DEDUCED FROM THE MOST SIMPLE AND EVIDENT PRINCIPLES;

#### TOGETHER WITH

#### SOME OF THE MOST USEFUL PROPERTIES OF NUMBERS, AND SUCH OTHER PARTICULARS AS ARE CALCULATED TO ELUCIDATE THE MORE ABSTRUSE AND INTERESTING PARTS OF THE SCIENCE.

---

### EDITED BY JOHN ROWBOTHAM, F.R.A.S.

---

### Eighteenth Edition, corrected, with Additions,

#### AMONG WHICH WILL BE FOUND

#### A NEW METHOD OF VERIFYING DATES, OF FINDING EASTER SUNDAY, AND OF DETERMINING THE MOON'S AGE, BY OLD OR NEW STYLE, AD INFINITUM.

## BY SAMUEL MAYNARD,

#### EDITOR OF KEITH'S AND BONNYCASTLE'S MATHEMATICAL WORKS, ETC. ETC.

---

## LONDON:

#### LONGMAN AND CO.; HAMILTON AND CO.; SIMPKIN, MARSHALL, AND CO.; F. AND J. RIVINGTON; WHITTAKER AND CO.; B. FEL-LOWES; MOULSTON AND CO.; ORR AND CO.; C. H. LAW; HALL AND CO.; AND AYLOTT AND JONES.

### 1851.

London:
Spottiswoodes and Shaw,
New-street-Square.

# PREFACE

## TO THE FIFTH EDITION.

Books of arithmetic have, of late, become so extremely numerous, that if the progress of the science were to be estimated from that circumstance alone, it might naturally be concluded that every possible improvement had been anticipated, and the subject wholly exhausted. But it has happened in this case, as in many others, that much has been promised and little effected. The greater part of these performances are so nearly alike, both in matter and method, that they appear to be little more than mere copies of each other, ill-digested, and embarrassed with such a variety of miscellaneous observations, as render them totally unfit for the purpose of teaching.

The principal object of a work of this kind, should be to provide the learner with a proper set of rules and examples, so methodised and arranged, that they may be readily transcribed, and fixed in the memory, without any other assistance from the master than that of explaining the nature of the process, and examining the truth of the operations. These I have endeavoured to supply; and, since the first publication of this treatise, have had the satisfaction to find that it has been generally approved by intelligent tutors, and introduced into several of the most respectable academies in the kingdom.

To render the work, therefore, still more complete, the present edition has not only been corrected and improved throughout, but in many places entirely re-written.—Every example in the book has, also, been separately examined, by two or three different persons, and the greatest care taken to avoid errors of the press; so that it is presumed few or none will be now found of any material consequence. To say more would be unnecessary; the plan of the work is already sufficiently known, and of its merits or defects, the public alone must determine.

JOHN BONNYCASTLE.

*Royal Military Academy, Woolwich.*

A 2

# PREFACE

## TO

## THE EIGHTEENTH EDITION.

----

In preparing the present edition of Bonnycastle's Arithmetic, the chief object of the Editor has been to secure accuracy. In revising the former impression some errors were detected which now no longer appear. Some improvements will also be found in a few of the earlier processes, and several new notes have been added. But the principal additions of any consequence will be found from pages 250 to 262, where new methods are given of Verifying Dates, and of finding Easter according to *new* or *old style*, for any given year whatsoever without limitation, and also of finding the Moon's age (according to the mean motion) on any assigned day whatever, before or after the Christian era. The examples given illustrating the methods, will sufficiently show their use and application.

SAMUEL MAYNARD.

*No. 8. Earl's Court, Leicester Square,*
*London, August 1. 1851.*

# TABLE OF CONTENTS.

# EXPLANATION

## OF

# THE CHARACTERS USED IN ARITHMETIC, &c.

---

+ denotes *plus* or *more.* The sign of *addition,* signifying that the numbers between which it is placed are to be added together. Thus, $9 + 6$ denotes that 6 is to be added to 9. In geometrical lines, also, $AB + CD$ signifies that the line $AB$ is to be increased by the line $CD$. Also $a + b$ denotes the sum of the quantities represented by $a$ and $b$, which must be of like kind.

— denotes *minus* or *less.* The sign of *subtraction,* signifying that the latter of the two numbers between which it is placed is to be taken from the former. Thus, $5 - 3$ denotes that the 3 is to be taken from the 5 ; in geometrical lines, also, $AB - CD$, signifies that the line $CD$ is to be taken from the line $AB$. Otherwise $a - b$ denotes their difference when $b$ is the less, and $b - a$ shows their difference when $a$ is the less, $b$ and $a$ being of course quantities of a like kind.

~ denotes *difference;* and is written between two numbers or quantities to denote their difference, when it does not appear which of them is the greater ;

as $\frac{13}{17} \sim \frac{91}{103}$, or $a \sim b$, $b$ and $a$ being of course quantities of like kind.

× or · denotes *into* or *by.* The sign of *multiplication,* signifying that the numbers between which it is placed are to be multiplied together. Thus. $8 \times 6$ denotes that 8 is to be multiplied by 6. Similarly in geometrical lines, $AB \times CD$, signifies that the numbers representing the line $AB$ and $CD$ are to be multiplied together: the same is likewise expressed, $AB \cdot CD$, which also, denotes the rectangle under $AB$ and $CD$. Again $a \times b$ expresses the product of the quantity $a$ by the number $b$, or of the quantity $b$ by the number $a$, and $a \cdot b$ or $ab$ signifies the same thing. Again, $5AB$ or $5a$ denotes that the quantity $AB$ or $a$ is to be taken 5 times ; and $7(a + b)$ is 7 times $a + b$ ; and these numbers 5 or 7, showing how often the quantities are to be taken or multiplied, are called the coefficients. The sign of multiplication between the coefficient and parentheses is very often left out, it being always understood that the quantities which are included by the parentheses are to be multiplied by the coefficient.

÷ denotes *divided by.* The sign of *division,* signifying that the former of the two numbers between which it is placed is to be divided by the latter. Thus, $8 \div 4$ denotes that 8 is to be divided by 4. This is also expressed by placing the dividend above a line, and the divisor below it. Thus, $\frac{8 \ numerator}{4 \ denominator}$ denotes that 8 is to be divided by 4. In geometrical lines, also, $AB \div CD$ signifies that the line $AB$ is to be divided by the line $CD$ ; or thus, $\frac{AB}{CD}$. Otherwise $a \div b$, or $\frac{a}{b}$ shows that the quantity or number represented by $a$ is to be divided by the number which is represented by $b$. Also $\frac{a}{b}$ is the reciprocal of $\frac{b}{a}$ ; and $\frac{1}{a}$ is the reciprocal of $a$, for the reciprocal of any number is that number inverted, or unity divided by it.

*Ratio* is the mutual relation of two numbers, or of two quantities, with respect to magnitude.

It is evident that this relation can exist only between quantities of a similar kind : thus a number can only be compared with a number ; a line with a line ; &c. &c. ; for it would be absurd to compare a certain number of feet with a certain number of pounds, &c.

The ratio of two numbers or of two quantities is expressed by placing a colon between them, as $1 : 2$ ; $a : b$ ; &c., and is called the ratio of 1 to 2 ; the ratio of $a$ to $b$ ; &c. respectively.

The first of the two terms of a ratio is called the *antecedent,* the other the *consequent*

*Proportion* is the equality or similitude of two or more ratios, and is denoted by a double colon placed between the ratios: thus if $a : b$ is the same as $1 : 2$, then the proportion is denoted by $a : b :: 1 : 2$, or $1 : 2 :: a : b$, and read "as $a$ is to $b$ so is 1 to 2," or "as 1 is to 2 so is $a$ to $b$."

In a proportion consisting of two ratios or four terms, the first and fourth terms are called the *extremes*, the second and third the *means*. When the means are equal, either of them is called a mean proportional between the extremes.

Proportion is often confounded with ratio; but they are quite different things: for, as above defined, ratio is the mutual relation of two quantities of one and the same kind; but proportion consists of two or more ratios, consequently of four or more quantities; of which the quantities or terms of any one ratio may be the same or different from those of any other ratio.

= denotes *equal to*; the sign of equality, signifying that the numbers or quantities (which must be of like kind) between which it is placed are equal to each other. Thus, 2 poles + 2 poles = 4 poles = 22 yards = 1 chain = 100 links.

―― denotes a *vinculum*; and ( ) denotes *parentheses*; [ ] denotes *crotchets*; and $\{\ \}$ denotes *braces*. These signs are made use of to connect two or more quantities together, and they are synonymous with regard to their application; for,

$$\overline{(7 + 4 - 5)} \times 8 = [(7 + 4) - 5] \times 8 = (11 - 5) \times 8 = 6 \times 8 = 48,$$
is the same as
$$[(7 + 4) - 5] \times 8 = (11 - 5) \times 8 = 6 \times 8 = 48,$$
or
$$\{(7 + 4) - 5\} \times 8 = (11 - 5) \times 8 = 6 \times 8 = 48.$$

The *vinculum*, or *parentheses*, which includes the 7 and 4, serves as a chain to link them together, or to connect two or more quantities into one, and shows that they are to be added together before the number 5 is subtracted; and the *crotchets*, and also the *braces*, show that the numerals which they include must first be operated upon, and the result multiplied by the number 8.

$^2$, $^3$, $^n$ denote *indices*, or *exponents*. These expressions, placed above a number to the right, show to what power it is understood to be raised; as $10^2$, $10^3$, $a^n$, &c., which represents the square and cube of 10; and also the $n$th power of $a$; thus, $10^2 = 10 \times 10 = 100$, and $10^3 = 10 \times 10 \times 10 = 1000$; also $a^n$, meaning that $a$ is a factor as often as there are units in $n$, whatever number $n$ may be.

$\sqrt{}$, $\sqrt[3]{}$, $\sqrt[n]{}$ denotes *radical signs*. Any one of these expressions placed before a number, represents that the number is to have its respective root extracted; it is also expressed by a fractional index, or exponent, placed over, and a little to the right of, the given number. Thus the square root of 36 is expressed by $\sqrt{36}$, or $(36)^{\frac{1}{2}}$; the cube root of 64 by $\sqrt[3]{64}$, or $(64)^{\frac{1}{3}}$; and the $n$th root of $a$ by $\sqrt[n]{a}$, or $a^{\frac{1}{n}}$, &c.

$^\circ$ ' " ''' '''' denote *degrees*, *minutes*, *seconds*, *thirds*, and *fourths*, when placed above a quantity to the right; thus, 70 *degrees*, 16 *minutes*, 34 *seconds*, 49 *thirds*, 57 *fourths*, are expressed by $70^\circ$, $16'$, $34''$, $49'''$, $57''''$. Also, one of these characters is made use of sometimes to denote a *repeating decimal*, when placed above the quantity to the right; thus, the *repeater* ·819444, &c., is expressed by ·8194', and the same dash denotes a *circulate*, when placed over the first and last figure to the right; thus, ·769230769230, &c. is expressed by 7·69230'. A dot placed over the figure in circulating decimals is frequently made use of instead of the dash. Again, some of these characters are made use of for lineal measure; thus, 10 *inches*, 8 *seconds*, 7 *thirds*, 5 *fourths*, are expressed by 10', 8'', 7''', 5''''.

The Italic letters $\pounds$, $l$, $s$, $d$, $f$, $q$, are taken from the Latin words, $\pounds$ or $l$. libræ, for pounds; $s$, solidi for shillings; $d$, denarii for pence; $f$, or $q$, quadrantes, for farthings.

$\therefore$ denotes *therefore*.

$\because$ denotes *because*.

$\angle$ denotes an *angle*; as $\angle$ A signifies the angle A.

$\perp$ denotes *perpendicular to*.

$>$ between quantities of like kind denotes *greater than*, as A $>$ B, shows that A is greater than B.

$<$ between quantities of like kind denotes *less than*, as A $<$ B, shows that A is less than B.

$\infty$ denotes *infinity*, viz. that the quantity standing before it is of an unlimited value; thus $a = \infty$ signifies that $a$ is equal to infinity, or that $a$ is infinitely great.

If $a = \infty$, and $b =$ a finite quantity, then $b \div a$ is infinitely small.

# ARITHMETIC.

ARITHMETIC is the science which treats of the nature of Numbers, and of their use in various kinds of calculations.

Its leading rules are Notation, Addition, Subtraction, Multiplication, and Division; from which all the rest are derived.

## Notation, and Numeration.

NOTATION is the method of expressing numbers by words or figures; and NUMERATION is the reading or writing any proposed sum or number.

The characters used for this purpose are the ten numeral figures, or digits, 0 cipher, 1 one, 2 two, 3 three, 4 four, 5 five, 6 six, 7 seven, 8 eight, 9 nine; by which, either singly or conjointly, all numbers can be expressed.

This is done by giving to each of these figures another value, besides its simple one, which is made to depend upon the place it stands in, when joined to others, as in the following table:

| &c. &c. | Hundreds of Millions. | Tens of Millions. | Millions. | Hundreds of Thousands. | Tens of Thousands. | Thousands. | Hundreds. | Tens. | Units. |
|---|---|---|---|---|---|---|---|---|---|
| | 9 | 8 | 7 | 6 | 5 | 4 | 3 | 2 | 1 |
| | | 9 | 8 | 7 | 6 | 5 | 4 | 3 | 2 |
| | | | 9 | 8 | 7 | 6 | 5 | 4 | 3 |
| | | | | 9 | 8 | 7 | 6 | 5 | 4 |
| | | | | | 9 | 8 | 7 | 6 | 5 |
| | | | | | | 9 | 8 | 7 | 6 |
| | | | | | | | 9 | 8 | 7 |
| | | | | | | | | 9 | 8 |
| | | | | | | | | | 9 |

Where it is to be observed, that the figure in the first place, reckoning from right to left, denotes only its simple value; that in the second place, ten times its simple value; that in the third, a hundred times its simple value; and so on: the value of any figure, in each successive place, being always ten times its preceding value.

Thus, in the number 1843, the 3 in the first place signifies only three; 4 in the second place signifies four tens, or forty; 8 in the third place is eight hundred; the 1 in the fourth place, one thousand; and the whole number is read thus, one thousand eight hundred and forty-three.

The *naught*, or *cipher*, stands for nothing of itself; but when joined to the right hand of other figures, it increases their value in the same tenfold proportion: thus, 8 signifies only eight; but 80 signifies eight tens, or eighty; 800 is ten times 80, or eight hundred, &c.

To this we may also add, that for the more easily reading of large numbers, it is usual to divide them into periods of 6 figures each; the first of which will be units, tens, hundreds, and thousands; the second, millions; the third, bi-millions, or billions; the fourth, tri-millions, or trillions, &c. as below.

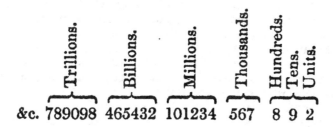

&c. 789098 465432 101234 567 8 9 2

Which number is read thus, seven hundred and eighty-nine thousand and ninety-eight trillions, four hundred and sixty-five thousand four hundred and thirty-two billions, one hundred and one thousand two hundred and thirty-four millions, five hundred and sixty-seven thousand eight hundred and ninety-two.

And by continuing the periods in a similar manner, to quadrillions, quintillions, &c. any number, however large, may be readily expressed and enumerated.

It may, likewise, be remarked, that the digits 1, 2, 3, 4, 5, 6, 7, 8, 9, having each a value of itself, are called significant figures, in order to distinguish them from the cipher, or zero, 0, which is naught, or of no value, when it stands alone.*

## EXAMPLES.

Write in figures the following numbers:—

(1.) Twenty-five.

(2.) One hundred and eighty.

(3.) Seven hundred and seventeen.

(4.) Eight hundred and sixty-seven.

(5.) Nine hundred and fifty-nine.

(6.) One thousand four hundred and thirty-three.

(7.) Fifty-four thousand six hundred and fifty.

(8.) One million, three hundred and twenty-seven thousand, five hundred and ninety-one.

(9.) Two millions, two hundred and twenty-two thousand, eight hundred and seventy-five.

(10.) Five millions, five hundred thousand, and fifteen.

(11.) Nine hundred and ninety-nine millions, seven hundred and seventy thousand, and fifty.

---

* The Romans, and other ancient nations, for want of being acquainted with the method of notation now used, which was first introduced into Europe by the Arabs about the year 1000, expressed numbers by means of the seven following capital letters of the alphabet:

Numbers I.   V.   X.   L.   C.   D.   M.

Value 1.   5.   10.   50.   100.   500.   1000.

And by repeating and combining these, any of the intermediate, or higher numbers, were denoted as follows:

Numbers II.   III.   IIII.   XX.   CC.   CCC.   MM.

Value 2.   3.   4.   20.   200.   300.   2000.

Also annexing a letter, or letters, of a lower value to one of a higher, denoted their sum:

As VI.   VIII.   XII.   XV.   XVII.   LXX.   DC.

Value 6.   8.   12.   15.   17.   70.   600.

And when a letter of a lower value was put before one of a higher, it denoted their difference:

As IV.   IX.   XIX.   XL.   XC.   CD.

4.   9.   19.   40.   90.   400.

Also, in the titles of some old books, we find IↃ put for D, or 500; and for every such Ↄ annexed, the value is increased tenfold; as IↃↃ is 5000, IↃↃↃ is 50000, &c.; CIↃ is also put for M, or 1000; and for every such C and Ↄ, the value is increased as before. Thus, CCIↃↃ is 10000, and CCCIↃↃↃ is 100000.

And if a bar be put over any number, it increases its value 1000 fold. Thus, $\overline{\text{V}}$ is 5000, $\overline{\text{X}}$ is 10000, $\overline{\text{L}}$ is 50000, and $\overline{\text{C}}$ 100000, &c.

(12.) Four hundred and seventy-nine millions, six hundred and twenty-seven thousand, and eighty-seven.

(13.) Eighteen billions, eight hundred and eighty-eight millions, eight hundred thousand, eight hundred and eighty-seven.

### Write in words the following numbers :

| | | | | | |
|---|---|---|---|---|---|
| (14.) | 27 | (20.) | 9090 | (26.) | 190851 |
| (15.) | 81 | (21.) | 10751 | (27.) | 940509 |
| (16.) | 170 | (22.) | 40848 | (28.) | 1207508 |
| (17.) | 1114 | (23.) | 85423 | (29.) | 8400018 |
| (18.) | 3064 | (24.) | 90600 | (30.) | 28043713 |
| (19.) | 9876 | (25.) | 110101 | (31.) | 111000111 |

## Simple Addition.

SIMPLE ADDITION is the method of collecting several numbers, of the same denomination, into one sum.

### RULE.*

1. Place the numbers under each other, so that units may stand under units, tens under tens, &c., and draw a line below them.

---

* This rule is founded on the known axiom that the whole is equal to the sum of all its parts. And the method of placing the numbers, and carrying for the tens, is evident from the nature of notation; for any other disposition of them would entirely alter their value : and carrying one for every ten, from an inferior line to a superior, is in consequence of a unit in the latter being equal in value to ten in the former.

It may here, also, be observed, that besides the method given in the text, there is another very ingenious one of proving addition, by casting out the nines; which is as follows:

RULE 1. Add all the figures in the uppermost row together, according to the order in which they stand; and having rejected as many nines as are contained in their sum, set down the remainder directly even with the rest of the figures.

2. Do the same with each of the other rows, and find the sum of all the remainders; then, if the excess of nines in this sum, taken as before, be equal to the excess of nines in the total sum, the work is right.

**EXAMPLE.**

| | | |
|---|---|---|
| 3782 | Excess of 9's | 2 |
| 5766 | | 6 |
| 8755 | | 7 |
| 18303 | | 6 |

This method depends upon a property of the number 9, which, excepting 3, belongs to none of the other digits; viz. that any number

2. Add up the figures in the column of units, and find how many tens are contained in their sum.

3. Set down what remains above the tens, or, if nothing remains, a cipher, and carry as many units, or ones, to the next column as there were tens.

4. Add up the second column, together with the number carried, in the same manner as the first; and proceed thus till the whole is finished.

### METHOD OF PROOF.

Draw a line below the uppermost row; and add all the rest together, setting their sum under the number to be proved.

Then add this last found number and the uppermost line together; and if the sum be the same as that found by the first addition, the work is right.

Or the same may be done otherwise, by beginning at the upper line and adding the numbers downwards; in the same manner as they were before added upwards; in which case, if the two sums agree, it may be presumed that the work is right.

---

divided by 9 will leave the same remainder as the sum of its figures, or digits, divided by 9; which may be shown thus:

Let there be any number, as 3467; which, being separated into its several parts, becomes $3000 + 400 + 60 + 7$; then if each of these parts be taken singly, we shall have $3000 = 3 \times 1000 = 3 \times (999 + 1) = 3 \times 999 + 3$; $400 = 4 \times 99 + 4$; and $60 = 6 \times 9 + 6$. Whence $3467 = 3 \times 999 + 4 \times 99 + 6 \times 9 + 3 + 4 + 6 + 7$; and, consequently, $3467 \div 9 = (3 \times 999 + 4 \times 99 + 6 \times 9 + 3 + 4 + 6 + 7) \div 9$. But $3 \times 999 + 4 \times 99 + 6 \times 9$ is evidently divisible by 9; therefore, if 3467 be divided by 9, it will leave the same remainder as $3 + 4 + 6 + 7$ divided by 9; and a similar mode of proceeding will hold for any other number; and generally let $a, b, c,$ &c. be the digits of any number beginning with units' place: then $N = a + b.10 + c.10^2 + $ &c.; $= a + b + b.9 + c + c.99 + $ &c.;

$$\therefore \frac{N}{9} = \frac{a+b+c}{9} + b + c.11;$$

$$\therefore \frac{N}{9} \text{ and } \frac{a+b+c}{9} \text{ have the same remainder.}$$

In the same manner this property may also be shown to belong to the number 3; but the preference is usually given to 9, on account of its being more convenient in practice.

Hence, from the demonstration here given, the reason of the rule itself is evident; for the excess of nines in two or more numbers being taken separately, and the excess of nines also taken out of the sum of the former excesses, it is plain that this last excess must be equal to the excess of nines contained in the total sum of all these numbers; the parts being equal to the whole.

## EXAMPLES.

| (1.) | 23456 | (2.) | 22345 | (3.) | 34578 |
|---|---|---|---|---|---|
| | 78901 | | 67890 | | 3750 |
| | 23456 | | 8752 | | 87 |
| | 78901 | | 340 | | 328 |
| | 23456 | | 350 | | 17 |
| | 78901 | | 78 | | 327 |
| | 307071 *Sum.* | | 99755 *Sum.* | | 39087 *Sum.* |
| | 283615 | | 77410 | | 4509 |
| | 307071 *Proof.* | | 99755 *Proof.* | | 39087 *Proof.* |

(4.) Add 8635, 2194, 7421, 5063, 2196, and 1245 together. *Ans.* 26754.

(5.) Add 24603, 298765, 47321, 58653, 64218, 5376, 9821, and 340 together. *Ans.* 509097.

(6.) Add 562163, 21964, 56321, 18536, 4340, 279, and 83 together. *Ans.* 663686.

(7.) Add 97684, 30768, 5015, 307, 36, and 15 together. *Ans.* 133825.

(8.) What is the sum of thirty-seven thousand and six, four hundred and twenty-nine thousand and nine, and two millions and thirty-six? *Ans.* 2466051.

(9.) How many shillings are there in a crown, a guinea, a moidore (or twenty-seven shilling piece), and six-and-thirty shillings? *Ans.* 89 *shillings.*

(10.) How many days are there in the first nine calendar months, when it is leap-year? *Ans.* 274 *days.*

(11.) How many days are there from the 19th day of April 1851 to the 28th day of November 1852, both days exclusive? *Ans.* 588 *days.*

(12.) Add together 2745678; twice forty thousand millions, four hundred and sixty-seven thousand and six; 3 times 47934576879; 87496; two thousand four hundred and seven; twice fifty thousand seven hundred and nine; and 4 times 4976378917. *Ans.* 243713117316.

(13.) To 3 times 427642874328, add 4 times ninety-six billions, four hundred and eighty-four thousand millions, seven hundred and ninety-six thousand, two hundred and fourteen; and 7428397862847428. *Ans.* 7815616794655268.

(14.) Add 4 times 718832864284 to twice sixteen billions, nine hundred and twenty-seven thousand millions, four thousand eight hundred and sixteen; and twice 47429865123, and 4923649328.　　　　　　　　*Ans.* 34241114846342.

(15.) A person born in 1852; at what year will he be 48 years of age?　　　　　　　　*Ans. In the year* 1900.

## Simple Subtraction.

SIMPLE SUBTRACTION is the method of finding the difference of any two numbers, of the same denomination, by taking the less from the greater.

### RULE.*

1. Place the less number under the greater, so that units may stand under units, tens under tens, &c., and draw a line below them.

2. Begin at the right-hand, and take each figure in the lower line, when it can be done, from that above it, and set down the remainder.

3. But if any of those figures be greater than those above them, add ten to the upper one, and then take the lower figure from it; observing, in this case, to carry one for the ten that was borrowed to the next lower figure; with which proceed as before; and so on till the whole is finished.

---

* 1. When all the figures of the least number, in this rule, are less than their corresponding figures in the greater, the difference of the figures, in the several like places, must, altogether, make the true difference sought; for, as the sum of the parts is equal to the whole, so, likewise, must the sum of the differences of all the similar parts be equal to the difference of the whole.

2. When any figure of the greater number is less than its corresponding figure in the least, the ten, which is added by the rule, is the value of a unit in the next higher place, by the nature of notation; and as the one which is added to the next figure of the less number diminishes the value of the greater accordingly, this is only taking from one place and adding as much to another, by which the total is not changed. So that, by this means, the larger number is resolved into such parts as are each greater than, or equal to, the similar parts of the less; and consequently the difference of the corresponding figures, taken together, will make up the difference of the whole, as before.

The truth of the method of proof is evident; for the difference of two numbers added to the less is manifestly equal to the greater.

### METHOD OF PROOF.

Add the remainder to the less number; and if the sum be equal to the greater, the work is right.

### EXAMPLES.

| (1.) | (2.) | (3.) |
|---|---|---|
| From 3287625 | From 5327467 | From 1234567 |
| Take 2343756 | Take 1008438 | Take  345678 |
| *Rem.*  943869 | *Rem.* 4319029 | *Rem.*  888889 |
| *Proof* 3287625 | *Proof* 5327467 | *Proof* 1234567 |

| (4.) | (5.) | (6.) |
|---|---|---|
| From 1472742 | From 4007632 | From 9069041 |
| Take 1251620 | Take  909876 | Take 1099876 |
| *Rem.*  221122 | *Rem.* 3097756 | *Rem.* 7969165 |
| *Proof* 1472742 | *Proof* 4007632 | *Proof* 9069041 |

(7.) From 2637804 take 2376982.        *Ans.* 260822.

(8.) From 3762162 take 826541.        *Ans.* 2935621.

(9.) From 8821360 take 378218.        *Ans.* 8443142.

(10.) What is the difference between thirteen thousand and thirteen, and eleven hundred and nine?        *Ans.* 11904.

(11.) What is the difference between two millions seven thousand and eighteen, and one hundred and five thousand and seventeen?        *Ans.* 1902001.

(12.) The Indian method of notation was first known in England about the year A.D. 1150; how long is it since to the year 1852?        *Ans.* 702 *years.*

(13.) Sir Isaac Newton was born in the year 1642, and died in 1727: how old was he at the time of his decease?        *Ans.* 85 *years.*

(14.) Homer, according to the Arundelian marbles, was born 2759 years ago (*viz.* 2759 years before 1852): how many years was that before the birth of Christ?        *Ans.* 907 *years.*

(15.) Christ was born about the year of the world 4000; the flood happened in the year A.M. 1656: how many years was the flood before Christ?        *Ans.* 2344 *years.*

(16.) The mariner's compass was invented in A.D. 1302,

printing in 1440; and America was discovered in 1492 : how many years were there between each of these discoveries ?

*Ans.* 138, 190, and 52 *years.*

(17.) A. was born when B. was 21 years of age : how old will A. be when B. is 47 ; and what will be the age of B. when A. is 60 ?     *Ans.* A. 26, and B. 81 *years.*

(18.) Gunpowder was invented in A.D. 1334, and the Reformation commenced in 1370 : how many years were there between, and how many are there since, each of these events, this being 1852 ?

*Ans.* 36 *yrs. between*, and 518 and 482 *since.*

(19.) The distance from London to Edinburgh, by the way of Newcastle, is 393 miles, and from London to Newcastle 272 miles : how many miles are there between Newcastle and Edinburgh ?     *Ans.* 121 *miles.*

(20.) * The knowledge of printing was introduced into England by William Caxton (who resided near Westminster Abbey) in A.D. 1474: how many years is it since ?

(21.) From 10000079000651741000530 7 take
    5788909807500007305.

(22.) From 72340005996867140087145 6 take
    3009788876793009 99537.

(23.) From 80100010891199900056 0724 take
    207912989900560769.

(24.) A gentleman has two sons, the age of the elder added to his, make 126 years, and the age of the younger son is equal to the difference between the age of the father and the elder son. Now, if the father be 80 years of age, how old are each of his sons ?     *Ans.* 46 *years* and 34 *years.*

## Simple Multiplication.

SIMPLE MULTIPLICATION is the method of finding what any given number of one denomination will amount to when repeated a certain number of times.

The number to be multiplied is called the Multiplicand.

The number you multiply by is called the Multiplier.

---

* In this and the three following examples, the learner will be able to see if his answer is correct. Thus, add the result obtained to the *lower* or substractive number; the sum, if correct, will be the *upper* number.

And the number found, after the work is finished, is called the Product.

Both the multiplier and multiplicand are, also, in general, called Terms, or Factors.

### Multiplication, Pence, and Shilling Table

| d. s. d. | l. s. d. | l. s. d. | l. s. d. | l. s. d. | l. s. d. | l. s. d. | l. s. d. | l. s. d. | l. s. d. | l. s. d. | l. s. d. |
|---|---|---|---|---|---|---|---|---|---|---|---|
| Pence 0.0.2 | 0.0.3 | 0.0.4 | 0.0.5 | 0.0.6 | 0.0.7 | 0.0.8 | 0.0.9 | 0.0.10 | 0.0.11 | 0.1.0 | |
| **1** | **2** | **3** | **4** | **5** | **6** | **7** | **8** | **9** | **10** | **11** | **12** |
| Shills. 0.2.0 | 0.3.0 | 0.4.0 | 0.5.0 | 0.6.0 | 0.7.0 | 0.8.0 | 0.9.0 | 0.10.0 | 0.11.0 | 0.12.0 | |
| 0.0.2 | 0.0.4 | 0.0.6 | 0.0.8 | 0.0.10 | 0.1.0 | 0.1.2 | 0.1.4 | 0.1.6 | 0.1.8 | 0.1.10 | 0.2.0 |
| **2** | **4** | **6** | **8** | **10** | **12** | **14** | **16** | **18** | **20** | **22** | **24** |
| 0.2.0 | 0.4.0 | 0.6.0 | 0.8.0 | 0.10.0 | 0.12.0 | 0.14.0 | 0.16.0 | 0.18.0 | 1.0.0 | 1.2.0 | 1.4.0 |
| 0.0.3 | 0.0.6 | 0.0.9 | 0.1.0 | 0.1.3 | 0.1.6 | 0.1.9 | 0.2.0 | 0.2.3 | 0.2.6 | 0.2.9 | 0.3.0 |
| **3** | **6** | **9** | **12** | **15** | **18** | **21** | **24** | **27** | **30** | **33** | **36** |
| 0.3.0 | 0.6.0 | 0.9.0 | 0.12.0 | 0.15.0 | 0.18.0 | 1.1.0 | 1.4.0 | 1.7.0 | 1.10.0 | 1.13.0 | 1.16.0 |
| 0.0.4 | 0.0.8 | 0.1.0 | 0.1.4 | 0.1.8 | 0.2.0 | 0.2.4 | 0.2.8 | 0.3.0 | 0.3.4 | 0.3.8 | 0.4.0 |
| **4** | **8** | **12** | **16** | **20** | **24** | **28** | **32** | **36** | **40** | **44** | **48** |
| 0.4.0 | 0.8.0 | 0.12.0 | 0.16.0 | 1.0.0 | 1.4.0 | 1.8.0 | 1.12.0 | 1.16.0 | 2.0.0 | 2.4.0 | 2.8.0 |
| 0.0.5 | 0.0.10 | 0.1.3 | 0.1.8 | 0.2.1 | 0.2.6 | 0.2.11 | 0.3.4 | 0.3.9 | 0.4.2 | 0.4.7 | 0.5.0 |
| **5** | **10** | **15** | **20** | **25** | **30** | **35** | **40** | **45** | **50** | **55** | **60** |
| 0.5.0 | 0.10.0 | 0.15.0 | 1.0.0 | 1.5.0 | 1.10.0 | 1.15.0 | 2.0.0 | 2.5.0 | 2.10.0 | 2.15.0 | 3.0.0 |
| 0.0.6 | 0.1.0 | 0.1.6 | 0.2.0 | 0.2.6 | 0.3.0 | 0.3.6 | 0.4.0 | 0.4.6 | 0.5.0 | 0.5.6 | 0.6.0 |
| **6** | **12** | **18** | **24** | **30** | **36** | **42** | **48** | **54** | **60** | **66** | **72** |
| 0.6.0 | 0.12.0 | 0.18.0 | 1.4.0 | 1.10.0 | 1.16.0 | 2.2.0 | 2.8.0 | 2.14.0 | 3.0.0 | 3.6.0 | 3.12.0 |
| 0.0.7 | 0.1.2 | 0.1.9 | 0.2.4 | 0.2.11 | 0.3.6 | 0.4.1 | 0.4.8 | 0.5.3 | 0.5.10 | 0.6.5 | 0.7.0 |
| **7** | **14** | **21** | **28** | **35** | **42** | **49** | **56** | **63** | **70** | **77** | **84** |
| 0.7.0 | 0.14.0 | 1.1.0 | 1.8.0 | 1.15.0 | 2.2.0 | 2.9.0 | 2.16.0 | 3.3.0 | 3.10.0 | 3.17.0 | 4.4.0 |
| 0.0.8 | 0.1.4 | 0.2.0 | 0.2.8 | 0.3.4 | 0.4.0 | 0.4.8 | 0.5.4 | 0.6.0 | 0.6.8 | 0.7.4 | 0.8.0 |
| **8** | **16** | **24** | **32** | **40** | **48** | **56** | **64** | **72** | **80** | **88** | **96** |
| 0.8.0 | 0.16.0 | 1.4.0 | 1.12.0 | 2.0.0 | 2.8.0 | 2.16.0 | 3.4.0 | 3.12.0 | 4.0.0 | 4.8.0 | 4.16.0 |
| 0.0.9 | 0.1.6 | 0.2.3 | 0.3.0 | 0.3.9 | 0.4.6 | 0.5.3 | 0.6.0 | 0.6.9 | 0.7.6 | 0.8.3 | 0.9.0 |
| **9** | **18** | **27** | **36** | **45** | **54** | **63** | **72** | **81** | **90** | **99** | **108** |
| 0.9.0 | 0.18.0 | 1.7.0 | 1.16.0 | 2.5.0 | 2.14.0 | 3.3.0 | 3.12.0 | 4.1.0 | 4.10.0 | 4.19.0 | 5.8.0 |
| 0.0.10 | 0.1.8 | 0.2.6 | 0.3.4 | 0.4.2 | 0.5.0 | 0.5.10 | 0.6.8 | 0.7.6 | 0.8.4 | 0.9.2 | 0.10.0 |
| **10** | **20** | **30** | **40** | **50** | **60** | **70** | **80** | **90** | **100** | **110** | **120** |
| 0.10.0 | 1.0.0 | 1.10.0 | 2.0.0 | 2.10.0 | 3.0.0 | 3.10.0 | 4.0.0 | 4.10.0 | 5.0.0 | 5.10.0 | 6.0.0 |
| 0.0.11 | 0.1.10 | 0.2.9 | 0.3.8 | 0.4.7 | 0.5.6 | 0.6.5 | 0.7.4 | 0.8.3 | 0.9.2 | 0.10.1 | 0.11.0 |
| **11** | **22** | **33** | **44** | **55** | **66** | **77** | **88** | **99** | **110** | **121** | **132** |
| 0.11.0 | 1.2.0 | 1.13.0 | 2.4.0 | 2.15.0 | 3.6.0 | 3.17.0 | 4.8.0 | 4.19.0 | 5.10.0 | 6.1.0 | 6.12.0 |
| 0.1.0 | 0.2.0 | 0.3.0 | 0.4.0 | 0.5.0 | 0.6.0 | 0.7.0 | 0.8.0 | 0.9.0 | 0.10.0 | 0.11.0 | 0.12.0 |
| **12** | **24** | **36** | **48** | **60** | **72** | **84** | **96** | **108** | **120** | **132** | **144** |
| 0.12.0 | 1.4.0 | 1.16.0 | 2.8.0 | 3.0.0 | 3.12.0 | 4.4.0 | 4.16.0 | 5.8.0 | 6.0.0 | 6.12.0 | 7.4.0 |

### RULE.*

1. Place the multiplier under the multiplicand, so that units may stand under units, tens under tens, &c., and draw a line below them.

---

* 1. When the multiplier, in this rule, is a single digit, it is plain that the product will be rightly determined by the method here given; for by multiplying every figure or part of the multiplicand by this digit,

2. Begin at the right hand, and multiply every figure in the multiplicand by the unit's figure in the multiplier, setting down the whole of such products as are less than ten directly under the figures that are multiplied.

3. But for those that surpass ten, or a number of tens, write down the excess only; or, if there be no excess, a cipher, and carry a unit for every ten that was borrowed to the product of the next two figures.

4. Proceed in the same manner with each of the other figures of the multiplier, observing to place the first figure of every line immediately under the figure multiplied by.

---

we in effect multiply the whole; and writing down the products which are less than ten, or the excess of tens, in the place of the figures multiplied, and carrying the number of tens to the product of the next place, is only collecting the similar parts of the respective products properly together, according to their values; whence the result so obtained must be evidently equal to the whole required product.

2. If the multiplier be a number consisting of more than one digit; after having found the product of the multiplicand by the first figure of the multiplier, as above, we suppose the multiplier to be divided into parts, and find, after the same manner, the product of the multiplicand by the second figure of the multiplier; but as the figure we are now multiplying by stands in the place of tens, the product will be ten times its simple value; and therefore the first figure of this product must be put in the place of tens, or, which is the same thing, directly under the figure we are multiplying by. And by proceeding in this manner, separately, with all the figures of the multiplier, it is evident that we shall multiply all the parts of the multiplicand by all the parts of the multiplier, or the whole of the multiplicand by the whole of the multiplier; whence these several products, being added together, will give the whole required product.

To this, the following examples are subjoined, in order to render the reason of the rule, and the method of proof above given, as obvious as possible.

| (1.) | | | | (2.) | | |
|---|---|---|---|---|---|---|
| 7565 Multiplicand | | | | 1375435 Multiplicand | | |
| 5 Multiplier | | | | 4567 Multiplier | | |
| 25 | = | 5 | × 5 | 9628045 | = | 7 times the multd. |
| 300 | = | 60 | × 5 | 8252610 | = | 60 times ditto. |
| 2500 | = | 500 | × 5 | 6877175 | = | 500 times ditto. |
| 35000 | = | 7000 | × 5 | 5501740 | = | 4000 times ditto. |
| 37825 | = | 7565 | × 5 | 6281611645 | = | 4567 times ditto. |

It may here, also, be observed, that besides the method of proving the

5. Then add all the lines of products together, according to the order in which they stand, and their sum will be the answer or whole product required.

NOTE. *When the multiplier does not exceed twelve, the product can be written down as it arises, at one operation.*

### EXAMPLES.

(1.) Mult.     375982        (2.) Mult.     789243
by          7              by         12

Product 2631874         Product 9470916

truth of the operation, as before given, there is another very convenient and easy one, by means of that peculiar property of the number 9, mentioned in Addition; which is performed thus:

RULE. Cast the nines out of each of the factors, as in Addition, and multiply the two remainders together; then, if the excess of nines in their product be equal to the excess of nines in the total product, the work is right.

### EXAMPLE.

4215 - - 3 = excess of 9's in multiplicand
878 - - 5 = ditto in the multiplier

            33720
            · 29505
            33720

3700770 - - 6 = ditto in the product:

which is equal to the excess of 9's in 3 × 5, or 15, which is 6.

*Demon. of the Rule.*—Let $9n + r$ and $9n' + r'$ be the two factors to be multiplied; then will their product, or $(9n + r) \times (9n' + r')$, be equal to $9^2 nn' + 9n'r + 9n'r + rr'$; and since the first three terms of this are, each, an exact number of 9's, it is evident that the excess of 9's in the fourth term $rr'$, will be the same as the excess of 9's in the whole product; but $r$ and $r'$ are the excess of 9's in the factors themselves, and $rr'$ is their product; whence the truth of the rule is obvious.

This method of proof, which is usually ascribed to DR. WALLIS, is of a much earlier date, being given by LUCAS DE BURGO, in his work entitled *Summa de Arithmetica*, &c. printed in folio at Venice, 1494; and though it is, in many respects, a very convenient rule, there are circumstances in which it may fail. Thus, if two or more figures should be transposed in the work, or the value of one figure be too great, and that of another as much too little, or if a 9 be set down instead of a 0, or the contrary, the excess of nines in these cases will evidently be the same as if the work was right.

## METHOD OF PROOF.

Make the former multiplicand the multiplier, and the multiplier the multiplicand; and if the product found from this operation be the same as before, the work is right.

### EXAMPLE WITH THE METHOD OF PROOF.

| Mult. | 2984 | | Mult. | 1342 |
|---|---|---|---|---|
| by | 1342 | | by | 2984 |
| | 5968 | | | 5368 |
| | 11936 | | | 10736 |
| | 8952 | | | 12078 |
| | 2984 | | | 2684 |
| | 4004528 *Prod. or Ans.* | | | 4004528 *Proof.* |

### CASE I.

### EXAMPLES FOR PRACTICE.

(3.) Multiply 24031042 by 2.

(4.) Multiply 51420034 by 2.

(5.) Multiply 32745675 by 2.

(6.) Multiply 374328756 by 3.

(7.) Multiply 5806342748 by 4.

(8.) Multiply 8435674567 by 5.

(9.) Multiply 2745675464 by 6.

(10.) Multiply 54328432847 by 8.

(11.) Multiply 8643597307 by 9.

(12.) Multiply 796534289 by 11.

(13.) Multiply 900909099 by 12.  *Ans.* 10810909188.

(14.) Multiply 732468756 by 15.  *Ans.* 10987031340.

(15.) Multiply 947137610 by 18.  *Ans.* 17048476980.

(16.) Multiply 273580961 by 23.  *Ans.* 6292362103.

(17.) Multiply 27501976 by 271.  *Ans.* 7453035496.

(18.) Multiply 82164973 by 3027.  *Ans.* 248713373271.

(19.) Multiply 62473864 by 27356.  *Ans.* 1709035023584.

(20.) Multiply thirty-three millions three hundred thousand and sixteen, by one hundred and twenty thousand and four.  *Ans.* 3996135120064.

### CASE II.

*When there are ciphers at the right of either or both factors.*

### RULE.

Multiply the other figures only, and place as many ciphers to the right of the product as are in both the factors.

And if, instead of being at the end, they are in any part of the multiplier, neglect them as before, observing to place the first figure of every product exactly under the figure you are multiplying by.

### EXAMPLES.

(1.) Mult.  426000
     by    22000

        852
        852

*Prod.* 9372000000

(2.) Mult.  8057069
     by    70050

   40285345
   56399483

*Prod.* 564397683450

(3.) Multiply 461200 by 72000.   *Ans.* 33206400000.

(4.) Multiply 815036000 by 70300.
                   *Ans.* 57297030800000.

(5.) Multiply 100000319 by 307000.
                   *Ans.* 30700097933000.

(6.) Multiply 37450080000 by 200804000.
                   *Ans.* 7520125864320000000.

(7.) Multiply 507040500 by 4734050.
                   *Ans.* 2400355079025000.

(8.) Multiply 27156084900000 by 90060573000.
          *Ans.* 2445692566530647700000000.

### CASE III.

*When the multiplier is the product of two or more numbers, each of which does not exceed 12.*

### RULE.*

Multiply the first by one of these numbers, and then the product thus arising by the other, and so on for the rest; and the result will be the answer required.

---

* The reason of this method is obvious; for any number multiplied by the component parts of another, must give the same product as if it were multiplied by that number at once.

Thus in Example the First, on next page, 5 times the given number multiplied by 5, make 25 times that number, as plainly as 5 times 5 make 25.

### EXAMPLES.

(1.) Multiply 123456789 by 25, or 5 times 5, which are equal to 25.

$$123456789$$
$$5 \times 5 = 25$$

$$617283945$$
$$5$$

3086419725 *the Product.*

(2.) Multiply 785432 by 36.     *Ans.* 28275552.
(3.) Multiply 472849 by 45.     *Ans.* 21278205.
(4.) Multiply 364111 by 56.     *Ans.* 20390216.
(5.) Multiply 4612319 by 72.     *Ans.* 332086968.
(6.) Multiply 7128368 by 96.     *Ans.* 684323328.
(7.) Multiply 9248374 by 108.     *Ans.* 998824392.
(8.) Multiply 8749056 by 120.     *Ans.* 1049886720.
(9.) Multiply 61835720 by 132.     *Ans.* 8162315040.
(10.) Multiply 123456789 by 1440.     *Ans.* 177777776160.

*Exercising the preceding Cases.*

(1.) Multiply 90929092909091 by 12.    *Ans.* 1091149114909092.
(2.) Multiply 758257742417 by 144.    *Ans.* 109189114908048.
(3.) Multiply 706540040670 by 13200.    *Ans.* 9326328536844000.
(4.) Multiply 560004759670 by 500400. *Ans.* 280226381738868000.
(5.) Multiply 600197560000 by 5079000.
          *Ans.* 3048403407240000000.
(6.) Multiply 67432586743285 by 4230564.
          *Ans.* 285277873903018762740.
(7.) Multiply 73258674325867 by 8674325.
          *Ans.* 635469550171726264775.
(8.) Multiply 30758006732586 by 60032580.
          *Ans.* 1846482499814507651880.
(9.) Multiply 67498708600325 by 7432567.
          *Ans.* 501688674085391784275.
(10.) Multiply 86432586743258 by 234567890.
          *Ans.* 20274309499608000785620

*Note* 1.*   *To multiply a whole number by a whole number and a fraction.* — Multiply first by the whole number ; then, for the fractional part, multiply by the numerator, and divide by the denominator : add this result to the first product, and the sum will be the whole product.

---

* The examples from 1 to 22, belonging to the following two notes, may be omitted until the young student is acquainted with *Case I.* Simple Division (*page 22.*).

(1.) Multiply 340235 by $23\frac{2}{3}$.

$$
\begin{array}{rl}
340235 & \\
23\frac{2}{3} & \\
\hline
1020705 & = \textit{product by } 3. \\
680470\phantom{0} & = \textit{product by } 20. \\
226823\frac{1}{3} & = \textit{product by } \frac{2}{3}. \\
\hline
8052228\frac{1}{3} & = \textit{Ans.}
\end{array}
$$

(2.) Multiply $467324\frac{2}{5}$ by 37.

$$
\begin{array}{rl}
467324\frac{2}{5} & \\
37 & \\
\hline
3271268 & = \textit{product by } 7. \\
1401972\phantom{0} & = \textit{product by } 30. \\
14\frac{4}{5} & = \textit{product of } 37 \textit{ by } \frac{2}{5}. \\
\hline
17291002\frac{4}{5} & = \textit{Ans.}
\end{array}
$$

(3.) Multiply 68746078 by $73\frac{5}{9}$. *Ans.* $5056655959\frac{5}{9}$.
(4.) Multiply 42004764 by $4\frac{1}{4}$. *Ans.* 178520247.
(5.) Multiply 64368943 by $731\frac{5}{11}$. *Ans.* $47082955943\frac{5}{11}$.
(6.) Multiply $76843978\frac{7}{8}$ by 243. *Ans.* $18673086866\frac{5}{8}$.
(7.) Multiply $34276842\frac{1}{2}$ by 432. *Ans.* 14807595960.
(8.) Multiply $46876389\frac{11}{12}$ by 325. *Ans.* $15234826722\frac{11}{12}$.

*Note* 2. *To multiply two numbers together when both contain fractions.*— Multiply the integral part of each by the denominator of its fraction, add in the numerator, then multiply these two sums together, and divide the product by the product of the denominators.

(9.) Multiply $642345\frac{2}{3}$ by $34\frac{3}{4}$.

$$
\begin{array}{rlr}
 & 642345\frac{2}{3} & 34\frac{3}{4} \\
 & 3 & 4 \\
\hline
 & 1927037 & 139 \\
 & 139 & \\
\hline
 & 17343333 = \textit{product by } 9. & \\
 & 25051481\phantom{0} = \textit{product by } 130. & \\
\hline
\textit{Product of denominators} = 12) & 267858143 & \\
\hline
 & 22321511\frac{11}{12} = \textit{Ans.} &
\end{array}
$$

(10.) Multiply $342703\frac{1}{2}$ by $41\frac{1}{3}$.

$$
\begin{array}{rlr}
 & 342703\frac{1}{2} & 41\frac{1}{3} \\
 & 2 & 3 \\
\hline
 & 685407 & 124 \\
 & 124 & \\
\hline
 & 2741628 = \text{product by } 4. & \\
 & 8224884\phantom{0} = \text{last product by } 30. & \\
\hline
\textit{Product of denominators} = 6) & 84990468 & \\
\hline
 & 14165078 = \textit{Ans.} &
\end{array}
$$

(11.) Multiply 76894686$\frac{8}{12}$ by 342$\frac{6}{13}$.    *Ans.* 26336430183$\frac{1}{4}$.
(12.) Multiply 56768763$\frac{7}{9}$ by 360$\frac{1}{4}$.    *Ans.* 20482169845$\frac{1}{35}$.
(13.) Multiply 42380470$\frac{11}{12}$ by 760$\frac{9}{11}$.   *Ans.* 32247685597$\frac{1}{4}$.
(14.) Multiply 987654321$\frac{6}{8}$ by 548$\frac{3}{4}$.   *Ans.* 541563790342$\frac{2}{37}$.
(15.) Multiply 60046874$\frac{4}{9}$ by 370$\frac{3}{8}$.    *Ans.* 22473366909$\frac{5}{8}$.
(16.) Multiply 54674073$\frac{12}{14}$ by 634$\frac{11}{121}$.   *Ans.* 34668332705$\frac{5}{41}$.

To multiply by 5, add a cipher to the multiplicand, and divide by 2, because 5 is $\frac{1}{2}$ of 10.

To multiply by 12$\frac{1}{2}$, add two ciphers to the multiplicand, and divide by 8, because 12$\frac{1}{2}$ is $\frac{1}{8}$ of 100.

To multiply by 25, add two ciphers to the multiplicand, and divide by 4, because 25 is $\frac{1}{4}$ of 100.

To multiply by 33$\frac{1}{3}$, add two ciphers to the multiplicand, and divide by 3, because 33$\frac{1}{3}$ is $\frac{1}{3}$ of 100.

To multiply by 125, add three ciphers to the multiplicand, and divide by 8, because 125 is $\frac{1}{8}$ of 1000.

To multiply by 250, add three ciphers to the multiplicand, and divide by 4, because 250 is $\frac{1}{4}$ of 1000.

(17.) Multiply 47687043 by 5, and perform the operation by division.
          *Ans.* 238435215.

(18.) Multiply 36746874 by 12$\frac{1}{2}$.   *Ans.* 459335925.
(19.) Multiply 68740632 by 25.   *Ans.* 1718515800.
(20.) Multiply 63074683 by 33$\frac{1}{3}$.   *Ans.* 2102489433$\frac{1}{3}$.
(21.) Multiply 23456789 by 125.   *Ans.* 2932098625.
(22.) Multiply 56732143 by 250.   *Ans.* 14183035750.

# Simple Division.

SIMPLE DIVISION is the method of finding how often one number is contained in another.

The number to be divided is called the Dividend.

The number you divide by is called the Divisor.

And the number of times the dividend contains the divisor is called the Quotient.

If the dividend contains the divisor any number of times, and some part or parts over, those parts are called the Remainder.

### RULE.*

1. Draw a small curved line on the right and left of the dividend, and write the divisor on the left.

---

* According to the rule here given, we resolve the dividend into parts, and find by trial the number of times the divisor is contained in

2. Find how many times the divisor is contained in as many figures of the dividend as are just necessary, and place the result on the right for the first figure of the quotient.

---

each of them; whence the only thing that remains to be proved is, that the several figures of the quotient, taken as one number, according to the order in which they are placed, is the true quotient of the whole dividend by the divisor; which may be shown thus:

The complete value of the first part of the dividend is, by the nature of notation, 10, 100, or 1000, &c. times the value it is taken for in the operation, according as there are 1, 2, 3, &c. figures standing after it; and consequently the true value of the quotient figure, belonging to that part of the dividend, is also 10, 100, or 1000, &c. times its simple value; which is likewise the true value of the quotient figure belonging to that part of the dividend, as found by the rule; since there are as many figures to be set after it as there are remaining figures in the dividend. Hence this first quotient figure, taken in its complete value, from the place it stands in, is the true quotient of the divisor for the first part of the dividend; and as the same mode of reasoning is equally applicable to every other step of the operation, it is plain that all the rest of the figures, taken in order, as they are placed by the rule, make one number, which is equal to the sum of the true quotient figures of all the several parts of the dividend; and, therefore, this is the true quotient of the whole dividend by the divisor.

Thus, if it were required to divide 8560 by 36, the work, according to the process here pointed out, will stand thus:

```
          Divisor 36)8560 ............ dividend.
1st part of the dividend   8500
          36 × 200 =       7200 ............ 200 the 1st quotient.

1st remainder ............  1300
             add...           60
                           ─────
2nd part of the dividend   1360
          36 × 30 =        1080 ............ 30 the 2nd quotient.

2nd remainder............    280
             add...           0
                           ─────
3rd part of the dividend    280
          36 × 7 =          252 ............ 7 the 3rd quotient.

Last remainder  .........    28 ............ 237 sum of all the quotients.
```

Which number, together with the remainder, considered as a part of another unit, is the answer.

To this we may also add the following method of proof, by casting out the nines:

RULE. Cast the nines out of the divisor and quotient, as in addition, and to the product of the two remainders add the remainder, if any, in

3. Multiply the divisor by this quotient figure; and having subtracted the product from that part of the dividend above mentioned, bring down the next figure of the dividend to the right of the remainder.

4. Divide the remainder, so increased, by the divisor, as before, for the second figure of the quotient; observing if it goes 0 times to put a cipher, and bring down another figure to the quotient.

5. Proceed with this result as with the former; and so on, till all the figures of the dividend are brought down; then the entire number in the quotient, together with the last remainder, if any, will be the answer.

*₊* When the divisor does not exceed 12, the quotient can be written down as it arises, immediately under the dividend.

*Note* 1. Half the sum of any two numbers, increased by half their difference, will give the greater number; and half their sum diminished by half their difference, will give the less number.

2. The quotient, arising from the division of the sum of two or more numbers, is equal to the sum of the quotients arising from the division of the parts, separately, by the same divisor.

---

the question; then, if the excess of nines in this result be equal to the excess of nines in the dividend, the work is right.

### EXAMPLE.

```
76)47380(623
   456
   ───
   178
   152
   ───
   260
   228
   ───
    32
```

Here 4 = excess of 9's in 76, and 2 = do. in 623; whence the excess in 2 × 4 + 32; or in 40 = 4, which is also the excess in 47380.

It may here likewise be further observed, that as it is sometimes difficult to find how often the divisor may be had in the numbers of the several steps of the operation, the best way will be to find how many times the first figure of the divisor is contained in the first, or first two figures of the dividend, and the answer, made less by one or two, will generally be the figure wanted. Besides, if, after subtracting the product of the divisor and quotient figure from the dividend, the remainder should be equal to or exceed the divisor, it is plain that the figure so found is too small, and must, therefore, be increased by a unit, or more, till the remainder is either 0, or less than the divisor.

3. Any three of the four following quantities of a division sum, *viz.*, divisor, dividend, quotient, and remainder, being given, the fourth may be found by the following formula. Let $d =$ the divisor; $D =$ the dividend; $q =$ the quotient; and $r =$ the remainder. Then we shall have

$$d = \frac{D - r}{q}; \quad D = (d \times q) + r; \quad q = \frac{D - r}{d}; \quad \text{and } r = D - (q \times d).$$

4. An even number cannot divide, or measure, an odd number, nor a greater a less.

5. A given number is divisible by 2, if the last digit is even : it is divisible by 4, if the last two digits are divisible by 4 ; it is divisible by 8, if the last three digits are divisible by 8 ; and in general it is divisible by $2^n$, if the last $n$ digits are divisible by $2^n$.

6. A number is divisible by 3, if the sum of the digits is divisible by 3 ; such number also may be divided by 6, if, besides this, the last digit is even ; it is divisible by 9, if the sum of the digits can be divided by 9. The method of proof by casting out the nines, in the preceding rules, depends upon this theorem.

7. Every number that has the last digit 5 or 0, such number is divisible by 5 in both cases, and by 10 in the latter case.

8. A number is divisible by 11, when the sum of the digits in the odd places (counting from the right or unit's place) be equal to the sum of the digits in the even places ; or if the difference of these sums be divisible by 11, the number itself is divisible by 11.

9. If any two numbers be separately divided by 9 or 3, and the two remainders multiplied together, and that product divided by 9 or 3, the last remainder will be the same as if you divided the product of the first two numbers by 9 or 3.

10. If any number ending with 1, 3, 7, or 9, be the numerator or denominator of a fraction, and will not divide by 3, 7, or 9, that fraction is *generally* in its lowest terms, for

| | |
|---|---|
| Every number must terminate in one or other of the ten digits - - } | 0.1.2.3.4.5.6.7.8.9. |
| But no even number can be a prime number ; hence take away - - } | .. 2 . 4 . 6 . 8 |
| We have remaining - - - | 0.1..3.5.7.9 |
| No number terminating in 0 or 5 can be prime - - - - } | 0. .... 5 .... . |
| Hence it follows that every prime number must terminate in one or other of these four digits - - } | .1. 3 ...7 . 9 |

But of such numbers none the sum of whose digits is a multiple of 3 can be prime. Nor any terminating in 1, 3, 7, 9, that is in any power, or multiple, of another number.

11. Every prime number is of one of the forms ; $8n + 1$, $8n + 3$, $8n + 5$, $8n + 7$ ; $12n + 1$, $12n + 5$, $12n + 7$, $12n + 11$ ; $4n \pm 1$ ; $6n \pm 1$ ; $16n \pm 1$, $16n \pm 3$, $16n \pm 5$, $16n \pm 7$ ; $60n \pm 1$, $60n \pm 7$, $60n \pm 11$, $60n \pm 13$, $60n \pm 17$, $60n \pm 19$, $60n \pm 23$, $60n \pm 29$.

12. When any prime number (above the number 3) is either increased or diminished by unity, the result is always divisible by 6. Thus, take

for example, $(173 + 1) \div 6 = 174 \div 6 = 29$, and $(5749 - 1) \div 6 = 5748 \div 6 = 958$.

13. When any set of numbers are placed in the form of fractions, with the sign of addition or subtraction between them, and should the whole of these numbers that are in the numerator and denominator contain a common divisor, they may be abbreviated by dividing each of them by the common divisor.

14. When the numerator is equal to the denominator, the fraction is equal to the integer, *thus* $\frac{3}{3} = 1$.

15. When the numerator is greater than the denominator, the fraction is greater than the integer, as $\frac{4}{3} = 1\frac{1}{3}$.

16. If the numerator and denominator of a fraction be either multiplied or divided by the same number, the product or quotient will be a new fraction, equal in value to the former; *thus*, $\frac{6}{8} \div \frac{2}{2} = \frac{3}{4}$, or $\frac{3}{4} \times \frac{7}{7} = \frac{21}{28}$, all of which have the same value, for $\frac{6}{8} = \frac{3}{4} = \frac{21}{28}$.

### METHODS OF PROOF.

Multiply the quotient by the divisor, and add the remainder, if any, to the product; then if this sum be equal to the dividend, the work is right.

*Or thus.*

If you add the remainder, and all the products of the several quotient figures by the divisor, together, according to the order in which they stand in the work, the sum will be equal to the dividend.

### EXAMPLES.

(1.)  6)823573

137262⅚

(2.)  8)1134789

141848⅝

(3.)  12)748277

62356$\frac{5}{12}$

(4.)  65)123456 (  1899
       65          65
      ────        ───
      584        9495
      520       11394
      ───          21
      645       ───────
      585       123456  *Proof.*
      ───
      606                750
      585                125
      ───                500
       21                875
      ───                103

(5.)  125)768478(6147
         750
         ───
         184
         125
         ───
         597
         500
         ───
         978
         875
         ───
         103

*Proof of the 5th Example* = 768478 = *Sum.*

## CASE I.

### EXAMPLES FOR PRACTICE.

(6.) Divide 37567892 by 2.

(7.) Divide 547485764 by 3.

(8.) Divide 65378376 by 4.

(9.) Divide 47823565 by 5.

(10.) Divide 2345678964 by 6.

(11.) Divide 1234567890 by 7.

(12.) Divide 9876543210 by 8.

(13.) Divide 1357975313 by 9.

(14.) Divide 570196382 by 12.

(15.) Divide 321768430 by 17. *Ans.* $18927554\frac{13}{17}$.

(16.) Divide 321147368 by 27. *Ans.* $11894346\frac{26}{27}$.

(17.) Divide 137896254 by 97. *Ans.* $1421610\frac{84}{97}$.

(18.) Divide 140637301 by 108. *Ans.* $1302197\frac{25}{108}$.

(19.) Divide 3405657254 by 345. *Ans.* $9871470\frac{104}{345}$.

(20.) Divide 5713070049 by 678. *Ans.* $8426357\frac{3}{678}$.

(21.) Divide 29383945593 by 8405. *Ans.* $3496007\frac{6758}{8405}$.

(22.) Divide 4637064283 by 57606. *Ans.* $80496\frac{11707}{57606}$.

(23.) Divide two hundred and sixty-seven millions and five, by twenty-three thousand and seventeen. *Ans.* $11600\frac{2805}{23017}$.

(24.) Divide two thousand millions, five hundred and eighty-four thousand and seventeen, by two hundred and nineteen thousand, five hundred and sixty-one.

*Ans.* $9111\frac{163746}{219561}$.

(25.) Divide 6754371495671594 by 678957.

*Ans.* $9948157977\frac{81605}{678957}$.

(26.) Divide 15241578750190521 by 123456789.

*Ans.* 123456789.

(27.) Divide 5124985845000455205689 by 569.

*Ans.* $9007005000000800009\frac{568}{569}$.

## CASE II.

*When ciphers are annexed to the divisor.*

### RULE.*

Cut off the ciphers from the divisor, and the same number of figures from the right hand of the dividend; then divide

---

\* The reason of this contraction is easy to conceive; for the cutting off an equal number of figures from the divisor and dividend is the same as dividing each of them by 10, 100, 1000, &c.; and it is evident that

the remaining figures by each other, as usual, and the quotient will be the answer in whole numbers.

And if any thing remains, after this division, place the figures cut off from the dividend to the right hand of it, and then set the result over the divisor, for the fractional part.

### EXAMPLES.

(1.) Divide 46748696 by 20.

$$2,0)4674869,6$$

$$233743\tfrac{16}{20} \; quotient.$$

(2.) Divide 31086917 by 7100.

$$71,00)310869,17(4378\tfrac{717}{7100} \; quotient.$$

$$284$$

$$268$$

$$213$$

$$556$$

$$497$$

$$599$$

$$568$$

$$31$$

(3.) Divide 7380964 by 23000.     *Ans.* 320$\frac{20964}{23000}$.

(4.) Divide 29628754963 by 35000.    *Ans.* 846535$\frac{34963}{35000}$.

(5.) Divide 1022047821 by 770000.    *Ans.* 1327$\frac{547821}{770000}$.

(6.) Divide 6641829640 by 678400.     *Ans.* 9790$\frac{523640}{678400}$.

(7.) Divide 1945638720186 by 1987500.   *Ans.* 978937$\frac{432686}{1987500}$.

(8.) Divide 5407002012686400000 by 5760090. *Ans.* 938700960000.

## CASE III.

*When the divisor is the product of two or more factors, each of which does not exceed 12.*

### RULE.*

Divide the dividend by each of the factors separately for the required quotient. Multiply each successive re-

---

as often as the whole divisor is contained in the whole dividend, so often must any part of the divisor be contained in a like part of the dividend. This method, therefore, is only introduced to avoid a needless repetition of ciphers, which would happen in the common way, as may be seen by working an example at large.

  * To explain this rule, it is only necessary to observe, that each remainder being expressed relatively to its own divisor only, it must

mainder after the first, by all the divisors preceding its
own; the sum of the products, together with the first remainder, will be the true remainder required.

### WORKED EXAMPLES.

(1.) Divide 310468357939 by 56, or 7 × 8.   Also, divide
486275971537 by 83160, or 11 . 9 . 7 . 6 . 5 . 4.

$$56 = 7 \times 8 \cdot\cdot \begin{cases} 7)\overline{310468357939} \\ \overline{8)44352622562 \cdot\cdot 5} \\ Quotient = \underline{5544077820 \cdot\cdot 2} \end{cases} = (7 \times 2) + 5 = 19 \; remainder.$$

*Again,*

$$\begin{matrix} 83160 = 11 \times \\ 9 \times 7 \times 6 \times 20 \end{matrix} \begin{cases} 11)\overline{486275971537} \\ 9)\overline{44206906503} \cdot\cdot 4 & \cdot \quad \cdot \quad \cdot \quad = \quad 4 \\ 7)\overline{4911878500} \cdot\cdot 3 = 11 \times 3 & \cdot \quad \cdot \quad = \quad 33 \\ 6)\overline{701696928} \cdot\cdot 4 = 11 \times 9 \times 4 & \cdot \quad = \quad 396 \\ 2,0)\overline{11694948,8} \cdot\cdot 0 \end{cases}$$

$$Quotient = \underline{5847474} \cdot\cdot 8 = 11 \times 9 \times 7 \times 6 \times 8 \quad = 33264$$

$$Remainder = \underline{33697}$$

(2.) Divide 750840623511 by 11340000, or 30000 . 6 . 7 . 9.

$$3,0000)\overline{75084062,3511}$$

$$6)\overline{25028020} \cdot\cdot\cdot\cdot 23511 \quad\quad = \quad 23511$$

$$7)\overline{4171336} \cdot\cdot\cdot\cdot 4 \times 30000 \quad \cdot \quad = \quad 120000$$

$$9)\overline{595905} \cdot\cdot\cdot\cdot 1 \quad 30000 \times 6 \quad = \quad 180000$$

$$Quotient = \underline{66211} \cdot\cdot\cdot\cdot 6 \times 30000 \times 6 \times 7 = 7560000$$

$$Remainder = \underline{7883511}$$

(3.) Divide 7014596 by 72. .        *Ans.* 97424$\frac{68}{72}$.
(4.) Divide 5130652 by 132.         *Ans.* 38868$\frac{76}{132}$.
(5.) Divide 83016572 by 240.        *Ans.* 345902$\frac{92}{240}$.
(6.) Divide 9241862172 by 315, or 9.7.5.   *Ans.* 29339244$\frac{12}{315}$.
(7.) Divide 1666444213 by 945, or 9.7.5.3.   *Ans.* 1763433$\frac{28}{945}$.

be multiplied by all the preceding divisors to render it the true
remainder, relatively to the product of its own divisor and all the preceding divisors.   This multiplication is not required in the first remainder, it being already expressed in its proper relation.   The first
remainder and subsequent products are changed in denomination, but
not in magnitude, by the subsequent divisions: and thus the sum of
these products and the first remainder will be the true remainder
required.

(8.) Divide 1642807347 by 6600, or 1100.6.      *Ans.* 248910$\frac{1147}{6600}$.
(9.) Divide 5482961147 by 1344, or 8.8.7.3.      *Ans.* 4079584$\frac{251}{1344}$.
(10.) Divide 764206043241 by 2744, or 8.7.7.7. *Ans.* 278500744$\frac{1705}{2744}$.
(11.) Divide 72146950640 by 96000, or 12000.8.   *Ans.* 751530$\frac{70640}{96000}$.
(12.) Divide 3332168411071 by 28224000, or 12000.8.7.7.6.
                                            *Ans.* 118061$\frac{11747071}{28224000}$.


## CASE IV.

*To perform division more concisely than by the rule generally used.*

### RULE.

Multiply the divisor by the quotient figures as before, and subtract each figure of the product from the dividend, as you produce it; always remembering to carry as many units to the next figure as were borrowed before.

### EXAMPLES.

(1.) Divide 3104675846 by 833.

833)3104675846(3727101$\frac{713}{833}$ *the quotient.*
   6056
   2257
   5915
    848
   1546
    713

(2.) Divide 47296478 by 83.        *Ans.* 569837$\frac{7}{83}$.
(3.) Divide 27085946 by 216.       *Ans.* 125397$\frac{194}{216}$.
(4.) Divide 29137062 by 5317.      *Ans.* 5479$\frac{5219}{5317}$.
(5.) Divide 62015735 by 7803.      *Ans.* 7947$\frac{5294}{7803}$.
(6.) Divide 43275628456 by 87346.  *Ans.* 495450$\frac{53756}{87346}$.


*Exercising the preceding Cases.*

(1.) Divide 719051047192776115211 by 12.
                          *Ans.* 59920920599398009600$\frac{11}{12}$.
(2.) Divide 889059669149224938948296297 4987 by 987.
                          *Ans.* 900800070060005004000 3002001.
(3.) Divide 4279788253402 5500424 by 425.
                          *Ans.* 10070090008006000$\frac{424}{425}$.
(4.) Divide 4500092301078221090166 by 11.11.12.
                          *Ans.* 3099237121954697720$\frac{730}{1452}$.
(5.) Divide 656458931996524171800 by 700489070.
                          *Ans.* 937143718740.

C

(6.) The remainder of a division sum is 76, the dividend 5130652, and the quotient 38868 ; what is the divisor?   (*See Note* 3. *page* 20.)                  *Ans.* 132.

(7.) The following certain quantities of a division sum being given, *viz.* the dividend 7014596, remainder 68, and divisor 72 ; required the quotient?  (*See Note* 3. *page* 20.)             *Ans.* 97424.

(8.) What number multiplied by 79 will give the same product as 158 by 87 ?                                      *Ans.* 174.

(9.) The divisor, quotient, and remainder of a division sum are 240, 345902, and 92 ; required the dividend?  (*See Note* 3. *page* 20.)             *Ans.* 83016572.

(10.) Required the remainder of a division sum whose dividend, quotient, and divisor, are 47296478, 569837, and 83 ?  (*See Note* 3. *page* 20.)             *Ans.* 7.

*Note* 17.   *To divide a whole number by a whole number with a fraction joined to it.* — Multiply the integral part of the divisor by the denominator of the fraction, add in the numerator, and note the sum; then multiply the dividend by the denominator of the fraction, and divide the product by the sum noted, and we shall have the true quotient. If the dividend contain a fraction, and not the divisor, then multiply both the whole numbers by the denominator of the fraction, taking care to add in the numerator of the fraction in the dividend.

| | |
|---|---|
| (1.) Divide 999642 by $37\frac{2}{11}$. | (2.) Divide $987654\frac{5}{12}$ by 43. |

```
37 2/11   999642          43     987654 5/12
11        11              12      12
_____             _____
409)10996062(26885 97/409 = Ans.    516)11851853(22968 365/516 = Ans.
    818                          1032
    ____                         ____
    2816                         1531
    2454                         1032
    ____                         ____
    3620                         4998
    3272                         4644
    ____                         ____
    3486                         3545
    3272                         3096
    ____                         ____
    2142                         4493
    2045                         4128
    ____                         ____
    97                           365
```

| | |
|---|---|
| (3.) Divide 42306778 by $264\frac{4}{7}$.    *Ans.* $159993\frac{403}{1851}$. | (6.) Divide $738004731\frac{1}{4}$ by 732.    *Ans.* $100820\frac{467}{1461}$. |
| (4.) Divide 32968767 by $125\frac{4}{5}$.    *Ans.* $262072\frac{547}{629}$. | (7.) Divide $6234767\frac{11}{13}$ by 643.    *Ans.* $96963\frac{541}{771}$. |
| (5.) Divide 95467348 by $436\frac{5}{19}$.    *Ans.* $218710\frac{866}{8293}$. | (8.) Divide $38706847\frac{5}{11}$ by 426.    *Ans.* $90861\frac{339}{2343}$. |

*Note* 18.  *To divide one number by another when both contain fractions* — Multiply the integral part of each by the denominator of its fraction, and add in the numerator; of these two sums, multiply that belonging to the dividend by the denominator in the divisor, and divide the product by the product of the other sum and denominator in the dividend.

(9.) Divide 990436$\frac{2}{3}$ by 68 $\frac{1}{7}$.

| 68$\frac{1}{7}$ | 990436$\frac{2}{3}$ |
|---|---|
| 7 | 8 |
| 481 | 7923491 |
| 8 | 7 |

3848 )55464437(14413$\frac{3213}{3848}$ = Ans.

```
3848
————
16984
15392
————
 15924
 15392
 ————
  5323
  3848
  ————
 14757
 11544
 ————
  3213
```

(10.) Divide 999420$\frac{4}{10}$ by 75$\frac{3}{13}$.

| 75$\frac{1}{4}$ | 999420$\frac{1}{4}$ |
|---|---|
| 4 | 2 |
| 301 | 1998841 |
| 2 | 4 |

602 ) 7995364(13281$\frac{101}{301}$ = Ans.

```
602
————
1975
1806
————
 1693
 1204
 ————
 4896
 4816
 ————
  804
  602
  ————
  202
```

(11.) Divide 6342067$\frac{2}{3}$ by 421$\frac{6}{7}$.
Ans. 150464$\frac{500}{2529}$.

(12.) Divide 5214676$\frac{2}{3}$ by 123$\frac{1}{4}$.
Ans. 42199$\frac{6443}{5920}$.

(13.) Divide 1234567$\frac{3}{4}$ by 672$\frac{2}{3}$.
Ans. 18355$\frac{1585}{10085}$.

(14.) Divide 23674328$\frac{4}{10}$ by 321$\frac{6}{8}$.
Ans. 73579$\frac{141}{2587}$.

(15.) Divide 52146075$\frac{11}{2}$ by 241$\frac{6}{8}$.
Ans. 215606$\frac{18881}{20318}$.

(16.) Divide 52704678$\frac{81}{729}$ by 234$\frac{49}{313}$.
Ans. 225096$\frac{3625}{14757}$.

*Note* 19. *All the variations that can take place in dividing a fraction by a whole number, are exhibited in the following example.*

(17.)

| 3)468248 |
|---|
| 4)156082$\frac{2}{3}$ |
| 2)39020$\frac{2}{3}$ |
| 5)19510$\frac{1}{3}$ |
| 6)3902$\frac{1}{15}$ |
| 650$\frac{31}{90}$ = Ans. |

*First.* The first divisor gives 2 over, therefore merely put down the 2 as the numerator, and the divisor for the denominator, thus, $\frac{2}{3}$.

*Secondly.* The second divisor gives 2 over, therefore multiply the denominator of the fraction by what is over (viz. 2), and add in the numerator; now, if you can divide this sum by the divisor, put the quotient for a new numerator, under which write the denominator for the true fraction.

*Thirdly.* The third divisor gives nothing over, in this case the numerator of the fraction can be divided by the divisor, and the quotient will be the new numerator, under which place the denominator for the true fraction.

*Fourthly,* The fourth divisor gives nothing over, therefore multiply the divisor by the denominator of the fraction for a new denominator, over which place the numerator for the true fraction.

*Fifthly,* The fifth divisor gives 2 over, therefore multiply the denominator of the fraction by what is over (viz. 2), and add in the numerator for a new numerator, then multiply the divisor by the denominator of the fraction for a new denominator; this will be the true fraction.

---

\* It should be remembered that the remainder is always of the same denomination as the dividend.

EXAMPLES FOR PRACTICE.

(1.) Divide 58764791 by 7. 5. 3. 4. & 6.      *Ans.* 23319$\frac{211}{2520}$.
(2.) Divide 97068747 by 8. 6. 7. 3. & 5.      *Ans.* 19259$\frac{1179}{1680}$.
(3.) Divide 65077677 by 7. 6. 5. 3. & 2.      *Ans.* 51648$\frac{17}{20}$.
(4.) Divide 98764007 by 9. 7. 5. 3. & 4.      *Ans.* 26128$\frac{167}{3780}$.
(5.) Divide 50694683 by 2. 4. 3. 5. & 6.      *Ans.* 70409$\frac{203}{720}$.
(6.) Divide 98765432 by 9. 8. 7. 6. 5. 4. 3. & 2.      *Ans.* 272$\frac{7759}{15360}$.
(7.) Divide 32454063 by 7. 9. 5. 11. 3. & 6.      *Ans.* 5202$\frac{497}{8910}$.
(8.) Divide 123456789 by 12. 11. 9. 8. 7. 6. 5. & 4.      *Ans.* 154$\frac{11821}{887040}$.

# Compound Addition.

COMPOUND ADDITION is the method of collecting several numbers of different denominations into one sum.

### RULE.*

1. Place the numbers so that those of the same denomination may stand directly under each other, and draw a line below them.

2. Add up the figures in the lowest denomination, and find how many units, or ones, of the next higher denomination are contained in their sum.

3. Set down the remainder, and carry the rest to the next denomination, which add up as before, and so on through all the denominations to the highest; then this sum, together with the several parts before found, will be the answer required.

The method of proof is the same as in Simple Addition.

### TABLES OF MONEY.

2 Farthings make 1 Halfpenny   $\frac{1}{2}$.
4 Farthings —— 1 Penny      *d.*
12 Pence     —— 1 Shilling   *s.*
20 Shillings —— 1 Pound    *l.*

$\frac{1}{4}d.=1$ Farthing.   $\frac{1}{2}d.=2$ Farthings.   $\frac{3}{4}d.=3$ Farthings.

---

* This rule is also evident from what has been said in Simple Addition; for, in the adding of money, as 1 in the pence is equal to 4 in the farthings, 1 in the shillings to 12 in the pence, and 1 in the pounds to 20 in the shillings, it is plain that carrying as directed is nothing more than providing a method of placing the money arising from each column properly in the scale of denominations; and this reasoning will hold good in the addition of compound numbers of any denomination whatever.

Farthings.

4= 1 Penny.

48= 12= 1 Shilling.

960=240=20=1 Pound.

N.B.—The present gold coins in circulation in England, are the Sovereign, valued at 20s., and the Half-Sovereign 10s. The silver coins are the Crown, or 5s. piece ; the Half-Crown 2s. 6d.; the Shilling 12d.; the Sixpenny piece 6d. ; the Four-penny piece 4d., and the Threepenny piece 3d. The copper coins are the Penny, equal 4 farthings ; the Half-Penny, 2 farthings ; the Farthing piece, 4 of which make a Penny ; and the Half-Farthing, 8 of which make a Penny.

## IMAGINARY ENGLISH COINS.

| GOLD COINS. | s. | d. | | s. | d. |
|---|---|---|---|---|---|
| | | | An Angel, value............ | 10 . | 0 |
| A Moidore, value ........... | 27 . | 0 | A Noble....................... | 6 . | 8 |
| A Jacobus ..................... | 25 . | 0 | SILVER COINS. | | |
| A Carolus ............ ........ | 23 . | 0 | A Tester...................... | 0 . | 6 |
| A Mark ...................... | 13 . | 4 | A Groat ....................... | 0 . | 4 |

The following statement is the full weight of gold and silver coins in troy weight : —

| GOLD COINS.—Old Coinage. | dwt. | gr. | SILVER COINS.—Old Coinage. | dwt. | gr. |
|---|---|---|---|---|---|
| Guinea.............. weighs | 5 . | $9\frac{30}{33}$ | Crown...............weighs | 19 . | $8\frac{16}{31}$ |
| Half-guinea .................. | 2 . | $16\frac{31}{33}$ | Half-crown.............. | 9 . | $16\frac{8}{31}$ |
| Seven-shilling piece........ | 1 . | $19\frac{13}{33}$ | Shilling ...................... | 3 . | $20\frac{28}{31}$ |
| | | | Sixpence..................... | 1 . | $22\frac{14}{31}$ |
| New Coinage. | | | New Coinage. | | |
| Sovereign .................. | 5 . | $3\frac{171}{623}$ | Crown....................... | 18 . | $4\frac{4}{11}$ |
| Half-sovereign ............ | 2 . | $13\frac{397}{623}$ | Half-crown.............. | 9 . | $2\frac{2}{11}$ |
| Double-sovereign......... | 10 . | $6\frac{342}{623}$ | Shilling ...................... | 3 . | $15\frac{3}{11}$ |
| Five-sovereign piece..... | 25 . | $16\frac{242}{623}$ | Sixpence........ ........... | 1 . | $19\frac{7}{11}$ |
| | | | Fourpence .................. | 1 . | $5\frac{1}{11}$ |
| | | | Threepence................. | . | $21\frac{9}{11}$ |

The relative proportion between gold and silver in the English coins, according to the mint regulations, both of the old and new coinage.— The *old coinage* is as any weight of gold is to an equal weight of silver as 15·2376 to 1. The *new coinage* is as 14·3124 to 1.

*Note.*—Gold coins are allowed by *law* to pass under the above full weight. Thus the guinea, weighing 5 dwt. 8 gr. ; the sovereign, 5 dwt. 2¾ gr. ; and their divisions, in proportion, are a legal tender.

The standard of gold coin is 22 parts of pure gold, and 2 parts of copper, or some other alloy, melted together.* From a pound of standard gold are coined 44½ guineas, 89 half-guineas, 133¼ seven-shilling pieces. Also 46¾ sovereigns, with divisions and multiples in proportion. Hence the mint price of gold is 3*l.* 17*s.* 10½*d.* per ounce, or 46*l.* 14*s.* 6*d.* per pound troy. There is no alteration, either in weight or fineness, from former coinages, the sovereign, or 20*s.* piece, being 20/21 of the weight and value of a guinea.†

The current silver coin is 11 oz. 2 dwt. of pure silver, and 18 dwt. of copper. The new coin is minted at 5*s.* 6*s.* per ounce, or 3*l.* 6*s.* per pound troy: thus, from 1 lb. troy of this standard are now coined 13½ crowns, 26⅗ half-crowns, 66 shillings, or 132 sixpences.

It should be stated that the new silver coin is not a legal tender for any sum above 40 shillings, and in the year 1816 gold coins were declared to be the only legal tender in all payments beyond that sum.

The copper money is coined in the proportion of 24 pence to the pound avoirdupois. Thus the penny should weigh 10⅔ drams, or 291¾ troy grains, and the other pieces in proportion. Copper pence, half-pence, and farthings, are not a legal tender for more than 12 pence, and the half-farthings for not more than the value of sixpence.

| SHILLINGS AND PENCE TABLES. | | | | | | | |
|---|---|---|---|---|---|---|---|
| *s.* | *l.* | *s.* | *d.* | | *s.* | *d.* | *s.* | *d.* |
| 20 are 1 . 0 | | | 12 make 1 | | 20 are 1 . 8 |
| 30 | 1 . 10 | | 24 | 2 | 30 | 2 . 6 |
| 40 | 2 . 0 | | 36 | 3 | 40 | 3 . 4 |
| 50 | 2 . 10 | | 48 | 4 | 50 | 4 . 2 |
| 60 | 3 . 0 | | 60 | 5 | 60 | 5 . 0 |
| 70 | 3 . 10 | | 72 | 6 | 70 | 5 . 10 |
| 80 | 4 . 0 | | 84 | 7 | 80 | 6 . 8 |
| 90 | 4 . 10 | | 96 | 8 | 90 | 7 . 6 |
| 100 | 5 . 0 | | 108 | 9 | 100 | 8 . 4 |
| 110 | 5 . 10 | | 120 | 10 | 110 | 9 . 2 |
| 120 | 6 . 0 | | 132 | 11 | 120 | 10 . 0 |

* Any quantity of gold, as a pennyweight, is supposed to be divided into twenty-four equal parts called *carats.* When the whole is pure, it is said to be 24 carats fine; when 23 grains are pure and one is alloy, it is said to be 23 carats fine, and so on. Wrought gold is of two standards; the one 22 carats, the same as the coin, and the other 18 carats fine. The latter commenced in 1798, and is used chiefly in watch cases and rings.

† The guinea varied in its current price from 20 shillings up to 30 until the year 1717, when, by the recommendation of Sir Isaac Newton, it was fixed at 21 shillings, its present rate.

## EXAMPLES OF MONEY.

(1.)    l.    s.    d.
173 . 13 . 5

87 . 17 . 7¾
75 . 18 . 7½
25 . 17 . 8¼
10 . 10 . 10½
2 . 5 . 7

Sum 376 . 3 . 10

202 . 10 . 5

Proof 376 . 3 . 10

(2.)    l.    s.    d.
705 . 17 . 3½

354 . 17 . 2¾
175 . 17 . 3¾
87 . 19 . 7½
52 . 12 . 7¾
27 . 10 . 5¼

1404 . 14 . 6½

698 . 17 . 3

1404 . 14 . 6½

(3.)    l.    s.    d.
1275 . 12 . 4

700 . 10 . 10½
25 . 13 . 3¾
5 . 17 . 7¾
0 . 18 . 8
0 . 17 . 0

2009 . 9 . 10

733 . 17 . 6

2009 . 9 . 10

(4.)    l.    s.    d.
228 . 14 . 6
327 . 18 . 4½
579 . 12 . 6¾
109 . 18 . 10
730 . 10 . 1½
185 . 14 . 2

Sum

(5.)    l.    s.    d.
678 . 13 . 6¼
287 . 6 . 2
438 . 15 . 0¼
325 . 17 . 2
840 . 12 . 9¼
426 . 17 . 8½

(6.)    l.    s.    d.
678 . 5 . 10
87 . 10 . 9¾
123 . 8 . 8
47 . 16 . 9
307 . 2 . 0
187 . 16 . 10¼

(7.)    l.    s.    d.
368 . 10 . 3
257 . 10 . 5
88 . 11 . 4½
33 . 10 . 0
12 . 13 . 5
8 . 8 . 8½

Sum

Proof

(8.)    l.    s.    d.
567 . 8 . 9
259 . 16 . 8¾
287 . 16 . 7¾
87 . 15 . 4
25 . 16 . 8
24 . 10 . 2

(9.)    l.    s.    d.
1728 . 10 . 8½
457 . 10 . 6
328 . 19 . 9¾
478 . 12 . 2½
238 . 14 . 10
50 . 10 . 6¼

c 4

(10.) A. owes B. for bread 9*l.* 6*s.* 3¾*d.* ; for cheese, 4*l.* 3*s.* for tea, 10*l.* 9*s.* 5*d.* ; for butter, 3*l.* 0*s.* 2¼*d.* ; for sugar, 125*l.* 0*s.* 2½*d.* ; and for other articles, 26*l.* 13*s.* 6¾*d.*  What is the amount of the whole debt?     *Ans.* 178*l.* 12*s.* 8¼*d.*

# EXAMPLES OF WEIGHTS AND MEASURES.

## TROY WEIGHT.*

24 Grains (*gr.*)    make 1 Pennyweight *dwt.*
20 Pennyweights —— 1 Ounce     *oz.*
12 Ounces        —— 1 Pound     *lb.*
100 lbs.=1 Hundred Weight, and 2000 lbs.=1 Ton.

Grains.
24=   1 Pennyweight.
480=   20= 1 Ounce.
5760=240=12=1 Pound.

According to an Act of Parliament passed the 13*th* of August, 1834, the only articles that are allowed to be sold by Troy Weight are *Gold, Silver, Platina, Diamonds,* or other *Precious Stones,* and *Drugs* when sold by retail. †

### ASSAY WEIGHTS.

| *Gold.* | *Silver.* |
|---|---|
| 4 Grains make............ 1 Carat | 20 dwts. make ............... 1 oz. |
| 24 Carats ................. 1 Pound | 12 oz............................ 1 lb. |

But the carat used in weighing diamonds is nearly equal to 3⅛ grains, for an ounce troy is equal to 151¼ carats.

### EXAMPLES.

| | (1.) lb. | oz. | dwt. | gr. | | (2.) lb. | oz. | dwt. | gr. |
|---|---|---|---|---|---|---|---|---|---|
| Add | 14 . | 6 . | 12 . | 13 | Add | 10 . | 8 . | 11 . | 17 |
| | 17 . | 5 . | 3 . | 12 | | 42 . | 5 . | 16 . | 12 |
| | 15 . | 0 . | 9 . | 16 | | 12 . | 2 . | 14 . | 18 |
| | 2 . | 7 . | 15 . | 20 | | 51 . | 6 . | 0 . | 22 |
| | 13 . | 2 . | 10 . | 19 | | 24 . | 9 . | 17 . | 17 |
| | 4 . | 1 . | 5 . | 21 | | 29 . | 4 . | 18 . | 22 |
| *Sum* | 66 . | 11 . | 18 . | 5 | *Sum* | 171 . | 2 . | 0 . | 12 |

* *Imperial Troy Weight.*—Standard : One cubic inch of distilled water, at 62° Fahrenheit's thermometer, the barometer being 30 inches, weighs 252·458 grains troy.
   † The original of all weights, used in England, was a grain of wheat,

| (3.) | *lb.* | *oz.* | *dwt.* | *gr.* |
|---|---|---|---|---|
| Add | 100 . | 10 . | 19 . | 20 |
| | 32 . | 6 . | 0 . | 5 |
| | 80 . | 3 . | 2 . | 1 |
| | 7 . | 0 . | 0 . | 9 |
| | 0 . | 11 . | 19 . | 23 |
| | 0 . | 0 . | 8 . | 9 |
| *Sum* | 221 . | 8 . | 10 . | 19 |

| (4.) | *lb.* | *oz.* | *dwt.* | *gr.* |
|---|---|---|---|---|
| Add | 71 . | 6 . | 13 . | 14 |
| | 91 . | 11 . | 9 . | 12 |
| | 30 . | 6 . | 6 . | 13 |
| | 94 . | 7 . | 3 . | 18 |
| | 42 . | 10 . | 15 . | 20 |
| | 31 . | 0 . | 0 . | 21 |
| *Sum* | 362 . | 6 . | 10 . | 2 |

| (5.) | *lb.* | *oz.* | *dwt.* | *gr.* |
|---|---|---|---|---|
| Add | 49 . | 8 . | 7 . | 10 |
| | 56 . | 3 . | 13 . | 23 |
| | 99 . | 11 . | 19 . | 1 |
| | 29 . | 9 . | 9 . | 0 |
| | 30 . | 10 . | 3 . | 2 |
| | 10 . | 0 . | 18 . | 20 |

| (6.) | *lb.* | *oz.* | *dwt.* | *gr.* |
|---|---|---|---|---|
| Add | 27 . | 10 . | 17 . | 18 |
| | 117 . | 9 . | 12 . | 14 |
| | 133 . | 6 . | 13 . | 15 |
| | 240 . | 11 . | 13 . | 15 |
| | 330 . | 0 . | 19 . | 8 |
| | 220 . | 0 . | 0 . | 23 |

(7.) What is the sum of 48 lb. 11 oz. 18 dwt. 21 gr. ; 42 lb. 10 oz. 14 dwt. ; 40 lb. 9 oz. 16 dwt. 20 gr. ; 36 lb. 8 oz. 15 dwt. 22 gr. ; 38 lb. 10 oz. 10 dwt. ; and 53 lb. 17 dwt. 13 gr. ?*

## AVOIRDUPOIS WEIGHT. †

| 16 Drams (*dr.*) | make 1 Ounce | *oz.* |
|---|---|---|
| 16 Ounces | —— 1 Pound | *lb.* |
| 14 Pounds | —— 1 Stone ‡ | *st.* |
| 28 Pounds, or 2 Stones | —— 1 Quarter | *qr.* |
| 4 Quarters, or 8 Stones, or 112 *lbs.* | —— 1 Hundred Weight | *cwt.* |
| 20 Hundred Weight | —— 1 Ton | *ton.* |

taken out of the middle of the ear, and well dried, 32 of which were to be considered as a pennyweight. Goldsmiths and jewellers have a particular class of weights for gold and precious stones, viz. the carat and grain, and for silver the pennyweight and grain.

* For the answers to these and the other questions, see the Key.

† *Note.* 1 pound Avoirdupois is = 7000 grains Troy = 14 oz. 11 dwt. 16 grs. Troy, and 1 lb. Troy is = 5760 grains = 12 oz. Troy. Hence, the

A fother of lead is 19½ cwt. in London, but in the North it is 21 cwt., in some places 20 cwt., and in others 22 cwt.

Grains.
$27\frac{11}{32} =$   1 Dram.
$437\frac{1}{2} =$    16 =   1 Ounce.
7000 =    256 =   16 =   1 Pound.
196000 =  7168 =  448 =  28 = 1 Quarter.
784000 = 28672 = 1792 = 112 = 4 = 1 Hund. Wt.
15680000 = 573440 = 35840 = 2240 = 80 = 20 = 1 Ton.

Avoirdupois weight is the only weight that can be legally used in this kingdom for weighing all things of a coarse or drossy nature, as grocery wares, butter, cheese, meat, bread, corn, &c., and all metals, except gold and silver.

----

Troy pound is to the Avoirdupois pound in the ratio of 5760 grs. to 7000 grs., or of 144 to 175; and the Troy ounce is to the Avoirdupois ounce in the ratio of 480 grs. Troy to 437¼ grs. Troy, or of 192 to 175.

It is likewise to be remarked, that 56 lb. of old hay, 60 lb. of new, or 36 lb. of straw, make 1 truss, and 36 trusses make a load of hay or straw.

‡ *Observe*, although it is enacted by the 4 & 5 Will. 4. c. 49. sec. 12., that the stone shall consist of 14 lbs., and that all contracts made by any other stone shall be null and void; yet it is the established custom in London, notwithstanding the law, to buy and sell meat, especially in the wholesale market, at 8 lbs. to the stone.

### OTHER WEIGHTS USUALLY DENOMINATED BY MEASURES.

|  | lb. | oz. |
|---|---|---|
| A peck loaf of bread weighs | 17 | 6 |
| A half ditto | 8 | 11 |
| A quarter ditto | 4 | 5½ |
| A peck of flour is 1 stone | 14 | 0 |
| A bushel of ditto is 4 stone | 56 | 0 |
| A sack, or 5 bushels of ditto is 20 stone | 280 | 0 |
| A firkin of butter | 56 | 0 |

Although we speak of flour and bread, especially in London, as if they were sold by measure, they are in reality, and can, legally, only be sold by weight; the quartern loaf, as it is called when baked and sold to the public, should weigh 4 lbs.

## EXAMPLES.

| (1.) T. | cwt. | qr. | lb. | (2.) Cwt. | qr. | lb. | oz. | (3.) Qr. | lb. | oz. |
|---|---|---|---|---|---|---|---|---|---|---|
| 42 | 14 | 2 | 20 | 20 | 3 | 27 | 15 | 15 | 9 | 13 |
| 59 | 12 | 1 | 14 | 12 | 0 | 0 | 6 | 17 | 14 | 9 |
| 76 | 13 | 3 | 22 | 10 | 1 | 3 | 9 | 24 | 13 | 7 |
| 47 | 17 | 1 | 17 | 6 | 2 | 8 | 4 | 19 | 10 | 11 |
| 36 | 10 | 2 | 9 | 4 | 2 | 20 | 13 | 16 | 8 | 13 |
| 49 | 9 | 1 | 16 | 27 | 0 | 21 | 2 | 10 | 13 | 6 |
| 57 | 14 | 2 | 11 | 8 | 1 | 2 | 0 | 12 | 4 | 14 |
| 3 | 4 | 3 | 24 | 0 | 2 | 13 | 12 | 21 | 20 | 10 |
| 373 | 17 | 3 | 21 | 90 | 2 | 13 | 13 | 137 | 12 | 3 |

| (4.) Qr. | lb. | oz. | dr. | (5.) Cwt. | qr. | lb. | oz. | (6) Qr. | lb. | oz. |
|---|---|---|---|---|---|---|---|---|---|---|
| 1 | 25 | 14 | 9 | 12 | 1 | 10 | 10 | 19 | 7 | 12 |
| 2 | 20 | 1 | 15 | 8 | 2 | 6 | 0 | 17 | 9 | 8 |
| 3 | 6 | 7 | 3 | 19 | 3 | 15 | 5 | 14 | 26 | 5 |
| 0 | 18 | 12 | 11 | 7 | 0 | 20 | 14 | 13 | 20 | 13 |
| 2 | 27 | 3 | 2 | 11 | 1 | 27 | 11 | 15 | 17 | 9 |
| 1 | 19 | 8 | 1 | 5 | 2 | 19 | 7 | 18 | 12 | 11 |
| 3 | 0 | 15 | 5 | 13 | 1 | 18 | 9 | 19 | 16 | 3 |
| 2 | 0 | 0 | 13 | 7 | 0 | 5 | 10 | 21 | 15 | 14 |

| (7.) Qr. | lb. | oz. | dr. | (8.) Cwt. | gr. | lb. | oz. | (9.) Qr. | lb. | oz. |
|---|---|---|---|---|---|---|---|---|---|---|
| 3 | 25 | 10 | 8 | 51 | 3 | 19 | 0 | 48 | 20 | 13 |
| 2 | 5 | 3 | 11 | 17 | 0 | 26 | 15 | 17 | 12 | 9 |
| 1 | 2 | 14 | 0 | 18 | 1 | 12 | 8 | 16 | 14 | 7 |
| 0 | 26 | 12 | 15 | 12 | 2 | 0 | 14 | 20 | 19 | 8 |
| 1 | 0 | 5 | 1 | 14 | 1 | 0 | 10 | 23 | 2 | 14 |
| 2 | 4 | 6 | 7 | 13 | 2 | 0 | 13 | 21 | 1 | 10 |
| 1 | 9 | 8 | 7 | 10 | 1 | 20 | 12 | 14 | 17 | 0 |
| 7 | 0 | 5 | 6 | 18 | 1 | 2 | 9 | 10 | 17 | 12 |

(10.) A shopkeeper bought 3 qrs. 14 lb. of teas ; 1 qr. 23 lb. of coffee ; 3 cwt. 2 qrs. 5 lb. of sugars ; 2 qrs. 3 lb. 13 oz. 9 dr. of spices ; 13 cwt. 1 qr. 24 lb. of hops, and other articles weighing 3 cwt. 17 lb. 7 oz. 13 dr. What is the weight of the whole?

## APOTHECARIES' WEIGHT.

|  |  |  |  |
|---|---|---|---|
| 20 Grains (*gr.*) make | 1 Scruple | *sc.* or ℈j.* |
| 3 Scruples | —— 1 Dram† | *dr.* or ℨj. |
| 8 Drams | —— 1 Ounce | *oz.* or ℥j. |
| 12 Ounces | —— 1 Pound | *lb.* or lb. j. |

Grains.
20 =   1 Scruple.
60 =   3 = 1 Dram.
480 =  24 =  8 = 1 Ounce.
5760 = 288 = 96 = 12 = 1 Pound.

The standard for this weight is the same as that of Troy weight, but with different divisions, the ounce being divided into 8 drams or 24 scruples.. Medicines are compounded by this weight; but drugs are usually bought and sold by avoirdupois weight.

### EXAMPLES.

| (1.) | lb. | oz. | dr. | sc. |
|---|---|---|---|---|
|  | 24 | 7 | 2 | 1 |
|  | 17 | 11 | 7 | 2 |
|  | 36 | 6 | 5 | 0 |
|  | 15 | 9 | 7 | 1 |
|  | 9 | 3 | 4 | 1 |
|  | 16 | 10 | 3 | 2 |
|  | 4 | 0 | 1 | 1 |
|  | 125 | 1 | 7 | 2 |

| (2.) | Oz. | dr. | sc. | gr. |
|---|---|---|---|---|
|  | 11 | 2 | 1 | 17 |
|  | 7 | 4 | 2 | 14 |
|  | 4 | 0 | 1 | 19 |
|  | 2 | 5 | 2 | 11 |
|  | 10 | 1 | 2 | 16 |
|  | 8 | 7 | 1 | 13 |
|  | 9 | 0 | 0 | 11 |
|  | 53 | 7 | 2 | 1 |

| (3.) | Dr. | sc. | gr. |
|---|---|---|---|
|  | 3 | 2 | 15 |
|  | 0 | 1 | 13 |
|  | 2 | 2 | 11 |
|  | 7 | 0 | 17 |
|  | 5 | 2 | 14 |
|  | 6 | 1 | 0 |
|  | 0 | 0 | 19 |
|  | 27 | 0 | 9 |

| (4.) | lb. | oz. | dr. | sc. |
|---|---|---|---|---|
|  | 17 | 6 | 5 | 2 |
|  | 33 | 9 | 1 | 0 |
|  | 20 | 8 | 7 | 1 |
|  | 86 | 11 | 3 | 2 |
|  | 90 | 4 | 0 | 0 |
|  | 32 | 10 | 6 | 2 |

| (5.) | Oz. | dr. | sc. | gr. |
|---|---|---|---|---|
|  | 8 | 5 | 1 | 8 |
|  | 7 | 6 | 2 | 13 |
|  | 11 | 7 | 0 | 0 |
|  | 10 | 0 | 0 | 16 |
|  | 1 | 2 | 2 | 3 |
|  | 0 | 7 | 1 | 19 |

| (6.) | Dr. | sc. | gr. |
|---|---|---|---|
|  | 7 | 1 | 17 |
|  | 4 | 0 | 3 |
|  | 0 | 2 | 10 |
|  | 4 | 1 | 12 |
|  | 6 | 0 | 0 |
|  | 7 | 2 | 19 |

* Physicians chiefly make use of the latter characters, in the above table, in writing their prescriptions.

† *Dram*, which is sometimes written *drachm*, is a contraction from *drachma*.

(7.) An Apothecary made a composition of five ingredients; the first weighed 3 lb. 7 oz.; the second, 1 oz. 7 dr. 13 gr.; the third, 7 lb. 2 sc.; the fourth, 11 lb. 3 dr. 1 sc.; and the fifth, 5 lb. 5 oz. 2 dr. 1 sc. 7 gr. What was the weight of the whole?

## WOOL WEIGHT.*

| 7 | Pounds (*lb*). | make 1 Clove | *cl.* |
|---|---|---|---|
| 14 | Pounds, or 2 Cloves | —— 1 Stone | *st.* |
| 28 | Pounds, or 2 Stone | —— 1 Tod | *td.* |
| 6½ | Tods | —— 1 Wey | *wy.* |
| 2 | Weys, or 364 lbs. | —— 1 Sack | *sa.* |
| 12 | Sacks, or 4368 lbs. | —— 1 Last | *la.* |

And a Pack of wool is 12 score, or 240 pounds.

Pounds.
```
   7 =   1 Clove.
  14 =   2 =   1 Stone.
  28 =   4 =   2 =   1 Tod.
 182 =  26 =  13 =   6½ = 1 Wey.
 364 =  52 =  26 =  13  = 2 = 1 Sack.
4368 = 624 = 312 = 156  = 24 = 12 = 1 Last.
```

### EXAMPLES.

| (1.) | *La.* | *sa.* | *wy.* | *td.* |
|---|---|---|---|---|
| | 21 | 9 | 1 | 5 |
| | 18 | 7 | 0 | 4 |
| | 9 | 10 | 1 | 6 |
| | 7 | 11 | 1 | 3 |
| | 8 | 1 | 0 | 2 |
| | 66 | 5 | 0 | 0½ |

| (2.) | *Wy.* | *td.* | *st.* | *cl.* |
|---|---|---|---|---|
| | 11 | 4 | 1 | 1 |
| | 0 | 2 | 0 | 1 |
| | 21 | 6 | 1 | 1 |
| | 0 | 5 | 0 | 0 |
| | 0 | 4 | 1 | 1 |
| | 35 | 3½ | 1 | 0 |

| (3.) | *St.* | *cl.* | *lb.* |
|---|---|---|---|
| | 20 | 1 | 6 |
| | 13 | 0 | 2 |
| | 15 | 0 | 5 |
| | 10 | 1 | 6 |
| | 7 | 0 | 3 |
| | 67 | 1 | 1 |

* The stone formerly varied in weight in different counties. In Gloucestershire it was 15 lb., and in Herefordshire only 12 lb.

The same may also be said with respect to a stone of meat, which, in London, is 8 lb., but in the northern counties, and some other parts of the kingdom, 16 lb.; though 14 lb. is the only legal standard.

(4.) *La.  sa.  wy.  td.*
```
29 . 8 . 1 . 4
19 . 7 . 1 . 6
 8 . 6 . 0 . 5
 0 . 10 . 1 . 3
 0 . 0 . 0 . 6
84 . 9 . 1 . 2
```

(5.) *Wy.  td.  st.  cl.*
```
20 . 2 . 1 . 1
13 . 4 . 0 . 1
17 . 5 . 1 . 0
 9 . 3 . 1 . 1
 4 . 6 . 1 . 0
 3 . 0 . 1 . 1
```

(6.) *St.  cl.  lb.*
```
15 . 1 . 4
16 . 0 . 3
19 . 0 . 2
10 . 1 . 1
 8 . 0 . 4
 7 . 1 . 2
```

(7.) *Sa.  wy.  td.  st.*
```
45 . 1 . 3 . 1
17 . 0 . 6 . 0
28 . 1 . 0 . 1
13 . 0 . 5 . 1
 9 . 1 . 4 . 1
 5 . 0 . 3 . 1
 2 . 1 . 0 . 1
```

(8.) *La.  wy.  td.  st.*
```
16 . 5 . 4 . 1
14 . 3 . 2 . 1
19 . 9 . 5 . 0
17 . 2 . 1 . 1
 6 . 8 . 6 . 1
 4 . 7 . 3 . 1
 4 . 12 . 4 . 0
```

(9.) *Sa.  wy.  lb.*
```
14 . 1 . 4
13 . 0 . 5
10 . 1 . 3
 7 . 0 . 4
 8 . 0 . 3
 6 . 1 . 0
 5 . 0 . 3
```

## LONG MEASURE, OR MEASURES OF LENGTH.

| | | | |
|---|---|---|---|
| 3 | Barley-corns (*b. c.*)* | make 1 Inch | *in.* |
| 12 | Inches | —— 1 Foot | *ft.* |
| 3 | Feet, or 36 inches | —— 1 Yard | *yd.* |
| 6 | Feet, or 2 yards | —— 1 Fathom | *fth.* |
| 5½ | Yards=1 Perch or | —— 1 Pole or Rod | *po.* |
| 40 | Poles | —— 1 Furlong | *fur.* |
| 8 | Furlongs, or 1760 yards | —— 1 Mile | *mi.* |
| 3 | Miles | —— 1 League | *lea.* |
| 60 | Geographical miles, or } 69½ British miles } | —— 1 Degree | *deg. or* ° |

*Obs.* Among mechanics the *inch* is usually divided into *eighths.* By the officers of the revenue, and by scientific persons, it is divided into *tenths, hundredths,* &c. Formerly it was made to consist of 12 parts called *lines.*

---

\* The length of 3 barley-corns was formerly reckoned an inch, but a barley-corn being no exact standard of measure, it was determined by an act of parliament, passed June 17th, 1824, that the standard for the

Bar.

$$3 = \qquad 1 \text{ Inch.}$$
$$36 = \qquad 12 = \qquad 1 \text{ Foot.}$$
$$108 = \qquad 36 = \qquad 3 = \qquad 1 \text{ Yard.}$$
$$594 = \qquad 198 = \qquad 16\tfrac{1}{2} = \qquad 5\tfrac{1}{2} = \qquad 1 \text{ Pole.}$$
$$23760 = \quad 7920 = \quad 660 = 220 = 40 = 1 \text{ Furlong.}$$
$$190080 = 63360 = 5280 = 1760 = 320 = 8 = 1 \text{ Mile.}$$

## EXAMPLES.

| (1.) Mi. fur. po. yds. | (2.) Po. yds. ft. in. | (3.) Yds. ft. in. |
|---|---|---|
| 72 . 7 . 38 . 2 | 20 . 4 . 2 . 11 | 19 . 2 . 9 |
| 51 . 5 . 20 . 3 | 10 . 1 . 1 . 8 | 17 . 0 . 5 |
| 20 . 4 . 39 . 5 | 13 . 2 . 0 . 7 | 18 . 1 . 7 |
| 12 . 0 . 6 . 4 | 31 . 0 . 1 . 10 | 12 . 0 . 1 |
| 21 . 2 . 0 . 1 | 12 . 5 . 2 . 0 | 24 . 1 . 10 |
| 32 . 1 . 5 . 3 | 5 . 3 . 1 . 6 | 20 . 2 . 11 |
| 210 . 5 . 31 . 1½ | 94 . 1½ . 1 . 6 | 113 . 0 . 7 |

| (4.) Mi. fur. po. yds. | (5.) Lea. mi. fur. po. | (6.) Mi. fur. po. |
|---|---|---|
| 37 . 3 . 14 . 2 | 13 . 1 . 7 . 10 | 13 . 7 . 30 |
| 28 . 4 . 17 . 3 | 40 . 2 . 6 . 30 | 15 . 0 . 19 |
| 17 . 4 . 4 . 3 | 15 . 1 . 0 . 12 | 17 . 1 . 10 |
| 10 . 5 . 6 . 3 | 29 . 0 . 7 . 29 | 19 . 2 . 15 |
| 29 . 2 . 2 . 2 | 64 . 1 . 0 . 17 | 14 . 1 . 16 |
| 30 . 0 . 0 . 4 | 98 . 2 . 5 . 0 | 20 . 5 . 8 |

measure of length shall be the *imperial standard yard* of 36 inches, when compared with the length of the pendulum vibrating seconds of mean time in the latitude of London, in a vacuum, at the level of the sea, being in the proportion of 36 to 39·1393 inches.

The standard yard, formerly preserved at the House of Commons, was destroyed by the fire which consumed the two houses of parliament in 1834 ; so that the country is now without a legal standard of measure, except the one constructed for the *Royal Astronomical Society* of London.

It may also be observed, in addition to the measures given above, that a *Hand,* which is used in estimating the height of horses, is 4 inches.

| (7.) Po. | yds. | ft. | in. | | (8.) Mi. | fur. | po. | yds. | | (9.) Fur. | po. | yds. |
|---|---|---|---|---|---|---|---|---|---|---|---|---|
| 35 | 4 | 2 | 11 | | 56 | 7 | 19 | 4 | | 28 | 3 | 2 |
| 12 | 2 | 1 | 8 | | 13 | 3 | 36 | 5 | | 29 | 5 | 3 |
| 16 | 5 | 2 | 0 | | 81 | 0 | 10 | 2 | | 20 | 7 | 0 |
| 24 | 0 | 1 | 9 | | 91 | 6 | 25 | 0 | | 13 | 5 | 4 |
| 38 | 3 | 2 | 10 | | 70 | 4 | 13 | 3 | | 22 | 7 | 0 |
| 0 | 0 | 1 | 6 | | 60 | 0 | 38 | 2 | | 20 | 1 | . |

(10.) From A. to B. is 3 mi. 2 fur. 7 p.; from B. to C. 17 mi. 13 p.; from C. to D. 7 fur. 10 p. 5 yds.; and from D. to E. 5 mi. 33 p. 1 yd. 7 in.  What is the distance from A. to E.?

## CLOTH MEASURES.

| 2¼ | Inches | make 1 Nail | nl. |
|---|---|---|---|
| 4 | Nails | —— 1 Quarter of a Yard | qr. |
| 3 | Quarters | —— 1 Flemish Ell* | fl. |
| 4 | Quarters | —— 1 Yard | yd. |
| 5 | Quarters | —— 1 English Ell | en. |
| 6 | Quarters | —— 1 French Ell* | fr. |

Inches.
$2\frac{1}{4} =$ 1 Nail.
$9 = 4 =$ 1 Quarter.
$36 = 16 = 4 =$ 1 Yard.
$27 = 12 = 3 =$ 1 Flem. Ell.
$45 = 20 = 5 =$ 1 Eng. Ell.
$54 = 24 = 6 =$ 1 French Ell.

### EXAMPLES.

| (1.) Fl. e. | qrs. | nl. | in. | | (2.) Yds. | qrs. | nl. | in. | | (3.) En. e. | qrs. | nl. | in. |
|---|---|---|---|---|---|---|---|---|---|---|---|---|---|
| 65 | 1 | 3 | 1 | | 20 | 3 | 1 | 1 | | 97 | 2 | 2 | 1 |
| 26 | 2 | 1 | 2 | | 38 | 2 | 0 | 1 | | 58 | 1 | 3 | 2 |
| 24 | 0 | 1 | 0 | | 28 | 2 | 0 | 2 | | 20 | 4 | 2 | 1 |
| 82 | 2 | 3 | 1 | | 45 | 1 | 3 | 1 | | 9 | 3 | 0 | 2 |
| 33 | 0 | 3 | 0 | | 63 | 0 | 2 | 0 | | 0 | 4 | 3 | 1 |
| 7 | 1 | 2 | 1 | | 8 | 2 | 1 | 2 | | 0 | 2 | 2 | 2 |
| 240 | 0 | 3 | 0½ | | 205 | 0 | 2 | 0¼ | | 188 | 0 | 0 | 0 |

* Flemish and French ells are now seldom used, nor is the English ell, except nominally in measures of width.

| (4.) Fr. e. qrs. nl. | (5.) Yds. qrs. nl. in. | (6.) En. e. qrs. nl. |
|---|---|---|
| 126 . 4 . 2 | 85 . 2 . 3 . 1 | 950 . 3 . 3 |
| 233 . 5 . 3 | 92 . 3 . 2 . 2 | 837 . 4 . 2 |
| 87 . 1 . 2 | 86 . 1 . 1 . 0 | 903 . 2 . 1 |
| 32 . 3 . 1 | 7 . 0 . 2 . 1 | 250 . 1 . 0 |
| 25 . 2 . 0 | 0 . 3 . 1 . 2 | 501 . 0 . 3 |
| 16 . 0 . 2 | 0 . 0 . 2 . 1 | 69 . 3 . 2 |

(7.) A merchant bought four parcels of cloth; the first contained 400 English ells, 1 qr. 3 nls.; the second, 976 Eng. ells, 3 qrs.; the third, 765 Eng. ells, 2 qrs. 1 nl.; the fourth, 43 Eng. ells, 2 qrs. How many ells, &c. were there in the whole?

## SQUARE MEASURE, OR MEASURES OF SURFACE.

| | | | |
|---|---|---|---|
| 144 | Square Inches | make 1 Square Foot | sq. ft. |
| 9 | Square Feet | —— 1 Square Yard | sq. yd. |
| 30¼ | Square Yards | —— 1 Square Pole | sq. po. |
| 40 | Square Poles | —— 1 Rood | sq. rd. |
| 4 | Roods, or 4840 Sq. Yards —— 1 Acre | | ac. |
| 640 | Acres | —— 1 Square Mile | sq. mi. |

Also 100 square feet, among carpenters and other workmen, make a square of flooring, roofing, &c.

Sq. Inches.
```
     144=      1 Sq. Foot.
    1296=      9  =   1 Sq. Yard.
   39204=    272¼=  30¼=   1 Sq. Pole.
 1568160=10890  =1210 =  40=1 Rood.
6272640=43560  =4840 =160=4=1 Acre.
```

By this measure, land, and all husbandmen's and gardeners' work are measured; also all kinds of artificers' work,

---

* Land is usually measured by a chain, called, after its inventor, GUNTER's *chain*; which is 4 poles, or 22 yards, or 66 feet long, and consists of 100 links, each of which is 7·92 inches. Also 10 square chains, that is 10 chains in length and one in breadth, make an acre.

as boards, glass, pavements, plastering, wainscotting, tiling, flooring, and all dimensions of length and breadth only.

### EXAMPLES.

| (1.) *Rd.* | *po.* | *yds.* | *ft.* |
|---|---|---|---|
| 3 | 38 | 26 | 7 |
| 2 | 15 | 13 | 5 |
| 1 | 2 | 6 | 2 |
| 0 | 1 | 9 | 4 |
| 2 | 0 | 0 | 3 |
| 3 | 20 | 30 | 8 |
| 12 | 38 | 26½ | 2 |

| (2.) *Acr.* | *rd.* | *po.* |
|---|---|---|
| 382 | 1 | 34 |
| 618 | 3 | 14 |
| 100 | 1 | 27 |
| 74 | 2 | 19 |
| 63 | 1 | 31 |
| 55 | 3 | 38 |
| 1295 | 3 | 3 |

| (3.) *Acr.* | *rd.* | *po.* |
|---|---|---|
| 721 | 2 | 15 |
| 94 | 3 | 32 |
| 36 | 2 | 29 |
| 59 | 3 | 28 |
| 265 | 0 | 17 |
| 27 | 0 | 30 |
| 1205 | 1 | 31 |

| (4.) *Rd.* | *po.* | *yds.* | *ft.* |
|---|---|---|---|
| 2 | 1 | 28 | 6 |
| 3 | 30 | 10 | 7 |
| 1 | 38 | 30 | 3 |
| 0 | 18 | 0 | 2 |
| 1 | 0 | 12 | 0 |
| 1 | 20 | 13 | 3 |

| (5.) *Acr.* | *rd.* | *po.* |
|---|---|---|
| 409 | 1 | 36 |
| 81 | 3 | 20 |
| 94 | 2 | 10 |
| 8 | 0 | 17 |
| 0 | 3 | 39 |
| 0 | 3 | 25 |

| (6.) *Acr.* | *rd.* | *po.* |
|---|---|---|
| 4061 | 0 | 24 |
| 2731 | 2 | 3 |
| 841 | 3 | 19 |
| 96 | 2 | 39 |
| 85 | 0 | 10 |
| 40 | 1 | 0 |

(7.) A surveyor, having measured four pieces of land, found one to contain 7 acres, 3 roods, 24 poles; another, 18 acres, 1 rood, 16 poles; the third, 20 acres, 5 poles, 8 yards; and the fourth, 15 acres, 24 yards, 7 feet. How many acres, &c. were surveyed?

## MEASURES OF SOLIDITY AND CAPACITY.

### CUBIC OR SOLID MEASURE.

| | |
|---|---|
| 1728 Cubic Inches | make 1 Cubic Foot. |
| 27 Cubic Feet | —— 1 Cubic Yard. |
| 40 Feet of rough timber | |
| 50 Feet of hewn or squared do. } | —— 1 Load or Ton. |
| 42 Cubic Feet | —— 1 Ton of shipping. |

By this measure, stone, timber, and all works that have length, breadth, and thickness, are measured.

## EXAMPLES.

| (1.) | Yd. | ft. | in. | | (2.) | Yd. | ft. | in. | | (3.) | Yd. | ft. | in. |
|---|---|---|---|---|---|---|---|---|---|---|---|---|---|
| | 27 . | 19 . | 72 | | | 247 . | 19 . | 120 | | | 49 . | 17 . | 12 |
| | 23 . | 21 . | 5 | | | 495 . | 18 . | 560 | | | 39 . | 16 . | 7 |
| | 40 . | 9 . | 18 | | | 140 . | 22 . | 60 | | | 84 . | 19 . | 27 |
| | 26 . | 20 . | 90 | | | 790 . | 16 . | 108 | | | 46 . | 13 . | 12 |
| | 108 . | 26 . | 4 | | | 401 . | 7 : | 25 | | | 51 . | 20 . | 48 |
| | 227 . | 14 . | 189 | | | 2076 . | 1 . | 873 | | | 272 . | 4 . | 106 |

| (4.) | Yd. | ft. | in. | | (5.) | Yd. | ft. | in. | | (6.) | Yd. | ft. | in. |
|---|---|---|---|---|---|---|---|---|---|---|---|---|---|
| | 729 . | 13 . | 107 | | | 706 . | 22 . | 19 | | | 56 . | 13 . | 9 |
| | 904 . | 17 . | 24 | | | 437 . | 16 . | 8 | | | 49 . | 19 . | 19 |
| | 381 . | 12 . | 11 | | | 539 . | 18 . | 29 | | | 57 . | 17 . | 18 |
| | 209 . | 18 . | 17 | | | 406 . | 17 . | 20 | | | 28 . | 18 . | 13 |
| | 195 . | 20 . | 21 | | | 407 . | 17 . | 38 | | | 56 . | 10 . | 10 |
| | 206 . | 17 . | 10 | | | 591 . | 17 . | 91 | | | 19 . | 19 . | 9 |

## WINE MEASURE.*

| 4 Gills | make | 1 Pint | pt. |
|---|---|---|---|
| 2 Pints | —— | 1 Quart | qt. |
| 4 Quarts | —— | 1 Gallon | gal. |
| 42 Gallons | —— | 1 Tierce | tier. |
| 84 Gals. or 2 Tierces | —— | 1 Puncheon | pun. |
| 63 Gallons | —— | 1 Hogshead | hhd. |
| 126 Gals. or 2 Hhds. | —— | 1 Pipe or Butt | pi. |
| 252 Gals. or 2 Pipes | —— | 1 Tun | tn. |

* Besides these measures there are some others, as an anker, chiefly used for brandy, which contains from 9 to 10 gallons; and a rundlet, that holds from 18 to 20 gallons.

It may be observed, from the merchants' wine measures, that a pipe of different sorts of wine does not always consist of the same quantity. Thus a pipe of Port is 115 gallons, a pipe or rather a butt of sherry is 108 gallons, a pipe of Madeira or Cape is 92 gallons.

THE WINE MERCHANTS' MEASURES are as follows: but it is the practice to gauge all such vessels, and charge them, as well as the duty, according to their actual contents.

115 Gallons make 1 Pipe of Port.
108 Gallons —— 1 Butt of Sherry.
117 Gallons —— 1 Pipe of Lisbon.
105 Gallons —— 1 Pipe of Malaga.
100 Gallons —— 1 Pipe of Teneriffe or Vidonia.
92 Gallons —— 1 Pipe of Madeira.
92 Gallons —— 1 Pipe of Cape.
46 Gallons —— 1 Hhd. of Claret.
30 Gallons —— 1 Aum of Hock.

Pints.

$$2 = 1 \text{ Quart.}$$
$$8 = 4 = 1 \text{ Gallon.}$$
$$336 = 168 = 42 = 1 \text{ Tierce.}$$
$$504 = 252 = 63 = 1\tfrac{1}{2} = 1 \text{ Hogshead.}$$
$$672 = 336 = 84 = 2 = 1\tfrac{1}{3} = 1 \text{ Puncheon.}$$
$$1008 = 504 = 126 = 3 = 2 = 1\tfrac{1}{2} = 1 \text{ Pipe,}$$
$$2016 = 1008 = 252 = 6 = 4 = 3 = 2 = 1 \text{ Tun.}$$

By this measure all kinds of spirits, as well as cider, mead, vinegar, oil, honey, &c. are measured.

*Note.* — The *imperial gallon*, with its divisions, is the only legal standard measure of capacity for *wine, ale, beer, spirits,* and all *sorts of liquids,* as well as all *dry goods.*

According to the *Act,* the *imperial standard gallon* contains 10 lbs. avoirdupois of distilled water, and its cubic content equals 277·273843570, or nearly 277¼ cubic inches. The old wine gallon, which is now abolished, contained 231 cubic inches, and the old ale or beer gallon 282 cubic inches. Therefore, 5 gallons by the new or imperial measure are nearly equal to 6 gallons of the old wine measure, and 60 gallons imperial measure are nearly equal to 59 gallons of the old beer measure.

#### EXAMPLES.

| (1.) Pi. | hhd. | gal. | qt. | (2.) Hhd. | gal. | qt. | pt. | (3.) Hhd. | gal. | qt. |
|------|------|------|------|------|------|------|------|------|------|------|
| 1 | 1 | 27 | 3 | 64 | 22 | 2 | 1 | 27 | 14 | 2 |
| 0 | 1 | 60 | 1 | 21 | 17 | 3 | 1 | 47 | 13 | 1 |
| 1 | 0 | 34 | 0 | 73 | 61 | 2 | 1 | 25 | 17 | 0 |
| 0 | 1 | 37 | 2 | 63 | 45 | 1 | 1 | 16 | 13 | 3 |
| 1 | 1 | 52 | 1 | 40 | 20 | 3 | 1 | 17 | 7 | 2 |
| 1 | 0 | 48 | 0 | 27 | 16 | 2 | 0 | 18 | 5 | 1 |
| 1 | 0 | 42 | 2 | 94 | 50 | 3 | 1 | 27 | 0 | 0 |
| 9 | 0 | 50 | 1 | 385 | 46 | 3 | 0 | 178 | 8 | 1 |

| (4.) Tun. | pi. | hhd. | gal. |
|---|---|---|---|
| 83 | 1 | 1 | 62 |
| 32 | 0 | 0 | 12 |
| 80 | 1 | 1 | 40 |
| 91 | 1 | 0 | 20 |
| 53 | 1 | 1 | 55 |
| 42 | 1 | 0 | 0 |
| 9 | 0 | 1 | 10 |

| (5.) Tun. | pun. | tier. | gal. |
|---|---|---|---|
| 61 | 2 | 1 | 40 |
| 53 | 1 | 0 | 39 |
| 48 | 2 | 1 | 13 |
| 32 | 0 | 0 | 10 |
| 25 | 1 | 1 | 9 |
| 17 | 2 | 0 | 41 |
| 8 | 1 | 1 | 0 |

| (6.) Hhd. | gal. | qt. |
|---|---|---|
| 48 | 16 | 3 |
| 59 | 17 | 1 |
| 28 | 14 | 0 |
| 50 | 50 | 3 |
| 46 | 19 | 0 |
| 23 | 2 | 2 |
| 14 | 1 | 1 |

| (7.) Tun. | pun. | tier. | gal. |
|---|---|---|---|
| 56 | 2 | 0 | 41 |
| 32 | 1 | 1 | 16 |
| 48 | 2 | 1 | 10 |
| 25 | 0 | 0 | 38 |
| 10 | 2 | 1 | 19 |
| 8 | 0 | 1 | 0 |
| 0 | 2 | 0 | 40 |

| (8.) Hhd. | gal. | qt. | pt. |
|---|---|---|---|
| 53 | 12 | 2 | 1 |
| 91 | 61 | 3 | 1 |
| 81 | 0 | 2 | 1 |
| 90 | 15 | 0 | 0 |
| 8 | 6 | 2 | 1 |
| 0 | 57 | 1 | 0 |
| 0 | 0 | 3 | 1 |

| (9.) Gal. | qt. | pt. |
|---|---|---|
| 49 | 3 | 1 |
| 57 | 0 | 0 |
| 69 | 2 | 1 |
| 43 | 1 | 1 |
| 57 | 0 | 1 |
| 41 | 0 | 0 |
| 37 | 1 | 0 |

## ALE AND BEER MEASURE.

| 2 Pints | make 1 Quart | qt. |
|---|---|---|
| 4 Quarts | —— 1 Gallon | gal. |
| 8 Gallons | —— 1 Firkin of Ale | a. fir. |
| 9 Gallons | —→ 1 Firkin of Beer | b. fir. |
| 18 Gals. or 2 Firkins | —— 1 Kilderkin | kil. |
| 36 Gals. or 2 Kilderkins | —— 1 Barrel | bar. |
| 54 Gals. or 1½ Barrels | —— 1 Hogshead | hhd. |
| 72 Gals. or 2 Barrels | —— 1 Puncheon | pun. |
| 108 Gals. or 2 Hogsheads | —— 1 Butt | butt. |
| 2 Butts or 4 Hogsheads | —— 1 Tun | tun. |

Pints.

$$2 = 1 \text{ Quart.}$$
$$8 = 4 = 1 \text{ Gallon.}$$
$$72 = 36 = 9 = 1 \text{ Firkin.}$$
$$144 = 72 = 18 = 2 = 1 \text{ Kilderkin.}$$
$$288 = 144 = 36 = 4 = 2 = 1 \text{ Barrel.}$$
$$432 = 216 = 54 = 6 = 3 = 1\tfrac{1}{2} = 1 \text{ Hogshead.}$$
$$576 = 288 = 72 = 8 = 4 = 2 = 1\tfrac{1}{3} = 1 \text{ Punch.}$$
$$864 = 432 = 108 = 12 = 6 = 3 = 2 = 1\tfrac{1}{2} = 1 \text{ Butt.}$$

In London, they reckon only 8 gallons for the firkin of ale, and 32 for the barrel; but in all other parts of England, for ale, and beer, 9 gallons make a firkin, and 36 gallons a barrel.

*Note.* The old ale gallon contained 282 cubic inches; but the Imperial standard gallon contains only 277·274 cubic inches, the same as for wine.

### EXAMPLES.

| (1.) *But. hhd. bar. kil.* | (2.) *Fir. gal. qt.* | (3.) *Hhds. fir. gal. qt.* |
|---|---|---|
| 56 . 1 . 1 . 1 | 47 . 6 . 2 | 45 . 2 . 7 . 3 |
| 19 . 0 . 1 . 1 | 39 . 3 . 1 | 36 . 3 . 6 . 2 |
| 30 . 1 . 0 . 1 | 37 . 4 . 0 | 95 . 1 . 5 . 1 |
| 47 . 1 . 1 . 0 | 29 . 5 . 2 | 86 . 1 . 4 . 3 |
| 25 . 1 . 1 . 1 | 13 . 1 . 1 | 17 . 3 . 4 . 0 |
| 15 . 1 . 1 . 1 | 10 . 0 . 0 | 10 . 0 . 2 . 3 |
| 196 . 1 . 1 . 1 | 177 . 2 . 2 | 291 . 1 . 4 . 0 |

| (4.) *But. hhd. gal. qt.* | (5.) *Hhds. gal. qt.* | (6.) *Hhds. gal. qt. pt.* |
|---|---|---|
| 1 . 1 . 27 . 3 | 39 . 27 . 3 | 90 . 50 . 2 . 1 |
| 0 . 1 . 51 . 2 | 48 . 17 . 0 | 19 . 35 . 3 . 0 |
| 1 . 0 . 39 . 1 | 82 . 10 . 1 | 78 . 16 . 1 . 1 |
| 1 . 1 . 12 . 0 | 17 . 11 . 0 | 16 . 3 . 0 . 1 |
| 0 . 1 . 9 . 3 | 10 . 10 . 1 | 9 . 52 . 3 . 0 |
| 1 . 0 . 28 . 3 | 16 . 0 . 2 | 8 . 13 . 2 . 1 |

| (7.) *Fir. gal. qt. pt.* | (8.) *Kil. gal. qt.* | (9.) *Kil. gal. qt. pt.* |
|---|---|---|
| 7 . 6 . 3 . 1 | 39 . 15 . 3 | 2 . 17 . 3 . 1 |
| 5′ . 7 . 2 . 0 | 26 . 17 . 2 | 1 . 16 . 2 . 0 |
| 2 . 3 . 1 . 1 | 37 . 10 . 1 | 0 . 10 . 1 . 1 |
| 6 . 2 . 3 . 1 | 49 . 11 . 2 | 1 . 8 . 0 . 1 |
| 5 . 5 . 1 . 0 | 50 . 9 . 0 | 2 . 6 . 3 . 1 |

(10.) A brewer sent to an innkeeper, at one time, 5 hogsheads, 1 barrel, 20 gallons of beer; at another, 9 kilderkins, 1 firkin; and at another, 1 tun, 3 hogsheads, 50 gallons; how many tuns, hogsheads, &c. did he send in all?

## DRY MEASURE.

| | | |
|---|---|---|
| 2 Pints (*pt.*) | make 1 Quart | *qt.* |
| 2 Quarts | ——— 1 Pottle | *pot.* |
| 4 Quarts, or 2 Pottles | ——— 1 Gallon | *gal.* |
| 2 Gallons | ——— 1 Peck | *pck.* |
| 4 Pecks, or 8 Gallons | ——— 1 Bushel | *bu.* |
| 4 Bushels | ——— 1 Coom, or Sack | *coom.* |
| 8 Bushels, or 2 Cooms | ——— 1 Quarter | *qr.* |
| 5 Quarters | ——— 1 Wey or Load | *wey.* |
| 10 Quarters, or 2 Weys | ——— 1 Last | *last.* |

*Obs. Herrings* are measured by the barrel of 26⅜ gallons, or by the cran of 37½ gallons.

*Note.* For the late coal measure 3 bushels, heaped up, made a sack, and 12 sacks, or 36 bushels, a chaldron; but, by the present regulations, coals are sold by the hundred-weight, or by the ton, and not by measure. A sack of coals should weigh 224 lbs.

Pints.
```
    8=    1 Gallon.
   16=    2=   1 Peck.
   64=    8=   4=  1 Bushel.
  256=   32=  16=  4=  1 Coom.
  512=   64=  32=  8=  2=  1 Quarter.
 2560=  320= 160= 40= 10=  5= 1 Wey.
 5120=  640= 320= 80= 20= 10= 2= 1 Last.
```

By this measure corn, seeds, roots, salt, charcoal, oysters, &c., and all dry goods are measured.

The imperial bushel contains 80 lb. by weight of distilled water, and its content equals 2218·192 cubic inches, being eight times that of a gallon. The *imperial heaped bushel* contains 2815·4887 cubic inches, the cone being 19½ inches diameter, and height 6 inches; but heaped measure was abolished by an act of parliament passed August 13th, 1834. See 4 & 5 Will. 4. c. 49. s. 4. The late Winchester bushel, formerly used for dry measure, was 18½ in. wide, and 8 in. deep; its contents were 2150·42 cubic inches.

32 Winchester bushels nearly make 31 imperial bushels.

### EXAMPLES.

(1.) *Lst. wey qr. coom.*
27 . 0 . 3 . 1
36 . 1 . 4 . 1
91 . 1 . 2 . 0
95 . 0 . 4 . 1
86 . 1 . 3 . 1
71 . 1 . 0 . 1
40 . 1 . 2 . 1
———
450 . 1 . 1 . 0

(2.) *Bush. pck. gal.*
27 . 3 . 0
14 . 0 . 1
17 . 2 . 1
48 . 1 . 0
19 . 0 . 1
20 . 0 . 0
29 . 1 . 1
———
176 . 1 . 0

(3.) *Qr. bush. pck. gal.*
19 . 4 . 2 . 1
12 . 7 . 3 . 1
11 . 5 . 2 . 1
98 . 4 . 1 . 0
25 . 3 . 2 . 1
8 . 2 . 1 . 1
0 . 6 . 0 . 1
———
177 . 2 . 2 . 0

(4.) *W. qr. bush. pck.*
93 . 4 . 7 . 3
91 . 1 . 7 . 2
73 . 3 . 2 . 1
59 . 2 . 3 . 1
27 . 0 . 0 . 0
0 . 4 . 6 . 3
2 . 3 . 2 . 1
———

(5.) *Pck. gal. pot.*
49 . 1 . 1
59 . 0 . 1
60 . 1 . 0
56 . 0 . 1
55 . 1 . 1
17 . 0 . 1
12 . 1 . 0
———

(6.) *Qr. bush. pck. gal.*
80 . 6 . 3 . 1
89 . 5 . 2 . 0
46 . 4 . 1 . 1
37 . 7 . 3 . 1
18 . 3 . 2 . 1
0 . 4 . 3 . 0
7 . 2 . 1 . 1
———

(7.) *Lst. wey qr. coom.*
99 . 1 . 4 . 1
65 . 1 . 3 . 1
49 . 0 . 2 . 0
83 . 1 . 2 . 1
16 . 0 . 0 . 0
———

(8.) *Qr. bush. pck.*
60 . 3 . 2
37 . 0 . 3
56 . 7 . 2
50 . 6 . 0
23 . 4 . 0
———

(9.) *Lst. qr. bush. pck.*
72 . 6 . 7 . 2
37 . 9 . 6 . 3
68 . 4 . 2 . 1
38 . 3 . 0 . 2
17 . 7 . 5 . 3
———

(10.) A corn merchant exported 18 lasts, 2 qr. 5 bu. of wheat; 29 lasts, 6 qr. 7 bu. of rye; 15 lasts, 9 qr. 3 bu. of beans; and 46 lasts, 6 bu. of oats. How many lasts, &c. were exported in the whole?

## MEASURES OF TIME.

| | | |
|---|---|---|
| 60 Seconds (*sec.*) | make 1 Minute | *m. or min.* |
| 60 Minutes | —— 1 Hour | *hr.* |
| 24 Hours | —— 1 Day | *d.* |
| 7 Days | —— 1 Week | *w.* |
| 4 Weeks | —— 1 Month | *mo.* |
| 12 Calendar Months, or 13 Common Months, or 52 Weeks } | —— 1 Year | *yr.* |

Seconds.
```
     60 = 1 Minute.
   3600 =      60 =    1 Hour.
  86400 =    1440 =   24 =   1 Day.
 604800 =   10080 =  168 =   7 = 1 Week.
2419200 =   40320 =  672 =  28 = 4 = 1 Month.
31557600 = 525960 = 8766 = 365¼ = 1 Year.
```

The tropical or solar year is usually reckoned at 365¼ days; but its accurate length, as determined by astronomical observation, is 365 d. 5 h. 48 min. 48 sec.*

---

* The civil year consists of 365 days for three years together, and of 366 days every fourth, or leap year; except when the number that denotes a complete century, as the 17th, 18th, 19th, and 21st, is not divisible by 4, in which case it must be reckoned as a common year.

Hence, if the date of any year, for the whole of the present century, be exactly divisible by 4, it is leap year; and if it be not divisible by 4, the remainder shows how many years have passed since the last leap year.

It may here, also, be observed that the length of each of the 12 calendar months may be easily recollected by means of the following verse:

Thirty days hath September, April, June, and November,
And all the rest have thirty-one, excepting February alone,

which last month has twenty-eight days in common years, and twenty-nine when it is leap year. So that January has 31 days, February 28, March 31, April 30, May 31, June 30, July 31, August 31, September 30, October 31, November 30, December 31.

D

## EXAMPLES.

| (1.) Yr. | Com. mo. | w. | d. |
|---|---|---|---|
| 76 . | 8 . | 3 . | 6 |
| 57 . | 11 . | 2 . | 3 |
| 34 . | 9 . | 3 . | 5 |
| 57 . | 6 . | 1 . | 2 |
| 35 . | 10 . | 2 . | 4 |
| 56 . | 9 . | 3 . | 3 |
| 20 . | 6 . | 1 . | 2 |
| 339 . | 11 . | 2 . | 4 |

| (2.) Hr. | min. | sec. |
|---|---|---|
| 20 . | 37 . | 40 |
| 17 . | 20 . | 35 |
| 21 . | 16 . | 34 |
| 16 . | 27 . | 46 |
| 22 . | 19 . | 52 |
| 19 . | 22 . | 16 |
| 21 . | 31 . | 37 |
| 138 . | 56 . | 20 |

| (3.) Mo. | w. | d. |
|---|---|---|
| 19 . | 2 . | 6 |
| 6 . | 1 . | 4 |
| 22 . | 3 . | 5 |
| 7 . | 2 . | 3 |
| ·2 . | 1 . | 6 |
| 17 . | 3 . | 2 |
| 11 . | 3 . | 4 |
| 88 . | 3 . | 2 |

| (4.) D. | h. | m. | sec. |
|---|---|---|---|
| 24 . | 14 . | 48 . | 20 |
| 65 . | 5 . | 48 . | 55 |
| 87 . | 23 . | 15 . | 39 |
| 86 . | 23 . | 30 . | 0 |
| 79 . | 7 . | 48 . | 0 |
| 15 . | 22 . | 41 . | 14 |
| 4 . | 12 . | 25 . | 21 |

| (5.) Hr. | m. | sec. |
|---|---|---|
| 29 . | 51 . | 52 |
| 27 . | 18 . | 16 |
| 39 . | 19 . | 10 |
| 27 . | 17 . | 17 |
| 18 . | 19 . | 20 |
| 13 . | 13 . | 9 |
| 21 . | 23 . | 29 |

| 6.) M. | w. | d. |
|---|---|---|
| 10 . | 2 . | 4 |
| 3 . | 1 . | 5 |
| 11 . | 3 . | 6 |
| 2 . | 3 . | 3 |
| 7 . | 2 . | 2 |
| 2 . | 0 . | 5 |
| 5 . | 2 . | 3 |

| (7.) M. | w. | d. | h. |
|---|---|---|---|
| 47 . | 2 . | 3 . | 20 |
| 89 . | 3 . | 1 . | 19 |
| 12 . | 2 . | 5 . | 18 |
| 27 . | 3 . | 6 . | 12 |
| 19 . | 1 . | 4 . | 3 |
| 3 . | 0 . | 0 . | 1 |
| 6 . | 1 . | 1 . | 7 |
| 5 . | 0 . | 0 . | 12 |

| (8.) D. | h. | min. |
|---|---|---|
| 11 . | 11 . | 9 |
| 31 . | 13 . | 17 |
| 50 . | 14 . | 13 |
| 29 . | 17 . | 14 |
| 56 . | 16 . | 10 |
| 27 . | 18 . | 51 |
| 0 . | 11 . | 10 |
| 13 . | 16 . | 9 |

| (9.) W. | d. | h. |
|---|---|---|
| 10 . | 6 . | 16 |
| 8 . | 5 . | 15 |
| 7 . | 0 . | 13 |
| 6 . | 1 . | 18 |
| 3 . | 2 . | 17 |
| 2 . | 1 . | 21 |
| 3 . | 3 . | 20 |
| 0 . | 6 . | 12 |

## FOREIGN MEASURES OF LENGTH.

English Feet.
The Paris Foot....................................... 1·065747
Rhinland Foot....................................... 1·033
Rhinland Rood=12 Rhinland Feet .........12·396

English Yards.
One French Metre=39·370089 Eng. Inches=1·093614
One French Toise, or 6 Paris Feet = 6·394479
    English Feet.................................... 2·131493
One French League, 2282 Toises, 25 to a
    Degree.......................................4864·067026
Brabant League, 2800 Toises .................5968·
Italian Mile, 60 to a Degree...................2029·
German Mile, 15 to a Degree ...............8116·

Also, from the measurements carried on through France and a part of Spain, the French mathematicians make ¼ of the whole terrestrial meridian 5130740 toises in length ; and the ten millionth part of this, or ·513074 toise is the metre, or standard for measures of length now adopted in that country, the length of which is 3·28084075 English feet.

# Compound Subtraction.

COMPOUND SUBTRACTION is the method of finding the difference between any two numbers consisting of several denominations.

### RULE. *

1. Place the less number under the greater, so that the parts which are of the same denomination may stand directly under each other, and draw a line below them.

2. Begin at the right hand, and take each number in the lower line, when it can be done, from that above it, and set the remainder under it.

3. But if any of these numbers be greater than those above them, add as many to the upper number as will make one of

---

* The reason of this rule will readily appear from what has been said in simple subtraction ; for the borrowing depends upon the same principle, and differs from it only, as the numbers to be subtracted are of different denominations.

the next higher denomination, and then subtract the lower number from it, setting down the remainder as before.

4. Carry the unit borrowed to the next number in the lower line, which subtract from that above it, in the same manner as the last; and so on, till the whole is finished; then the several remainders, taken together, will be the difference required.

The method of proof is by adding the remainder to the less number, as in simple subtraction; then, if the sum is equal to the greater, the work is right.

### EXAMPLES OF MONEY.

| (1.) | l. | s. | d. |
|---|---|---|---|
| From | 9 | . 8 | . 6½ |
| Take | 4 | . 3 | . 4¼ |
| Rem. | 5 | . 5 | . 2¼ |

| (2.) | l. | s. | d. |
|---|---|---|---|
| From | 16 | . 12 | . 8¾ |
| Take | 10 | . 11 | . 6¼ |
| Rem. | 6 | . 1 | . 2½ |

| (3.) | l. | s. | d. |
|---|---|---|---|
| From | 21 | . 13 | . 4¾ |
| Take | 18 | . 9 | . 8½ |
| Rem. | 3 | . 3 | . 8¼ |

| (4.) | l. | s. | d. |
|---|---|---|---|
| From | 136 | . 12 | . 3 |
| Take | 95 | . 15 | . 2 |
| Rem. | 40 | . 17 | . 1 |
| Proof | 136 | . 12 | . 3 |

| (5.) | l. | s. | d. |
|---|---|---|---|
| From | 386 | . 2 | . 7 |
| Take | 197 | . 8 | . 7 |
| Rem. | 188 | . 14 | . 0 |
| Proof | 386 | . 2 | . 7 |

| (6.) | l. | s. | d. |
|---|---|---|---|
| From | 860 | . 0 | . 7¼ |
| Take | 99 | . 12 | . 8½ |
| Rem. | 760 | . 7 | . 10¾ |
| Proof | 860 | . 0 | . 7¼ |

| (7.) | l. | s. | d. |
|---|---|---|---|
| From | 45 | . 16 | . 9¾ |
| Take | 13 | . 8 | . 5¼ |

| (8.) | l. | s. | d. |
|---|---|---|---|
| From | 8 | . 12 | . 10¼ |
| Take | 5 | . 16 | . 9¼ |

| (9.) | l. | s. | d. |
|---|---|---|---|
| From | 453 | . 6 | . 2¼ |
| Take | 165 | . 12 | . 10¾ |

(10.) From 15l. 7s. 10d. take 6l. 4s. 5d.

(11.) From 284l. 9s. 8d. take 192l. 19s. 3d.

(12.) From 474l. 0s. 6¼d. take 72l. 17s. 7½d.

(13.) From 1097l. 14s. 7¾d. take 596l. 12s. 9½d.

(14.) A tradesman had owing to him 849l. 6s. 8¾d., and received at one time 56l. 2s. 6d., at another 32l. 17s. 5½d., at a third 101l. 6s. 2d. What remains due to him?

*Ans.* 659l. 0s. 7¼d.

## TROY WEIGHT.

| (1.) | *lb.* | *oz.* | *dwt.* | *gr.* |
|------|-------|-------|--------|-------|
| From | 37 . | 3 . | 14 . | 11 |
| Take | 14 . | 2 . | 10 . | 9 |
| *Rem.* | 23 . | 1 . | 4 . | 2 |

| (2.) | *lb.* | *oz.* | *dwt.* | *gr.* |
|------|-------|-------|--------|-------|
| From | 218 . | 9 . | 10 . | 8 |
| Take | 59 . | 10 . | 15 . | 20 |
| *Rem.* | 158 . | 10 . | 14 . | 12 |

| (3.) | *lb.* | *oz.* | *dwt.* | *gr.* |
|------|-------|-------|--------|-------|
| From | 373 . | 0 . | 0 . | 0 |
| Take | 248 . | 10 . | 18 . | 21 |

| (4.) | *lb.* | *oz.* | *dwt.* | *gr.* |
|------|-------|-------|--------|-------|
| From | 508 . | 7 . | 17 . | 21 |
| Take | 436 . | 2 . | 13 . | 9 |

| (5.) | *lb.* | *oz.* | *dwt.* | *gr.* |
|------|-------|-------|--------|-------|
| From | 151 . | 6 . | 0 . | 8 |
| Take | 116 . | 8 . | 12 . | 15 |

| (6.) | *lb.* | *oz.* | *dwt.* | *yr.* |
|------|-------|-------|--------|-------|
| From | 986 . | 0 . | 16 . | 0 |
| Take | 719 . | 6 . | 9 . | 18 |

(7.) From 637 lb. 9 oz. 8 gr. take 288 lb. 1 oz. 9 dwt. 20 gr.
(8.) From 8947 lb. take 5398 lb. 6 oz. 18 dwt. 12 gr.

## AVOIRDUPOIS WEIGHT.

| (1.) | *T.* | *cwt.* | *qr.* | *lb.* | *oz.* |
|------|------|--------|-------|-------|-------|
| From | 7 . | 14 . | 1 . | 3 . | 6 |
| Take | 2 . | 6 . | 3 . | 4 . | 11 |
| *Rem.* | 5 . | 7 . | 1 . | 26 . | 11 |

| (2.) | *Cwt.* | *qr.* | *lb.* | *oz.* | *dr.* |
|------|--------|-------|-------|-------|-------|
| From | 4 . | 2 . | 12 . | 10 . | 8 |
| Take | 2 . | 3 . | 16 . | 15 . | 3 |
| *Rem.* | 1 . | 2 . | 23 . | 11 . | 5 |

| (3.) | *T.* | *cwt.* | *qr.* | *lb.* | *oz.* |
|------|------|--------|-------|-------|-------|
| From | 21 . | 14 . | 2 . | 20 . | 13 |
| Take | 16 . | 12 . | 1 . | 24 . | 14 |

| (4.) | *Cwt.* | *qr.* | *lb.* | *oz.* | *dr.* |
|------|--------|-------|-------|-------|-------|
| From | 7 . | 1 . | 13 . | 3 . | 8 |
| Take | 4 . | 3 . | 19 . | 6 . | 10 |

(5.) *T. cwt. qr. lb. oz.*
From   15 . 1 . 1 . 0 . 9
Take   12 . 0 . 2 . 23 . 12
_____

_____

(6.) *Cwt. qr. lb. oz. dr.*
From   84 . 1 . 19 . 2 . 0
Take   57 . 0 . 21 . 9 . 11
_____

_____

(7.) Bought 2 ton, 5 cwt. 1 qr. 7 lb. of sugar; and sold 1 ton, 19 cwt. 20 lb.   What remains?

## APOTHECARIES' WEIGHT.

(1.) *lb.   oz. dr. sc. gr.*
From   24 . 8 . 7 . 2 . 18
Take   17 . 7 . 6 . 1 . 13
_____
Rem.    7 . 1 . 1 . 1 . 5

(2.) *lb.   oz.   dr. sc.   gr.*
From    8 . 4 . 7 . 0 . 14
Take    0 . 8 . 7 . 2 . 19
_____
Rem.    7 . 7 . 7 . 0 . 15

(3.) *lb.   oz.   dr. sc.   gr.*
From   20 . 5 . 6 . 2 . 10
Take   13 . 9 . 7 . 1 . 14
_____

_____

(4.) *lb.   oz.   dr.   sc.   gr.*
From    8 . 9 . 6 . 2 . 18
Take    6 . 6 . 5 . 1 . 12
_____

_____

(5.) *lb.   oz.   dr. sc.   gr.*
From    8 . 3 . 2 . 1 . 7
Take    0 . 10 . 7 . 0 . 15
_____

_____

(6.) *lb.   oz.   dr.   sc.   gr.*
From    7 . 0 . 0 . 0 . 0
Take    2 . 8 . 3 . 2 . 13
_____

_____

## WOOL WEIGHT.

(1.) *La.   sa.   wy. td.   st.*
From   218 . 7 . 1 . 5 . 1
Take    79 . 10 . 1 . 6 . 1
_____
Rem.   138 . 8 . 1 . 5½ . 0

(2.) *Sa.   wy. td.   st.*
From   37 . 1 . 3 . 0
Take   18 . 1 . 5 . 1
_____
Rem.   18 . 1 . 3½ . 1

(3.) *La. sa. wy. td. st.*
From 28 . 9 . 1 . 4 . 1
Take 16.11 . 1 . 6 . 1

————————————

————————————

(4.) *Wy. td. st. cl. lb.*
From 98 . 4 . 1 . 0 . 5
Take 63 . 5 . 1 . 1 . 6

————————————

————————————

(5.) *Wy. td. st. cl. lb.*
From 63 . 0 . 0 . 0 . 0
Take 40 . 5 . 1 . 1 . 5

————————————

————————————

(6 ) *Sa. wy. td. st.*
From 65 . 1 . 6 . 1
Take 48 . 1 . 3 . 0

————————————

————————————

## LONG MEASURE.

(1.) *Lea. mi. fur. po. yd.*
From 20 . 2 . 7 . 38 . 4
Take 10 . 1 . 6 . 9 . 3

*Rem.* 10 . 1 . 1 . 29 . 1

————————————

(2.) *Po. yd. ft. in. b.c.*
From 37 . 3 . 2 . 10 . 1
Take 20 . 2 . 2 . 11 . 2

*Rem.* 17 . 0 . 2 . 10 . 2

————————————

(3.) *Mi. fur. po. yd. ft.*
From 100 . 2 . 6 . 4 . 2
Take 19 . 6 . 30 . 3 . 2

————————————

————————————

(4.) *Mi. fur. po. yd. ft.*
From 87 . 0 . 19 . 2 . 1
Take 9 . 6 . 31 . 4 . 1

————————————

————————————

(5.) *Lea. mi. fur. po. yd.*
From 160 . 1 . 3 . 20 . 2
Take 84 . 2 . 6 . 28 . 3

————————————

————————————

(6.) *Mi. fur. po. yd. ft. in.*
From 70 . 7 . 13 . 1 . 1 . 2
Take 20 . 0 . 14 . 2 . 2 . 8

————————————

————————————

(7.) From 50 lea. 2 m. 1 fur. take 19 lea. 18 pls. 4 yds.
(8.) From 72 m. 4 fur. take 12 m. 6 fur. 3 yds. 2 ft

## CLOTH MEASURE.

(1.) *Yds. qr. na. in.*
From 65 . 1 . 3 . 1
Take 13 . 2 . 1 . 2

Rem. 51 . 3 . 1 . 1¼

(2.) *E. e. qr. na. in.*
From 27 . 2 . 1 . 2
Take 13 . 3 . 2 . 1

Rem. 13 . 3 . 3 . 1

(3.) *E. e. qr. na. in.*
From 27 . 2 . 3 . 1
Take 14 . 3 . 2 . 2

(4.) *Fr. e. qr. na. in.*
From 37 . 0 . 1 . 2
Take 29 . 3 . 3 . 1

(5.) *Fl. e. qr. na. in.*
From 39 . 1 . 0 . 1
Take 19 . 1 . 2 . 2

(6.) *E. e. qr. na. in.*
From 48 . 2 . 1 . 1
Take 30 . 4 . 2 . 2

(7.) From 156 Eng. ells take 30 Eng. ells, 1 qr. 1 nl.
(8.) From 908 Fr. ells take 170 Fr. ells, 4 qrs. 3 nls.
(9.) From 856 yds. take 200 yds. 2 qrs. 1 nl. 1 in.

## SQUARE MEASURE.

(1.) *Ac. rd. pl. yd. ft.*
From 29 . 3 . 26 . 16 . 5
Take 12 . 2 . 18 . 20 . 6

Rem. 17 . 1 . 7 . 25¼ . 8

(2.) *Ac. rd. pl. yd. ft.*
From 47 . 2 . 10 . 10 . 7
Take 23 . 3 . 20 . 4 . 3

Rem. 23 . 2 . 30 . 6 . 4

(3.) *Ac. rd. pi. yd. ft.*
From 69 . 2 . 13 . 13 . 7
Take 30 . 3 . 28 . 30 . 4

(4.) *Ac. rd. pl. yd. ft.*
From 90 . 3 . 19 . 13 . 7
Take 63 . 3 . 38 . 10 . 3

(5.) *Ac. rd. pl. yd. ft.*
From 83 . 0 . 30 . 23 . 1
Take 26 . 3 . 36 . 27 . 2

(6.) *Ac. rd. pl. yd. ft.*
From 76 . 0 . 0 . 0 . 3
Take 38 . 2 . 30 . 3 . 8

(7.) From 780 ac. 2 rds. take 396 ac. 3 rds. 15 pls.
(8.) From 800 ac. take 100 ac. 2 rds. 8 ft.

## WINE MEASURE.

(1.) *Tun. pip. hhd. gal. qt.*
From 86 . 1 . 0 . 20 . 2
Take 48 . 1 . 1 . 50 . 3

*Rem.* 37 . 1 . 0 . 32 . 3

(2.) *Hhd. gal. qt. pt.*
From 98 . 40 . 2 . 1
Take 33 . 60 . 3 . 1

*Rem.* 64 . 42 . 3 . 0

(3.) *Tun. pun. tier. gal. qt.*
From 61 . 1 . 0 . 36 . 3
Take 18 . 2 . 1 . 31 . 2

(4.) *Tun. pip. hhd. gal. qt.*
From 90 . 1 . 0 . 30 . 1
Take 56 . 1 . 1 . 48 . 2

(5.) *T. hhd. gal. qt. pt.*
From 13 . 1 . 20 . 2 . 0
Take 9 . 0 . 38 . 3 . 1

(6.) *Tun. pun. tier. gal.*
From 89 . 1 . 1 . 25
Take 31 . 2 . 1 . 38

(7.) From 6 tuns, take 3 hhds. 15 gal. 3 qts.
(8.) From 28 tuns, 1 pun. take 15 tuns, 1 tier. 19 gal.

## ALE AND BEER MEASURE.

(1.) *Bar. kil. b.fir. gal. qt.*
From 21 . 1 . 1 . 6 . 3
Take 9 . 1 . 1 . 7 . 2

*Rem.* 11 . 1 . 1 . 8 . 1

(2.) *Hhd. b.fir. gal. qt.*
From 45 . 2 . 6 . 2
Take 21 . 3 . 7 . 3

*Rem.* 23 . 4 . 7 . 3

(3.) *Hhd. gal. qt. pt.*
From    200 . 0 . 0 . 0
Take    87 .50 . 2 . 1

(4.) *Butts. hhd. gal. qt.*
From    251 . 1 . 13 . 0
Take    111 . 1 . 48 . 3

(5.) *Hhd. kil. gal. qt. pt.*
From    100 . 1 . 12 . 1 . 1
Take    40 . 2 . 16 . 3 . 0

(6.) *Pun. b.fir. gal. qt.*
From    84 . 5 . 3 . 2
Take    26 . 7 . 6 . 1

(7.) From 12 tuns, 1 butt, take 8 tuns, 50 gal. 3 qts.
(8.) From 19 butt, 1 hhd. take 10 butt, 1 hhd. 40 gal.

## DRY MEASURE.

(1.) *Last. wey. qrs. cm. bus.*
From    136 . 1 . 2 . 1 . 3
Take    97 . 1 . 3 . 0 . 2

Rem.    38 . 1 . 4 . 1 . 1

(2.) *Qrs. bus. pe. gal.*
From    28 . 5 . 1 . 1
Take    19 . 6 . 3 . 0

Rem.    8 . 6 . 2 . 1

(3.) *Qrs. bus. pec. gal.*
From    155 . 3 . 2 . 0
Take    18 . 4 . 3 . 1

Rem.    136 . 6 . 2 . 1

(4.) *Wey. qrs. bus. pec.*
From    186 . 2 . 3 . 2
Take    42 . 4 . 6 . 3

Rem.    143 . 2 . 4 . 3

(5.) *Wey. qrs. bus. pec.*
From    112 . 1 . 3 . 2
Take    18 . 4 . 2 . 3

(6.) *Wey. qrs. bus. pec.*
From    190 . 3 . 2 . 3
Take    86 . 4 . 5 . 2

(7.) *Last. wey. qrs. cm.*
From    165 . 0 . 2 . 1
Take    46 . 1 . 3 . 1

(8.) *Qrs. bus. pec. pot.*
From    279 . 1 . 1 . 0
Take    34 . 2 . 1 . 3

(9.) From 20 weys or loads, take 8 loads, 3 qrs. 2 pec.
(10.) From 8 loads, 2 qrs. 1 coom, take 4 qrs. 3 bus. 2 pec.

## TIME.

(1.) *Wk. da. hr. min. sec.*

From   32 . 3 . 7 . 10 . 13
Take    3 . 2 . 10 . 30 . 9
-----
*Rem.*  29 . 0 . 20 . 40 . 4

(2.) *Yr. cal. mo. wk. da.*

From   176 . 8 . 3 . 4
Take    91 . 9 . 2 . 6
-----
*Rem.*  84 . 11 . 0 . 5

(3.) *Mo. wk. da. hr. min.*

From   12 . 1 . 2 . 14 . 19
Take    7 . 2 . 3 . 9 . 20
-----
*Rem.*   4 . 2 . 6 . 4 . 59

(4.) *Mo. wk. da. hr.*

From   93 . 2 . 1 . 0
Take   45 . 2 . 4 . 12
-----
*Rem.*  47 . 3 . 3 . 12

(5.) *Yr. mo. wk. da. hr*

From   1650 . 9 . 2 . 3 . 5
Take    486 . 2 . 3 . 5 . 7
-----

(6.) *Mo. wk. da. hr.*

From   18 . 0 . 4 . 10
Take    9 . 2 . 5 . 21
-----

(7.) From 400 years, take 98 years, 3 mo. 8 hr. 10 sec.
(8.) From 87 months, take 43 mo. 2 wk. 3 dys. 1 hr.
(9.) From 39 weeks, take 13 wks. 6 dys. 20 hrs. 11 min. 13 sec.

# Compound Multiplication.

COMPOUND MULTIPLICATION is the method of finding what any given number, of different denominations, will amount to, when repeated a certain proposed number of times.

### RULE.*

1. Set the multiplier under the lowest denomination of the multiplicand; and having multiplied the number in that place by it, find how many integers of the next higher denomination are contained in the product, and put down what remains.

---

* The product of a number consisting of several parts, or denominations, by any simple number whatever, will evidently be expressed by taking the product of that simple number, and each part by itself, as so

D 6

2. Carry the integers thus found to the product of the multiplier and the number in the next higher denomination, with which proceed as before; and so on through all the denominations to the highest; then this product, together with the several parts before found, will be the whole product required.

## CASE I.

*When the multiplier does not exceed* 12.

### EXAMPLES OF MONEY.

(1.) 9 lb. of tobacco at 4s. 8½d. per lb.

$$4s. \; 8\frac{1}{2}d.$$
$$9$$

£2. 2s. 4½d. *Answer.*

(2.) 3 lb. of green tea at 9s. 6d. per lb.
(3.) 5 lb. of loaf sugar at 1s. 3d. per lb.
(4.) 9 cwt. of cheese at 4l. 11s. 5d. per cwt.
(5.) 12 gallons of brandy at 19s. 6d. per gall.

## CASE II.

When the multiplier exceeds 12, and is a composite number, or the product of two or more numbers in the Multiplication table (*page* 10.), multiply, successively, by each of its parts, instead of the whole number at once.

### EXAMPLES.

(1.) 16 cwt. of cheese at 4l. 18s. 8d. per cwt.

$$4 \times 4 = 16$$

4 cwt. = 19   14   8
4

16 cwt. = 78l.   18s.   8d. *the answer.*

---

many distinct products; thus 25l. 12s. 6d. multiplied by 9, will be 225l. 108s. 54d. = (by taking the shillings from the pence, and the pounds from the shillings, and placing them in the shillings and pounds respectively we have) 230l. 12s. 6d., which is the same as the rule; and this will hold true when the multiplicand is any compound number whatever.

(2.) 28 yards of broadcloth at 19s. 4d. per yard.

*Ans. 27l. 1s. 4d.*

(3.) 35 firkins of butter at 2l. 15s. 3½d. per firkin.

*Ans. 96l. 15s. 2½d.*

(4.) 42 cwt. of tallow at 2l. 16s. 6d. per cwt.

*Ans. 118l. 13s.*

(5.) 64 gallons of brandy at 18s. 6d. per gallon.

*Ans. 59l. 4s.*

(6.) 96 quarters of rye at 2l. 3s. 4d. per quarter.

*Ans. 208l.*

(7.) 120 dozen of candles at 10s. 9d. per dozen.

*Ans. 64l. 10s.*

(8.) 132 yards of Irish cloth at 2s. 4d. per yard.

*Ans. 15l. 8s.*

(9.) 144 reams of paper at 1l. 6s. 4d. per ream.

*Ans. 189l. 12s.*

### CASE III.

When the multiplier is not a composite number, take that which is nearest to it, and multiply by its component parts, as before ; then add or subtract as many times the first line as the number so taken is greater or less than the given multiplier.

#### EXAMPLES.

(1.) 17 ells of Holland at 7s. 8½d. per ell.

$$
\begin{array}{ccc}
£. & s. & d. \\
0 . & 7 . & 8\frac{1}{2} \\
\end{array}
$$

$$4 \times 4 + 1 = 17$$

$$
\begin{array}{ccc}
1 . & 10 . & 10 = 4 \textit{ ells} \\
 & & 4 \\
\end{array}
$$

$$
\begin{array}{lll}
6 . & 3 . & 4 \;= 16 \textit{ ells} \\
0 . & 7 . & 8\frac{1}{2} = 1 \textit{ ell} \\
\end{array}
$$

£6. 11s. 0½d. *the answer.*

(2.) 23 ells of dowlas at 1s. 6½d. per ell. *Ans.* 1l. 15s. 5¼d.

(3.) 46 bushels of wheat at 8s. 7¼d. per bushel.

*Ans.* 19l. 15s. 9½d.

(4.) 59 yards of silk at 7s. 10d. per yard. *Ans.* 23l. 2s. 2d.

(5.) 94 pairs of silk stockings at 12s. 2d. per pair.

*Ans.* 57l. 3s. 8d.

(6.) 117 cwt. of Malaga raisins at 4*l.* 2*s.* 3*d.* per cwt.

Ans. 481*l.* 3*s.* 3*d.*

### EXAMPLES OF WEIGHTS, MEASURES, &c.

| (1.) *lb.*   *oz.*   *dwt.*   *gr.* | (2.) *lb.*   *oz.*   *dr.*   *sc.* | (3.) *Cwt.*   *qr.*   *lb.*   *oz.* |
|---|---|---|
| 21 . 1 . 17 . 13 | 2 . 4 . 2 . 2 | 27 . 1 . 13 . 12 |
| 4 | 7 | 12 |

| (4.) *Mi.*   *fr.*   *pls.*   *yds.* | (5.) *Yds.*   *qrs.*   *na.* | (6.) *Ac.*   *ro.*   *po.* |
|---|---|---|
| 24 . 3 . 20 . 2 | 127 . 2 . 2 | 27 . 2 . 1 |
| 6 | 8 | 9 |

| (7.) *T.*   *hhd.*   *gal.*   *pt.* | (8.) *Wy.*   *qr.*   *bus.*   *pck.* | (9.) *W.*   *d.*   *hr.*   *m.* |
|---|---|---|
| 29 . 1 . 20 . 3 | 27 . 1 . 7 . 2 | 113 . 6 . 20 . 59 |
| 5 | 7 | 11 |

# Compound Division.

COMPOUND DIVISION is the method of finding how often one given number is contained in another of different denominations.

### RULE.*

1. Place the divisor and dividend as in simple division.

2. Begin at the left-hand, or highest denomination of the dividend, which divide by the divisor, and set down the quotient.

---

* To divide a number consisting of several denominations by any simple number whatever, is evidently the same as dividing all the parts or numbers of which it is composed, by the same simple number. And this will be true when any of the parts are not an exact multiple of the divisor; for, by conceiving the number, by which it exceeds that multiple, to have its proper value, by being placed in the next lower denomination, the dividend will still be divided into similar parts, and the true quotient found as before: thus 25*l.* 12*s.* 3*d.* divided by 9 will be the same as 18*l.* 144*s.* 99*d.* divided by 9, which is equal to 2*l.* 16*s.* 11*d.* as by the rule; and the method of carrying from one denomination to another is exactly the same in other cases, as Weights and Measures.

3. If anything remains after this division, find how many integers of the next lower denomination it is equal to, and add them to the number, if any, which stands in that denomination.

4. Divide this number so found by the divisor, and set the quotient under its proper denomination.

5. Proceed in the same manner through all the denominations to the lowest; and the whole result thus obtained will be the answer required.

### CASE I.

*When the multiplier does not exceed 12.*

#### EXAMPLES OF MONEY.

(1.) Divide 225*l.* 2*s.* 4*d.* by 2.

$$2)225l. \ 2s. \ 4d.$$

*Ans.* 112*l.* 11*s.* 2*d.* the quotient.

(2.) Divide 751*l.* 14*s.* 7¾*d.* by 3.
(3.) Divide 821*l.* 17*s.* 9¾*d.* by 4.
(4.) Divide 2382*l.* 13*s.* 5½*d.* by 5.
(5.) Divide 28*l.* 2*s.* 1½*d.* by 6.
(6.) Divide 55*l.* 15*s.* 0¾*d.* by 7.
(7.) Divide 6*l.* 5*s.* 8*d.* by 8.
(8.) Divide 135*l.* 10*s.* 7*d.* by 9
(9.) Divide 21*l.* 18*s.* 4*d.* by 10.
(10.) Divide 227*l.* 10*s.* 5*d.* by 11.
(11.) Divide 1332*l.* 11*s.* 8½*d.* by 12.

### CASE II.

When the divisor is a composite number that exceeds 12, find what simple numbers, multiplied together, will produce it, and divide by them separately, as in simple division.

#### EXAMPLES.

(1.) What is a certain commodity per cwt. if 16 cwt. cost 30*l.* 18*s.* 8*d.* ?

$$4)30l. \ 18s. \ 8d.$$

$$4)7l. \ 14s. \ 8d.$$

1*l.* 18*s.* 8*d.* the answer.

(2.) Divide 85*l*. 6*s*. by 72.  *Ans. 1l. 3s. 8¼d.*
(3.) Divide 57*l*. 3*s*. 7*d*. by 35.  *Ans. 1l. 12s. 8d.*
(4.) Divide 31*l*. 2*s*. 10½*d*. by 99.  *Ans. 6s. 3½d.*
(5.) At 18*l*. 18*s*. per cwt., how much per lb.? *Ans. 3s. 4½d.*
(6.) If a quantity of tobacco, consisting of 20 hundred-weight, comes to 370*l*. 6*s*. 8*d*., what is that per hundred-weight?  *Ans. 18l. 10s. 4d.*
(7.) If a quantity of sugar, consisting of 264 pounds, cost 11*l*. 16*s*. 6*d*., what is the price per pound? *Ans. 10¾d.*

## CASE III.

If the divisor cannot be produced by the multiplication of two or more small numbers, divide by the whole divisor at once, after the manner of long division.

### EXAMPLES.

(1.) Divide 74*l*. 13*s*. 6*d*. by 17.

$$17)74l. \; 13s. \; 6d.(4l. \; 7s, \; 10d. \; Ans.$$
$$68$$
$$\overline{\phantom{00}}$$
$$6$$
$$20$$
$$\overline{\phantom{00}}$$
$$17)133(7s.$$
$$119$$
$$\overline{\phantom{00}}$$
$$14$$
$$12$$
$$\overline{\phantom{00}}$$
$$17)174(10d.$$
$$170$$
$$\overline{\phantom{00}}$$
$$4$$
$$\overline{\phantom{00}}$$

(2.) Divide 23*l*. 15*s*. 7¼*d*. by 37.  *Ans. 12s. 10¼d.*
(3.) Divide 199*l*. 3*s*. 10*d*. by 53.  *Ans. 3l. 15s. 2d.*
(4.) Divide 675*l*. 12*s*. 6*d*. by 138.  *Ans. 4l. 17s. 11d.*
(5.) Divide 315*l*. 3*s*. 10¼*d*. by 365.  *Ans. 17s. 3¼d.*

### EXAMPLES OF WEIGHTS AND MEASURES.

(1.) Divide 23 lb. 7 oz. 6 dwt. 12 gr. by 7.

*Ans. 3 lb. 4 oz. 9 dwt. 12 gr*

(2.) Divide 13 lb. 1 oz. 2 dr. 0 sc. 10 gr. by 12.
*Ans.* 1 *lb.* 1 *oz.* 0 *dr.* 2 *sc.* 10⅝ *gr.*

(3.) Divide 1061 cwt. 2 qr. by 28.
*Ans.* 37 *cwt.* 3 *qr.* 18 *lb.*

(4.) Divide 375 mi. 2 fur. 7. po. 2 yd. 1 ft. by 39.
*Ans.* 9 *mi.* 4 *fur.* 39 *po* 0 *yd.* 2 *ft.* 8 *in.*

(5.) Divide 571 yd. 2 qr. 1 nl. by 47.
*Ans.* 12 *yd.* 0 *qr.* 2 *nl.*

(6.) Divide 51 ac. 2 ro. 3 po. by 51.
*Ans.* 1 *ac.* 0 *ro.* 1 *po.* 19 *yds.*

(7.) Divide 10 tun. 2 hhd. 17 gall. 2 qt. of wine by 67.
*Ans.* 39 *gall.* 3 *qt.*

(8.) Divide 120 lasts, 1 qr. 1 bu. 2 pck. by 74.
*Ans.* 1 *last,* 6 *qr.* 1 *bu.* 3 *pck.*

(9.) Divide 120 mo. 2 we. 3 da. 5 ho. 20 min. by 111.
*Ans.* 1 *mo.* 0 *we.* 2 *da.* 10 *ho.* 12 *min.*

## Reduction.

REDUCTION is the method of converting numbers from one name or denomination to another, without altering their values.

### RULE.*

I. When the numbers are to be reduced from a higher denomination to a lower.

1. Multiply the number in the higher denomination by as many of the next lower as make an integer, or one, in that higher, and set down the product.

2. To this product add the number, if any, which was in this lower denomination before; and multiply the sum by as many of the next lower denomination as make an integer in the present one.

3. Proceed in the same manner through all the denominations to the lowest, and the number last found will be the value of all the numbers that were in the higher denominations taken together.

---

* The reason of this rule is obvious; for pounds are brought into shillings by multiplying them by 20, shillings into pence by multiplying them by 12, and pence into farthings by multiplying them by 4; and the contrary by division: and a similar rule will be true for the reduction of numbers consisting of any denominations whatever.

II. When the numbers are to be reduced from a lower denomination to a higher.

1. Divide the given number by as many of that denomination as makes one of the next higher, and set down what remains.

2. Divide this quotient by as many of the last denomination as make one of the next higher and set down what remains, as before.

3. Proceed in like manner through all the denominations to the highest; and the quotient last found, together with the several remainders, if any, will be of the same value as the number proposed.

### EXAMPLES.

(1.) In 1465*l.* 14*s.* 5*d.* how many farthings?

$$1465l.\ 14s.\ 5d.$$
$$20$$
_____

$$29314\ shillings.$$
$$12$$
_____

$$351773\ pence.$$
$$4$$
_____

$$1407092\ farthings = Ans.$$

(2.) Reduce 1407092 farthings into pounds.

$$4)1407092$$
_____

$$12)351773$$
_____

$$2,0)2931,4\text{-}5d.$$
_____

$$1465l.\ 14s.\ 5d.\ Ans.$$
_____

(3.) In 12*l.* how many farthings?        *Ans.* 11520.

(4.) In 6169 pence how many pounds?   *Ans.* 25*l.* 14*s.* 1*d.*

(5.) In 35 guineas how many farthings?    *Ans.* 35280 *f.*

(6.) How many French francs of 10*d.* each are there in 100*l.* ?        *Ans.* 2400.

(7.) In 213210 grains how many pounds troy?
*Ans. 37 lb. 3 dwt. 18 gr.*

(8.) In 1776 quarter-guineas how many sixpences?
*Ans. 18648.*

(9.) In 59 lb. 0 oz. 13 dwt. 5 gr. how many grains?
*Ans. 340157 grs.*

(10.) In 420 quarter-guineas how many moidores of 27s. each? *Ans. 81 moidores and 18s. over.*

(11.) In 231*l.* 16*s.* how many ducats at 4*s.* 9*d.* each?
*Ans. 976.*

(12.) It is required to reduce 1776 pieces, of thirty-six shillings each in value, to half-crowns. *Ans. 25574⅘.*

(13.) In 50807 moidores, how many pieces of coin, each 4*s.* 6*d.*? *Ans. 304842.*

(14.) In 274 marks, each 13*s.* 4*d.*, and 87 nobles, each 6*s.* 8*d.*, how many pounds? *Ans. 211l. 13s. 4d.*

(15.) How many times will a coach wheel of 18½ feet in circumference turn round between London and York, the distance being 197 miles? *Ans. 56224 32/37 times.*

(16.) In 35 tons, 17 cwt. 1 qr. 23 lb. 7 oz. 13 dr. how many drams? *Ans. 20571005.*

(17.) In 37 cwt. 2 qr. 17 lb. avoirdupois, how many lbs. troy, a lb. avoirdupois being equal to 14 oz. 11 dwt. 16 gr. troy? *Ans. 5124 lb. 9 oz. 18 dwts. 8 grs.*

(18.) How many barley-corns will reach round the world at the Equator, supposing its circumference, according to Schumacher, to be 24900 miles? *Ans. 4732992000.*

(19.) In 17 pieces of cloth, each containing 27 Flemish ells, how many yards? *Ans. 344 yds. 1 qr.*

(20.) If a person step at an average 2½ feet, how many steps will he take in walking 20 miles? *Ans. 42240.*

(21.) How many minutes have elapsed since the birth of Christ to the year 1852 inclusive, allowing the year to consist of 365¼ days? *Ans. 97407792 min.*

(22.) If 44¼ guineas weigh 1 lb. troy, and 48 half-pence a lb. avoirdupois, what is the difference between the weight of a guinea and a half-penny? *Ans. 15 gr. 11103/18992.*

(23.) How long would it require to count eight hundred millions of money, which is almost the national debt of this country at present, at a rate of 100*l.* a minute without intermission? *Ans. 15 yrs. 3 mo. 1 wk. 4 da. 13 h. 20 m.*

# The Rule of Three, or Simple Proportion.

THE RULE OF THREE is the method of finding a number that shall have the same proportion to one of three given numbers as there is between the other two.

## RULE.*

Consider which of the three given terms is of the same kind with the answer, or number to be found, and put it down the last in the proportion.

---

\* This rule, which has commonly been divided into two parts, as well as improperly stated, is here, for the sake of the learner, rendered equally applicable both to the Rule of Three Direct, and the Rule of Three Inverse. Its truth, as far as regards direct proportion, is founded on this obvious principle, that magnitudes or quantities of any kind vary in proportion to the varying parts of their cause. Thus, different quantities of goods bought are in proportion to the money laid out for each; the spaces gone over, by uniform motions, are in proportion to the times, &c.

When applied to ordinary inquiries it may also be made sufficiently evident, by attending only to principles already explained. Thus it is shown, in multiplication of money, that the price of one multiplied by the quantity is the price of the whole; and in division, that the price of the whole, divided by the quantity, is the price of one.

Hence, in all cases of valuing goods, &c. where one is the first term of the proportion, it is plain that the answer found by this rule, will be the same as that found by multiplication of money; and where one is the second or third term of the proportion it will be the same as that found by division of money.

Also, if the first term be any number whatever, it is plain that the product of the second and third terms will be greater or less than the true answer required, by as much as the price, in either of these terms, exceeds or falls short of the price of one, or as the first term differs from unity. Consequently this product, divided by the first term, will give the true answer required.

In like manner, when the proportion is inverse, or such that two of the four proposed numbers increase in the same proportion that the two others diminish, the truth of the rule may be made evident, from the principles of compound multiplication and division, as before. For example: If 6 men can do a piece of work in ten days, in how many days will 12 men do it?

Here 12 men : 6 men :: 10 days : $\dfrac{10 \times 6}{12} = 5$ days, the answer

Then, if it appears, from the nature of the question, that the answer will be greater than this number, put the greater of the other two terms in the middle, and the less first ; but if it will be less, put the less in the middle and the greater first.

Having thus stated the question, reduce the first two terms of the proportion, when necessary, to the same denomination, and the third to the lowest denomination mentioned in it.

Then multiply the second and third terms together, and divide the product by the first, and the quotient will be the answer, in the same denomination that the third term was reduced to; which must be brought again, if necessary, to the highest denomination it admits of, in order that the answer may be exhibited in its proper form.

### EXAMPLES.

1. What is the value of a pipe of port, consisting of 115 gallons, at the rate of 2*l*. 5*s*. a dozen, or 12 quarts?

| | |
|---|---|
| 12 *qts.* : 115 *galls.* :: 2*l.* 5*s.* | Or thus (*see note*) : |
|     4 *qts.* = 1 *gall.*  20*s.* | 12 *qts.* : 115 *galls.* :: 2 11/4 |
|     460 *qts.*    45*s.* |     4 *qts.* |
|     45 | 3 *qts.*  460 *qts.*  2*l.* |
|     2300 |     115 |
|     1840 |     3 |
| 12)20700 | 4)345 |
| 2,0)172,5 |    86*l.* 5*s.* = *Ans.* |
|   86*l.* 5*s.* = *Ans.* | |

where the product of the second and third terms, *i. e.* 6 times 10, or 60, is evidently the time in which one man would perform the work ; consequently 12 men will do it in one twelfth part of that time, or in 5 days; and the same mode of reasoning will apply to any other example of this kind.

*Note.* When it can be done, multiply and divide as in compound multiplication and division. And if the 1st term, and either the 2nd or 3rd, can be divided by any number without a remainder, let them be so divided, and the quotients used instead of them; which, in general, will much abridge the operation.

(2.) How many yards of calico, that is ell-wide, English, will line 26¼ yards of cotton that is 3 qrs. wide ?

| 1 *ell.* | : | 3 *qrs.* | :: | 26¼ *yds.* |
|---|---|---|---|---|
| 5 | | 105 | | 4 |

$\overline{5\,qrs.}$    5)$\overline{315}$    $\overline{105\,qrs.}$

     4)63 qrs.

     15¾ yds.

Ans. = 15 *yds.* 3 *qrs.*

Or thus (*see note* p. 69.) :

5 *qrs.* ( = 1 *ell.*) : 3 *qrs.* :: 26¼ *yds.*

    1 *qr.*    5¼     5¼ *yds,*

     15¾ *yds.*

Ans. = 15 *yds.* 3 *qrs.*

(3.) What is the value of a cwt. of sugar at 1s. 1½d. per lb. ?      *Ans.* 6*l.* 6*s.*

(4.) What is the value of a ton of coals, at 1s. 6½d. per cwt. ?      *Ans.* 1*l.* 10*s.* 10*d.*

(5.) What is the value of 1½ cwt. of coffee at 5½d. per oz. ?      *Ans.* 61*l.* 12*s.*

(6.) If 750 men are allowed 22500 rations of bread per month, how many rations will a garrison of 1200 men require?      *Ans.* 36000.

(7.) At 10½d. per lb. what is the value of a firkin of butter containing half a cwt.?      *Ans.* 2*l.* 9*s.*

(8.) What is the tax upon 745*l.* 14*s.* 8*d.* at 3*s.* 6*d.* in the pound?      *Ans.* 130*l.* 10*s.* 0¾d. ⅕ *f.*

(9.) If 10 workmen can finish a piece of work in 12 days, how many can do the same in 3 days?      *Ans.* 40 *men.*

(10.) How much in length that is 4½ inches broad will make a square foot, which is 12 inches long and 12 inches broad?      *Ans.* 32 inches, or 2 ft. 8 in.

(11.) At 3*l.* 9*s.* per tod, what is the value of a pack of wool weighing 2 cwt. 2 qrs. 13 lb. ?      *Ans.* 36*l.* 2*s.* 0¼d.

(12.) What can a person spend per week whose income is 700*l.* per annum ?      *Ans.* 13*l.* 9*s.* 2¾d.

(13.) How many yards of matting, 2 ft. 6 in. broad, will cover a floor that is 27 ft. long, and 20 ft. broad?      *Ans.* 72 *yards.*

(14.) What is the value of 2 qrs. 1 nl. of velvet at 19s. 8½d. per Eng. ell ?      *Ans.* 8s. 10¼d. $\frac{7}{10}$ *f.*

(15.) How many quarters of corn can I buy for 40 guineas at 8d. 6d. per bushel ?      *Ans.* 12 qrs. 2$\frac{14}{17}$ *bush.*

(16.) If an ounce of silver be worth 5s. 6d., what is the price of a tankard that weighs 1 lb. 10 oz. 10 dwts. 4 gr. ?      *Ans.* 6*l.* 3s. 9½d.

(17.) How much in length that is $13\frac{1}{2}$ poles in breadth must be taken to contain an acre, which is 40 poles long and 4 poles broad?  *Ans.* 11 po. 4 yds. 2 ft. $0\frac{2}{3}$ in.

(18.) If 1 Eng. ell, 2 qrs. of muslin cost 4s. 7d. what will $39\frac{1}{2}$ yards cost?  *Ans.* 5l. 3s. $5\frac{1}{4}$d.

(19.) What is the half-year's rent of 547 acres of land, at 1l. 11s. per annum per acre?  *Ans.* 423l. 18s. 6d.

(20.) At a guinea per week, how many months' board can I have for 100l.?  *Ans.* 23 mo. 3 wks. $1\frac{2}{3}$ du.

(21.) At 1l. 6s. 5d. per yard, what is the value of a piece of cloth containing $52\frac{3}{4}$ Eng. ells?  *Ans.* 87l. 1s. $10\frac{3}{16}$d.

(22.) How many yards of cloth, 3 qrs. wide, are equal in measure to 30 yds. 5 qrs. wide?  *Ans.* 50 yards.

(23.) How many yards of paper, of $1\frac{1}{4}$ yard wide, will be sufficient to hang a room, which is twenty yards in circumference, and 4 yards in height?  *Ans.* 64 yards.

(24.) How many yards of stuff, 3 qrs. broad, will line a cloak that is $5\frac{1}{2}$ yards in length and $1\frac{1}{4}$ yards broad?  *Ans.* 9 yds. 0 qr. $2\frac{2}{3}$ na.

(25.) If a servant's wages be 27 guineas a-year, how much will he have to receive for 95 days' service?  *Ans.* 7l. 7s. $6\frac{3}{4}$d. $\frac{45}{73}$f.

(26.) Supposing 32 bricks will pave a space that is a yard square, how many will it take to pave a kitchen that is 22 feet long and 18 feet wide?  *Ans.* 1408.

(27.) What is the value of a gold snuff-box that weighs 4 oz. 8 dwt. 9 gr. at the rate of 4l. 3s. $9\frac{1}{2}$d. per ounce?  *Ans.* 18l. 10s. 3d.

(28.) How many yards of calico that is ell wide will line 20 yards of cotton that is 3 qrs. wide?  *Ans.* 12 yards.

(29.) If the penny loaf weighs $4\frac{1}{2}$ ounces when flour is 4s. 9d. a peck, how much ought it to weigh when flour is 5s. 6d. a peck?  *Ans.* 3 oz. $14\frac{2}{11}$ dr.

(30.) What is the value of a chest of tea, weighing 2 cwt. 1 qr. 19 lb. at 8s. 6d. per lb.?  *Ans.* 115l. 3s. 6d.

(31.) What does 59 cwt. 2 qrs. 24 lb. of tobacco come to at 7l. 14s. 5d. per cwt.?  *Ans.* 461l. 0s. $10\frac{1}{4}$d.

(32.) How many Eng. ells of Holland may be bought for 100 guineas at the rate of 8s. $9\frac{1}{2}$d. per yard?  *Ans.* 191 *ells*, 0 qr. $1\frac{169}{211}$ nl.

(33.) Bought 12 pockets of hops, each weighing 1 cwt. 2 qrs. 17 lb.; what do they come to at 5l. 1s. 4d. per cwt.?  *Ans.* 100l. 8s. $6\frac{3}{4}$d.

(34.) Bought 3 casks of raisins, each weighing 2 cwt. 2 qrs. 25 lbs.; what will they come to at 5$l$. 1$s$. 8$d$. per cwt.?

*Ans.* 41$l$. 10$s$. 6$\frac{3}{4}d$.

(35.) If 12 men can reap a field of wheat in 3 days, in what time can the same work be performed by 25 men?

*Ans.* 1 *da.* 10 *h.* 33$\frac{3}{5}$ *m.*

(36.) If 3$\frac{3}{4}$ yards of cloth, of 1$\frac{1}{2}$ yard in width, will make a suit of clothes, how much will be requisite for the same purpose, when the cloth is only $\frac{3}{4}$ yard wide? *Ans.* 7$\frac{1}{2}$ *yards.*

(37.) If a person's income be 500 guineas a year, and he spends 19$s$. 7$d$. per day, one day with another, how much will he have saved at the year's end? *Ans.* 167$l$. 12$s$. 1$d$.

(38.) What is the value of 172 pigs of lead, each weighing 3 cwt. 2 qrs. 17$\frac{1}{2}$ lb. at 25$l$. 12$s$. 6$d$. per fother of 19$\frac{1}{2}$ cwt.?

*Ans.* 826$l$. 8$s$. 1$\frac{1}{2}d$.

· (39.) The rents of a whole parish amount to 1750$l$. and a rate is granted of 98$l$. 9$s$. 6$d$.; what is that in the pound?

*Ans.* 1$s$. 1$\frac{1}{2}d$.

· (40.) If my horse stands me in 1$s$. 11$d$. per day keeping, what will be the charge of 11 horses for the year?

*Ans.* 384$l$. 15$s$. 5$d$.

(41.) What must 40$s$. pay towards a tax, when 650$l$. 13$s$. 4$d$. is assessed at 83$l$. 12$s$. 4$d$.? *Ans.* 5$s$. 1$\frac{1}{2}d$.

(42.) If the cock of a large cistern will empty it in 27 minutes, how many such cocks will empty it in 5$\frac{1}{2}$ minutes?

*Ans.* 4$\frac{10}{11}$.

(43.) If 27 cows can be kept in a field for 12 days, how long can 40 cows feed upon the same quantity of pasture?

*Ans.* 8$\frac{1}{10}$ *days.*

(44.) If the soldiers in a besieged garrison have provisions sufficient for 5 months at the rate of 20 oz. per man a day, how long will they be able to hold out when they are reduced to 12 oz. a day? *Ans.* 8 *mo.* 9 *da.* 8 *ho.*

(45.) Bought 25 pieces of Holland, each containing 25 Eng. ells, for 300 guineas, what is that per yard? *Ans.* 8$s$. 0$\frac{3}{4}d$. $\frac{9}{125}f$.

· (46.) A bankrupt owes in all 1490$l$. 5$s$. 10$d$., and has in money, goods, and recoverable debts, 784$l$. 17$s$. 4$d$.; if these be delivered to his creditors, what will they get in the pound? *Ans.* 10$s$. 6$\frac{1}{4}d$. $\frac{20993}{35787}f$.

· (47.) If 15 ells of stuff, $\frac{3}{4}$ of a yard wide, cost 37$s$. 6$d$., what will 40 ells of the same stuff cost, being yard wide?

*Ans.* 6$l$. 13$s$. 4$d$.

(48.) If I buy 15 yards of cloth for 11 guineas, how many Flemish ells can I buy for 240*l*. 13*s*. 4*d*. at the same rate?

*Ans.* 416 *Flemish ells, 2 qrs.*

(49.) What is a quarter's rent of 500 acres of land, which is let for 1*l*. 15*s*. 6*d*. an acre per annum? *Ans.* 221*l*. 17*s*. 6*d*.

(50.) A factor bought 19 pieces of Holland cloth, which cost him 176*l*. 13*s*. at the rate of 5*s*. 3*d*. per ell Flemish; how many English ells did the 19 pieces contain?

*Ans.* 403 *ells, 3 qrs. 3 nl.*

(51.) If a gentleman's estate be worth 1384*l*. 16*s*. a year, and the land-tax be assessed at 2*s*. 9½*d*. per pound, what is his net annual income? *Ans.* 1191*l*. 10*s*. 1¼*d*.

(52.) If a person lend me 250*l*. for 7 months, how long ought I to lend him 300*l*. in return for his kindness?

*Ans.* 5 *mo.* 3 *we.* 2⅓ *da.*

(53.) How many Venetian ducats, at 4*s*. 4*d*. each, are equal in value to 730 rix-dollars, at 4*s*. 5¾*d*. each? *Ans.* 754 $\frac{59}{104}$.

(54.) Bought 4 bales of cloth, each containing 6 pieces, and each piece 27 yards, at 16*l*. 4*s*. per piece, what is the value of the whole, and the rate per yard?

*Ans.* 388*l*. 16*s*. *whole cost, at* 12*s*. *per yard.*

(55.) Bought 1000 Flemish ells of cloth for 90*l*., how must I sell it again per ell English to gain 10*l*. by the whole?

*Ans.* 3*s*. 4*d*.

(56.) Bought 3 tuns of oil for 151*l*. 14*s*., 85 gallons of which being damaged, I desire to know how I may sell the remainder per gallon, so as neither to lose nor gain by the bargain?

*Ans.* 4*s*. 6¼*d*. $\frac{25}{671}$ *f.*

(57). What quantity of water must I add to a hogshead of wine, value 33*l*., to reduce the first cost to 9*s*. per gallon?

*Ans.* 10 *gal.* 1 *q.* 0⅔ *pi.*

(58.) What does the whole pay of a man-of-war's crew, consisting of 640 sailors, amount to, for 32 months' service, each man's wages being 22*s*. 6*d*. per month? *Ans.* 23040*l*.

(59.) How many pieces of Holland, each containing 15 ells Flemish, may be bought for 30*l*. 16*s*. 5*d*. at the rate of 5*s*. 3*d*. per ell English? *Ans.* 13 *pieces,* 2$\frac{4}{63}$ *qrs. over.*

(60.) The circumference of the earth being 25000 miles; it is required to find at what rate per hour a body must be carried, to pass completely round it in 23 hours 56 minutes, which is the length of a sidereal day? *Ans.* 1044$\frac{204}{359}$ *miles.*

(61.) If the carriage of 30 cwt. of baggage cost 1*l*. 4*s*. for

E

20 miles, what will the carriage of 76 cwt. for 84 miles amount to, at the same rate? *Ans.* 12*l.* 15*s.* 4¼*d.* $\frac{7}{25}$*f.*

(62.) If a person spend as much in four months as he gains in three, how much can he lay by annually, supposing he gains 120*l.* 10*s.* every six months? *Ans.* 60*l.* 5*s.*

(63.) Shipped for Barbadoes 500 pairs of stockings at 3*s.* 6*d.* per pair, and 1650 yards of baize at 1*s.* 3*d.* per yard; and have received in return 348 gallons of rum at 6*s.* 8*d.* per gallon, and 750 lb. of indigo at 1*s.* 4*d.* per lb.; what remains due upon my adventure? *Ans.* 24*l.* 12*s.* 6*d.*

(64.) If a certain number of men can throw up an entrenchment in 10 days, when the day is 6 hours long, in what time would they do it when the day is 8 hours long? *Ans.* 7½ days.

(65.) A wall that is to be built to the height of 27 feet, was raised 9 feet by 12 men in 6 days; how many men must be employed to finish the wall in 4 days, at the same rate of working? *Ans.* 36.

(66.) If 30 men can perform a piece of work in 11 days, how many will accomplish another piece of work four times as large in a fifth part of the time? *Ans.* 600.

# Compound Proportion.

COMPOUND PROPORTION is the method of resolving, at one operation, such questions, as by the common Rule of Three would require two or more statings to be worked separately.

## RULE.*

Arrange the given terms or numbers mentioned in the question according to their proper statings, as taught in the Rule

---

* The reason of this rule may be readily shown from the nature of Simple Proportion: for every separate row in this case is a particular stating in the common Rule of Three; and therefore if all the separate dividends be collected together into one dividend, and all the divisors into one divisor, their quotient must be the answer sought. Thus, in example the first:

As 9 bush. : 24 bush. :: 16 horses : $\frac{24 \times 16}{9}$ horses,

And as 7 days : 6 days :: $\frac{24 \times 16}{9}$ horses : $\frac{24 \times 16 \times 6}{9 \times 7} = 36\frac{4}{7}$ horses, as by the rule.

of Simple Proportion; considering the third term, taken singly, as common to each stating.

Then, the continued product of all the second terms of these proportions, and the third, or common term, divided by the product of all the first terms, will give the answer required.

*Note.* When the same numbers are found in the divisor as in the dividend, they may be thrown out of each.

### EXAMPLES.

(1.) If 16 horses will consume 9 bushels of oats in 6 days, how many horses would consume 24 bushels in 7 days at the same rate?

$$\left\{ \begin{array}{l} 9 \text{ bushels} \\ 7 \text{ days} \end{array} \right\} : \left\{ \begin{array}{l} 24 \text{ bushels} \\ 6 \text{ days} \end{array} \right\} :: 16 \text{ horses} : \text{answer}.$$

Or $\dfrac{6 \times 24 \times 16}{9 \times 7} = \dfrac{2 \times 24 \times 16}{3 \times 7} = \dfrac{2 \times 8 \times 16}{1 \times 7} = \dfrac{256}{7} = 36\frac{4}{7}$ *Ans.*

(2.) If a family of 9 people spend 120*l.* in 8 months, how much will serve a family of 24 people 16 months at the same rate of living?    *Ans.* 640*l.*

(3.) If 8 men can dig 24 yards of earth in 6 days, how many men must there be to dig 18 yards in 3 days?    *Ans.* 12 *men.*

(4.) If 2 men can do $12\frac{3}{4}$ rods of ditching in $6\frac{1}{4}$ days, how many rods may be done by 18 men in 14 days?
    *Ans.* $247\frac{2}{13}$ *rods.*

(5.) If a regiment of soldiers, consisting of 939 men, will consume 351 quarters of wheat in 7 months, how many will consume 1464 quarters in 5 months at that rate?
    *Ans.* $5483\frac{23}{195}$ *men.*

(6.) If the carriage of 5 cwt. 3 qrs. for 150 miles cost 3*l.* 7*s.* 4*d.*, what must be paid for the carriage of 7 cwt. 2 qrs. 25 lb. for 64 miles, at the same rate?
    *Ans.* 1*l.* 18*s.* $7\frac{127}{2415}$ *d.*

(7.) If 540 tiles, each 12 inches square, will pave the floor of a certain building, how many will the same place require, when the tiles are 10 inches long, and 8 inches broad?
    *Ans.* 972.

(8.) If a person can travel 300 miles in 10 days, when the day is 12 hours long, how many days will it take him to travel 600 miles, when the day is 16 hours long?    *Ans.* 15 *days.*

E 2

(9.) If a barrel of beer be sufficient to last a family of 7 persons 12 days, how many barrels will be drunk out by a family of 14 persons in a year? *Ans.* 60⅚.

(10.) If the expense of 6 labourers for 21 weeks come to 120*l.*, what will be the expense of 14 labourers for 46 weeks, at the same rate? *Ans.* 613*l.* 6*s.* 8*d.*

(11.) If 50 men can throw up an entrenchment in 10 days, when the day is 8 hours long, in what time will 120 men do it when the day is 6 hours long? *Ans.* 5⅚ *days.*

(12.) If 1000 men, besieged in a town, with provisions for 28 days, at the rate of 18 oz. a day, per man, be reinforced with 600 men more, how many ounces a day must each man have that the provisions may last 42 days; this being the time at which they expect to be relieved? *Ans.* 7½ *ounces.*

(13.) If 6 tailors, on the approach of a general mourning, can make ten suits of clothes in 4 days, how many suits can 20 men make in 7 days, under the same circumstances?
*Ans.* 58⅓ *suits.*

(14.) If an iron bar, 5 feet long, 2½ inches broad, and 1¾ inch thick, weigh 45 lbs., how much will a bar of the same metal weigh, that is 7 feet long, 3 inches broad, and 2¼ inches thick? *Ans.* 97⅛ *lbs.*

(15.) If 248 men, in 5 days, of 11 hours each, can dig a trench 230 yards long, 3 wide, and 2 deep, in how many days, of 9 hours long, will 24 men dig a trench of 420 yards long, 5 wide, and 3 deep? *Ans.* 288 *days,* 2¹³⁄₂₃ *hrs.*

# Practice.

PRACTICE is a compendious method of working questions in the Rule of Three, when the first term is a unit or one; and is generally used among merchants and tradesmen, on account of its being the most easy and expeditious way of finding the value of any quantity of goods, or other commodities, from the known price of one of the articles.

The rule is commonly divided into several cases, in the treating of which it is to be observed, that an aliquot part of any number is such a part as, being taken a certain number of times, will exactly make that number; thus, ¼ is an aliquot part of 1, for being taken 4 times, or being multiplied by 4, it produces 1; and 2 is an aliquot part of 6, since, when taken 3 times, it makes 6, &c.

## TABLES OF THE ALIQUOT PARTS OF MONEY, WEIGHTS, AND MEASURES.

### A Table of the Aliquot Parts of Weights and Measures.

**AVOIRDUPOIS WEIGHT.**

*Of a Ton.*

cwt.
$$10 = \tfrac{1}{2}$$
$$5 = \tfrac{1}{4}$$
$$4 = \tfrac{1}{5}$$
$$2\tfrac{1}{2} = \tfrac{1}{8}$$
$$2 = \tfrac{1}{10}$$

*Of a Cwt.*

qr.   lb.
$$2 \text{ or } 56 = \tfrac{1}{2}$$
$$1 \text{ or } 56 = \tfrac{1}{4}$$
$$16 = \tfrac{1}{7}$$
$$14 = \tfrac{1}{8}$$
$$8 = \tfrac{1}{14}$$

*Of ½ Cwt. or 56lb.*

lb.
$$28 = \tfrac{1}{2}$$
$$14 = \tfrac{1}{4}$$
$$8 = \tfrac{1}{7}$$
$$7 = \tfrac{1}{8}$$

*Of a ¼ Cwt. or 28lb.*

lb.
$$14 = \tfrac{1}{2}$$
$$7 = \tfrac{1}{4}$$
$$4 = \tfrac{1}{7}$$
$$3\tfrac{1}{2} = \tfrac{1}{8}$$

*Of a Pound.*

oz.
$$8 = \tfrac{1}{2}$$
$$4 = \tfrac{1}{4}$$
$$2 = \tfrac{1}{8}$$

**TROY WEIGHT.**

*Of an Ounce.*

dwt.   gr.
$$10 . 0 = \tfrac{1}{2}$$
$$6 . 16 = \tfrac{1}{3}$$
$$5 . 0 = \tfrac{1}{4}$$
$$4 . 0 = \tfrac{1}{5}$$
$$3 . 8 = \tfrac{1}{6}$$
$$2 . 12 = \tfrac{1}{8}$$
$$2 . 0 = \tfrac{1}{10}$$
$$1 . 0 = \tfrac{1}{12}$$

*Of a Cwt.*

gr.
$$12 = \tfrac{1}{2}$$
$$8 = \tfrac{1}{3}$$
$$6 = \tfrac{1}{4}$$
$$4 = \tfrac{1}{6}$$
$$3 = \tfrac{1}{8}$$
$$2 = \tfrac{1}{12}$$

———

**LAND MEASURE.**

*Of an Acre.*

r.   p.
$$2 . 0 = \tfrac{1}{2}$$
$$1 . 0 = \tfrac{1}{4}$$
$$32 = \tfrac{1}{5}$$
$$20 = \tfrac{1}{8}$$
$$16 = \tfrac{1}{10}$$
$$8 = \tfrac{1}{20}$$

*Of a Rood.*

p.
$$20 = \tfrac{1}{2}$$
$$10 = \tfrac{1}{4}$$
$$8 = \tfrac{1}{5}$$
$$5 = \tfrac{1}{8}$$
$$4 = \tfrac{1}{10}$$
$$2 = \tfrac{1}{20}$$

**CLOTH MEASURE.**

*Of a Yard.*

qr.   n.
$$2 . 0 = \tfrac{1}{2}$$
$$1 . 0 = \tfrac{1}{4}$$
$$2 = \tfrac{1}{8}$$
$$1 = \tfrac{1}{16}$$

*Of an English Ell.*

qr.   n.
$$2 . 2 = \tfrac{1}{2}$$
$$1 . 1 = \tfrac{1}{4}$$
$$1 . 0 = \tfrac{1}{5}$$
$$2 = \tfrac{1}{10}$$
$$1 = \tfrac{1}{20}$$

*Of a Flemish Ell.*

qr.   n.
$$1 . 2 = \tfrac{1}{2}$$
$$1 . 0 = \tfrac{1}{3}$$
$$3 = \tfrac{1}{4}$$
$$2 = \tfrac{1}{6}$$
$$8 = \tfrac{1}{12}$$

*Of a French Ell.*

qr.   n.
$$3 . 0 = \tfrac{1}{2}$$
$$2 . 0 = \tfrac{1}{3}$$
$$1 . 2 = \tfrac{1}{4}$$
$$1 . 0 = \tfrac{1}{6}$$
$$3 = \tfrac{1}{8}$$
$$2 = \tfrac{1}{12}$$
$$1 = \tfrac{1}{24}$$

## A Table of the Aliquot Parts of Money.

| Of a Pound. | | | Of a Shilling. |
|---|---|---|---|
| s. d. £ | s. d. £ | d. £ | d. s. |
| 10 . 0 = $\frac{1}{2}$ | 1 . 3 = $\frac{1}{16}$ | 3 = $\frac{1}{80}$ | 6 = $\frac{1}{2}$ |
| 6 . 8 = $\frac{1}{3}$ | 1 . 0 = $\frac{1}{20}$ | 2½ = $\frac{1}{96}$ | 4 = $\frac{1}{3}$ |
| 5 . 0 = $\frac{1}{4}$ | 10 = $\frac{1}{24}$ | 2 = $\frac{1}{120}$ | 3 = $\frac{1}{4}$ |
| 4 . 0 = $\frac{1}{5}$ | 8 = $\frac{1}{30}$ | 1½ = $\frac{1}{160}$ | 2 = $\frac{1}{6}$ |
| 3 . 4 = $\frac{1}{6}$ | 7½ = $\frac{1}{32}$ | 1¼ = $\frac{1}{192}$ | 1½ = $\frac{1}{8}$ |
| 2 . 6 = $\frac{1}{8}$ | 6 = $\frac{1}{40}$ | 1 = $\frac{1}{240}$ | 1 = $\frac{1}{12}$ |
| 2 . 0 = $\frac{1}{10}$ | 5 = $\frac{1}{48}$ | ¾ = $\frac{1}{320}$ | ¾ = $\frac{1}{16}$ |
| 1 . 8 = $\frac{1}{12}$ | 4 = $\frac{1}{60}$ | ½ = $\frac{1}{480}$ | ½ = $\frac{1}{24}$ |
| 1 . 4 = $\frac{1}{15}$ | 3¾ = $\frac{1}{64}$ | ¼ = $\frac{1}{960}$ | ¼ = $\frac{1}{48}$ |

### CASE I.*

### *When the price is less than a penny.*

#### RULE.

(1.) Divide the given number by the aliquot parts of a penny, and then by 12 and by 20, and it will give the answer required.

#### EXAMPLES.

4506 at $\frac{3}{4}d$.

$\frac{1}{2}$ is $\frac{1}{2}$   2253
$\frac{1}{4}$ is $\frac{1}{2}$   1162$\frac{1}{2}$

12)3379$\frac{1}{2}$

2,0)28,1-7$\frac{1}{2}d$.

£14. 1s. 7$\frac{1}{2}d$.

| | | |
|---|---|---|
| (2.) | 3456 at $\frac{1}{4}d$. | Ans. 3l. 12s. |
| (3.) | 347 at $\frac{1}{2}d$. | Ans. 14s. 5$\frac{1}{2}d$. |
| (4.) | 846 at $\frac{3}{4}d$. | Ans. 2l. 12s. 10$\frac{1}{2}d$. |
| (5.) | 810 at $\frac{3}{4}d$. | Ans. 2l. 10s. 7$\frac{1}{2}d$. |

---

* As most of the following compendiums are only particular cases in a more general rule, it will be sufficient for their illustration, to explain the principles on which the rule itself is founded.

## CASE II.

*When the price is an aliquot part of a shilling.*

### RULE.

Divide the given number by the aliquot part, and the quotient will be the answer in shillings, which reduce into pounds as before.

### EXAMPLES.

(1.) 3*d.* is $\frac{1}{4}$   1728 at 3*d.*
_____

2,0)43,2
_____

£21. 12*s. the answer.*

_____

*General Rule.* 1. Suppose the price of the given quantity to be 1*l.* or 1*s.* &c. as it may happen; then will the quantity itself be the answer at the supposed price.

2. Divide the given price into aliquot parts, either of the supposed price, or of each other, and the sum of the quotients belonging to each, will be the true answer required.

### EXAMPLE.

What is the value of 526 yards of cloth, at 3*s.* 10¼*d.* per yard?

Here 526*l.*   would be the *Ans.* at 1*l. per yard.*

| | | | | | | | |
|---|---|---|---|---|---|---|---|
| 3*s.* 4*d.* is $\frac{1}{6}$ | 87*l.* . 13*s.* . . 4*d.* | | ditto at 0*l.* . 3*s.* . . 4*d.* per yard. |
| 4*d.* is $\frac{1}{10}$ | 8 . 15 . 4 | | ditto at 0 . 0 . 4 |
| 2*d.* is $\frac{1}{2}$ | 4 . 7 . 8 | | ditto at 0 . 0 . 2 |
| ¼*d.* is $\frac{1}{8}$ | 0 . 10 . 11½ | | ditto at 0 . 0 . 0¼ |

The full price £101 . 7 . 3½    ditto at 0 . 3 . 10¼

In the above example, it is plain, that the quantity 526 is the answer at 1*l.*: consequently, as 3*s.* 4*d.* is the $\frac{1}{6}$ of a pound, $\frac{1}{6}$ part of that quantity, or 87*l.* 13*s.* 4*d.*, is the price at 3*s.* 4*d.*   In like manner, as 4*d.* is the $\frac{1}{10}$ part of 3*s.* 4*d.* so $\frac{1}{10}$ of 87*l.* 13*s.* 4*d.* or 8*l.* 15*s.* 4*d.* is the answer at 4*d.* And by reasoning in this manner 4*l.* 7*s.* 8*d.* will appear to be the price at 2*d.* and 10*s.* 11¼*d.* the price at ¼*d.*   Hence, as the sum of all these parts is equal to the whole price (3*s.* 10¼*d.*), so the sum of the answers belonging to each price will be the answer at the full price required. And the same will be true of any example whatever.

(2.)    437 at 1*d*.          *Ans.* 1*l*. 16*s*. 5*d*.
(3.)    352 at 1½*d*.         *Ans.* 2*l*. 4*s*.
(4.)   5275 at 2*d*.          *Ans.* 43*l*. 19*s*. 2*d*.
(5.)   1776 at 3*d*.          *Ans.* 22*l*. 4*s*.
(6.)   6771 at 4*d*.          *Ans.* 112*l*. 17*s*.
(7.)    899 at 6*d*.          *Ans.* 22*l*. 9*s*. 6*d*.

### CASE III.

*When the price is pence and farthings, which are no aliquot parts of a shilling.*

### RULE.

Find what aliquot part of a shilling is nearest to the given price, and divide the proposed number by it.

Then consider what part the remainder is of this aliquot part and divide the former quotient by it; and so on for the next; then the several quotients, added together, will be the answer in shillings, which reduce into pounds as before.

### EXAMPLES.

(1.) 876 at 8½*d*.

6*d*. is ½ 438
2*d*. is ⅓ 146
½*d*. is ¼   36 . 6*d*.

2,0)62,0 . 6*d*.

£31. 0*s*. 6*d*. the answer.

(2.)    372 at 1¾*d*.          *Ans.* 2*l*. 14*s*. 3*d*.
(3.)    325 at 2⅓*d*.          *Ans.* 3*l*. 7*s*. 8½*d*.
(4.)    827 at 4½*d*.          *Ans.* 15*l*. 10*s*. 1½*d*.
(5.)   2700 at  7¼*d*.         *Ans.* 81*l*. 11*s*. 3*d*.
(6.)   2150 at  9¾*d*.         *Ans.* 87*l*. 6*s*. 10½*d*.
(7.)   1720 at 11½*d*.         *Ans.* 82*l*. 8*s*. 4*d*.

### CASE IV.

*When the price is any number of shillings under 20.*

### RULE.

1. If the price be an even number, multiply the given

number by half of it, doubling the first figure to the right hand for shillings, and the rest are pounds.

2. When it is an odd number, find for the greatest even number as before, to which add $\frac{1}{20}$ of the given number for the odd shilling, and the sum will be the answer.

EXAMPLES.

(1.) 243 at 4s.
        2
        _____

£48. 12s. *the answer.*

(2.) 566 at 7s.
        3
        _____

            169 . 16
1s. is $\frac{1}{20}$  28 .  6
        _____

£198.    2s. *the answer.*

| | | | |
|---|---|---|---|
| (3.) | 2757 at 1s. | *Ans.* | 137*l.* 17*s.* |
| (4.) | 2643 at 2s. | *Ans.* | 264*l.* 6*s.* |
| (5.) | 3271 at 5s. | *Ans.* | 817*l.* 15*s.* |
| (6.) | 872 at 8s. | *Ans.* | 348*l.* 16*s.* |
| (7.) | 372 at 11s. | *Ans.* | 204*l.* 12*s.* |
| (8.) | 5271 at 14s. | *Ans.* | 3689*l.* 14*s.* |
| (9.) | 3142 at 17s. | *Ans.* | 2670*l.* 14*s.* |
| (10.) | 264 at 19s. | *Ans.* | 250*l.* 16*s.* |

CASE V.

*When the price is any number of shillings and pence.*

RULE.

If the price be an aliquot part of a pound divide the given quantity by that part, and the quotient will be the answer in pounds.

But if it be not an exact aliquot part, find first for the shillings, and then take parts for the pence.

e 5

## EXAMPLES.

(1.) 3s. 4d. is ⅙ 329 at 3s. 4d.

£54. 16s. 8d. *the answer.*

(2.) 765 at 5s. 9d.

| 5s. is ¼ | 191 . 5 |
| 6d. is 1/10 | 19 . 2 . 6 |
| 3d. is ½ | 9 . 11 . 3 |

£219. 18s. 9d. *the answer.*

(3.) 7150 at 1s. 8d.       *Ans.* 595*l.* 16s. 8d.
(4.) 2715 at 2s. 6d.       *Ans.* 339*l.* 7s. 6d.
(5.) 3150 at 3s. 4d.       *Ans.* 525*l.* 0s. 0d.
(6.) 2710 at 6s. 8d.       *Ans.* 903*l.* 6s. 8d.
(7.) 7211 at 1s. 3d.       *Ans.* 450*l.* 13s. 9d.
(8.) 2701 at 3s. 2d.       *Ans.* 427*l.* 13s. 2d.
(9.)   969 at 19s. 11d.       *Ans.* 964*l.* 19s. 3d.

## CASE VI.

*When the price is shillings, pence, and farthings.*

### RULE.

Divide the price into the aliquot parts of a pound, or of each other, and the sum of the quotients belonging to each aliquot part, will be the answer required.

### EXAMPLES.

(1.) 244 at 5s. 8½d.

| 5s. | ¼ | ˙61 |
| 6d. | 1/10 | 6 . 2 |
| 2d. | ⅓ | 2 . 0 . 8 |
| ½d. | ¼ | 0 . 10 . 2 |

£69. 12s. 10d. *the answer.*

| | | | | | |
|---|---|---|---|---|---|
| (2.) 875 at 1s. $4\frac{3}{4}d$. | *Ans.* | 61*l.* | 1*s.* | $4\frac{1}{4}d$. |
| (3.) 7524 at 3s. $5\frac{1}{2}d$. | *Ans.* | 1301*l.* | 0*s.* | 6*d.* |
| (4.) 3715 at 9s. $4\frac{1}{2}d$. | *Ans.* | 1741*l.* | 8*s.* | $1\frac{1}{2}d$. |
| (5.) 2572 at 13s. $7\frac{1}{2}d$. | *Ans.* | 1752*l.* | 3*s.* | 6*d.* |
| (6.) 1603 at 16s. $10\frac{1}{2}d$. | *Ans.* | 1352*l.* | 10*s.* | $7\frac{1}{2}d$. |
| (7.) 2710 at 19s. $2\frac{1}{2}d$. | *Ans.* | 2602*l.* | 14*s.* | 7*d.* |
| (8.) 430 at 19s. $6\frac{1}{4}d$. | *Ans.* | 419*l.* | 13*s.* | $11\frac{1}{2}d$. |

### CASE VII.

*When the price is pounds and shillings, or pounds, shillings, pence, and farthings.*

### RULE.

Multiply the quantity proposed by the number of pounds, and work for the rest by some of the former rules; then the sums added together will give the answer required.

### EXAMPLES.

(1.) 428 at 3*l.* 4*s.* $6\frac{1}{2}d$.

| | |
|---|---|
| | 3 |
| | 1284 |
| 4*s.* is $\frac{1}{5}$ | 85 . 12 |
| 6*d.* is $\frac{1}{8}$ | 10 . 14 |
| $\frac{1}{2}d$. is $\frac{1}{12}$ | 0 . 17 . 10 |
| | £1381. 3*s.* 10*d.* *the answer.* |

| | | | | |
|---|---|---|---|---|
| (2.) 137 at 1*l.* 17*s.* $6\frac{1}{4}d$. | *Ans.* 257*l.* | 0*s.* | $4\frac{1}{4}d$. |
| (3.) 947 at 4*l.* 15*s.* $10\frac{1}{4}d$. | *Ans.* 4538*l.* | 13*s.* | $10\frac{3}{4}d$. |
| (4.) 457 at 14*l.* 17*s.* $9\frac{1}{2}d$. | *Ans.* 6804*l.* | 10*s.* | $9\frac{1}{2}d$. |
| (5.) 713 at 19*l.* 19*s.* $11\frac{3}{4}d$. | *Ans.* 14259*l.* | 5*s.* | $1\frac{3}{4}d$. |

### CASE VIII.

*When the quantity of which the price is required is a whole number, with parts annexed.*

### RULE.

Work for the whole number according to the former rules, to which add $\frac{1}{4}$, $\frac{1}{2}$, or any other part of the price, that the question requires, for the answer.

(1.) $234\frac{3}{4}$ at 5s. 8d.

| | |
|---|---|
| 5s. is $\frac{1}{4}$ | 58 . 10 |
| 6d. is $\frac{1}{10}$ | 5 . 17 |
| 2d. is $\frac{1}{3}$ | 1 . 19 |
| for $\frac{1}{2}$ | 0 . 2 . 10 |
| for $\frac{1}{4}$ | 0 . 1 . 5 |

£66.    10s.    3d. the answer.

(2.) $273\frac{1}{4}$ at 0l.  2s.  6d.        Ans.  34l.  3s.  $1\frac{1}{2}$d.
(3.) $937\frac{1}{2}$ at 3l. 17s. 8d.        Ans. 3640l. 12s.  6d.
(4.) $139\frac{3}{4}$ at 1l. 19s. 4d.        Ans. 274l. 16s. 10d.
(5.) $371\frac{3}{4}$ at 4l. 13s. 7d.        Ans. 1739l.  9s.  $7\frac{1}{4}$d.
(6.) $284\frac{1}{3}$ at 2l. 10s. 6d.        Ans. 718l.  7s.  3d.

CASE IX.

*When the quantity of which the value is required is of several denominations.*

RULE.

Multiply the given price by the highest denomination, as in compound multiplication; and take the proper parts of the price for the lower denominations, as in the former rules.

EXAMPLES.

(1.) 8 cwt. 2 qr. 16 lb. at 2l. 5s. 6d.

2l.  5s.  6d.
8

| | |
|---|---|
| | 18 . 4 . 0 |
| 2 qr. is $\frac{1}{2}$ | 1 . 2 . 9 |
| 14 lb. is $\frac{1}{4}$ | 0 . 5 . $8\frac{1}{4}$ |
| 2 lb. is $\frac{1}{7}$ | 0 . 0 . $9\frac{3}{4}$ |

£19.    13s.    3d. the answer.

(2.) 37 cwt. 2 qrs. 14 lb. at 7l. 10s. 9d. per cwt.
                    Ans. 283l. 11s. $11\frac{1}{2}$d.
(3.) 17 cwt. 1 qr. 12 lb. at 1l. 19s. 8d. per cwt.
                    Ans. 34l. 8s. 6d.

(4.) 23 cwt. 3 qrs. 8 lb. at 3*l*. 19. 11*d*. per cwt.
*Ans*. 95*l*. 3*s*. 8¾*d*.

(5.) 39 cwt. 0 qr. 10 lb. at 1*l*. 17*s*. 10*d*. per cwt.
*Ans*. 73*l*. 18*s*. 10¼*d*.

## PROMISCUOUS QUESTIONS.

(1.) 73 cwt. 1 qr. of sugar, at 5*l*. 15*s*. 7*d*. per cwt.?
*Ans*. 423*l*. 6*s*. 5¾*d*.

(2.) 17 tons, 2 cwt. 3 qrs. 12 lb. at 9*l*. per ton?
*Ans*. 154*l*. 5*s*. 8¼*d*.

(3.) 3 qrs. 12½ lb. at 2*l*. 16*s*. 10*d*. per cwt.?
*Ans*. 2*l*. 8*s*. 11¼*d*.

(4.) 9 tods, 1 stone of wool, at 3*l*. 10*s*. 6*d*. per tod?
*Ans*. 33*l*. 9*s*. 9*d*.

(5.) 125 yards, 3 qrs. of cloth, at 19*s*. 8½*d*. per yard?
*Ans*.123*l*. 18*s*. 3¾*d*.

(6.) 713 acres, 3 roods, 39 pls. at 3*l*. 17*s*. 6*d*. per acre?
*Ans*. 2766*l*. 14*s*. 6*d*.

(7.) 24 gals. 3 qts. of oil, at 7*s*. 4½*d*. per gallon?
*Ans*. 9*l*. 2*s*. 6¼*d*.

(8.) 57 hhds. 41 gals. of ale, at 3*l*. 10*s*. 6*d*. per hhd.?
*Ans*. 203*l*. 12*s*. 0¼*d*.

(9.) 43 qrs. 5 bu. of wheat, at 3*l*. 8*s*. 6*d*. per quarter?
*Ans*. 149*l*. 8*s*. 3¾*d*.

(10.) 14 gallons of brandy, at 22*s*. 6*d*. per gallon?
*Ans*. 15*l*. 15*s*. 0*d*.

(11.) 2 cwt. 2 qrs. 9 lb. of tea, at 7*s*. 6*d*. per lb.?
*Ans*. 108*l*. 7*s*. 6*d*.

(12.) 7 cwt. 1 qr. 13 lb. of cheese, at 4*l*. 17*s*. 6*d*. per cwt. ?
*Ans*. 35*l*. 18*s*. 2*d*.

(13.) What is the hire of a house for 9 months and 11 days. at 12*l*. 10*s*. per month?　　*Ans*. 117*l*. 8*s*. 2½*d*.

# Tare and Tret.

TARE and TRET are practical rules for deducting certain allowances, which are made by merchants and tradesmen in selling their goods by weight.

GROSS WEIGHT is the whole weight of the goods, together with the box, barrel, bag, &c. that contains them.

TARE is an allowance made to the buyer for the weight of the box, barrel, bag, &c., which contains the goods bought; and is either at so much per box, &c., or at so much per cwt., or at so much in the whole.

TRET is an allowance of 4 lb. in every 104 lb. or $\frac{1}{26}$ part of the whole, for waste, dust, &c.

CLOFF is an allowance, after tare and tret are deducted, of 2lb. upon every 3 cwt. that the weight may hold good when sold by retail.

SUTTLE is when the allowance of tare only is deducted from the gross weight, the remainder being then called Tare Suttle.

NEAT WEIGHT is what remains after all allowances are made.*

### CASE I.

*When the tare is at so much for the whole.*

### RULE.

Subtract the tare from the gross weight, and the remainder will be the neat weight required.

### EXAMPLES.

(1.) What is the neat weight of 38 barrels of raisins, weighing 133 cwt. 2 qrs. 9 lb. allowing 3 cwt. 1 qr. 17 lb. for tare?

$$
\begin{array}{r}
\textit{cwt. qrs. lb.} \\
133 \, . \, 2 \, . \; 9 \\
3 \, . \, 1 \, . 17 \\
\hline
\end{array}
$$

*Diff.*$=130 \, . \, 0 \, . \, 20=$*the answer.*

(2.) What is the neat weight of 24 barrels of figs, weighing 45 cwt. 1 qr. 17 lb., allowing 2 cwt. 1 qr. 18 lb. for tare?   *Ans.* 42 *cwt.* 3 *qrs.* 27 *lb.*

(3.) What is the neat weight of 45 hhds. of tobacco, each weighing 4 cwt. 3 qrs. 19 lb. tare being allowed upon the whole at 3 cwt. 2 qrs.?   *Ans.* 217 *cwt.* 3 *qrs.* 15 *lb.*

---

\* It may here be observed, that several sorts of goods have their Tares ascertained, in a Table annexed to the *Book of Rates.*

## CASE II.

*When the tare is at so much per box, barrel, bag, &c.*

### RULE.*

Multiply the number of boxes, barrels, &c. by the tare; then subtract the product from the gross, and the remainder will be the neat weight required.

### *Or thus,*

Subtract the tare of the box, barrel, &c. from its gross weight, and multiply the difference by the number of the boxes, barrels, &c.

### EXAMPLES.

(1.) What is the neat weight of 7 frails of raisins, each weighing 5 cwt. 2 qrs. 5 lb. gross, tare 23 lb. per frail?

$$
\begin{array}{ccc}
cwt. & qrs. & lb. \\
5 & . \; 2 \; . & 5 = gross, \; per \; frail. \\
 & & 23 = tare, \; per \; frail. \\
\hline
Diff. = 5 & . \; 1 \; . & 10 = neat, \; per \; frail. \\
 & & 7 \\
\hline
Ans. = 37 & . \; 1 \; . & 14 \; prod. = total \; neat \; weight. \\
\hline
\end{array}
$$

(2.) What is the neat weight of 241 barrels of figs, each weighing 3 qrs. 19 lb. gross, tare 10 lb. per barrel?

*Ans.* 22413 *lb.*

(3.) What is the neat weight of 14 hhds. of tobacco, each weighing 5 cwt. 2 qrs. 17 lb. gross, tare 100 lb. per hhd?

*Ans.* 66 *cwt.* 2 *qrs.* 14 *lb.*

(4.) What is the neat weight of 17 bags of cotton yarn, each weighing 2 cwt. 3 qrs. 4 lb. gross, tare 9 lb. per bag?

*Ans.* 45 *cwt.* 3 *qrs.* 27 *lb.*

---

* It is manifest that this, as well as every other case in the rule, is only an application of the rules of Proportion and Practice; which have been already sufficiently explained; and therefore any farther illustration of the method of proceeding is unnecessary.

## CASE III.

### *When the tare is at so much per cwt.*

#### RULE.

Divide the gross weight by the aliquot parts of a cwt., then subtract the sum of the quotients from the gross, and the remainder will be the neat weight required.

#### EXAMPLES.

(1.) Gross 173 cwt. 3 qrs. 17 lb., tare 16 lb. per cwt.: how much neat?

$$
\begin{array}{r}
\textit{cwt.} \quad \textit{qrs.} \quad \textit{lb.} \\
173 \, . \, 3 \, . \, 17 \; \textit{gross.} \\
16 \; \textit{lb. is } \tfrac{1}{7} \quad 24 \, . \, 3 \, . \, 10 \\
\hline
\textit{Diff.}=149 \, . \, 0 \, . \, 7 = \textit{the answer.} \\
\hline
\end{array}
$$

(2.) What is the neat weight of 7 barrels of potash, each weighing 201 lb. gross, tare being at 10 lb. per cwt.?

*Ans.* 1281 *lb.* 6 *oz.*

(3.) What is the neat weight of 25 barrels of figs, each weighing 2 cwt. 1 qr. gross, tare 16 lb. per cwt.?

*Ans.* 48 *cwt.* 0 *qr.* 24 *lb.*

(4.) What is the value of the neat weight of 13 hhds. of sugar, at 4*l.* 13*s.* 6*d.* per cwt., each weighing 4 cwt. 3 qrs. 17 lb. gross, tare 13 lb. per cwt.?     *Ans.* 263*l.* 6*s.* 6*d.*

## CASE IV.

### *When an allowance is made both for tare and tret.*

#### RULE.

Find for the tare, and subtract it from the gross weight, by the foregoing rules; then the remainder, or suttle divided by 26, will give the tret; which being subtracted from the suttle, leaves the neat weight required.

The reason for dividing by 26 is, because 4 lb. is $\frac{1}{26}$ of 104 lb.

### EXAMPLES.

(1.) What is the neat weight of 9 cwt. 2 qr. 17 lb. gross, tare 37 lb., and tret as usual?

$$
\begin{array}{ccc}
cwt. & qr. & lb. \\
9 . & 2 . & 17 \ gross. \\
37 \ lb. = 0 . & 1 . & 9 \ tare. \\
\hline
26)9 . & 1 . & 8 \ suttle. \\
0 . & 1 . & 12 \ tret. \\
\hline
\end{array}
$$

*Diff.*=8 . 3 . 24 *the answer.*

(2.) What is the neat weight of 152 cwt. 1 qr. 3 lb. gross, tare 10 lb. per cwt., and tret as usual?
*Ans.* 133 *cwt.* 1 *qr.* 10 *lb.* 15 *oz.*

(3.) What is the neat weight of 7 casks of pruens, each weighing 3 cwt. 1 qr. 5 lb. gross, tare 17$\frac{1}{2}$ lb. per cwt., and tret as usual? *Ans.* 18 *cwt.* 2 *qr.* 23 *lb.* 10 *oz.*

(4.) What is the neat weight of 3 hhd. of sugar, weighing as follows: No. I., 4 cwt. 0 qr. 5 lb. gross, tare 73 lb.; No. II., 3 cwt. 2 qr. gross, tare 56 lb.; and No. III., 2 cwt. 3 qr. 17 lb. gross, tare 47 lb., allowing tret for each as usual?
*Ans.* 8 *cwt.* 2 *qr.* 4 *lb.*

### CASE V.

*When tare, tret, and cloff, are all allowed.*

### RULE.

Deduct tare and tret as before : then divide the remainder, or suttle, by 168, and the quotient will be the cloff; which being subtracted from the suttle, leaves the neat weight.

The reason for dividing by 168 is, that 168 is the $\frac{1}{2}$ of 3 cwt., or of 112 × 3 = 336 lbs.

### EXAMPLES.

(1.) What is the neat weight of a hhd. of tobacco, weighing 15 cwt. 3 qr. 20 lb. gross, tare 7 lb. per cwt., and tret and cloff as usual?

$$
\begin{array}{r}
cwt. \quad qr. \quad lb. \\
15 \ . \ 3 \ . \ 20 \ gross.
\end{array}
$$

7 *lb.* is $\frac{1}{16}$ 0 . 3 . 27 *tare.*

26)14 . 3 . 21
    0 . 2 .  8 *tret.*

168)14 . 1 . 13 *suttle.*
     0 . 0 .  9 *cloff.*

*Diff.* = 14 . 1 .  4 = *the answer.*

(2.) What is the neat weight of 19 barrels of molasses, each containing 13 cwt. 1 qr. 17 lb. gross, tare 13 lb. per cwt., and tret and cloff as usual: and what is the value at 5¾*d.* per lb?      *Ans.* 24095 *lb.*, and value 577*l.* 5*s.* 6¼*d.*

(3.) 29 parcels, each weighing 3 cwt. 0 qr. 14. lb. gross ; what is the value of the neat weight at 1*l.* 11*s.* 6*d.* per cwt., allowing 8 lb. per cwt. for tare, and tret and cloff as usual?      *Ans.* 126*l.* 13s. 7¾*d.*

(4.) What is the value of the neat weight of 5 hhds. of tobacco, each weighing 5 cwt. 2 qr. 25 lb. gross, at 8*l.* 12*s.* 6*d.* per cwt., allowing 8 lb. per cwt. for tare, tret as usual, and cloff 2 lb. per hhd?      *Ans.* 219*l.* 11*s.* 9¾*d.*

# Bills of Parcels.

## A Hosier's Bill.

(1.)      Mr. Thomas Williams,

           Bought of Richard Simpson, Jan. 4. 1852.

|  |  | *s.* | *d.* |  |
|---|---|---|---|---|
| 8 Pairs of worsted stockings, | at | 4 . | 6 | *per pr.* |
| 5 Pairs of thread ditto, | at | 3 . | 2 | |
| 3 Pairs of black silk ditto, | at | 14 . | 0 | |
| 6 Pairs of black worsted ditto | at | 4 . | 2 | |
| 4 Pairs of fine cotton ditto, | at | 7 . | 6 | |
| 2 Yards of flannel, | at | 1 . | 8 | *per yd.* |
| 6 Yards of fleecy hosiery, | at | 2 . | 10 | |

£8 . 9 . 2

## A MERCER'S BILL.

(2.)　　Mr. William George,

　　　　　　Bought of Peter Thomson, July 13. 1852.

|  |  | s. | d. |  |
|---|---|---|---|---|
| 15 | Yards of satin, | at 9 | . 6 | *per yard.* |
| 18 | Yards of velvet, | at 17 | . 4 | |
| 12 | Yards of brocade, | at 19 | . 8 | |
| 16 | Yards of sarcenet, | at 3 | . 2 | |
| 13 | Yards of velvet, | at 27 | . 6 | |
| 23 | Yards of lustre, | at 6 | . 3 | |
| 30 | Yards of plush, | at 8 | . 0 | |

£74 . 2 . 5

## A LINEN-DRAPER'S BILL.

(3.)　　Mr. Henry Morris,

　　　　　　Bought of Caleb Windsor, March 8. 1852.

|  |  | s. | d. |  |
|---|---|---|---|---|
| 40 | Ells of dowlas, | at 1 | . 6 | *per ell.* |
| 34 | Ells of diaper, | at 1 | . $4\frac{1}{2}$ | |
| 31 | Ells of Holland, | at 5 | . 8 | |
| 39 | Yards of cloth, | at 2 | . 4 | *per yard.* |
| $17\frac{1}{2}$ | Yards of muslin, | at 7 | . $2\frac{1}{2}$ | |
| $13\frac{3}{4}$ | Yards of cambric, | at 10 | . 6 | |
| 27 | Yards of printed linen, | at 2 | . 5 | |
| 43 | Yards of Welsh flannel, | at 2 | . 2 | |
| 27 | Yards of cotton, | at 2 | . 4 | |
| 50 | Yards of tape, | at 0 | . $2\frac{1}{2}$ | |

£43 . 15 . $9\frac{1}{4}$

## A Milliner's Bill.

(4.)　　Mrs. Matthewson,

　　　　Bought of Simon Percy, June 18. 1852.

| | *l.* | *s.* | *d.* | |
|---|---|---|---|---|
| 15 Yards of Dresden lace, | at 0 | 13 | 3½ | *per yd.* |
| 18 Yards of fine lace, | at 0 | 12 | 3 | |
| 5 Pairs of kid gloves, | at 0 | 2 | 2 | *per pr.* |
| 12 Opera fans, | at 0 | 3 | 6 | *each.* |
| 2 Patent laced cloaks, | at 3 | 3 | 0 | |
| 4 Dozen pairs of thread gloves, | at 0 | 1 | 3 | *per pr.* |
| 6 Yards of Persian, | at 0 | 2 | 6 | *per yd.* |
| 12 Yards of ribbon, | at 0 | 0 | 8½ | |
| 21 Yards of edging, | at 0 | 1 | 6 | |
| 36½ Yards of gauze, | at 0 | 2 | 2 | |

£39 . 12 . 9½

## A Woollen-Draper's Bill.

(5.)　　Mr. John Page,

　　　　Bought of Jacob Goodson, May 1. 1852.

| | *l.* | *s.* | *d.* | |
|---|---|---|---|---|
| 17 Yards of fine serge, | at 0 | 3 | 9 | *per yd.* |
| 18 Yards of drugget, | at 0 | 9 | 0 | |
| 15 Yards of superfine cloth, | at 1 | 2 | 0 | |
| 16 Yards of black cloth, | at 0 | 18 | 0 | |
| 25 Yards of shalloon, | at 0 | 1 | 9 | |
| 17 Yards of drab, | at 0 | 17 | 6 | |
| 20 Yards of ladies' cloth, | at 0 | 16 | 3 | |
| 5 Yards of kerseymere, | at 0 | 17 | 0 | |

£79 . 15 . 0

## A GROCER'S BILL.

(6.)     Mr. Nathaniel Parsons,

Bought of William Smith, Aug. 6. 1852.

|  |  | s. | d. |  |
|---|---|---|---|---|
| 24½ | lbs. of fine green tea, | at 18 . | 6 | *per lb.* |
| 24¼ | lbs. of imperial tea, | at 24 . | 0 | |
| 35¾ | lbs. of best hyson, | at 13 . | 10 | |
| 17 | lbs. of coffee, | at 5 . | 4 | |
| 25 | lbs. of best loaf sugar, | at 1 . | 1½ | |
| 137 | lbs. of soft sugar, | at 0 . | 7½ | |
| 12 | cakes of chocolate, | at 5 . | 6 | *per cake.* |
| 20 | lbs. of raisins, | at 1 . | 2 | *per lb.* |
| 15½ | lbs. of cocoa, | at 3 . | 4 | |

£93 . 15 . 2½

## A WINE-MERCHANT'S BILL.

(7.)     Mr. Thomas Greville,

Bought of John Simes, April 3. 1852.

|  |  | s. | d. |  |
|---|---|---|---|---|
| 12½ | Dozens of Port, | at 4 . | 6 | *per bottle.* |
| 3½ | Dozens of Lisbon, | at 4 . | 3 | |
| 2 | Dozens of claret, | at 8 . | 6 | |
| 4½ | Dozens of sherry, | at 5 . | 6 | |
| 1½ | Dozens of Burgundy, | at 10 . | 6 | |
| 6 | Dozens of Vidonia, | at 4 . | 6 | |
| 9 | Dozens of Bucellas, | at 3 . | 8 | |
| 8 | Gallons of brandy, | at 22 . | 6 | *per gall.* |
| 5 | Gallons of rum, | at 17 . | 6 | |
| 4 | Gallons of Hollands, | at 21 . | 6 | |

£130 . 17 . 0

### A Cheesemonger's Bill.

(8.) Mr. Edward Patteson,

Bought of Stephen Cross, Sept. 1. 1852.

|  | s. | d. |
|---|---|---|
| 8 lbs. of Cambridge butter, | at 0 . | 10 *per lb.* |
| 17 lbs. of new cheese, | at 1 . | 0 |
| $\frac{1}{3}$ firkin of buttter, wt. 28 lbs. | at 0 . | $9\frac{1}{2}$ |
| 6 Cheshire cheeses, wt. 127 lbs. | at 0 . | 11 |
| 2 Warwickshire ditto, wt. 15 lbs. | at 0 . | 9 |
| 2 lbs. of cream cheese, | at 1 . | 6 |
| 12 lbs. of Stilton cheese, | at 1 . | 8 |

£9 . 16 . 6

## Vulgar Fractions.

A FRACTION is any part or parts of a unit or of something considered as a whole; and it represented by two numbers, placed one above the other, with a line drawn between them; as $\frac{1}{2}$, $\frac{2}{3}$, $\frac{3}{4}$, &c.

The number below the line is called the *denominator*, and shows how many equal parts the integer or whole is divided into. And the number above the line is the *numerator*, which shows how many of those parts are expressed by the fraction.

Thus, $\frac{2}{3}$ denotes that some whole quantity, considered as a unit, is divided into 3 equal parts, and that the fraction expresses 2 of those parts.

Fractions are either proper, improper, simple, compound, mixed, or complex.

1. A *proper fraction* is when the numerator is less than the denominator; as $\frac{3}{4}$, $\frac{4}{5}$, $\frac{5}{7}$, &c.

2. An *improper fraction* is when the numerator is equal to, or greater than, the denominator; as, $\frac{5}{5}$, $\frac{8}{3}$, $\frac{130}{21}$, &c.

3. A *simple fraction* is that which is expressed singly, or without any reference to others, as $\frac{6}{7}$, $\frac{17}{9}$, &c.

4. A *compound fraction* is the fraction of a fraction, as $\frac{1}{2}$ of $\frac{2}{3}$, of $\frac{3}{4}$, of $\frac{5}{6}$, &c.

5. A *mixed number* is that which is composed of a whole number and a fraction, as $8\frac{1}{5}$, $17\frac{6}{13}$, &c.

6. A *complex fraction* is that which has a fraction, or a mixed number, in either, or both, of its terms ; as

$$\frac{\frac{1}{2}}{5}, \text{ or } \frac{7}{9\frac{1}{4}}, \text{ or } \frac{3\frac{1}{8}}{13}, \text{ or } \frac{2\frac{1}{2}}{7\frac{1}{3}}, \&c.$$

*Note.* Any whole number, as 5, may be expressed like a fraction, by writing 1 under it as a denominator, thus $\frac{5}{1}$.

## REDUCTION OF VULGAR FRACTIONS.

REDUCTION OF VULGAR FRACTIONS is the method of changing them from one form, or denomination, to another, in order to prepare them for the operations of addition, subtraction, &c.

### CASE I.

*To abbreviate or reduce fractions to their lowest terms.*

#### RULE.*

Divide the terms of the given fraction by any number that will divide each of them without a remainder, and these quo-

---

* It is evident that by dividing the numerator and denominator of any fraction, equally by any number that will divide them without a remainder, the result will give another fraction equal to the former : and if these divisions be performed as often as can be done, or the greatest common divisor be found by the second part of the rule, the terms of the resulting fraction must be the least possible. For it is a universal *axiom* in fractions, *that* if you multiply or divide both the numerator and denominator of a fraction by the same number, its value is not altered. (*See Note* 16. *page* 21.)

*Note.* When both the terms of any given fraction end with an even number, they can be each divided by 2 ; and if one of them ends with a 5, and the other with a 0, or both of them with a 5, they can each be divided by 5.

Also, when the numerator and denominator of any fraction both end with 0's, an equal number of them may be left out of each, without altering the result. Thus $\frac{20}{50} = \frac{2}{5}$; and $\frac{300}{1400} = \frac{3}{14}$.

Which simple rules it will be necessary for the learner to keep in his memory, as they greatly facilitate the reduction required.

And in cases where a division of this kind cannot be used, the number proper for that purpose must be found by trial, or by having recourse either to the second part of the above rule, or to some of the theorems respecting the properties of numbers, given at the end of the present work (*or see Notes from* 4 *to* 12. *page* 20.)

tients again in the same manner; and so on, till it appears that there is no number greater than 1, which will divide them; and the resulting fraction will be in its lowest terms.

### Or,

Divide the greater term of the fraction by the less, and this divisor by the remainder; and so on, dividing each divisor by the last remainder, till nothing remains; then if the numerator and denominator of the given fraction be each divided by the number so found, it will reduce it to its lowest terms.

### EXAMPLES.

(1.) Reduce $\frac{144}{240}$ to its lowest terms.

$$\overset{(2)}{ } \quad \overset{(2)}{ } \quad \overset{(3)}{ } \quad \overset{(2)}{ } \quad \overset{(2)}{ } \; divisors.$$

$$\frac{144}{240}=\frac{72}{120}=\frac{36}{60}=\frac{12}{20}=\frac{6}{10}=\frac{3}{5}=the\ answer.$$

*Or thus,*

$$\overset{(12)}{ } \quad \overset{(4)}{ } \; divisors.$$

$$\frac{144}{240}=\frac{12}{20}=\frac{3}{5}=Ans.$$

*Or thus,*

$$144)240(1$$
$$\quad\; 144$$
$$\quad\;\overline{\hspace{1.5cm}}$$
$$96)144(1; \; hence \; 48)\tfrac{144}{240}=\tfrac{3}{5}, as\ before.$$
$$\;\; 96$$
$$\quad\overline{\hspace{1.5cm}}$$
$$48)96(2$$
$$\;\; 96$$

(2.) Reduce $\frac{48}{272}$ to its lowest terms.        *Ans.* $\frac{3}{17}$.

(3.) Reduce $\frac{192}{576}$ to its lowest terms.        *Ans.* $\frac{1}{3}$.

---

It may here also be observed, that when numbers with the sign of addition or subtraction between them, are to be divided by any number, each of the numbers must be divided. Thus $\dfrac{4+8+10}{2}=2+4+5=11$; but when they have the sign of multiplication between them, only one of them must be divided. Thus $\dfrac{3\times8\times10}{2\times6}=\dfrac{3\times4\times10}{1\times6}=\dfrac{1\times4\times10}{1\times2}=$

$\dfrac{1\times2\times10}{1\times1}=\dfrac{20}{1}=20.$   *Or thus,* $\dfrac{\overset{4}{\cancel{3}}\times\overset{5}{\cancel{8}}\times\cancel{10}}{\cancel{2}\times\cancel{6}}=\dfrac{20}{1}=20.$

(4.) Reduce $\frac{825}{960}$ to its lowest terms.        *Ans.* $\frac{55}{64}$.
(5.) Reduce $\frac{252}{364}$ to its lowest terms.        *Ans.* $\frac{9}{13}$.
(6.) Reduce $\frac{1344}{1536}$ to its lowest terms.        *Ans.* $\frac{7}{8}$.
(7.) Reduce $\frac{1449}{1764}$ to its lowest terms.        *Ans.* $\frac{23}{28}$.
(8.) Reduce $\frac{1408}{1664}$ to its lowest terms.        *Ans.* $\frac{11}{13}$.
(9.) Reduce $\frac{7631}{28415}$ to its lowest terms.        *Ans.* $\frac{13}{45}$.
(10.) Reduce $\frac{42237}{75582}$ to its lowest terms.        *Ans.* $\frac{19}{34}$.

## CASE II.

*To reduce a mixed number to its equivalent improper fraction.*

### RULE.*

Multiply the whole number by the denominator of the fraction, and add the numerator to the product; then this sum placed above the denominator will form the fraction required.

### EXAMPLES.

(1.) Reduce $27\frac{2}{9}$ to its equivalent improper fraction.

$$27\frac{2}{9} = \frac{(27 \times 9) + 2}{9} = \frac{245}{9} = Ans.$$

*Or thus,*
$$\begin{array}{r} 27 \\ 9 \text{ } multiply. \\ \hline 243 \\ 2 \text{ } add. \\ \hline \frac{245}{9} = Answer. \end{array}$$

(2.) Reduce $19\frac{3}{4}$ to its equivalent improper fraction.
        *Ans.* $\frac{79}{4}$.

(3.) Reduce $22\frac{1}{5}$ to an improper fraction.        *Ans.* $\frac{111}{5}$.
(4.) Reduce $514\frac{5}{16}$ to an improper fraction.        *Ans.* $\frac{8229}{16}$.
(5.) Reduce $100\frac{19}{59}$ to an improper fraction.        *Ans.* $\frac{5919}{59}$.
(6.) Reduce $47\frac{5}{13}$ to an improper fraction.        *Ans.* $\frac{616}{13}$.

---

* All fractions represent a division of the numerator by the denominator, and may consequently be taken as proper and adequate expressions for the quotient. Thus the quotient of 2 divided by 3 is $\frac{2}{3}$; from which the rule is manifest; for if any number be multiplied and divided by the same number, it is evdent that the quotient must be the same as the quantity first proposed

F

### CASE III.

*To reduce an improper fraction to its equivalent whole or mixed number.*

#### RULE.*

Divide the numerator by the denominator, and the quotient will be the integer or whole number required: and if there be any remainder, place it over the denominator, to the right hand of the former, for the fractional part.

#### EXAMPLES.

(1.) Reduce $\frac{981}{16}$ to its equivalent whole or mixed number.

$$16)981(61\tfrac{5}{16} = Answer.$$
$$96$$
$$\overline{\phantom{0}}$$
$$21$$
$$16$$
$$\overline{\phantom{0}}$$
$$5$$

(2.) Reduce $\frac{56}{8}$ to its equivalent whole or mixed number.

                                       *Ans.* 7.

(3.) Reduce $\frac{1245}{22}$ to its equivalent whole or mixed number.

                                       *Ans.* $56\tfrac{13}{22}$.

(4.) Reduce $\frac{3848}{21}$ to its equivalent whole or mixed number.

                                       *Ans.* $183\tfrac{5}{21}$.

(5.) Reduce $\frac{5907}{25}$ to its equivalent whole or mixed number.

                                       *Ans.* $236\tfrac{7}{25}$.

(6.) Reduce $\frac{621613}{514}$ to its equivalent whole or mixed number.

                                       *Ans.* $1209\tfrac{187}{514}$.

### CASE IV.

*To reduce a compound fraction to an equivalent simple one.*

#### RULE.†

If any of the proposed quantities be integers, or mixed numbers, reduce them to improper fractions, by *Case II.*, then mul-

---

   \* This rule is plainly the reverse of the former, and has its reason in the nature of Common Division.

   † That a compound fraction may be represented by a simple one is evident, since a part of a part must be equal to some part of the whole.

tiply all the numerators together for a numerator, and all the denominators together for a denominator ; and the former product placed over the latter will be the simple fraction required.

*Note.* If two or more factors that are equal to each other be found both in the numerator and denominator, they may be struck out of each, and when it can be done, any two terms of the fraction may be divided by the same number, and the quotients used instead of them.

### EXAMPLES.

(1.) Reduce $\frac{2}{3}$ of $\frac{3}{4}$ of $\frac{8}{11}$ to a simple fraction.

$$\frac{2 \times 3 \times 8}{3 \times 4 \times 11} = \frac{48}{132} = \frac{4}{11} = \textit{the answer.}$$

*Or thus,*

$$\frac{2 \times 3 \times 8}{3 \times 4 \times 11} = \frac{2 \times 8}{4 \times 11} = \frac{2 \times 2}{11} = \frac{4}{11} = \textit{Answer, as before.}$$

*Or by cancelling,* that is by finding any number that will divide a number both in the numerator and denominator, as per note.

$$\frac{2 \times 3 \times \overset{2}{\cancel{8}}}{\cancel{3} \times \cancel{4} \times 11} = \frac{2 \times 2}{11} = \frac{4}{11} = \textit{Answer as before.}$$

(2.) Reduce $\frac{2}{3}$ of $\frac{3}{4}$ to a simple fraction.      *Ans.* $\frac{1}{2}$.
(3.) Reduce $\frac{4}{7}$ of $\frac{8}{9}$ to a simple fraction.      *Ans.* $\frac{32}{63}$.
(4.) Reduce $\frac{2}{3}$ of $\frac{3}{5}$ of $\frac{5}{8}$ to a simple fraction.      *Ans.* $\frac{1}{4}$.

---

The truth of the rule for this reduction may be shown as follows : —
Let the compound fraction to be reduced be $\frac{2}{3}$ of $\frac{4}{7}$. Then $\frac{1}{3}$ of $\frac{4}{7} = \frac{4}{7} \div 3 = \frac{4}{21}$, and consequently $\frac{2}{3}$ of $\frac{4}{7} = \frac{4}{21} \times 2 = \frac{8}{21}$, as by the rule ; and the like will be found to be true in all cases.

If the compound fraction consists of three or more fractions, the two first may be reduced to a single one, and then that single one and the third to another ; and so on for any number of them.

It may here also be observed, that a whole number may be reduced to an equivalent fraction, having a given denominator, by multiplying it by the given denominator, and then putting the same denominator under the product.

Thus, if it were required to reduce 5 to a fraction, having 7 for its denominator, we shall have $\frac{5 \times 7}{7} = \frac{35}{7}$ ; and if 9 is to be reduced to a fraction having 11 for its denominator, the answer is $\frac{99}{11}$.

(5.) Reduce $\frac{2}{3}$ of $9\frac{1}{8}$ to a simple fraction.      *Ans.* $\frac{11}{3}=3\frac{2}{3}$.

(6.) Reduce $\frac{3}{100}$ of $12\frac{6}{7}$ to a simple fraction.      *Ans.* $\frac{27}{70}$.

(7.) Reduce $\frac{4}{5}$ of $\frac{7}{8}$ of $10\frac{1}{2}$ to a simple fraction. *Ans.* $\frac{147}{20}=7\frac{7}{20}$.

## CASE V.

*To reduce fractions of different denominators to others of an equal value, that shall have a common denominator.*

### RULE 1.*

If any of the proposed quantities be integers, mixed numbers, or compound fractions, reduce them to simple fractions by the former rules.

Then multiply each numerator of these fractions by all the denominators, except its own, for a new numerator, and all the denominators together for a common denominator.

### EXAMPLES.

(1.) Reduce $\frac{1}{2}$, $\frac{3}{5}$, and $\frac{4}{7}$ to equivalent fractions, having a common denominator.

$$1 \times 5 \times 7 = 35 \; \textit{the new numerator for } \tfrac{1}{2}$$
$$3 \times 2 \times 7 = 42 \; \ldots \ldots \ldots \textit{ditto  for } \tfrac{3}{5}$$
$$4 \times 2 \times 5 = 40 \; \ldots \ldots \ldots \textit{ditto  for } \tfrac{4}{7}$$
$$\overline{2 \times 5 \times 7 = 70 \; \textit{the common denominator.}}$$

*Therefore, the new equivalent fractions are* $\frac{35}{70}$, $\frac{42}{70}$, *and* $\frac{40}{70}$ *the answer; because* $\frac{35}{70}=\frac{1}{2}$; $\frac{42}{70}=\frac{3}{5}$; *and* $\frac{40}{70}=\frac{4}{7}$.

(2.) Reduce $\frac{2}{3}$ and $\frac{4}{5}$ to fractions having a common denominator.      *Ans.* $\frac{10}{15}$ *and* $\frac{12}{15}$.

---

* By placing the terms of the fractions, and the numbers by which they are multiplied, properly under each other, it will be seen that the numerator and denominator of each of them are multiplied by the same number, and consequently their values are not altered. Thus, in the first example :

$$\frac{1}{2}\Big|\frac{\times 5 \times 7}{\times 5 \times 7} \; ; \; \frac{3}{5}\Big|\frac{\times 2 \times 7}{\times 2 \times 7} \; ; \; \frac{4}{7}\Big|\frac{\times 2 \times 5}{\times 2 \times 5}$$

given above, the common denominator is a multiple of all the denominators, and consequently may be divided by any of them, without leaving a remainder. Hence it is manifest that proper parts may be taken for all the numerators as required.

A common denominator may often be more readily found, by multiplying the numerator and denominator of each of the fractions by such numbers as will make the denominators the same in them all. Thus, if the fractions be $\frac{2}{3}$ and $\frac{3}{4}$, the terms of the first being multiplied by 4, will give $\frac{8}{12}$, and the terms of the second, multiplied by 3, will give $\frac{9}{12}$, each of which have the same denominator.

(3.) Reduce $\frac{1}{2}$, $\frac{1}{3}$, and $\frac{1}{4}$ to fractions having a common denominator. *Ans.* $\frac{12}{24}$, $\frac{8}{24}$, and $\frac{6}{24}$.

(4.) Reduce $\frac{1}{2}$, $\frac{2}{3}$, $\frac{5}{6}$, and $\frac{7}{8}$ to fractions having a common denominator. *Ans.* $\frac{144}{288}$, $\frac{192}{288}$, $\frac{240}{288}$, $\frac{252}{288}$.

(5.) Reduce $\frac{1}{3}$, $\frac{3}{5}$, $5\frac{1}{2}$, and $\frac{2}{19}$, to a common denominator. *Ans.* $\frac{190}{570}$, $\frac{342}{570}$, $\frac{3135}{570}$, $\frac{60}{570}$.

(6.) Reduce $\frac{11}{13}$, $\frac{3}{4}$ of $1\frac{1}{4}$, $\frac{9}{11}$, and $\frac{5}{7}$, to a common denominator. *Ans.* $\frac{13552}{16016}$, $\frac{15015}{16016}$, $\frac{13104}{16016}$, $\frac{11440}{16016}$.

## RULE 2.

*To reduce fractions to others that shall have the least common denominator.*

1. Divide the product of any two of the denominators by the greatest divisor of each of the factors, and proceed in the same manner with the product of the quotient thus arising, and another denominator; and so on to the last quotient, which will be the least common denominator sought.

2. Divide the common denominator thus found by the denominator of each fraction, and multiply the quotient by the numerator; then these products, taken in order, will be the numerators of the fractions required.

### EXAMPLES.

(1.) Reduce $\frac{1}{2}$, $\frac{3}{4}$, and $\frac{5}{6}$, to fractions having the least common denominator.

*Here* $\dfrac{2 \times 4}{2} = 4$; $\dfrac{4 \times 6}{2} = 12$ *the least common denominator.*

*And* $\dfrac{12}{2} \times 1 = 6$; $\dfrac{12}{4} \times 3 = 9$; $\dfrac{12}{6} \times 5 = 10$ *the numerators.*

*Whence* $\frac{6}{12}$, $\frac{9}{12}$, and $\frac{10}{12}$ *are the fractions required.*

(2.) Reduce $\frac{7}{12}$ and $\frac{11}{18}$ to fractions, having the least common denominator. *Ans.* $\frac{21}{36}$, $\frac{22}{36}$.

(3.) Reduce $\frac{1}{2}$, $\frac{2}{3}$, $\frac{3}{4}$, and $\frac{5}{6}$, to fractions having the least common denominator. *Ans.* $\frac{6}{12}$, $\frac{8}{12}$, $\frac{9}{12}$, $\frac{10}{12}$.

(4.) Reduce $\frac{2}{5}$, $\frac{2}{3}$, $\frac{5}{9}$, and $\frac{7}{10}$, to fractions having the least common denominator. *Ans.* $\frac{36}{90}$, $\frac{60}{90}$, $\frac{50}{90}$, $\frac{63}{90}$.

(5.) Reduce $\frac{1}{7}$, $\frac{3}{8}$, $\frac{4}{9}$, $\frac{5}{24}$, and $\frac{7}{72}$, to fractions having the least common denominator. *Ans.* $\frac{72}{504}$, $\frac{189}{504}$, $\frac{224}{504}$, $\frac{105}{504}$, $\frac{49}{504}$.

(6.) Reduce $\frac{1}{3}$, $\frac{3}{4}$, $\frac{5}{6}$, $\frac{7}{8}$, $\frac{11}{16}$, and $\frac{17}{24}$, to equivalent fractions, having the least common denominator possible. *Ans.* $\frac{16}{48}$, $\frac{36}{48}$, $\frac{40}{48}$, $\frac{42}{48}$, $\frac{33}{48}$, $\frac{34}{48}$.

## CASE VI.

*To reduce a fraction of one denomination to that of another which shall have the same value.*

### RULE.*

When the reduction is from a less name to a greater, multiply the denominator by all the different denominations, from that given to the one sought; but if it be from a greater name to a less, multiply the numerator by all the denominations, as before, and it will give the fraction required.

### EXAMPLES.

(1.) Reduce $\frac{5}{6}$ of a penny to the fraction of a pound.

$$\frac{5}{6 \times 12 \times 20} = \frac{1}{6 \times 12 \times 4} = \frac{1}{288} = the\ ans.\ required.$$

(2.) Reduce $\frac{7}{18}$ of a pound to the fraction of a penny.

$$\frac{7 \times 20 \times 12}{18} = \frac{7 \times 10 \times 12}{9} = \frac{7 \times 10 \times 4}{3} = \frac{280}{3} = Ans.$$

$$Or\ thus,\quad \frac{7 \times 20 \times \overset{2}{\cancel{12}}}{\underset{3}{\cancel{18}}} = \frac{7 \times 20 \times 2}{3} = \frac{280}{3} = Ans.$$

Here it is to be observed, that 12 in the numerator and 18 in the denominator are both divisible by 6.

(3.) Reduce $\frac{2}{3}$ of a farthing to the fraction of a pound.

Ans. $\frac{1}{1440}$.

(5.) Reduce $\frac{5}{9}$ of a pound to the fraction of a penny.

Ans. $\frac{400}{3}$.

(5.) Reduce $\frac{4}{5}$ of a dwt. to the fraction of a pound troy.

Ans. $\frac{1}{300}$.

(6.) Reduce $\frac{6}{7}$ of a pound avoirdupois to the fraction of a cwt.

Ans. $\frac{3}{392}$.

(7.) Reduce $\frac{5}{48}$ of a mile to the fraction of a yard. Ans. $\frac{550}{3}$.

(8.) Reduce $\frac{3}{13}$ of a month to the fraction of a day. Ans. $\frac{84}{13}$.

(9.) Reduce 7s. 3d. to the fraction of a pound.† Ans. $\frac{29}{80}$.

---

* The reason of this practice is explained in the rule for reducing compound fractions to simple ones.

† Quantities of this sort are best reduced to the fraction required, by bringing them to their lowest denomination, for a numerator, and then

(10.) Reduce 6 fur. 16 po to the fraction of a mile. *Ans.* $\frac{4}{5}$.
(11.) Reduce $\frac{2}{7}l$. to the fraction of a guinea. *Ans.* $\frac{40}{147}$.
(12.) Reduce $\frac{5}{8}$ of a crown to the fraction of a guinea.
*Ans.* $\frac{25}{168}$.
(13.) Reduce $\frac{5}{6}$ of half-a-crown to the fraction of a shilling. *Ans.* $\frac{25}{12}$.
(14.) Reduce $\frac{6}{7}$ of a moidore to the fraction of a crown.
*Ans.* $\frac{162}{35}$.

### CASE VII.

*To find the value of a fraction in the known parts of the integer.*

#### RULE.*

Multiply the numerator by the parts in the next inferior denomination, and divide the product by the denominator; and if any thing remains, multiply it by the next inferior denomination, and divide by the denominator as before; and so on as far as can be done; then the quotients, placed in order, will be the answer required.

#### EXAMPLES.

(1.) What is the value of $\frac{5}{7}$ of a shilling?

$$5$$
$$12 \text{ pence} = 1 \text{ shilling.}$$

$$7)\overline{60}$$

$$8d. \quad 4 = \tfrac{4}{7} \text{ of one penny over.}$$
$$4 \text{ farthings} = 1d.$$

$$7)\overline{16}$$

$$2\tfrac{2}{7}f. \qquad\qquad\qquad Ans. \ 8\tfrac{1}{2}d. \ \tfrac{2}{7}f.$$

---

putting the integer, reduced to the same denomination, under it, for a denominator.

Thus 7s. 3d. = 87d. and 1l. = 240d.; therefore $\frac{87}{240} = \frac{29}{80} =$ the answer.

* The numerator of a fraction which arises after any operation is performed, may be considered as a remainder, and the denominator as a divisor; whence this rule has its reason in the nature of Compound Division, and the valuation of remainders in the Rule of Three; which have been already sufficiently explained.

F 4

(2.) What is the value of $\frac{3}{8}$ of a pound sterling ? *Ans.* 7s. 6d.
(3.) What is the value of $\frac{2}{9}$ of a guinea?        *Ans.* 4s. 8d.
(4.) What is the value of $\frac{4}{7}$ of half-a-crown? *Ans.* 1s. $5\frac{1}{7}$d.
(5.) What is the value of $\frac{13}{19}$ of a moidore? *Ans.* 18s. $5\frac{13}{19}$d.
(6.) What is the value of $\frac{2}{5}$ of a pound troy? *Ans.* 7 oz. 4 dwts.
(7.) What is the value of $\frac{4}{7}$ of a pound avoirdupois ?
                          *Ans.* 9 oz. $2\frac{2}{7}$ dr.
(8.) What is the value of $\frac{5}{9}$ of an ell English ?
                          *Ans.* 2 qrs. $3\frac{1}{9}$ na.
(9.) What is the value of $\frac{2}{15}$ of a hhd. of ale ?
                          *Ans.* 7 gal. 0 qt. $1\frac{3}{5}$ pt.
(10.) What is the value of $\frac{7}{8}$ of a ton of wine ?
                          *Ans.* 3 hhds. 31 gal. 2 qt.
(11.) What is the value of $\frac{7}{9}$ of a cwt. ?
                          *Ans.* 3 qr. 3 lb. 1 oz. $12\frac{4}{9}$ dr.
(12.) What is the value of $\frac{7}{13}$ of a day ?
                          *Ans.* 12 ho. 55 min. $23\frac{1}{13}$ sec.
(13.) What is the value of $\frac{3}{7}$ of a mile ?
                          *Ans.* 3 fur. 17 po. 0 yd. 2 ft. $4\frac{2}{7}$ in.

### CASE VIII.

*To reduce a complex fraction to an equivalent simple one.* ·

#### RULE.

Multiply each of its terms by the denominator of the fractional part, if there be only one ; or first by one denominator
and then by another, if there be more than one, and the
result will be the simple fraction required.

#### EXAMPLES.

(1.) Reduce the complex fractions $\frac{2\frac{1}{2}}{7}$ and $\frac{3\frac{1}{4}}{6\frac{1}{3}}$, to simple
fractions.

*First,* $\quad \frac{2\frac{1}{2}}{7} = \frac{(2 \times 2) + 1}{7 \times 2} = \frac{5}{14} = $ *1st Ans.*

*Second,* $\frac{3\frac{1}{4}}{6\frac{1}{3}} = \frac{[(3 \times 4) + 1] \times 3}{[(6 \times 3) + 1] \times 4} = \frac{13 \times 3}{19 \times 4} = \frac{39}{76} = $ *2nd Ans.*

(2.) Reduce the complex fraction $\frac{4}{5\frac{1}{4}}$ to a simple fraction.
                          *Ans.* $\frac{16}{21}$.

(3.) Reduce the complex fraction $\frac{9\frac{1}{6}}{3}$ to a simple one.
                          *Ans.* $\frac{46}{15}$.

(4.) Reduce the complex fraction $\dfrac{2\frac{1}{8}}{3\frac{1}{6}}$ to a simple one.

$Ans.\ \frac{51}{76}.$

(5.) Reduce the complex fraction $\dfrac{7\frac{1}{2}}{9\frac{5}{6}}$ to a simple one.

$Ans.\ \frac{45}{59}.$

(6.) Reduce the complex fraction $\dfrac{20\frac{1}{9}}{22\frac{1}{12}}$ to a simple fraction.

$Ans.\ \frac{724}{795}.$

## ADDITION OF VULGAR FRACTIONS.

### RULE.*

Reduce such of the fractions as require it to simple ones, and such as are of different denominations to those of the same name; then bring the fractions, so prepared, to a common denominator, and the sum of the numerators, placed over this denominator. will be the sum of the fractions required.

*Note.* When large mixed numbers, or mixed numbers and fractions, are to be added together, it will be best to bring the fractional parts only to a common denomination, and then annex their sum to that of the whole numbers, carrying for the units, if any, as usual.

### EXAMPLES.

(1.) Add $\frac{2}{3}$ and $\frac{3}{4}$ together.

*Here* $\frac{2}{3}=\frac{8}{12}$, *for* $\frac{2}{3}\times\frac{4}{4}=\frac{8}{12}$; *and* $\frac{3}{4}=\frac{9}{12}$, *for* $\frac{3}{4}\times\frac{3}{3}=\frac{9}{12}$.

*Whence* $\frac{8}{12}+\frac{9}{12}=\frac{17}{12}=1\frac{5}{12}=Ans.$

*Or thus,*

$\left.\begin{array}{l} 2\times4=8 \\ 3\times3=9 \end{array}\right\}$ *numerators*

*Sum of the numerators* $=17$

*Common denom.* $3\times4=\dfrac{\phantom{3\times4=}}{12}=1\frac{5}{12}=Ans.\ as\ before.$

---

* Fractions that have different denominators not of the same kind, and therefore cannot be incorporated with each other; but when they are reduced to a common denominator, and by that means, made parts of the same thing, their sum, or difference, may then be as properly expressed by the sum or difference of the numerators, as the sum or difference of any two quantities whatever, by the sum or difference of their individuals; whence the reason of the rules, both for addition and subtraction, is manifest.

To this we may add, that the bringing of fractions to a common de-

(2.) Required the sum of $2\frac{1}{3}$, $\frac{4}{5}$, and $\frac{1}{2}$ of $\frac{3}{4}$.

*First, $2\frac{1}{3}=\frac{7}{3}$, and $\frac{1}{2}$ of $\frac{3}{4}=\frac{3}{8}$.*

*Therefore the fractions are $\frac{7}{3}$, $\frac{4}{5}$, and $\frac{3}{8}$.*

*Hence* $\left.\begin{array}{l}7\times5\times8=280\\4\times3\times8=\phantom{0}96\\3\times3\times5=\phantom{0}45\end{array}\right\}$ *numerators.*

*Sum of the numerators* $\ldots\ldots=\overline{421}$
*Common denominators* $3\times5\times8=\overline{120}$ $=3\frac{61}{120}=$ *the answer.*

*Or thus, by Note,* $\dfrac{1}{3}+\dfrac{4}{5}+\dfrac{3}{8}=\dfrac{40}{120}+\dfrac{96}{120}+\dfrac{45}{120}=\dfrac{181}{120}=1\frac{61}{120}$.

*Then* $2+1\frac{61}{120}=3\frac{61}{120}=$*the answer as before.*

(3.) Required the sum of $\frac{3}{7}$ and $\frac{5}{11}$.     *Ans.* $\frac{68}{77}$.
(4.) Required the sum of $\frac{1}{2}$, $\frac{1}{3}$, and $\frac{1}{4}$.     *Ans.* $1\frac{1}{12}$.
(5.) Required the sum of $\frac{2}{5}$ and $9\frac{1}{4}$.     *Ans.* $9\frac{13}{20}$.
(6.) Add $\frac{5}{8}$, $7\frac{1}{2}$, and $\frac{1}{3}$ of $\frac{3}{4}$ together.     *Ans.* $8\frac{3}{8}$.
(7.) What is the sum of $\frac{3}{5}$, $\frac{4}{5}$ of $\frac{1}{3}$, and $\frac{3}{20}$?     *Ans.* $1\frac{1}{60}$.
(8.) What is the sum of $\frac{9}{10}$ of $6\frac{7}{8}$, $\frac{4}{7}$ of $\frac{1}{2}$, and $7\frac{1}{2}$?
     *Ans.* $13\frac{109}{112}$.
(9.) Required the sum of $55\frac{1}{2}$, $109\frac{6}{7}$, and $2\frac{9}{10}$.   *Ans.* $168\frac{9}{35}$.
(10.) Add $\frac{1}{7}l$. $\frac{2}{9}s$. and $\frac{5}{12}d$. together.     *Ans.* 3s. $1\frac{1}{4}d.$ $\frac{10}{21}f.$
(11.) Add $\frac{2}{3}$ of a yard, $\frac{3}{4}$ of a foot, and $\frac{3}{8}$ of a mile together.
     *Ans.* $660\frac{11}{12}$ *yds., or* 660 *yds.* 2 *ft.* 9 *in.*
(12.) Add $\frac{1}{3}$ of a week, $\frac{1}{4}$ of a day, and $\frac{1}{2}$ an hour together.
     *Ans.* $2\frac{29}{48}$ *days, or* 2 *da.* $14\frac{1}{2}$ *hrs.*
(13.) Required the sum of $1000\frac{2}{3}$, $74\frac{5}{9}$, and $6\frac{2}{45}$.   *Ans.* 1081.
(14.) Required the sum of $\frac{5}{9}$ of a guinea, and $\frac{3}{8}$ of a moidore.
     *Ans.* 1l. 1s. $9\frac{1}{2}d.$
(15.) What is the sum of $\frac{2}{7}$ of $15l.$, $3\frac{3}{7}l.$, $\frac{1}{3}$ of $\frac{5}{7}$ of $\frac{3}{4}$ of a $l.$,
and $\frac{2}{3}$ of $\frac{3}{7}$ of a shilling?     *Ans.* 7l. 17s. $5\frac{1}{7}d.$
(16.) What is the sum of $\frac{4}{7}$ of a cwt., $8\frac{5}{6}$ lb., and $3\frac{9}{10}$ oz.?
     *Ans.* 2 *qrs.* 17 *lb.* 1 *oz.* $3\frac{11}{15}$ *drs.*
(17.) What is the sum of $3\frac{1}{2}$ English ells, $4\frac{1}{2}$ yards, and $\frac{5}{7}$
of a nail?     *Ans.* 8 *yds.* 3 *qrs.* $2\frac{5}{7}$ *na.*
(18.) What is the sum of $\frac{3}{4}$ of a hhd. of ale, $2\frac{5}{7}$ gallons, and
$\frac{3}{4}$ of $\frac{4}{5}$ of a pint?     *Ans.* 43 *gal.* $2\frac{11}{35}$ *pts.*

---

nominator is only requisite in addition and subtraction; no such operation being necessary in any of the other rules.

(19.) What is the sum of $4\frac{9}{16}$ miles, $\frac{2}{7}$ of a furlong, and $\frac{3}{8}$ of $1\frac{1}{2}$ yd.? *Ans.* 4 *mi.* 4 *fur.* $173\frac{53}{70}$ *yds.*

## SUBTRACTION OF VULGAR FRACTIONS.

### RULE.

Reduce the fractions, when necessary, to a common denominator, as in addition: then the difference of the numerators, placed over the common denominator, will give the difference of the fractions required.

But when they consist of large mixed numbers, or mixed numbers and fractions, subtract them according to the method mentioned in the former rule.

### EXAMPLES.

(1.) What is the difference of $\frac{3}{4}$ and $\frac{5}{7}$?

$$Here \frac{3}{4}=\frac{21}{28}; \ and \ \frac{5}{7}=\frac{20}{28}.$$

$$Therefore \ \frac{21}{28}-\frac{20}{28} \ or \ \frac{21-20}{28}=\frac{1}{28}=Answer.$$

$$Or \ thus, \left. \begin{array}{l} 3\times7=21 \\ 5\times4=20 \end{array} \right\} numerators.$$

$Difference\ of\ the\ numerators=1$
$Denominators \ldots\ldots 4\times7=\overline{28}$ = *the answer as before.*

(2.) What is the difference between $\frac{2}{3}$ and $\frac{2}{9}$ of $\frac{3}{7}$?

$$Here \ \frac{2}{9} of \frac{3}{7}=\frac{6}{63}=\frac{2}{21}; \ and \ \frac{2}{3}=\frac{14}{21}, for \ \frac{2\times7}{3\times7}=\frac{14}{21},$$

$$Therefore \ \frac{14}{21}-\frac{2}{21}=\frac{12}{21}=\frac{4}{7}=the\ answer.$$

(3.) Required the difference of $\frac{2}{3}$ and $\frac{7}{9}$.　　*Ans.* $\frac{1}{9}$.
(4.) Required the difference of $\frac{7}{11}$ and $\frac{8}{13}$.　　*Ans.* $\frac{3}{143}$.
(5.) Required the difference of $\frac{97}{100}$ and $\frac{3}{7}$.　　*Ans.* $\frac{379}{700}$.
(6.) Required the difference of 169 and $14\frac{3}{7}$.　*Ans.* $154\frac{4}{7}$.
(7.) Required the difference of $214\frac{1}{4}$ and $\frac{2}{3}$ of 19. *Ans.* $201\frac{7}{12}$.
(8.) Required the difference between $\frac{1}{2}$ of a pound and $\frac{3}{4}$ of a shilling.　　　　　　　*Ans.* 9s. 3d.
(9.) Required the difference between $\frac{2}{5}$ of an ounce and $\frac{7}{8}$ of a pennyweight.　　　　*Ans.* 11 *dwts.* 3 *grs.*
(10.) Required the difference between $\frac{2}{3}$ of a league and $\frac{7}{10}$ of a mile.　　　*Ans.* 1 *mi.* 2 *fur.* 16 *po.*

(11.) Required the difference between $\frac{7}{8}$ of a guinea and $\frac{2}{3}$ of a moidore. *Ans.* $4\frac{1}{2}d.$

(12.) Required the difference between $8\frac{9}{10}$ cwt. and 1 qr. $2\frac{3}{7}$ lb. *Ans.* 8 *cwt.* 2 *qrs.* $14\frac{13}{35}$ *lbs.*

## MULTIPLICATION OF VULGAR FRACTIONS.

### RULE.*

Prepare the fractions, by reducing such as require it to simple ones, as in the former rules; then multiply the numerators together for a numerator, and the denominators for a denominator, and it will give the product required.

*Note.* When one of the factors is a large mixed number, and the other a whole number, it will be best to multiply the parts of the former separately, observing to carry for units to the whole numbers, when necessary.

It may here also be further observed, that in the multiplication of whole numbers, the product will be always greater than either of the factors; but if two proper fractions be multiplied together, the product will be less than either of the factors.

### EXAMPLES.

(1.) Required the product of $\frac{4}{5}$ and $\frac{7}{8}$.

$$\frac{4 \times 7}{5 \times 8} = \frac{28}{40} = \frac{7}{10} = Ans.; \quad or \quad \frac{4}{5} \times \frac{7}{8} = \frac{1}{5} \times \frac{7}{2} = \frac{7}{10} = Ans.;$$

$$or \quad \frac{4 \times 7}{7 \times 8} = \frac{7}{10} = Ans. \text{ as before.}$$
$$2$$

(2.) Required the continued product of $2\frac{1}{2}$, $\frac{1}{8}$, and $\frac{1}{3}$ of $\frac{5}{6}$.

Here $2\frac{1}{2} = \frac{5}{2}$; and $\frac{1}{3}$ of $\frac{5}{6} = \frac{5}{18}$.

Then $\dfrac{5 \times 1 \times 5}{2 \times 8 \times 18} = \dfrac{25}{288} = the\ answer.$

---

\* Multiplication by a fraction implies the taking some part or parts of the multiplicand, and is therefore truly expressed by a compound fraction. Thus $\frac{3}{4}$ multiplied by $\frac{5}{8}$, is the same as $\frac{3}{4}$ of $\frac{5}{8}$; and as the directions in the rule agree with the method already given to reduce these fractions to simple ones, it is evidently right.

Again, let $\frac{a}{b}$ be multiplied by $\frac{c}{d}$. Let $\frac{a}{b} = x$; $\frac{c}{d} = y$; $\therefore \frac{a}{b} \times \frac{c}{d} = xy$; because $a = bx$, $c = dy$; $\therefore$ by multiplication $ac = bdxy$, or $\frac{ac}{bd} = xy = \frac{a}{b} \times \frac{c}{d}$.

(3.) Multiply $\frac{4}{15}$ by $\frac{5}{24}$.     *Ans.* $\frac{1}{18}$.

(4.) Multiply $4\frac{1}{2}$ by $\frac{1}{8}$.     *Ans.* $\frac{9}{16}$.

(5.) Multiply $\frac{1}{2}$ of 7 by $\frac{1}{2}$.     *Ans.* $1\frac{3}{4}$.

(6.) Multiply 13 by $2\frac{1}{2}$.     *Ans.* $32\frac{1}{2}$.

(7.) Multiply $1017\frac{2}{3}$ by 35.     *Ans.* $35618\frac{1}{3}$.

(8.) Multiply $\frac{52}{3}$ by $\frac{1}{2}$ of 5.     *Ans.* $43\frac{1}{3}$.

(9.) Multiply $\frac{2}{9}$ of $\frac{3}{8}$ by $\frac{5}{8}$ of $3\frac{2}{7}$.     *Ans.* $\frac{23}{84}$.

(10.) Multiply $4\frac{1}{2}$, $\frac{3}{4}$ of $\frac{1}{7}$, and $18\frac{4}{5}$, continually together.
         *Ans.* $9\frac{9}{140}$.

(11.) Required the product of $\frac{2}{3}$, $3\frac{1}{4}$, 5, and $\frac{3}{4}$ of $\frac{3}{5}$.
         *Ans.* $4\frac{7}{8}$.

(12.) What is the continued product of 5, $\frac{2}{3}$, $\frac{2}{7}$ of $\frac{3}{5}$, and $4\frac{1}{6}$?     *Ans.* $2\frac{8}{21}$.

(13.) What is the continued product of 14, $\frac{5}{6}$, $\frac{4}{5}$ of 9, and $6\frac{2}{7}$?     *Ans.* 528.

(14.) Required the continued product of $14\frac{7}{8}$, $2\frac{1}{2}$, and $\frac{1}{3}$ of $4\frac{1}{7}$?     *Ans.* $51\frac{17}{48}$.

(15.) Required the continued product of $101\frac{1}{3}$ $202\frac{1}{2}$, $5\frac{1}{6}$, and $\frac{1}{2}$ of $7\frac{1}{4}$.     *Ans.* $383644\frac{3}{63}$.

(16.) Required the continued product of $\frac{1}{5}$ of $5\frac{1}{2}$, $\frac{2}{9}$ of 11, and $\frac{13}{204}$.     *Ans.* $\frac{1573}{9180}$.

## DIVISION OF VULGAR FRACTIONS.

### RULE.*

Reduce the fractions, when necessary, to simple ones, as in the former rules ; then invert the divisor, and proceed as in multiplication.

When the dividend is a mixed number, and the divisor a whole number, it will be best to divide the parts of the

---

* The reason of this rule may be shown thus: suppose it were required to divide $\frac{3}{4}$ by $\frac{2}{5}$; then $\frac{3}{4} \div 2$ is manifestly $\frac{1}{2}$ of $\frac{3}{4}$ or $\frac{3}{4 \times 2}$ ; but $\frac{2}{5} = \frac{1}{5}$ of 2, therefore $\frac{1}{5}$ of 2, or $\frac{2}{5}$, must be contained 5 times as often in $\frac{3}{4}$ as 2 is; that is $\frac{3 \times 5}{4 \times 2} = 1\frac{7}{8}$ the answer ; which is agreeable to the rule ; and the same will take place in all cases whatever.

*Note.* A fraction is multiplied by an integer, by dividing the denominator by it, or multiplying the numerator. And a fraction is divided by an integer, by dividing the numerator by it, or multiplying the denominator.

former separately, observing to carry for units to the fractional part, when necessary.

## EXAMPLES.

(1.) It is required to divide $\frac{4}{7}$ by $\frac{3}{5}$.

$$\frac{4}{7} \div \frac{3}{5} = \frac{4}{7} \times \frac{5}{3} = \frac{20}{21} = Answer.$$

(2.) It is required to divide $\frac{1}{5}$ of 19 by $\frac{2}{3}$ of $\frac{3}{4}$.

*Here $\frac{1}{5}$ of $19 = \frac{19}{5}$, and $\frac{2}{3}$ of $\frac{3}{4} = \frac{6}{12} = \frac{1}{2}$.*

*Then* $\dfrac{19}{5} \times \dfrac{2}{1} = \dfrac{38}{5} = 7\frac{3}{5}$  *the quotient required.*

(3.) Divide $\frac{4}{7}$ by $\frac{2}{3}$.  *Ans. $\frac{6}{7}$.*
(4.) Divide $3\frac{1}{6}$ by $9\frac{1}{2}$.  *Ans. $\frac{1}{3}$.*
(5.) Divide $9\frac{1}{6}$ by $\frac{1}{2}$ of 7.  *Ans. $2\frac{13}{21}$.*
(6.) Let 5 be divided by $\frac{7}{10}$.  *Ans. $7\frac{1}{7}$.*
(7.) Let $\frac{7}{8}$ be divided by 4.  *Ans. $\frac{7}{32}$.*
(8.) Let $\frac{1}{2}$ of $\frac{4}{9}$ be divided by $\frac{2}{3}$ of $\frac{3}{4}$.  *Ans. $\frac{4}{9}$.*
(9.) Let $5205\frac{1}{6}$ be divided by 12.  *Ans. $433\frac{23}{30}$.*
(10.) It is required to divide 100 by $4\frac{7}{8}$.  *Ans. $20\frac{20}{39}$.*
(11.) It is required to divide $\frac{3}{4}$ of $\frac{7}{8}$ by $\frac{2}{3}$.  *Ans. $\frac{63}{64}$.*
(12.) It is required to divide $\frac{5}{8}$ of 50 by $4\frac{1}{3}$.  *Ans. $9\frac{8}{13}$.*

## RULE OF THREE IN VULGAR FRACTIONS.

### RULE.*

State the question as in the common Rule of Three, and reduce all the terms, if necessary, to simple fractions, and the first two to such as are of the same denomination.

Then multiply the last two terms of the proportion, and the reciprocal of the first term (i. e. *the first term inverted*) continually together, and the product will be the answer, in the same denomination that the last term was reduced to.

---

* This rule depends upon the same principles as the common Rule of Three ; and in the practical application of it, according to the method here given, the determination of the greater or less of the two first terms, which is necessary in the process there described, will be most readily seen by bringing them, when in the same denomination, to a common denominator, and then observing which has the greater or less numerator.

### EXAMPLES.

(1.) If $\frac{3}{5}$ of a yard cost $\frac{7}{12}$ of a £, what will $\frac{6}{15}$ of an English ell cost?

*First $\frac{3}{5}$ of a yard $=\frac{3}{5}$ of $\frac{4}{1}$ of $\frac{1}{5}=\frac{12}{25}$ of an ell.*

*Then $\dfrac{12}{25}$ ell $:$ $\dfrac{6}{15}$ ell $::$ $\dfrac{7}{12}$ £.*

*And $\dfrac{6}{15}\times\dfrac{7}{12}\times\dfrac{25}{12}=\dfrac{35}{72}l.=9s.\ 8\frac{1}{2}d.\ \frac{2}{3}f.=$the answer.*

(2.) What quantity of shalloon, that is $\frac{3}{4}$ yard wide, will line $9\frac{1}{2}$ yards of cloth that is $2\frac{1}{2}$ yards wide?

*First $2\frac{1}{2}$ yds. $=\frac{5}{2}$; and $9\frac{1}{2}$ yds. $=\frac{19}{2}$.*

*Then $\dfrac{3}{4}$ yd. $:$ $\dfrac{5}{2}$ yd. $::$ $\dfrac{19}{2}$ yd.*

*And $\dfrac{5}{2}\times\dfrac{19}{2}\div\dfrac{3}{4}=\dfrac{5}{1}\times\dfrac{19}{1}\times\dfrac{4}{3}=\dfrac{95}{2}=31\frac{2}{3}$ yds. $=$ the answer.*

(3.) If $\frac{2}{3}$ of an ell of Holland cost $\frac{1}{3}l.$ what will $12\frac{2}{3}$ ells cost?                               *Ans. 7l. 0s. 8$\frac{3}{4}$d. $\frac{6}{9}$f.*

(4.) If $\frac{5}{8}$ of a cwt. cost $4\frac{7}{9}l.$ what will $4\frac{1}{2}$ lb. cost?
                               *Ans. 6s. 1$\frac{1}{2}$d. $\frac{6}{7}$f.*

(5.) How much in length that is $7\frac{7}{9}$ inches broad will make a square foot?        *Ans. 18$\frac{18}{35}$ inches.*

(6.) If $\frac{3}{16}$ of a ship cost 273l. 2s. 6d. what is $\frac{5}{32}$ of her worth?                       *Ans. 227l. 12s. 1d.*

(7.) If $\frac{5}{8}$ of a gallon of wine cost $\frac{5}{8}l.$ what will $\frac{5}{8}$ of a tun cost?                               *Ans. 140l.*

(8.) How much in length that is $11\frac{1}{12}$ poles broad will make a square acre?          *Ans. 13$\frac{61}{143}$ po.*

(9.) How many yards of ell-wide flannel are sufficient to line a cloak, containing $18\frac{7}{8}$ yds. of camlet $\frac{3}{4}$ of a yd. wide?
                       *Ans. 11 yds. 1 qr. 1$\frac{1}{2}$ na.*

(10.) A person who possessed a $\frac{3}{5}$ share of a coal mine, sold $\frac{3}{4}$ of his interest in it for 1710l., what was the reputed value of the whole mine?          *Ans. 3800l.*

(11.) If the penny loaf weigh $6\frac{9}{10}$ oz., when wheat is 5s. a bushel, what ought it to weigh when it is 8s. 6d. per bushel?
                               *Ans. 4$\frac{1}{17}$ oz.*

(12.) A mercer bought $3\frac{1}{2}$ pieces of silk, each containing

$24\frac{1}{3}$ yards, at 6s. $0\frac{1}{2}d$. per yard, what does the whole come to? *Ans.* 25l. 14s. $6\frac{1}{2}d$. $\frac{1}{3}f$.

(13.) Agreed for the carriage of $2\frac{1}{2}$ tons of goods $2\frac{9}{10}$ miles for $\frac{3}{40}$ of a guinea, what is that per cwt. for a mile? *Ans.* $\frac{378}{725}$ *of a farthing.*

(14.) If a coat and waistcoat can be made of $3\frac{3}{4}$ yards of broad cloth of $1\frac{1}{2}$ yard in breadth, how many yards of stuff of $\frac{5}{8}$ yd. in breadth will it require to fit the same person? *Ans.* 9 *yds.*

(15.) If, when the days are $13\frac{5}{8}$ hours long, a traveller performs his journey in $35\frac{1}{2}$ days, in how many days will he perform the same journey when the days are $11\frac{9}{10}$ hours long? *Ans.* $40\frac{815}{952}$ *days.*

(16.) A regiment of soldiers, consisting of 976 men, are to be new clothed, each coat to contain $2\frac{1}{2}$ yds. of cloth that is $1\frac{5}{8}$ yd. wide, and to be lined with shalloon $\frac{7}{8}$ yd. wide; how many yards of shalloon will line them? *Ans.* 4531 *yds.* 1 *qr.* $2\frac{6}{7}$ *na.*

## Decimal Fractions.

A DECIMAL FRACTION is that which has for its denominator a unit, with as many ciphers annexed to it as the numerator has places; and is usually expressed by writing the numerator only, with a point placed before it, on the left hand.

Thus $\frac{5}{10}$, $\frac{25}{100}$, $\frac{75}{1000}$, &c. are decimal fractions, which are expressed by ·5, ·25, and ·075; and in reading them, the first is called 5-tenths, the second 25-hundredths, and the third 75-thousandths of a unit.

Ciphers to the right-hand of decimals make no alteration in their value; for ·5, ·50, ·500, &c. are the same as $\frac{5}{10}$, $\frac{50}{100}$, $\frac{500}{1000}$, which are each equal to $\frac{1}{2}$; but if they are placed on the left hand of the decimal, they decrease its value in a tenfold proportion. Thus, ·5, ·05, ·005, &c. are 5-tenths, 5-hundredths, 5-thousandths, &c. respectively. Also 2·7 is 2 and 7-tenths, and 32·04 is 32 and 4-hundredths.*

---

* As the values of the figures, in notation of whole numbers, increase in a tenfold proportion, from the right hand to the left, so in decimals, their values decrease in a ten-fold proportion, from the left-hand to the right; hence the operations in all the leading rules are performed in the same manner in both cases; observing only, in the latter, to point off the proper number of decimals in the result.

## ADDITION OF DECIMALS.

### RULE.

Arrange the numbers according to the value of their places, or so that all the decimal points may fall directly under each other.

Then find their sum as in whole numbers, and point off as many places for decimals as are equal to the greatest number of decimal places in any one of the given numbers.

### EXAMPLES.

(1.) Find the sum of $25·074 + 1·8254 + 125· + ·0567876 + 1776·111$.

$$
\begin{array}{r}
25·074 \\
1·8254 \\
125· \\
·0567876 \\
1776·111 \\
\hline
1928·0671876 \;\textit{the sum.} = Ans.
\end{array}
$$

(2.) Find the sum of $376·25 + 86·125 + 637·4725 + 6·5 + 358·865 + 41·02$.       *Ans.* 1506·2325.

(3.) Required the sum of $3·5 + 47·25 + 927·01 + 2·0073 + 1·5$.       *Ans.* 981·2673.

(4.) Required the sum of $276· + 54·321 + ·65 + 112· + 1·25 + ·0463$.       *Ans.* 444·2673.

(5.) Required the sum of $·01 + 2·19 + ·307 + ·009 + 1·0768$.       *Ans.* 3·5928.

## SUBTRACTION OF DECIMALS.

### RULE.

Set the numbers under each other according to the value of their places; then, beginning at the right-hand, subtract as in whole numbers, and point off the decimals as in addition.*

---

\* This method of setting the numbers under each other, according to the value of their places, is only necessary in addition and subtraction.

### EXAMPLES.

(1.) Find the difference of 2464·21 and 327·07643.

$$
\begin{array}{r}
2464 \cdot 21 \\
327 \cdot 07643 \\
\hline
\end{array}
$$

2137·13357 *the difference.*=*Ans.*

(2.) From 127·62 take 13·725.      *Ans.* 113·895.
(3.) From 6213·725 take 162·25.      *Ans.* 6051·475.
(4.) From 3760·279 take 423·0076.      *Ans.* 3337·2714.
(5.) From 30·7265 take ·007598.      *Ans.* 30·718902.
(6.) From 100·011 take 2·07568.      *Ans.* 97·93532.

## MULTIPLICATION OF DECIMALS.

### RULE.*

Place the factors under each other, and multiply them together as in whole numbers.

Then point off as many figures from the product as there are decimal places in both the factors; observing, if there be not enough, to put as many ciphers to the left-hand of them, as will supply the deficiency.

### EXAMPLES.

(1.) Multiply 42·35      (2.) Multiply ·02534
       by 6·842               by   ·03256

$$
\begin{array}{r}
8470 \\
16940 \\
33880 \\
25410 \\
\hline
\end{array}
\qquad
\begin{array}{r}
15204 \\
12670 \\
5068 \\
7602 \\
\hline
\end{array}
$$

*Ans.*=289·75870      *Ans.*= ·0008250704 *the product.*

---

\* To prove the truth of the rule, let ·9776 and ·823 be the numbers to be multiplied; then, since these are equivalent to $\frac{9776}{10000}$ and $\frac{823}{1000}$, it follows that $\frac{9776}{10000} \times \frac{823}{1000} = \frac{8045648}{10000000} = \cdot 8045648$ by the nature of notation; which product consists of as many places as there are ciphers; that is, of as many places as are in both the factors, agreeably to the rule: and the same will be found to be true of any two numbers whatever.

(3.) Multiply 79·347 by 23·15.     *Ans.* 1836·88305.
(4.) Multiply ·63478 by ·8204.     *Ans.* ·520773512.
(5.) Multiply ·385746 by ·00464.     *Ans.* ·00178986144.
(6.) Multiply 4·987642 by ·098765.     *Ans.* ·492604462130.
(7.) Multiply 3·8567 by ·0041.     *Ans.* ·01581247.

### CASE II.

*To contract the operation, so as to retain only as many decimals in the product as may be thought necessary.*

### RULE.

Put the unit's figure of the multiplier under that figure of the multiplicand whose place is the last to be retained in the product, and dispose of the rest so that they may all stand in a contrary order to that in which they are usually placed.

Then, in multiplying, reject all the figures to the right-hand of the multiplying digit, and set down the products so that their right-hand figures may fall in a straight line directly under each other, observing to increase the first figure of every line with what would arise by carrying 1 from 5 to 14; 2 from 15 to 24; 3 from 25 to 34, &c., from the product of the two preceding figures, when you begin to multiply; and the sum will be the product required.

### EXAMPLES.

(1.) It is required to multiply 27·14986 by 92·41035, and to retain only four places of decimals in the product.

| *Contracted.* | *Common way.* |
|---|---|
| 27·14986 | 27·14986 |
| 53014·29 | 92·41035 |
| | |
| 24434874 | 13,574930 |
| 542997 | 81\|44958 |
| 108599 | 2714\|986 |
| 2715 | 108599\|44 |
| 81 | 542997\|2 |
| 14 | 24434874\| |
| | |
| *Ans.*=2508·9280 | 2508·9280\|650510 = *Ans.* |

(2.) Multiply 245·378263 by 72·4385, reserving only 5 places of decimals in the product.     *Ans.* 17774·83332.

(3.) Multiply 128·67845 by 38·2463, reserving only 3 places of decimals in the product.      *Ans.* 4921·476.

(4.) Multiply 8634·875 by 843·7527, reserving only the integers in the product.      *Ans.* 7285699

(5.) Multiply ·248264 by ·725234, reserving 6 figures 5 figures, and 4 figures in the product respectively.

           *Ans.* ·180049, ·18005, *and* ·1800.

## DIVISION OF DECIMALS.

### RULE.*

1. Divide as in whole numbers, and point off, from the right-hand of the quotient, as many places for decimals, as the decimal places in the dividend exceed those in the divisor; observing, if there be not so many as the rule requires, to supply the defect by prefixing ciphers.

2. If there should be a remainder after division, or more decimal places in the divisor than there are in the dividend, ciphers may be annexed to the dividend, and the quotient carried on to any extent required.†

*Note.* The decimal places in the dividend, when necessary, must always be made equal to those in the divisor, before the operation is begun; and, in this case, the quotient, to that extent, will be a whole number.

### EXAMPLES.

<table>
<tr><td align="center">(1.)</td><td align="center">(2.)</td></tr>
<tr><td align="center">·5)12·678945</td><td align="center">1·2)·0482796</td></tr>
<tr><td align="center">25·35789 = Ans.</td><td align="center">·040233 = Ans.</td></tr>
</table>

---

* The reason of pointing off as many decimal places in the quotient as the places in the dividend exceed those of the divisor, is evident; for since the number of decimal places in the dividend is equal to those in the divisor and quotient taken together, by the nature of multiplication, it follows that the quotient contains as many places as those in the dividend exceed those in the divisor.

† Another way to know the place of the decimal point in the quotient, is by making the first figure of it to occupy the same place of integers, or decimals, as that figure of the dividend does which stands over the place of units of the first product.

(3.)

17·9)·48624097(·0271643
1282     [ = *Ans.*
294
1150
769
537
000
&c.

(4.)

·2685)27·0000(100·55865
15000     [ = *Ans.*
15750
23250
17700
15900
24750
&c.

(5.) Divide 2·345678 by 6.      *Ans.* ·3909463′, &c.
(6.) Divide 17·084597 by ·024.      *Ans.* 711·858, &c.
(7.) Divide 234·70525 by 64·25.      *Ans.* 3·653.
(8.) Divide ·8727587 by ·162.      *Ans.* 5·38739, &c.
(9.) Divide 298·89 by ·1107.      *Ans.* 2700.
(10.) Divide 14 by ·7854.      *Ans.* 17·825, &c.

## CASE II.

*To contract the rule by diminishing the divisor at every step of the process.*

### RULE.

Take as many of the left-hand figures of the divisor as are equal to the number of integers and decimals that are to be in the quotient, and find how many times they will go in the first figures of the dividend, as usual.

Then consider each remainder as a new dividend; and in dividing, leave out, continually, one figure to the right-hand of the divisor, remembering to carry for the increase of the figures cut off, as in the rule for contracted multiplication, before given.

*Note.* When there are not so many figures in the divisor as there are to be in the quotient, begin the operation with all the figures as usual, and continue it until the number of figures in the divisor, and those that remain to be found in the quotient, are equal; after which, use the method of contraction above described.

### EXAMPLES.

(1.) Divide 2508·928065051 by 92·41035, so as to have only 4 places of decimals in the quotient.

(1.)

*Contracted way.*

$$92 \cdot 41035)2508 \cdot 928065051(27 \cdot 1498 = Ans.$$

660721
13849
4608
912
80
6

*Common way.*

$$92 \cdot 41035)2508 \cdot 928065051(27 \cdot 1498 = Ans.$$

660721|06
13848|615
4607|5800
911|16605
79|472901
5|544621

(2.) Divide 721·17562 by 2·257432, so as to retain only 3 places of decimals in the quotient.          *Ans.* 319·467.

(3.) Divide 12·169825 by 3·14159, so as to preserve only 5 places of decimals in the quotient.          *Ans.* 3·87377.

(4.) Divide 87·076326 by 9·365407 so as to preserve only 7 places of decimals in the quotient.          *Ans.* 9·2976553.

(5.) Divide 40·076745 by 2·9586, so as to retain the integers only in the quotient.          *Ans.* 13.

## REDUCTION OF DECIMALS.

### CASE I.

*To reduce a vulgar fraction to its equivalent decimal.*

### RULE.*

Annex as many ciphers to the numerator as may be thought necessary; then divide by the denominator, and point off as

---

* Let the given vulgar fraction, of which the decimal expression is required, be $\frac{7}{8}$. Then since every decimal fraction has 10, 100, or 1000, &c. for its denominator, and that the denominator, of one of two equal fractions is to its numerator, as the denominator of the other to its

many decimal places in the quotient for the answer, as there were ciphers annexed.

### EXAMPLES.

(1.) Reduce $\frac{5}{24}$ to a decimal.

$$4)5\cdot000000$$

$$6)1\cdot250000$$

$$\cdot2083'33\ \&c.=Ans.$$

(2.) Reduce $\frac{1}{4}$, $\frac{1}{2}$, and $\frac{3}{4}$ to decimals. *Ans.* ·25, ·5, and ·75.
(3.) What is the decimal value of $\frac{3}{8}$? *Ans.* ·375.
(4.) Required the decimal value of $\frac{1}{25}$. *Ans.* ·04.
(5.) Required the decimal value of $\frac{3}{192}$. *Ans.* ·015625.
(6.) Let $\frac{275}{3842}$ be expressed decimally. *Ans.* ·071577.
(7.) Let $\frac{13}{1728}$ be expressed decimally. *Ans.* ·0075231.

---

numerator; it follows that $13:7::1000\ \&c.:\dfrac{7\times1000\ \&c.}{13}=\dfrac{7000\ \&c.}{13}$
$=\cdot53846$, the numerator of the decimal required; which is the same as by the rule.

If the right hand figure of the denominator of the fraction to be reduced be an even number, a 0, or a 5, the quotient will consist of some exact number of decimals; but if it be either 3, 7, or 9, there will always be a remainder after division; and consequently the decimal will never terminate. In such cases, therefore, the division may be continued to as many places of figures only as are thought necessary.

The following method of converting a vulgar fraction, of which the denominator is a prime number, into a decimal, consisting of a great number of figures, is given by Colson, p. 162. of his *Commentary on Sir. I. Newton's Treatise of Fluxions, quarto,* 1736.

A modification of Colson's method of developing an incommensurable fraction is given in Maynard's *Solutions to Colenso's Arithmetic.* (*See foot note,* p. 115.)

#### EXAMPLE.

Let $\frac{1}{29}$ be the fraction which is to be converted into an equivalent decimal.

Then, by dividing in the common way, till the remainder becomes a single figure, we shall have $\frac{1}{29}=\cdot03448\frac{8}{29}$ for the complete quotient; and if this equation be multiplied by the numerator 8, it will give $\frac{8}{29}=\cdot27584\frac{64}{29}$, or rather $\frac{8}{29}=\cdot27586\frac{6}{29}$; which being substituted for the fraction in the first equation, will make $\frac{1}{29}=\cdot0344827586\frac{6}{29}$. Again, let this equation be multiplied by 6, and it will give $\frac{6}{29}=\cdot2068965517\frac{7}{29}$; and, therefore, by substituting as before, $\frac{1}{29}=\cdot03448275862068965517\frac{7}{29}$; and so on, for any number of figures.

## CASE II.

*To reduce numbers of different denominations to their equivalent decimal values.*

### RULE.*

Reduce both the given number and the integer to which it is referred, to the same denomination; then divide the former of these by the latter, as in the case of a vulgar fraction, and the quotient will be the equivalent decimal required.

### *Or,*

Write the given numbers perpendicularly under each other, in order, from the least to the greatest, for dividends.

Then, opposite to each dividend, on the left-hand, place such a number for a divisor as will bring it to the next superior denomination, and draw a line between them.

---

* The reason of this rule may be explained from the first example; thus three farthings is $\frac{3}{4}$ of a penny, which, brought to a decimal, is ·75d.; consequently 9¾d. may be expressed by 9·75d.; but 9·75 is $\frac{975}{100}$ of a penny, or $\frac{975}{1200}$ of a shilling, which, when brought to a decimal, is ·8125s.; and therefore 15s. 9¾d. may be expressed by 15·8125s.; in like manner, 15·8125s. $= \frac{158125}{10000}$ of a shilling $= \frac{158125}{200000}$ of a pound, which, by bringing it to a decimal, is $=$ ·790625l. as by the rule.

It may here, also, be further observed, that the decimal value of any number of shillings, pence, and farthings can be found by inspection, as follows:

Put down half the greatest even number of shillings for the first decimal figure, and the farthings in the given pence and farthings possess the second and third places; observing to increase the second place by 5, if the shillings are odd, and the third place by 1, when the farthings exceed 12, and by 2 when they exceed 37.

Thus, the value of 15s. 8½d. in the decimal parts of a pound, will be found as below:

·7   $= \frac{1}{2}$ *of* 14s.
·05 *for the odd shilling.*
·034 $=$ *farthings in* 8½d.
·001 *for the excess of* 12.

·785l. $=$ *decimal required.*

This done, begin with the uppermost number, and set down the quotient of each division, as decimal parts, on the right-hand of the dividend next below it; and proceed in this manner to the last quotient, which will give the answer as before.

## EXAMPLES.

(1.) Reduce 15*s.* 9¾*d.* to the decimal of a pound.

*Here* 15*s.* 9¾*d.*=759 *farthings, and* 20*s.*=960 *farthings.*
*Whence* $\frac{759}{960}$=·790625*l. the decimal required.*

*Or,*

$$4 | 3·00$$

$$12 | 9·7500$$

$$20 | 15·8125$$

·790625*l.*=*the answer, as before.*

(2.) Reduce 9*s.* to the decimal of a pound.    *Ans.* ·45.

(3.) Reduce 19*s.* 5½*d.* to the decimal of a pound.
*Ans.* ·972916′.

(4.) Reduce 2 qrs. 14 lb. to the decimal of a cwt. *Ans.* ·625.

---

The reason of which rule may be shown thus: As shillings are so many 20*ths* of a pound, the half of them must be so many 10*ths*, and consequently will occupy the place of 10*ths* in the decimals; but when they are odd, their half will always consist of 2 figures, the first of which will be half the even number next less, and the second a 5; which confirms the rule as far as it respects shillings.

Again, farthings are so many 960*ths* of a pound; and had it happened that 1000, instead of 960, had made a pound, it is plain that any number of farthings would have made so many thousandths, and might have taken their place in the decimal accordingly: but 960 increased by $\frac{1}{24}$ part of itself is=1000; consequently any number of farthings, increased by their $\frac{1}{24}$ part, will be an exact decimal expression for them: whence, if the number of farthings be more than 12, a $\frac{1}{24}$ part is greater than ½, and therefore 1 must be added; and when the number of farthings is more than 37, a $\frac{1}{24}$ part is greater than 1½*d.* for which 2 must be added; and thus the rule is shown to be just.

The reverse of this rule, or method of finding the value of any decimal parts of a pound by inspection, is also as follows:

Double the first figure, or place of tenths, for shillings, and if the second be 5, or more than 5, reckon another shilling; then call the

(5.) Reduce 3 qrs. 2 na. to the decimal of a yard.

*Ans.* ·875.

(6.) Reduce 17 yds. 1 ft. 6 in. to the decimal of a mile.

*Ans.* ·0099431'8'.

(7.) Reduce 1 rd. 14 po. to the decimal of an acre.

*Ans.* ·3375.

(8.) Reduce 1 gall. of wine to the decimal of a hhd.

*Ans.* ·0'15873'.

(9.) Reduce 3 bu. 1 peck to the decimal of a quarter.

*Ans.* ·40625.

(10.) Reduce 10 wk. 2 da. to the decimal of a year.

*Ans.* ·1'97802'.

(11.) Reduce 10 oz. 18 dwts. 16 grs. to the decimal of a lb.

*Ans.* ·91'1111.

## CASE III.

### *To find the value of any given decimal in terms of the integer.*

#### RULE.

Multiply the given decimal by the number of parts in the next less denomination, and point off as many places to the right-hand as there are places in the decimal.

Then multiply the figures so pointed off, by the parts in the next inferior denomination, reserving as many places to the right-hand as before ; and proceed in this manner through all the denominations to the last, when the several figures standing on the left of the decimal point will be the answer required.

#### EXAMPLES.

(1.) Find the value of ·37623 of a pound.

---

figures in the second and third places, after 5 is deducted, so many far-things, abating 1 when they are above 12, and 2 when above 37, and the result will be the answer.

Thus, the value of ·785*l.* may be found by inspection, as below.

> 14*s.* . ,   = *double of* 7.
> 1*s.* . . . *for the* 5 *in the place of tenths.*
> 0*s.* 8¾*d.* = 35 *farthings.*
> 0*s.*   ¼*d* *for the excess of* 12, *abated.*

> 15*s.* 8½*d.* = *the answer.*

$$·37623$$
$$20$$

*Shillings* 7·52460
$$12$$

*Pence* 6·29520
$$·4$$

*Farthings* 1·18080          *Ans.* 7s. 6¼d. $\frac{113}{625}$f.

(2.) What is the value of ·625 of a shilling ?     *Ans.* 7½d.
(3.) Required the value of ·83229 of a pound. *Ans.* 16s. 7¾d.
(4.) Required the value of ·6725 of a cwt.
                              *Ans.* 2 qrs. 19 lb. 5 oz.
(5.) What is the value of ·61 of a pipe of wine?
                              *Ans.* 1 hhd. 13 gal. 3 qts.
(6.) What is the value of ·0625 of a barrel of beer ?
                              *Ans.* 2 gal. 1 qt.
(7.) Required the value of ·67 of a league ?
                    *Ans.* 2 mi. 0 fur. 3 po. 1 yd. 3 in. 2 b.c.
(8.) Required the value of ·42857 of a month ?
          *Ans.* 1 we. 4 da. 23 ho. 59 min. 56$\frac{68}{125}$ sec.
(9.) It is required to find the value of ·785 of a year, consisting of 365¼ days.     *Ans.* 286 da. 17 ho. 18⅗ min.

## RULE OF THREE IN DECIMALS.

### RULE.

State the question as in the common rule of three, and
reduce the inferior denominations of such of the terms as are
compound, to the decimal parts of their integer, and the first
two terms to the same denomination.

Then multiply the two last terms of the proportion together,
and divide the product by the first term, and it will give the
answer, in the same denomination that the last term was reduced to.

### EXAMPLES.

(1.) What is the value of 57¾ yards of muslin, at 11s. 6d.
per ell?

a 2

$$1\!\cdot\!25 \; yd. \; : \; 57\!\cdot\!75 \; yds. \; :: \; 11\!\cdot\!5s.$$

$$11\!\cdot\!5$$

To find the decimals.

4)3·00

·75 $=\frac{3}{4}$

12)6·0

·5 $=\frac{6}{12}$

An ell $=1\frac{1}{4}$ yd.

4)1·0

·25 $=\frac{1}{4}$

∴ $1\frac{1}{4}$ yd. $=1\!\cdot\!25$ yds.

28875
5775
5775

1·25)664·125(   (20)
625 ·   531·3

      £26·565
391    20
375

     s. 11·300
162    12
125

     d. 3·600
375    4
375

    far. 2·400

Ans. 26l. 11s. 3½d. ⅖f.

(2.) If an oz. of silver cost 5s. 6d. what is the price of a tankard that weighs 1 lb. 10 oz. 10 dwts. 4 gr.?  Ans. 6l. 3s. 9½d.

(3.) If I buy 14 yards of cloth for 10 guineas, how many ells Flemish can I purchase for 283l. 17s. 6d. at the same rate?  Ans. 504 ells, 2 qrs.

(4.) What is the value of a pack of wool, weighing 3 cwt. 2 qrs. 19 lb. at 1l. 2s. 6d. per tod of 14 lb.? Ans. 33l. 0s. 6¼d. ⅝f.

(5.) If 250l. 10s. gain 12l. 10s. 6d. in 12 months, what principal will gain an equal sum in 7½ months? Ans. 400l. 16s.

(6.) How many English ells of Holland may be bought for 25l. 18s. 1¾d. at 7s. 9½d. per yard? Ans. 53 Eng. ells, 1 qr.

(7.) If the carriage of 4½ cwt. of goods, for 50 miles, cost 1l. 2s. 9d., how far can I have 14¼ cwt. carried for the same money? Ans. 15 mi. 6 fur. 12 po. 3 yds. 1 ft. 5 in.

(8.) If 1 Eng. ell, 2 qrs. of muslin cost 4s. 7d., what will 39½ yards cost? Ans. 5l. 3s. 5¼d. ⅝f.

(9.) Bought 12 pockets of hops, each weighing 1 cwt. 2 qrs. 17 lbs., what do they come to at 5l. 1s. 4d. per cwt.? Ans. 100l. 8s. 6¾d. ³⁄₇f.

# Circulating Decimals.

CIRCULATING or RECURRING DECIMALS, are such as are distinguished by the continual repetition of the same figure or figures.*

1. A *simple circulate, or repetend,* is that where one figure only is repeated, as ·111 &c. or ·333 &c.; which are denoted by ·1′ and ·3′.

2. A *compound circulate, or repetend,* is that which has the same figures circulating alternately; as ·0101 &c. ·123123 &c. which are denoted by ·0′1′ and ·1′23′.

3. A *mixed circulate, or repetend,* is that which has other figures in it besides those that are repeated: as ·28333 &c. and 5·2321321 &c.; which are represented by ·283′ and 5·23′21′

## REDUCTION OF CIRCULATING DECIMALS.

### CASE I.

*To reduce an unmixed simple or compound repetend to its equivalent vulgar fraction.*

### RULE.†

Take the significant figures in the given decimal, considered as whole numbers, for the numerator, and as many nines as there are recurring places in the repetend for the denominator;

---

* *Circulating decimals* are produced from such vulgar fractions, as, when their numerators are divided by their denominators, will never terminate; thus $\frac{2}{3} = \dfrac{2\cdot0000 \text{ &c.}}{3} = ·6′66$ &c. *ad infinitum,* and $\frac{3}{7} = \dfrac{3\cdot000000 \text{ &c.}}{7}$ = ·4′28571′428571 &c., where the figures 428571 will be repeated without end.

And although the repetends of many expressions of this kind will consist of a great number of figures, yet every circulating decimal whatever is equal to some vulgar fraction, and *vice versâ.*

† If unity, with ciphers annexed to it, be divided by 9 *ad infinitum,* the quotient will be 1 continually; *i. e.* if $\frac{1}{9}$ be reduced to a decimal, it will produce the circulate ·1′; and since ·1′ is the decimal equivalent to $\frac{1}{9}$, we shall have ·2′ = $\frac{2}{9}$, ·3′ = $\frac{3}{9}$, and so on till ·9′ = $\frac{9}{9}$ = 1.

Hence, every single repetend is equal to a vulgar fraction, whose numerator is the repeating figure, and denominator 9.

Again, $\frac{1}{99}$ and $\frac{1}{999}$, being reduced to decimals, make ·0′1′0101 &c. and

G 3

observing only, that when there are any integral figures in the circulate, as many ciphers must be annexed to the numerator as the highest place of the repetend is distant from the decimal point.

### EXAMPLES.

(1.) Required the least vulgar fraction that is equal to ·6′.

*Here* $·6′ = \frac{6}{9} = \frac{2}{3} = $ *the answer.*

(2.) Required the least vulgar fraction that is equal to ·3′6′.

*Here* $·3′6′ = \frac{36}{99} = \frac{4}{11} = $ *the answer.*

(3.) It is required to reduce ·3′ to its equivalent vulgar fraction.  *Ans.* $\frac{1}{3}$.

(4.) It is required to reduce ·0′9′ to its least equivalent vulgar fraction.  *Ans.* $\frac{1}{11}$.

(5.) It is required to reduce ·0′4′ to its equivalent vulgar fraction.  *Ans.* $\frac{4}{99}$.

(6.) Required the least vulgar fraction that is equal to ·7′69230′.  *Ans.* $\frac{10}{13}$.

(7.) It is required to reduce 2′·06′ to its equivalent vulgar fraction.  *Ans.* $\frac{2060}{999}$.

(8.) It is required to reduce ·1′42857′ to its least equivalent vulgar fraction.  *Ans.* $\frac{1}{7}$.

(9.) It is required to reduce 4′2·63′ to its equivalent vulgar fraction.  *Ans.* $\frac{142100}{3333}$.

### CASE II.

*To reduce a mixed circulate or repetend to its equivalent vulgar fraction.*

### RULE.*

Subtract the finite part of the expression, considered as a whole number, from the whole mixed repetend, taken in the same manner, for the numerator; and to as many

---

·0′01′001 &c, *ad infinitum*, which are = ·0′1′ and ·0′01′; that is, $\frac{1}{99}$ = ·0′1′ and $\frac{1}{999}$ = ·0′01′; consequently $\frac{2}{99}$ = ·0′2′; $\frac{3}{99}$ = ·0′3′ &c.; and $\frac{2}{999}$ = ·0′02′; $\frac{3}{999}$ = ·0′03′ &c.; and the same will hold universally.

* The reason of the rule for a mixed circulate, is similar to that for a simple one; for if we consider it as separated into its finite and

nines as there are repeating places in the circulate, annex as many ciphers as there are finite decimal places for the denominator.

EXAMPLES.

(1.) What is the vulgar fraction equivalent to ·138′?

$$Here \; ·138' = \frac{138-13}{900} = \frac{125}{900} = \frac{5}{36} = the \; answer.$$

(2.) Required the vulgar fraction equivalent to 2·41′8′.

$$Here \; \frac{2418-24}{990} = \frac{2394}{990} = \frac{1197}{495} = \frac{133}{55} = 2\frac{23}{55} = the \; answer.$$

(3.) Required the least vulgar fraction equivalent to ·026′.

$$Here \; ·026' = \frac{26-2}{900} = \frac{24}{900} = \frac{8}{300} = \frac{2}{75} = the \; answer.$$

---

circulating parts, the same principle will be seen to run through them both.

Thus the mixed circulate ·16′ consists of the finite decimal ·1, and the repetend ·06′: but ·1 $= \frac{1}{10}$, and ·06′ $= ·1 \times ·6' = \frac{1}{10} \times \frac{6}{9} = \frac{6}{90}$, whence the decimal ·16′ is equal to $\frac{1}{10} + \frac{6}{90} = \frac{9}{90} + \frac{6}{90} = \frac{15}{90} = \frac{16-1}{90}$, which is the same as by the rule; and a similar mode of reasoning will hold in all other cases.

It may here also be observed, that the truth of the answer, in either of these rules, may be proved, by converting the vulgar fraction into its equivalent decimal.

If it should be required to find whether the decimal equivalent to a given vulgar fraction be finite or infinite, and how many places the repetend will consist of, it may be done by the following rule:

Reduce the given fraction to its least terms, and divide the denominator by 10, 5, and 2, in their order, each as often as possible; then if the whole denominator, vanish after these divisions, the second will be finite; as is always the case with every vulgar fraction, whose denominator is 2, 5, or their multiples. But if there be a remainder, divide 9999 &c. by the result last obtained, till nothing remains, and the number of 9's used will show the number of places in the repetend; which will begin after as many places of figures as there were 10's, 5's, and 2's divided by.

The reason of which rule may be shown thus:

In dividing 1·0000 &c. by any prime number, except 2 or 5, the figures in the quotient will begin to repeat over again as soon as the remainder is 1; and since 9999 &c. is less than 10000 &c. by 1, therefore 9999 &c. divided by any number except 2 and 5, or their multiples, will leave 0 for a remainder, when the repeating figures are at that period. But whatever number of repeating figures we have when the dividend is 1, there

(4.) What is the least vulgar fraction equivalent to ·53′?

$Ans. \frac{8}{15}.$

(5.) What is the least vulgar fraction equivalent to ·59′25′?

$Ans. \frac{16}{27}.$

(6.) Required the least vulgar fraction equivalent to ·0098′7′.

$Ans. \frac{163}{16500}.$

(7.) Required the least vulgar fraction equivalent to 4·75′43′.

$Ans. \frac{7916}{1665}.$

(8.) What is the least vulgar fraction equivalent to ·0084′97133′?

$Ans. \frac{83}{9768}.$

## ADDITION OF CIRCULATING DECIMALS.

### RULE.

Convert the given decimals into their equivalent vulgar fractions, by the methods already explained, and find their sum according to the rule for the addition of vulgar fractions; then this sum, reduced to decimals, will give the answer required.

### EXAMPLES.

(1.) It is required to add together ·3′ and ·1′35′.

---

will be exactly the same number when the dividend is any other number; for the product of any circulating number, by any other given number, will consist of the same number of repeating figures as before.

Thus, let ·5′076′5076 &c. be a circulate whose repeating part is 5076; then every repetend (5076) being equally multiplied, must produce the same product: for though these products will consist of more places, yet the overplus in each, being similar, will be carried to the next, by which means each product will be equally increased, and consequently every four places will continue alike; and the same will hold for any other number.

Hence, it appears, that the dividend may be altered at pleasure, provided it be still prime to the denominator, and the number of places in the repetend will still be the same; thus $\frac{1}{11}$ = ·0′9′, and $\frac{3}{11}$, or $\frac{1}{11} \times 3$ = ·2′7′, where the number of places in each are alike: and the same will be true in all other instances.

The rule is chiefly of use in certain cases where the determination of the repetend, by common division, when it consists of a great number of places, would be found very troublesome; as, for instance, in converting $\frac{1}{290}$ to its equivalent circulating decimal, which is = ·00′3448275 86206896551724137931′: and other fractions might be given, where the repeating figures of its equivalent decimal would be still more numerous; but every vulgar fraction whatever is equal to some decimal; which is either finite, or a simple, compound, or mixed repetend.

*Here* $\cdot 3' = \dfrac{3}{9} = \dfrac{1}{3}$, *and* $\cdot 1'35' = \dfrac{135}{999} = \dfrac{45}{333} = \dfrac{5}{37}$.

*Whence* $\dfrac{1}{3} + \dfrac{5}{37} = \dfrac{37 + 15}{111} = \dfrac{52}{111} = 4'68' =$ *the answer.*

(2.) Required the sum of $\cdot 3'6'$ and $\cdot 0'9'$.　　Ans. $\cdot 4'5'$.

(3.) Required the sum of $\cdot 6'$ and $\cdot 1'42857'$. *Ans.* $\cdot 8'09523'$.

(4.) Required the sum of $\cdot 3'$, $\cdot 9'45'$, and $\cdot 7'69230'$.

　　　　　　　　　　　　Ans. $2 \cdot 0'48510'$.

(5.) Required the sum of $67 \cdot 3'45'$, $8 \cdot 6'21'$, $\cdot 2'4'$, and $\cdot 8'$.

　　　　　　　　　　　　Ans. $77 \cdot 0'98280'$.

(6.) Find the sum of $\cdot 5'$, $\cdot 2'5'$, $17 \cdot 47'$, $9 \cdot 6'51'$, and $67 \cdot 34'5'$.

　　　　　　　　　　　　Ans. $95 \cdot 28'29647'$.

## SUBTRACTION OF CIRCULATING DECIMALS.*

### RULE.

Convert the given decimals into vulgar fractions, as in addition, and find their difference according to the rule for the subtraction of vulgar fractions; then this difference, reduced to a decimal, will be the answer required.

### EXAMPLES.

(1.) Find the difference of 4.75 and $\cdot 375'$.

*Here* $4 \cdot 75 = 4\tfrac{3}{4}$, *and* $\cdot 375' = \dfrac{375 - 37}{900} = \dfrac{338}{900} = \dfrac{169}{450}$.

*Hence* $4\tfrac{3}{4} - \dfrac{169}{450} = 4\dfrac{337}{900} = 4 \cdot 374' =$ *the answer.*

(2.) From $\cdot 42'7'$ take $\cdot 03'4'$.　　　　　*Ans.* $\cdot 39'2'$.

(3.) From $24 \cdot 38'4'$ take $9 \cdot 07'2'$.　　　*Ans.* $15 \cdot 31'2'$.

(4.) From $82 \cdot 8'546'$ take $8 \cdot 7'2'$.　　　*Ans.* $74 \cdot 1'274'$.

(5.) From $476 \cdot 32'$ take $84 \cdot 7697'$.　　*Ans.* $391 \cdot 5524'$.

(6.) From $3 \cdot 856'4'$ take $\cdot 0382'$.　　　*Ans.* $3 \cdot 8182'4'$.

(7.) From $127 \cdot 4627'$ take $4'8 \cdot 6'$.　　*Ans.* $78 \cdot 8141'29'$.

---

\* As the circulates, both in this rule and those of addition, multiplication, and division, are converted into vulgar fractions, the reason of the operations, in each of these cases, is obvious; and though they are not so concise, in some cases, as those arising out of the rules given by several authors on this subject, it is presumed that they will be found more clear and satisfactory to the learner.

## MULTIPLICATION OF CIRCULATING DECIMALS.

### RULE.

Convert both the factors into their equivalent vulgar fractions, and find the product of those fractions as usual; then reduce the vulgar fraction, expressing the product, to an equivalent decimal, and it will be the answer required.

### EXAMPLES.

(1.) Multiply ·3′6′ by ·23′.

$$Here \ ·3'6' = \frac{36}{99} = \frac{4}{11}.$$

$$And \ ·23' = \frac{23}{90}.$$

$$Hence \ \frac{4}{11} \times \frac{23}{90} = \frac{92}{990} = 09'2' = the \ answer.$$

| | |
|---|---|
| (2.) Multiply 37·23′ by ·26′. | *Ans.* 9·928′. |
| (3.) Multiply 7·7′2′ by ·2′97′. | *Ans.* 2·2′97′. |
| (4.) Multiply 3·9′73′ by 8. | *Ans.* 31·7′91′. |
| (5.) Multiply 8574·3′ by 87·5′. | *Ans.* 750730·5′18′. |
| (6.) Multiply 48·76 by 3′2·41′. | *Ans.* 1580·4′696′. |
| (7.) Multiply 39640 by ·7′0503′. | *Ans.* 27947·6′6867′. |
| (8.) Multiply 74·0367 by 4·75′. | *Ans.* 352·08564. |

(9.) Multiply 421·4′21′ by ·002′.

*Ans.* ·9′364920476031587142698253 80′.

## DIVISION OF CIRCULATING DECIMALS.

### RULE.

Convert both the divisor and dividend into their equivalent vulgar fractions, and find their quotient as usual; then reduce the vulgar fraction, expressing this quotient, to its equivalent decimal, and it will be the answer required.

### EXAMPLES.

(1.) Divide ·6′ by 2·3′.

$$Here \ ·6' = \frac{6}{9} = \frac{2}{3}, \ and \ 2·3' = \frac{23-2}{9} = \frac{21}{9} = \frac{7}{3}.$$

$$Hence \ \frac{2}{3} \div \frac{7}{3} = \frac{2}{3} \times \frac{3}{7} = \frac{2}{7} = ·285714' = the \ answer.$$

(2.) Divide 3394·626′ by 764·5′.     *Ans.* 4·44.
(3.) Divide ·042 by ·036′.     *Ans.* 1·14′5′.
(4.) Divide 6·188′10′ by 4·2′97′.     *Ans.* 1·44.
(5.) Divide 5·7648′ by ·68.     *Ans.* 8·47′.
(6.) Divide 234·6′ by ·7′.     *Ans.* 301·7′14285′.
(7.) Divide 1327·8719′ by 7·684′.     *Ans.* 172·8.
(8.) Divide 41·9′717′ by 34·1′234′.     *Ans.* 1·23.

# Duodecimals.*

DUODECIMALS, or *Cross Multiplication*, is a rule made use of by workmen and artificers, for finding the contents of their works.

In which cases, the dimensions are usually taken in feet and inches, and the contents are estimated in square feet or square inches.

Several kinds of artificer's work are computed by different measures, viz.

1. Glazing and mason's flatwork, by the foot.
2. Painting, paving, plastering, &c. by the yard.
3. Partitioning, flooring, roofing, tiling, &c. by the square of 100 feet.
4. Brickwork, &c. by the rod of 16½ feet, the square of which is 272¼.

*Note.* Bricklayers always value their work at the rate of a brick and a half thick; and if the wall be more or less, it must be reduced to that thickness.

### RULE.

1. Set the two dimensions that are to be multiplied together, one under the other, so that feet may stand under feet, inches under inches, &c.
2. Multiply each term in the multiplicand, beginning at

---

* *Duodecimals* are fractions whose denominators are 12, or its multiples: the division and subdivision of the integer being 12*ths*, instead of 10*ths*, as in the decimal scale; so that what are commonly called inches, in any result, are so many 12*ths* of a square foot; the parts so many square inches, or 144*ths* of a square foot, and so on.

the lowest, by the feet in the multiplier, and set the results under their corresponding terms, observing to carry 1 for every 12, from each lower denomination to the one next higher.

3. Multiply, in like manner, all the terms of the multiplicand by the inches in the multiplier, and set the result one place farther to the right than that of the product by the feet, carrying 1 for every 12, as before; and so on, for any lower denomination: then the sum, found as in compound addition, will be the answer required.

Or, instead of multiplying by the several denominations, as above, take such aliquot parts of the multiplicand as there are of a foot, and add the several results together, as before, for the answer.

### EXAMPLES.

(1.) Multiply 4 ft. 7 in. by 6 ft. 4 in.

|  | | | | | | |
|---|---|---|---|---|---|---|
| *4 ft. 7 in.* | | | | *Or 4 ft. 7 in.* | | |
| *6 ft. 4 in.* | | | | 6 | | |

| 27 . 6 | | | | 27 . 6 | | |
|---|---|---|---|---|---|---|
| 1 . 6 . 4 *in.* | | | *4 in.* $\frac{1}{3}$ | 1 . 6 . 4 *in.* | | |

29 *ft.* 0 *pts.* 4 *in.* = *the Ans.*          29 *ft.* 0 *pts.* 4 *in.* = *Ans.*
                                                            *as before.*

(2.) Multiply 13 ft. 3¾ in. by 5 ft. 5½ in.

$$13\,ft.\ 3\tfrac{3}{4}\,in.$$
$$5$$

$$66\ .\ 6\tfrac{3}{4}$$
$$4\ in.\ \tfrac{1}{3}\quad 4\ .\ 5\tfrac{1}{4}$$
$$1\ in.\ \tfrac{1}{4}\quad 1\ .\ 1\tfrac{5}{16}$$
$$\tfrac{1}{2}\ in.\ \tfrac{1}{2}\quad 0\ .\ 6\tfrac{21}{32}$$

$$72\,ft.\ 7\tfrac{31}{32}\,pts. = Ans.$$

(3.) Multiply 9 ft. 6 in. by 4 ft. 7 in.    *Ans.* 43 *ft.* 6½ *pts.*
(4.) Multiply 12 ft. 5 in. by 6 ft. 8 in.    *Ans.* 82 *ft.* 9⅓ *pts.*
(5.) Multiply 35 ft. 4½ in. by 12 ft. 3 in.
                                        *Ans.* 433 *ft.* 4⅛ *pts.*
(6.) Multiply 64 ft. 6 in. by 8 ft. 9¼ in.   *Ans.* 565 *ft.* 8⅝ *pts.*

(7.) What is the price of a marble slab, whose length is, 5 ft. 7 in. and breadth 1 ft. 10 in., at 6s. per foot?

*Ans. 3l. 1s. 5d.*

(8.) A room is to be ceiled, whose length is 74 ft. 9 in. and width 11 ft. 6 in.: what will it come to at 3s. 10d. per yard?

*Ans. 18l. 6s. 1½d. ⅝f.*

(9.) What will the paving a court-yard come to at 4¾d. per yard, the length being 58 ft. 6 in. and breadth 54 ft. 9 in.?

*Ans. 7l. 0s. 10¼d. ⅝f.*

(10.) A room is 97 ft. 8 in. about, and 9 ft. 10 in. high, what will the painting of it come to at 2s. 8¾d. per yard?

*Ans. 14l. 11s. 2½d. $\frac{161}{162}$f.*

(11.) A piece of wainscotting is 8 ft. 3 in. long, and 6 ft. 6 in. broad: what will it come to at 6s. 7½d per yard?

*Ans. 1l. 19s. 5½d. ¾f.*

(12.) A house has 3 tiers of windows, 3 in a tier; the height of the first tier is 7 ft. 10 in., of the second 6 ft. 8 in., and of the third 5 ft. 4 in., and the breadth of each is 3 ft. 11 in.: what will the glazing of them come to at 14d. per foot?

*Ans. 13l. 11s. 10½d. ⅓f.*

(13.) What will the tiling of a barn cost at 25s. 6d. per square, the length being 43 ft. 10 in. and the breadth 27 ft. 5 in. on the flat, the eave boards projecting 16 inches on each side?

*Ans. 24l. 9s. 5½d. $\frac{21}{200}$f.*

(14.) How many square rods (272¼ sq.ft.=1 sq. rod) are there in a wall 62½ ft. long, 14 ft. 8 in. high, and 2½ bricks thick?

*Ans. 5 rods, 166 sq. ft. 76 sq. in.*

(15.) If a garden wall be 254 feet round, and 12 ft. 7 in. high, and 3 bricks thick, how many rods does it contain?

*Ans. 23 rods, 130 sq. ft. 84 sq. in.*

## Involution, or the Raising of Powers.

INVOLUTION, or the *raising of powers,* is the method of finding the square, cube, &c. of any given number.

A power of a number, is the product arising from multiplying it by itself, a certain number of times.

The index, or exponent, of a power, is the number that denotes that power.

Thus, $4 \times 4 = 4^2 = 16 =$ the square of 4; and $5 \times 5 \times 5 = 5^3$

=125=the cube of 5; where the indices, or exponents, are 2 and 3.*

### RULE.

Multiply the given number once by itself, for the square; twice by itself, for the cube; three times, for the fourth power; and so on.

Or, if it be a high power that is to be found, multiply any two or more of the inferior powers together that will produce that power, and the result will give the answer, as before.

### EXAMPLES.

(1.) It is required to find the square of 13.

$$
\begin{array}{r}
13 \\
13 \\
\hline
39 \\
13 \\
\hline
169 = Answer.
\end{array}
$$

* TABLE of the first NINE POWERS OR NUMBERS.

| 1st | 2d. | 3d. | 4th. | 5th. | 6th. | 7th. | 8th. | 9th. |
|---|---|---|---|---|---|---|---|---|
| 1 | 1 | 1 | 1 | 1 | 1 | 1 | 1 | 1 |
| 2 | 4 | 8 | 16 | 32 | 64 | 128 | 256 | 512 |
| 3 | 9 | 27 | 81 | 243 | 729 | 2187 | 6561 | 19683 |
| 4 | 16 | 64 | 256 | 1024 | 4096 | 16384 | 65536 | 262144 |
| 5 | 25 | 125 | 625 | 3125 | 15625 | 78125 | 390625 | 1953125 |
| 6 | 36 | 216 | 1296 | 7776 | 46656 | 279936 | 1679616 | 10077696 |
| 7 | 49 | 343 | 2401 | 16807 | 117649 | 823543 | 5764801 | 40353607 |
| 8 | 64 | 512 | 4096 | 32768 | 262144 | 2097152 | 16777216 | 134217728 |
| 9 | 81 | 729 | 6561 | 59049 | 531441 | 4782969 | 43046721 | 387420489 |

(2.) Required the 3rd and 4th power of 19.

$$
\begin{array}{r}
19 \\
19 \\
\hline
171 \\
19 \\
\hline
361 \;\textit{the square.} \\
19 \\
\hline
3249 \\
361 \\
\hline
\end{array}
$$

1st Ans.=6859 *the cube, or third power.*

$$
\begin{array}{r}
19 \\
\hline
61731 \\
6859 \\
\hline
\end{array}
$$

2nd Ans.=130321 *the fourth power.*

(3.) It is required to find the 5th power of 11.

| | |
|---|---|
| $\begin{array}{r} 11 \\ 11 \\ \hline 121 \\ 11 \\ \hline 1331 \\ 121 \\ \hline 1331 \\ 15972 \\ \hline 161051 = Ans. \\ \hline \end{array}$ | $Or,$ $\begin{array}{r} 11 \\ 11 \\ \hline 121 \\ 121 \\ \hline 121 \\ 242 \\ 121 \\ \hline 14641 \\ 11 \\ \hline 161051 = Ans. \; \text{as before.} \\ \hline \end{array}$ |

(4.) It is required to find the 3d power of 35. *Ans.* 42875.

(5.) It is required to find the 4th power of $\frac{3}{4}$.    *Ans.* $\frac{81}{256}$.

(6.) It is required to find the 5th power of ·029.

*Ans.* ·000000020511149.

(7.) It is required to find the 6th power of 6·03

*Ans.* 48073·293078275529.

(8.) It is required to find the 7th power of 3⅖.

*Ans.* $\frac{4103338673}{78125}$, or 5252·3350144.

# Evolution, or the Extracting of Roots.*

EVOLUTION is the reverse of Involution ; being the method of finding the square root, cube root, &c. of any given number.

The root of any number, or power, is such a number, as being multiplied into itself a certain number of times will produce that power.

Thus 2 is the square root of 4, because $2 \times 2 = 4$ ; and 4 is the cube root of 64, because $4 \times 4 \times 4 = 64$ ; and so on.

Any power of a given number may be found exactly, but there are many numbers of which a given root cannot be accurately determined ; although, by means of decimals, we can approximate towards it, to any assigned degree of exactness.

An incomplete root of this kind is called a surd root, and one which is perfectly accurate is called a rational root.

Thus, the square root of 2 is a surd root; but the square root of 4 is rational, being equal to 2 : also the cube root of 8 is a rational root, being equal to 2 ; but the cube root of 9 is a surd, or such as cannot be exactly found.

---

* Roots are sometimes denoted by writing the character $\sqrt{}$ before the number, or power, with the index of the root against it: thus, the square root of 70 is $\sqrt{70}$, and the cube root of it is $\sqrt[3]{70}$ ; the index 2 being always omitted when the square root is designated.

If the root consists of several numbers, with the sign $+$ or $-$ between them, the numbers are usually placed within parentheses, to show that the root of the whole is to be taken ; thus the square root of $4 + 3$ is $\sqrt{(4 + 3)}$, and the cube root of $28 - 13$ is $\sqrt[3]{(28 - 13)}$.

But roots of all kinds are frequently designated like powers, by means of fractional indices placed at the right-hand corner of the number.

Thus, the square root of 5 is denoted by $5^{\frac{1}{2}}$, the cube root of 19 by $19^{\frac{1}{3}}$ and the fourth root of $40 - 12$ by $(40 - 12)^{\frac{1}{4}}$, &c. The reason of which method is sufficiently plain: for since $\sqrt{a}$ is a geometrical mean between 1 and $a$, so ½ is an arithmetical mean between 0 and 1 ; and therefore as 2 is the index of the square of $a$, ½ will be the proper index of its square root ; and in the same manner it will appear that ⅓ is the proper index of the cube root of $a$, ¼ of the biquadrate of $a$, and so on.

## TO EXTRACT THE SQUARE ROOT OF A GIVEN NUMBER.

### RULE.*

1. Divide the given number into periods of two figures each, by putting a point over the place of units, another over the place of hundreds, and so on, over every second figure, to the left in integers, and to the right in decimals.

2. Find the square root of the first period, or if it has no exact root, that of the square number next less, and set it on the right hand of the given number, after the manner of a quotient figure in division.

3. Subtract the square of this part of the root, from the

---

* In order to show the reason of the rule, it will be proper to premise the following : —

*Lemma.* The product of any two numbers can have at most but as many places of figures as are in both the factors, and at least but one less.

The truth of which may be shown thus : Take two numbers consisting of any number of places of figures, that shall be the least possible of those places *viz.* unity with ciphers, as 1000 and 100 ; then, their product will be 1 with as many ciphers annexed as are in both the numbers, *viz.* 100000 : but 100000 has one place less than 1000 and 100 together have ; and, since 1000 and 100 were taken the least possible, the product of any other two numbers, of the same number of places, will be greater than 100000 ; consequently the product of any two numbers can have, at least, but one place less than both the factors.

Again, take two numbers, of any number of places of figures, that shall be the greatest possible of those places, as 999 and 99. Then, since 999 × 99 is less than 999 × 100, and 999 × 100 (= 99900) contains only as many places of figures as are in 999 and 99, it is evident that 999 × 99 or the product of any other two numbers consisting of the same number of places, cannot have more places of figures than are in both its factors.

Hence, a square number cannot have more places of figures than double the places of the root, and, at least, but one less. And a cube number cannot have more places of figures than triple the places of the root, and, at least, but two less : whence the method of pointing the figures for the square and cube root is obvious.

Having premised this, the truth of the rule may be shown algebraically, thus :

Suppose N, the number whose square root is to be found, to consist of two periods, and let the figures of the root be denoted by $a$ and $b$.

Then $(a+b)^2 = a^2 + 2ab + b^2 = $ N, the given number ; and to find the

said period, and to the remainder annex the following period, for a dividend.

4. Double the figure of the root above found for a divisor, and find how often it is contained in the dividend, exclusive of the place of units; and set the result both in the quotient and divisor.

5. Subtract the product of this quotient figure and the divisor, thus augmented, from the dividend, and bring down the next period to the remainder, for a new dividend.

6. Divide this new dividend by double the figures already in the root, for another figure; and proceed in this manner, through all the periods to the last; observing that there will be as many integral figures in the root as there are points over the integral part of the given number, and as many decimals as there are points over the decimal part.

It is also to be remarked, that when the figures belonging to the given number are exhausted, the operation may be continued at pleasure by annexing two ciphers to the remainder, for each operation; and that the best way of doubling the root is by adding the last figure of it to the last divisor.

## EXAMPLES.

(1.) Required the square root of 5499025.

---

square root of N is the same as to find the square root of $a^2 + 2ab + b^2$; the method of doing which is as follows:

$$1st \; divisor \; a)a^2 + 2ab + b^2(a + b \; the \; root = \sqrt{N}$$
$$a^2$$

---

$$2nd \; divisor \; 2a + b)2ab + b^2$$
$$2ab + b^2$$

---

$$* \qquad *$$

Or the same may be shown universally, thus:

$$(a+b+c+d+e \; \&c.)^2 = a^2 + \{2a+b\}b + \{2(a+b)+c\}c + \{2(a+b+c) + d\}d + \{2(a+b+c+d)+e\}e \; \&c.$$

### Or,

$$(a+b+c+d+e \; \&c.)^2 = a^2 + (2a+b)b + (A+b+c)c + (B+c+d)d + (c+d +e)e \; \&c.$$

Where it is to be observed, that A is the coefficient of $b$ in the 2d term, B that of $c$ in the 3d term, c that of $d$ in the 4th term, and so on; which is the same as the rule.

$$5|49|90|25(2345 \text{ } the \text{ } root. = Ans.$$
$$4 = 2 \times 2$$

$$43|149$$
$$3|129 = 43 \times 3$$

$$464|2090$$
$$4|1856 = 464 \times 4$$

$$4685)23425$$
$$23425 = 4685 \times 5$$

*

*Note* 1. When the root is to be extracted to a considerable number of places, the work may be abbreviated, thus :

Proceed in the extraction after the common method, till you have found half the required number of figures in the root, when they are even, or one more than half, when they are odd; and for the rest divide the last remainder, with the other part of the number annexed to it, by its corresponding divisor, and the two results, when united, will be the answer.

(2.) Required the square root of 14876·2357.

$$1|48|76|·23|57(121·96$$
$$1$$

$$22|48$$
$$2|44$$

$$241|476$$
$$1|241$$

$$2429|23523$$
$$9|21861$$

$$24386|166257$$
$$6|146316$$

$$24392)19941(8175$$
$$427$$
$$183$$
$$12$$
$$0$$

*Hence,* 121·968175 *is the root required.*

*Note* 2. An easy and expeditious method of extracting the square root, where the given number does not exceed eight figures, by means of Barlow's New Mathematical Tables. (*See* Table I., *8vo. ed.* 1814.)

A similar method also is given for extracting the cube root at p. 149.

### EXAMPLE 1.

Find the square root of ·3236068 to seven places of decimals.

*First,* Look for the nearest less square tabular number to the given number (·32360680) in *column* 3., *Table I.*, page 95., and it will be found to be ·32353344, observing at the same time the root or number ·5688 in *column* 1., which corresponds to it. Then subtract this nearest less square tabular number from the given number (viz. ·32360680 and ·32353344), and the difference equals ·00007336; now make this difference a dividend, and place the root ·5688 in the quotient, and double it for a divisor; then proceed by common simple division to obtain the answer. *Thus,*

·32360680 *the number in the example.*
·32353344 *the nearest less tabular square number.*

$$
\begin{array}{l}
1\cdot1376)\,000073360 \quad (\cdot5688644 = Ans. \\
\qquad\quad 68256 \qquad\qquad 2 \\
\overline{\qquad\qquad\quad} \\
\qquad\quad 51040 \quad 1\cdot1376\ the\ divisor. \\
\qquad\quad 45504 \quad \overline{\qquad\qquad} \\
\overline{\qquad\qquad\quad} \\
\qquad\quad 55360 \\
\qquad\quad 45504 \\
\overline{\qquad\qquad\quad} \\
\qquad\quad\ 9856
\end{array}
$$

### EXAMPLE 2.

Find the square root of 320·3644 to five places of decimals.

320·3644
320·0521

$$
\begin{array}{l}
35\cdot78 \,)\ \cdot31230 \ (\ 17\cdot89872 = Ans. \\
\qquad\ 28624 \qquad\qquad 2 \\
\overline{\qquad\qquad} \\
\qquad\ 26060 \quad 35\cdot78\ the\ divisor. \\
\qquad\ 25046 \quad \overline{\qquad\quad} \\
\overline{\qquad\qquad} \\
\qquad\ 10140 \\
\qquad\ \ 7156 \\
\overline{\qquad\qquad} \\
\qquad\ \ 2984
\end{array}
$$

(3.) Required the square root of 106929.     *Ans.* 327.

(4.) Required the square root of 152399025.  *Ans.* 12345.

(5.) Required the square root of 119550669121.

                                            *Ans.* 345761.

(6.) Required the square root of 368863. *Ans.* 607·34092 &c.

(7.) Required the square root of 3·1721812.

*Ans.* 1·78106 &c.

(8.) Required the square root of $\frac{5}{12}$. *Ans.* ·645497 &c.

(9.) Required the square root of $6\frac{3}{4}$. *Ans.* 2·5298 &c.

(10.) Required the square root of 10. *Ans.* 3·162277 &c.

(11.) Required the square root of ·00032754. *Ans.* ·01809 &c.

# The Extraction of the Cube Root.

## RULE 1.*

1. Separate the given number into periods of three figures each, by putting a point over every third figure from the place of units, towards the left-hand in integers, and to the right-hand in decimals.

2. Find the cube root of the first period, or if it has no exact root, the one next less, and set it on the right-hand of the given number, after the manner of a quotient figure in division.

3. Subtract the cube of this figure of the root, from the said period, and to the remainder annex the following period; which call the resolvend.

4. Under this resolvend, put three times the figure of the root above found, and three times its square, observing to remove the latter one place to the left; and call their sum the divisor.

5. Seek how often this divisor is contained in the resolvend, exclusive of the place of units, and set the result in the quotient next after the figure of the root before found.

6. Under the divisor put the cube of this last quotient figure, the square of it multiplied by three times the former figure or figures, and the triple of it by the square of the

---

* The reason of pointing the given number, as directed in the rule, is obvious from what has been said in the lemma made use of in demonstrating the square root; and the rest of the operation will be best understood from the following analytical process:

Suppose N, the given number, to consist of two periods, and let the figures in the root be denoted by $a$ and $b$.

Then $(a+b)^3 = a^3 + 3a^2b + 3ab^2 + b^3 = $ N = the given number; and to

former, each removed one place to the left, and call their sum the subtrahend.

7. Subtract the subtrahend from the resolvend, and to the remainder bring down the next period for a new resolvend, with which proceed as before; and so on, till the whole is finished; observing that the last figure of the root, in each operation, must be so taken that the subtrahend shall be less than the resolvend.

*Or the same may be done otherwise, thus :*

1. Point the given number, and find the first figure of the root as before.

2. Subtract the cube of the first figure of the root, thus found, from the first period on the left-hand, and annex the following period to the remainder for a dividend.

3. Divide this dividend by 3 times the square of the figure of the root above determined, and the first figure of the quotient will be the second figure of the root.

4. Subtract the cube of these two figures of the root from the first two periods on the left, and to the remainder annex the following period, for a new dividend, which divide by three

---

find the cube root of N is the same as to find the cube root of $a^3 + 3a^2b + 3ab^2 + b^3$; the method of doing which is as follows :

$$a^3 + 3a^2b + 3ab^2 + b^3 (a + b \text{ the root.}$$
$$a^3$$

$$\overline{3a^2b + 3ab^2 + b^3 \text{ resolvend.}}$$

$$3a^2$$
$$\quad + 3a$$

$$\overline{3a^2 \ + 3a \text{ divisor.}}$$

$$3a^2b$$
$$\quad + 3ab^2$$
$$\qquad + b^3$$

$$\overline{3a^2b + 3ab^2 + b^3 \text{ subtrahend.}}$$

Or, the truth of the rule may be shown universally, thus :

$$(a+b+c+d \ \&c.)^3 = a^3 + \left\{3a^2 + 3ab + b^2\right\} b + \left\{3(a+b)^2 + 3c(a+b) + c^2\right\} c$$
$$+ \left\{3(a+b+c)^2 + 3d(a+b+c) + d^2\right\} d, \&c. \quad \text{Or,}$$
$$(a+b+c+d \ \&c.)^3 = a^3 + \left\{3a^2 + 3ab + b^2\right\} b + \left\{A + 2b(a+b) + ab + 3c\right.$$
$$(a+b) + c^2\right\} c + \left\{B + 2c(a+b+c) + c(a+b) + 3d(a+b+c) + d^2\right\} d \ \&c.$$

Where A is the coefficient of $b$ in the 2d term, B that of $c$ in the 3d term, c that of $d$ in the 4th term, and so on.

times the square of the part of the root thus found; and so on till the whole is finished.

*Note.* The same rule must be observed for continuing the operation and pointing for decimals as in the square root, except that, in this case, three ciphers must be annexed to the remainder instead of two.

(1.) Required the cube root of 48228544.

48|228|544(364 *Ans.*

$27 = 3^3 = 3 \times 3 \times 3 = a^3$, because $a = 3$.

———

21228 *resolvend* $= 3a^2b + 3ab^2 + b^3$.

———

$9 = 3 \times 3 = 3a$
$27 = 3 \times 3^2 = 3 \times 3 \times 3 = 3a^2$

———

279 *divisor* $= 3a^2 + 3a$.   Then $b = 6$.

———

$216 = 6^3 = 6 \times 6 \times 6 = b^3$
$324 = 3 \times 3 \times 6^2 = 9 \times 6 \times 6 = 3ab^2$
$162 = 3 \times 3^2 \times 6 = 3 \times 3 \times 3 \times 6 = 3a^2b$

———

19656 *subtrahend* $= 3a^2b + 3ab^2 + b^3$.

———

1572544 *second resolvend.*
——— Here beginning again with the formula, $a = 36$
$108 = 3 \times 36 = 3a$
$3888 = 3 \times 36^2 = 3 \times 36 \times 36 = 3a^2$

———

38988 *second divisor* $= 3a^2 + 3a$.   Then $b = 4$.

———

$64 = 4^3 = 4 \times 4 \times 4 = b^3$
$1728 = 3 \times 36 \times 4^2 = 3ab^2$
$15552 = 3 \times 36^2 \times 4 = 3 \times 36 \times 36 \times 4 = 3a^2b$

———

1572544 *second subtrahend* $= 3a^2b + 3ab^2 + b^3$.

In the above solution it may be seen that the Editor has arranged the numbers according to the formula; and in the new edition of the "Key" it will be seen that he has adopted the same principle, in order to show one uniform system of solution.

| 0 | 0 | 48\|228\|544(364 |
|---|---|---|
|   |   | 27 |
| 3 | 9 |  |
| 6 | 27 | 21228 |
| 96 | 3276 | 19656 |
| 102 | 3888 |  |
| 1084 | 389136 | 1562544 |
|   |   | 1556544 |

. . . . . . .

(2.) Required the cube root of 41278·242816 by the latter rule.

$$41|278|{\cdot}242{,}816(34{\cdot}56 \; root. = Ans.$$
$$27$$

$$3^2 \times 3 = 27)14278(4$$

$$41278$$
$$34^3 = 39304$$

$$34^2 \times 3 = 3468)1974242(5$$

$$41278242$$
$$345^3 = 41063625$$

$$345^2 \times 3 = 357075)214617816(6$$

$$41278242816$$
$$3456^3 = 41278242816$$

. . . . . . . . . . .

## A NEW METHOD OF EXTRACTING THE CUBE ROOT OF ANY GIVEN NUMBER.*

### RULE 2.

*First.* Divide the given number into periods of three figures each, as in the common method, and find the nearest cube to the first period, subtract it therefrom, and put the root in the quotient; then thrice the square of this root will be the trial divisor for finding the next figure.

*Second.* Multiply the root figure or figures already found by 3, and prefix the product to the next new root figure

---

* This method of extracting the cube root is decidedly the best, and is certainly the shortest that has been discovered; it was first proposed in the Appendix (pp. 252, 253.) to Dr. CHARLES HUTTON's *Arithmetic,* 12mo. by the Editor, ALEXANDER INGRAM of Leith, printed by G. Ross, Edinburgh, 1807.

(which will be seen by the trial divisor); then multiply this number by the aforesaid new root figure, and place the product two figures to the right, below the trial divisor, and add it to the trial divisor; this sum will be the true divisor.

*Third.* Under this divisor, write the square of the last root figure, which add to the two sums above, and the result is the next trial divisor; the true divisor is found as before directed.

*Note.* — After the first or second decimal place in the root is found, the square of the root figure used in forming the trial divisor may be omitted, and also those two figures that are placed to the right of the trial divisor, in forming the true divisor, as the value of these figures will be too small for their omission to affect the truth of the result. But if the number of decimals in the root is required to be very great, these omissions must not be made till after the third or fourth decimal in the root is found.

### Examples.

(1.) Extract the cube root of the number 12326391.

$$12|326|391(231 = Ans.$$

| | |
|---|---|
| True divisor $2^3$ .................. $= 8$ | |
| | $\overline{\phantom{xx}}$ |
| Trial divisor...$2^2 \times 3 = 12$ | $4326$ |
| $63 \times 3 = 189$ | |
| | $\overline{\phantom{xx}}$ |
| True divisor ......... $= 1389 \times 3 = 4167$ | |
| $3^2 = \phantom{0}9$ | $159391$ |
| | $\overline{\phantom{xx}}$ |
| Trial divisor......... $= 1587$ | |
| $691 \times 1 = \phantom{00}691$ | |
| | $\overline{\phantom{xx}}$ |
| True divisor ......... $= 159391 \times 1 = 159391$ | |
| | $\overline{\phantom{xx}}$ |
| | $\cdots\cdots$ |
| | $\overline{\phantom{xx}}$ |

Here the nearest root of the first period of 12 is 2; hence, by the Rule, thrice the square of this root figure, or $2^2 \times 3 = 12$, the trial divisor. Now with this divisor, we see that 3 must be the next figure of the root, then $2 \times 3 = 6$, and 3 (the new root figure) with 6 prefixed, is 63; this multiplied by the new root figure 3, gives 189, which being placed two figures to the right of the trial divisor (as directed in the Rule), and added to it, gives the true divisor, 1389. To form the next trial divisor, add the square of the last root figure, 3, to the two sums above it, viz. 1389, 189, and we have $9 + 1389 + 189 = 1587$, for the next trial divisor. The next figure in the root is evidently 1; then with this new root figure, 1, and with three times the preceding part of the root prefixed is 691, for $23 \times 3 = 69$, and 1 with 69 prefixed is 691, which being placed two figures to the right of the trial divisor, and added to it, gives 159391, for the true divisor.

(2.) Extract the cube root of 9 to about fifteen places of decimals.

H

True divisor = 2³............................................ ................

Trial divisor = 2² × 3 = 12

608 × 8 = 4864

True divisor = 124864 × 8........................................................

8² = 64

Trial divisor = 129792

624008 × 8 = 4992064

True divisor = 129796992064 × 8....................................

8² = 64

Trial divisor = 129801984+192

6240243 × 3 = 18720729

True divisor = 12980217139929 × 3................................

3² = 9

Trial divisor = 12980235860667

62402498 × 8 = 499219984

True divisor = 1298024085286684 × 8.............................

8² = 64

Trial divisor = 1298024584506632

624025142 × 2 = 1248050284

True divisor = 129802459698713484 × 2..........................

2³ = 4

Trial divisor = 129802460946763772

6240251463 × 3 = 18720754389

True divisor = 12980246113397131589 × 3.....................

3² = 9

Trial divisor = 12980246132117885887

624025146905 × 5 = 3120125734525

True divisor = 12980246132429898604525 × 5...............

5² = 25

Trial divisor = 12980246132741911039075

6240251469151 × 1 = 6240251469151

True divisor = 1298024613274815128376651 × 1.............

1² = 1

Trial divisor = 1298024613275439143684803

62402514691539 × 9 = 561622632223851

True divisor = 129802461327600766316804151 × 9..........

9² = 81

Trial divisor = 12980246132756238894028083

6240251469155704 × 4 = 24961005876622816

True divisor = 1298024613276564885049157452816 × 4....

4² = 16

Trial divisor = 12980246132756738115020934075648

62402514691557121 × 1 = 62402514691557121

True divisor = 12980246132756567443552718099121921 × 1.

9 ( 2·0800838230519041, &c. = *Ans.*

..................... = 8

        1000000

... ............... = 998912

        1088000000000

............... ... = 1038375936512

        49624063488000

..................... = 38940651419787

        10683412068213000

..................... = 10384192682293472

        299219385919528000

...................... = 259604919397426968

        39614466522101032000

........................ = 38940738340191394767

        673728181909637233000000

............................. = 6490123066214949230022625

        247158752881423099773750000

.......................... = 12980246132748151285376651

        1173562915539415869199834900

........................... = 116822215194840068968512373590

        5340763591015179514711164100000000

.................................... = 51921084531062595401984629811264

        1486551379089199745127011188736000

............................. = 1298024613276567443552718099121921

        1885267658126323015742930896140779

н 2

*Or thus, contraction, by the Note (see also Contracted Division of Decimals,* p. 117.)

$$9 \ ( \ 2{\cdot}080083823051904^*$$

True divisor $= 2^3$ ............................. $= 8$

_____

Trial divisor $= 2^2 \times 3 = 12$          1000000
            $608 \times 8 = 4864$

True divisor $= 124864 \times 8$ ......... $= 998912$
            $8^2 = 64$

_____

                                          1088000000000

Trial divisor $= 129792$
$624008 \times 8 = 4992064$

True divisor $= 129796992064 \times 8$ ...... $= 1038375936512$
            $8^2 = 64$

_____

                                          49624063488

Trial divisor $= 129801984192$
$62402,4 \times 3 = 187207$

True divisor $= 12980217139,9 \times 3$ ......... $= 38940651420$

Trial divisor $= 12980235861$          10683412068
$624,0 \times 8 = 4992$

True divisor $= 1298024085,3 \times 8$ ......... $= 10384192682$

Trial divisor $- 1298024585$          299219386
$6,2 \times 2 = 12$

True divisor $= 129802459,7 \times 2$ .............. $= 259604919$

            $12,98,0,2,46,1$          39614467
                                     38940738

                                      _____

                                       673729
                                       649012

                                      _____

                                        24717
                                        12980

                                      _____

                                        11737
                                        11682

                                      _____

                                          55
                                          52

                                      _____

                                           3

_____

* Another figure might have been obtained, viz. 2, but, on account of the extent to which the root has been carried, this figure could not

*Note.* — An easy and expeditious method of extracting the cube root, by means of Barlow's New Mathematical Tables, (*see* TABLE 1., *Octavo Edition*, 1814) which is similar to the rule given to find the square root, *see Note* 2., p. 139., in the Arithmetic, both of these rules may be depended on in giving the roots true to seven figures, if the given number in the examples is within the limits of the table.   These two methods of extracting the square and cube root will be found to have a pre-eminence over logarithms, the computation being more *simple*, and each operation is performed in much less time.

*Example* 1.   Find the cube root of 98003·449.

*First,* Look for the nearest less cube tabular number to the given number (98003·449000) in column 4. of TABLE 1., p. 77., and it will be found to be 97972·181000, observing at the same time the root or number 46·10 in column 1. which corresponds to it; then subtract this nearest less cube tabular number from the given number, (viz. 98003·449000 and 97972·181000), and the difference equals 31·268000; now make this difference a dividend, and place the root 46·10 in the quotient. Then multiply the square of this root or quotient by 3, viz. $46·10^2$ × 3 = 6375·6300; *or rather thus*, see squares opposite the number 46·10 in column 3., we have 2125·2100 which × by 3 = 6375·6300 for a divisor, then proceed by common simple division to obtain the answer. Thus —

$$98003·449000 \text{ the number in the example.}$$
$$97972·181000 \text{ the nearest less tabular cube number.}$$

$$46·10^2 × 3 = 6375·6300)31·2680000(46·10490 = Ans.$$
$$25\ 5025200$$

$$576548000$$
$$573806700$$

$$27413000$$

*Example* 2.   Find the cube root of 2.

$$2·000000000 \text{ the number in the example.}$$
$$1·995616979 \text{ the nearest less tabular cube number.}$$

$$1·259^2 × 3 = 4·755243)·0043831210(1·259921 = Ans.$$
$$42797187$$

$$0340230$$
$$9510486$$

$$8297440$$
$$4755243$$

$$3542197$$

have been depended on as true; all the fifteen places, however, that we have found, are true to the last figure. (*See the previous solution,* pp. 146, 147.)

(3.) What is the cube root of 389017 ?　　*Ans.* 73.
(4.) What is the cube root of 1092727 ?　　*Ans.* 103.
(5.) What is the cube root of 27054036008 ? *Ans.* 3002.
(6.) What is the cube root of 122615327232 ? *Ans.* 4968.
(7.) What is the cube root of 1·740992427 ? *Ans.* 1·203.
(8.) Required the cube root of 146708·483. *Ans.* 52·74 &c.
(9.) Required the cube root of 171·46776406. *Ans.* 5·555 &c.
(10.) Required the cube root of ·0001357. *Ans.* ·05138 &c.
(11.) Required the cube root of $13\frac{2}{3}$. 　*Ans.* 2·3908 &c.
(12.) It is required to find the cube root of $71\frac{1}{3}$.

*Ans.* 4·1432464 &c.

### RULE 3.*

Find, by trials, the nearest rational root of the given number, and call it the assumed root.

Then, as twice the cube of the assumed root, added to the

---

* The methods usually given for extracting the cube root are so tedious and difficult to be remembered, that arithmeticians have long wished for a rule that would be more ready and convenient in practice. In consequence of which, several eminent mathematicians, both of our own country and abroad, have been led to devise approximating rules for this purpose; but no one, that I have yet seen, is so simple in its form, or seems so well adapted to general use, as that given above.

That it converges very fast may be easily shown as follows: Let $N =$ the given number, $a^3$ the cube of the assumed root $a$, and $x$ the correction; then $2a^3 + N : 2N + a^3 :: a : a + x =$ root by the rule; and consequently $(2a^3 + N) \times (a + x) = (2N + a^3) \times a$; or, by substituting $(a + x)^3$ for $N$, and then multiplying, $2a^4 + 2a^3x + a^4 + 4a^3x + 6a^2x^2 + 4ax^3 + x^4 = 2aN + a^4$.

Whence, by transposing the terms, and dividing the whole by $2a$, we shall have $N = a^3 + 3a^2x + 3ax^2 + x^3 + x^3 + \frac{x^4}{2a}$; which, by neglecting the terms $x^3 + \frac{x^4}{2a}$ as being very small, becomes $N = a^3 + 3a^2x + 3ax^2 + x^3 =$ to the known cube of $a + x$.

This rule I received, nearly 30 years ago, from a person who informed me that he had it from the late Mr. JAMES DODSON, at the time he was mathematical master of Christ's Hospital; but I have since found that it is exactly the same as Dr. HALLEY's rational formula, except that it is more commodiously expressed.

The irrational formula of the same author, for the cube root, is $\frac{1}{2}a + \frac{1}{2} \sqrt{\frac{4N - a^3}{3a}}$, which is something more accurate than the former, being less erroneous in point of excess than the other is in defect; so that if an arithmetical or geometrical mean be taken between these two results, it will be nearer the truth than either of them.

given number, is to twice the given number, added to the
cube of the assumed root, so is the assumed root to the root
required, nearly.

And by taking the number last found for the assumed root
and repeating the operation as often as may be thought necessary, in the same manner as before, the root may be
determined to any degree of exactness required.

### EXAMPLES.

1. Let it be required to find the cube root of 12484.

*Here the nearest rational root, as found by trial, is* 23, *and
its cube is* 12167.

$$\textit{Whence } 12167 \qquad\qquad 12484$$
$$2 \qquad\qquad\qquad 2$$
$$23^3 \times 2 = 24334 \qquad\quad 24968$$
$$12484 \qquad\qquad\quad 12167$$
$$\overline{36818} \quad : \quad \overline{37135} \quad :: \quad 23$$
$$23$$
$$\overline{111405}$$
$$74270$$

$$36818)854105(23\cdot198$$
$$11774$$
$$729$$
$$361$$
$$30$$
$$1$$

*Ans.* 23·198, *the root required, which is true to the last
place of decimals.*

2. Let it be required to find the cube root of 2.

*Here the nearest rational root is* 1, *and its cube is also* 1.

*Whence* $(1 \times 2) + 2 = 4$, *and* $(2 \times 2) + 1 = 5$.

*Therefore* $4 : 5 :: 1 : \frac{5}{4} = 1\cdot25 = \textit{root nearly}.$

*Again, the cube of* $\frac{5}{4} = \frac{125}{64}.$

*Whence* $\dfrac{125 \times 2}{64} + 2 : (2 \times 2) + \dfrac{125}{64} :: \dfrac{5}{4}.$

*Or* $\dfrac{378}{64} : \dfrac{381}{64} :: \dfrac{5}{4} : \dfrac{381 \times 5 \times 64}{64 \times 4 \times 378} = \dfrac{381 \times 5}{378 \times 4} = \dfrac{127 \times 5}{126 \times 4} = \dfrac{635}{504}$

$= 1\cdot259921$ &c. $= \textit{root, which is true to the last figure.}$

H 4

(1.) Required the cube root of 5.     *Ans.* 1·709975 &c.
(2.) Required the cube root of 81.     *Ans.* 4·326748 &c.
(3.) Required the cube root of 132.     *Ans.* 5·091643 &c.
(4.) Required the cube root of 576.     *Ans.* 8·320335 &c.
(5.) Required the cube root of 30·625.     *Ans.* 3·128662 &c.
(6.) Required the cube root of ·00533.     *Ans.* ·174679 &c.
(7.) Required the cube root of 5592.     *Ans.* 17·7496 &c.
(8.) Required the cube root of $51\frac{1}{8}$.     *Ans.* 3·711457 &c.

## TO EXTRACT THE ROOTS OF POWERS IN GENERAL.

### RULE.*

Let N be the given power or number, whose root is to be

---

* The demonstration of this rule, of which that for the cube root is only a particular case, may be easily derived from the binomial theorem, as follows:

Let N = given number, $n$ = index of the root, $r$ = nearest rational root, and $x$ = remaining part.

Then $N = (r + x)^n = r^n + n r^{n-1}x + n . \dfrac{n-1}{2} r^{n-2}x^2$, &c. by evolution.

And $\dfrac{N-r^n}{n r^{n-1}} = x + \dfrac{n-1}{2} . \dfrac{x^2}{r}$ &c.; where, on account of the smallness of $\dfrac{n-1}{2} . \dfrac{x^2}{r}$, the first term $x$ may be considered as nearly $= \dfrac{N-r^n}{n r^{n-1}}$.

But $N - r^n$ is also $= n r^{n-1}x + n . \dfrac{n-1}{2} r^{n-2}x^2$ &c. $= \left(n r^{n-1} + n . \dfrac{n-1}{2} r^{n-2}x\right)x$; whence, by substituting the former value of $x$ in this equation, we shall have $N - r^n = \left(n r^{n-1} + \dfrac{n-1}{2} . \dfrac{N-r^n}{r}\right)x = \dfrac{(n+1)r^n + (n-1)N}{2r} \times x$; consequently $x = \dfrac{(N-r^n) \times 2r}{(n+1)r^n + (n-1)N}$, and $r + x = r + \dfrac{(N-r^n) \times 2r}{(n+1)r^n \times (n-1)N}$ $= \dfrac{(n+1)N + (n-1)r^n}{(n+1)r^n + (n-1)N} \times r$; which is the expression required, and when converted into an analogy is the same as the rule.

It may here also be observed, that the fourth root of any number is equal to the square root of the square root of that number; and that the sixth root is equal to the square root of the cube root; and so on.

The proof of all roots is by involution, and then by casting out the nines as in multiplication.

The following theorems may likewise sometimes be found useful in extracting the root of a vulgar fraction: $\sqrt{\dfrac{a}{b}} = \dfrac{\sqrt{a}}{\sqrt{b}} = \dfrac{\sqrt{ab}}{b} = \dfrac{a}{\sqrt{ab}}$; $\sqrt[3]{\dfrac{a}{b}}$ $= \dfrac{\sqrt[3]{ab^2}}{b} = \dfrac{a}{\sqrt[3]{a^2b}}$, &c.

found, $n$ the index of that power, $r$ the assumed root, and A its power.

Then, as the sum of $n+1$ times A and $n-1$ times N is to the sum of $n+1$ times N and $n-1$ times A, so is the assumed root $r$ to the root required, nearly.

That is $(n+1)$A$+(n-1)$N $:(n+1)$N$+(n-1)$A $:: r :$ the true root, nearly.

$Or \dfrac{n+1}{2}$A $+\dfrac{n-1}{2}$N $:$ N $\infty$ A $:: r :$ the correction, which,

added to, or subtracted from, the assumed root, according as it was taken too little, or too great, will give the true root nearly, as before.

And, by repeating the operation with the root last found, as often as may be thought necessary, the answer may be determined to any degree of accuracy required.

### EXAMPLES.

(1.) It is required to find the 5th root of 2.

Assume the root$=1$, and its 5th power will, also, be 1.

*Then* N$=2$, A$=1$, $n=5$, *and* $r=1$,

*Whence*
$(n+1)$A$=6$ $\qquad$ $(n+1)$N$=12$
$(n=1)$N$=8$ $\qquad$ $(n-1)$A$=\;4$

$\qquad\quad\overline{\;\;14\;\;}$ $\qquad\qquad\;\;\overline{\;\;16\;\;}$

*Therefore* $14:16::1:\dfrac{16}{14}=\dfrac{8}{7}=1\tfrac{1}{7}=1\cdot142857$ *the root.*

*nearly.*

*Again, assume the root* $=\dfrac{8}{7}$, *and its 5th power will be* $\dfrac{32768}{16807}$.

*Then* N$=2$; A$=\dfrac{32768}{16807}$; $n=5$; *and* $r=\dfrac{8}{7}$.

*Whence* $\dfrac{n+1}{2}$A $=\dfrac{98304}{16807}$; $\dfrac{n-1}{2}$N$=4=\dfrac{67228}{16807}$;

*and* N$-$A$=2-\dfrac{32768}{16807}=\dfrac{846}{16807}$.

*And therefore* $\dfrac{98304}{16807}+\dfrac{67228}{16807}:\dfrac{846}{16807}::\dfrac{8}{7}$.

H 5

$$Or\ 165532 : 846 :: \frac{8}{7} : \frac{846 \times 8}{165532 \times 7} = \frac{846 \times 2}{41383 \times 7} = \frac{1692}{289681}$$
$$=0.005841.$$

*Consequently* $0.005841 + 1.142857 = 1.148698 = root\ re-$ *quired.*

(2.) What is the 3d root of ½ or ·5?     *Ans.* ·793700 &c.
(3.) What is the 4th root of 2?     *Ans.* 1·18920 &c.
(4.) What is the 4th root of 97·41?     *Ans.* 3·141599 &c.
(5.) What is the 6th root of 21035·8?     *Ans.* 5·25403 &c.
(6.) What is the 6th root of 2?     *Ans.* 1·12246 &c.
(7.) What is the 7th root of 21035·8?     *Ans.* 4·14539 &c.
(8.) What is the 7th root of 2?     *Ans.* 1·10408 &c.
(9.) What is the 8th root of 21035·8?     *Ans.* 3·47033 &c.
(10.) What is the 8th root of 2?     *Ans.* 1·09050 &c.
(11.) What is the 9th root of 21035·8?     *Ans.* 3·02223 &c.
(12.) What is the 9th root of 2?     *Ans.* 1·08005 &c.
(13.) What is the 365th root of 1·05?     *Ans.* 1·00013 &c.

## Simple Interest.

SIMPLE INTEREST is an allowance made by the borrower of any sum of money to the lender, according to a certain rate per annum; which, by law, must not exceed 5 per cent., that is 5*l.* for the use of 100*l.* for a year; 10*l.* for the use of it for 2 years; and so on.

*Principal* is the money lent.

*Rate* is the sum per cent. agreed on.

*Amount* is the principal and interest added together.

### RULE.*

Multiply the principal by the rate, and divide the product by 100, and the quotient will be the interest for 1 year.

Or, the interest for 1 year at 5 per cent. is 1-20th of the principal; and at 4 per cent. is 1-25th of the principal.

---

* It is customary, in some cases of this kind, to consider the time elapsed in different ways.

Thus, for instance, in the courts of law, interest is always computed in years, quarters, and days; which indeed is the only equitable method; but in computing the interest of the public bonds of the South Sea and India Companies, and in the Bank of England, &c. the time is generally taken in calendar months and days, and on Exchequer bills in quarters of a year and days.

Then multiply the interest for a year by the number of years given, and the product will be the interest for that time.

If there be any smaller portions of time, as months, or days, they must be worked for by the aliquot parts of a year, or by the rule of three.

When this is done, if the interest, so found, be added to the principal, it will give the amount, or the whole sum which is due.

## EXAMPLES.

(1.) What is the interest of 284*l.* 10*s.* for 2½ years at 5 per cent. per annum?

$$\begin{array}{ccl} £ & s. & \\ 284 & . 10 & \textit{principal.} \\ & 5 & \textit{interest.} \end{array}$$

$$1,00)14,22 . 10$$

$$\begin{array}{cccl} 14 & . 4 & . 6d. & \textit{one year's interest.} \\ & 2\frac{1}{2} & \textit{years.} \end{array}$$

$$\begin{array}{cccl} 28 & . 9 & . 0 & \textit{for 2 years.} \\ 7 & . 2 & . 3 & \textit{for } \frac{1}{2} \textit{ year.} \end{array}$$

$$\begin{array}{cccl} 35 & . 11 & . 3 & \textit{the interest required.} \\ 284 & . 10 & . 0 & \textit{principal.} \end{array}$$

$$£320 . 1 . 3 \textit{ the amount.}$$

*Or thus:*

$5l. = \frac{1}{20}$ *of* 100.

$$\begin{array}{ccc} £ & s. & d. \\ \frac{1}{20})284 & . 10 & . 0 \end{array}$$

$£14 . 4 . 6$ *one*

*year's int. as before.*

The principle upon which interest is calculated is the same as the Rule of Three; for the above example might be stated thus,

As 100*l.* : 5*l.* :: 284*l.* 10*s.* : 14*l.* 4*s.* 6*d.* *one year's interest.*

(2.) What is the interest of 230*l.* 10*s.* for 1 year, at 4 per cent. per annum? *Ans.* 9*l.* 4*s.* 4¾*d.*

(3.) What is the interest of 547*l.* 15*s.* for 3 years, at 5 per cent. per annum? *Ans.* 82*l.* 3*s.* 3*d.*

(4.) What is the amount of 690*l.* for 3 years, at 4½ per cent. per annum? *Ans.* 783*l.* 3*s.*

(5.) What is the interest of 205*l.* 15*s.* for ¼ year, at 4 per cent. per annum? *Ans.* 2*l.* 1*s.* 1¾*d.*

(6.) What is the amount of 120*l.* 10*s.* for 2½ years, at 4¾ per cent. per annum? *Ans.* 134*l.* 16*s.* 2¼*d.*

(7.) What is the interest of 47*l.* 10*s.* for 4 years and 52 days, at 4⅓ per cent? *Ans.* 8*l.* 17*s.* 1*d*¼.

(8.) What is the amount of 200 guineas, for 4 years, 7 months, and 25 days, at 4½ per cent? *Ans.* 253*l.* 19*s.* 2¼*d.*

(9.) A gentleman left his niece by will 558*l.* 15*s.* to be paid her with interest at 4 per cent. when she came of age, which was in 5 years, 9 months, and 21 days; what has she to receive in all? *Ans.* 688*l.* 10*s.* 11½*d.*

(10.) What is the interest due upon an India bond of 500*l.* value, at 3½ per cent. per annum, from September 30. 1852, to June 18. 1853 (*or* 261 *days*)? *Ans.* 12*l.* 10*s.* 3¼*d.*

(11.) What is the interest due upon an Exchequer bill of 450*l.* at 3¾ per cent. per annum for 2¾ years, and 67 days? *Ans.* 49*l.* 10*s.* 0¾*d.*

## COMMISSION, BROKERAGE, INSURANCE, AND BUYING AND SELLING OF STOCK.*

COMMISSION is an allowance of so much per cent. to a factor or correspondent abroad for buying and selling goods for his employer.

BROKERAGE is a similar allowance made to a person called a Broker, for assisting merchants or factors in procuring or disposing of goods.

INSURANCE is a per-centage, given to certain persons, or offices, who engage to make good the loss of ships, houses, or merchandise, which may happen from storms or fire.

---

* Stocks are of different kinds, as Bank stock, 3 per cent. reduced, 3 per cent. consols, omnium, &c.; the prices of which vary according to the circumstances of the times, and the rumours that prevail with respect to war or peace.

When the price of any particular stock, as, for instance, the 3 per cent. consols, is said to be 90⅛, the meaning is that 90*l.* 2*s.* 6*d.* must be paid on that day, for 100*l.* of this stock; and in this case the purchaser may be considered as having 100*l.* in the Bank for which he is to receive annually 3*l.* or two half-yearly dividends of 1*l.* 10*s.* each; and so on for any larger sum.

Omnium is a term that denotes the several kinds of stock, &c. by which Government pay those who agree to advance a certain sum of money, by way of loan; and when it is said to be at so much premium, as, for instance, 1½ per cent., the meaning is, that if a person purchase 100*l.* of this loan, he must pay 1*l.* 10*s.* more than the original leader.

BUYING AND SELLING OF STOCK is the purchasing or disposing of a certain sum of money in the Bank of England, or in the capital of some trading company, according to the rate per cent. which they may sell for at any given time.

The method of working questions that may occur in either of these rules, is the same as in simple interest.

### EXAMPLES.

(1.) What is the commission on 500*l.* 13*s.* 6*d.* at 3½ per cent. ?

$$
\begin{array}{r}
£ \quad s. \quad d. \\
500 \ . \ 13 \ . \ 6 \\
3 \\
\hline
1502 \ , \ \ 0 \ . \ 6 \\
250 \ . \ \ 6 \ . \ 9 \\
\hline
1,00)17,52 \ . \ \ 7 \ . \ 3 \\
\hline
£17 \ . \ 10 \ . \ 5\tfrac{1}{2} = \textit{the answer.}
\end{array}
$$

(2.) What is the brokerage on 610*l.* 10*s.* 4*d.* at 5*s.* or ¼ per cent. ?

$$
\begin{array}{r}
£ \quad s. \quad d. \\
5s. \text{ is } \tfrac{1}{4} \ 610 \ . \ 10 \ . \ 4 \\
\hline
1,00)1,52 \ . \ 12 \ . \ 7 \\
\hline
£1 \ . \ 10 \ . \ 6\tfrac{1}{4} = \textit{the answer.}
\end{array}
$$

(3.) What is the insurance on 874*l.* 14*s.* 2*d.* at 12½ per cent. ?

$$
\begin{array}{r}
£ \quad s. \quad d. \\
874 \ . \ 14 \ . \ 2 \\
\hline
10 \text{ is } \tfrac{1}{10} \ \ 87 \ . \ \ 9 \ . \ \ 5 \\
2 \text{ is } \tfrac{1}{5} \ \ 17 \ . \ \ 9 \ . \ 10\tfrac{1}{2} \\
\tfrac{1}{2} \text{ is } \tfrac{1}{4} \ \ \ 4 \ . \ \ 7 \ . \ \ 5\tfrac{1}{2} \\
\hline
£109 \ . \ \ 6 \ . \ \ 9 = \textit{the answer.}
\end{array}
$$

(4.) What is the purchase of 2054*l.* 16*s.* East India stock, at 110¼ per cent.?

$$
\begin{array}{ccc}
 & \pounds & s. & d. \\
10 \; is \; \tfrac{1}{10} \quad 2054 & . & 16 & . & 0 \\
205 & . & 9 & . & 7 \\
\tfrac{1}{4} \; is \; \tfrac{1}{40} \quad\;\; 5 & . & 2 & . & 8\tfrac{3}{4} \\
\hline
\pounds 2265 & . & 8 & . & 3\tfrac{3}{4} = the\;answer.
\end{array}
$$

(5.) My correspondent writes me word that he has bought goods on my account to the value of 754*l.* 16*s.* What does his commission come to at 2½ per cent.? *Ans.* 18*l.* 17*s.* 4¾*d.*

(6.) What must I allow my correspondent for disbursing on my account 529*l.* 18*s.* 5*d.* at 2¼ per cent.?

*Ans.* 11*l.* 18*s.* 5½*d.*

(7.) If I allow my factor 7⅝ per cent. for commission, what may he demand on the laying out of 1200*l.*? *Ans.* 91*l.* 10*s.*

(8.) What does the commission on 950*l.* come to at 3⅞ per cent.? *Ans.* 36*l.* 16*s.* 3*d.*

(9.) If I allow my broker 3¾ per cent., what may he demand when he sells goods to the value of 876*l.* 5*s.* 10*d.*

*Ans.* 32*l.* 17*s.* 2½*d.*

(10.) What is the brokerage of 879*l.* 18*s.* at ⅜ per cent.?

*Ans.* 3*l.* 5*s.* 11¾*d.*

(11.) If a broker sells goods to the amount of 508*l.* 17*s.* 10*d.*, what is his demand at 1½ per cent.? *Ans.* 7*l.* 12*s.* 8*d.*

(12.) What is the brokerage of 1087*l.* 15*s.* 6½*d.* at 1⅝ per cent.? *Ans.* 17*l.* 13*s.* 6¼*d.*

(13.) If a broker sells goods to the amount of 1000 guineas, what is his demand at ⅝ per cent.? *Ans.* 6*l.* 11*s.* 3*d.*

(14.) If I allow a broker 1¼ per cent., what is his demand for disposing of goods to the value of 729*l.* 10*s.* 6*d.*?

*Ans.* 9*l.* 2*s.* 4½*d.*

(15.) What is the insurance of 900*l.* at 10¾ per cent.?

*Ans.* 96*l.* 15*s.*

(16.) What is the insurance of 1200*l.* at 7⅝ per cent.?

*Ans.* 91*l.* 10*s.*

(17.) What is the insurance of an East India ship and cargo, valued at 35727*l.* 17*s.* 6*d.* at 17⅞ per cent.?

*Ans.* 6386*l.* 7*s.* 1¾*d.*

(18.) What is the purchase of 156*l*. 15*s*. 3 per cent. annuities, at 74½ per cent.? *Ans.* 116*l*. 15*s*. 6¾*d*.

(19.) What is the purchase of 816*l*. 12*s*. Bank annuities, at 89¾ per cent.? *Ans.* 729*l*. 16*s*. 8½*d*.

(20.) What is the purchase of 987*l*. 15*s*. India stock, at 113⅞ per cent.? *Ans.* 1124*l*. 16*s*.

(21.) Bought 650*l*. Bank annuities, at 90⅜ per cent., and paid brokerage ⅛ per cent.; what did the whole amount to? *Ans.* 588*l*. 5*s*.

(22.) What does 2400*l*. capital stock in the three per cent. consolidated Bank annuities come to, at 84⅛ per cent.? *Ans.* 2019*l*.

(23.) What is the value of 50*l*. per annum in the long annuities, which will terminate in 18 years, at 12⅜ years' purchase? *Ans.* 618*l*. 15*s*.

# Discount.

DISCOUNT is an allowance made for the payment of any sum of money before it becomes due, according to a certain rate per cent. agreed on between the parties concerned.

The *present worth* of any sum, or debt, due some time hence, is such a sum, as, if put out to interest for that time, at a certain rate per cent., would amount to the sum or debt then due.

In business, the usual method of estimating the discount of any note or bill is, to deduct the interest of the sum for the given time at 5 per cent.; or to reckon a penny a pound for every month the bill has to run; but the only accurate way is as follows:

### RULE.*

As the amount of 100*l*. for the given rate and time is to the interest of 100*l*. for that time, so is the given sum, or debt, to the discount required.

And if the discount be subtracted from the given sum, the remainder will be the present worth.

---

* That an allowance ought to be made for paying money before it becomes due, which is supposed to bear no interest till after it is due, is evident; for if I keep the money in my own hands till it is due, it is plain I can make advantage of it by putting it out to interest for that

*Or, to find the present worth, and hence the discount.*

As the amount of 100*l.* for the given rate and time is to 100*l.*, so is the given sum, or debt, to the present worth.

And if the present worth be subtracted from the given sum, the remainder will be the discount required.

### EXAMPLES.

(1.) What are the discount and present worth of 500*l.* due 2 years hence, at 5 per cent. ?

Interest of £100 for 2 years $= 5 \times 2 = $ £10.

|  | £ | £ | £ |
|---|---|---|---|
| Then | 110 | : 10 :: | 500 |
|  |  | 500 | |

Now, by deducting the discount from the 500*l.*, we have the present worth.

11,0)500,0

*Discount,* £45 . 9*s.* 1$\frac{1}{11}$*d.*

|  | £ | *s.* | *d.* |
|---|---|---|---|
| Thus | 500 . | 0 . | 0 |
|  | 45 . | 9 . | 1$\frac{1}{11}$ |

*Present worth,* £454 . 10 . 10$\frac{10}{11}$

---

time ; but if I pay it before it is due, it is giving that benefit to another. Hence, it only remains to inquire what discount ought, in this case, to be allowed ; and here some debtors may say, that since, by not paying the money till it becomes due, they can employ it at interest, therefore, by paying it before it is due, they shall lose that advantage, and for that reason all such interest ought to be discounted ; but this mode of reasoning is not just, for they cannot be said to lose that interest till the time the debt becomes due arrives ; whereas we are to consider what would properly be lost at present, by paying the debt before it becomes due ; and this can, in point of equity or justice, be no other than such a sum as, being put out to interest till the debt becomes due, would amount to the interest of the debt for that time. It is, besides, plain, that the advantage arising from discharging a debt, due some time hence, by a present payment, according to the principles here mentioned, is exactly the same as employing the whole sum at interest till the time the debt becomes due arrives ; for if the discount allowed for present payment be put out to interest for that time, its amount will be the same as the interest of the whole debt for the same time. Thus, the discount of 105*l.* due one year hence, reckoning interest at 5 per cent., will be 5*l.*, and 5*l.* put out to interest at 5 per cent. for one year, will amount to 5*s.*, which, with the 5*l.* discount on 105*l.*, is exactly equal to the interest of 105*l.* for one year at 5 per cent.

The truth of the rule for working is evident from the nature of simple interest ; for since the debt may be considered as the amount of

*Or to find the present worth, and hence the discount.*

£    £    £
110 : 100 :: 500
      500

———

11,0)5000,0

———

£454. 10s. 10$\frac{10}{11}$d. <sup>present worth.</sup>

———

Now, by deducting the present worth from the 500*l.*, we have the discount.

£   *s.*   *d.*

Thus   500 . 0 . 0
      454 . 10 . 10$\frac{10}{11}$

———

*The discount* £45 . 9 . 1$\frac{1}{11}$ <sup>as before.</sup>

(2.) What is the present worth of 150*l.* payable in $\frac{1}{4}$ year, discounting at 5 per cent.?    *Ans.* 148*l.* 2*s.* 11$\frac{1}{2}$*d.*

(3.) What is the present worth of 75*l.* due 15 months hence, at 5 per cent.?    *Ans.* 70*l.* 11*s.* 9*d.*

(4.) What is the discount on 85*l.* 10*s.* due September the 8th, this being July the 4th, reckoning interest at 5 per cent. per annum?    *Ans.* 15*s.* 3$\frac{3}{4}$*d.*

(5.) What ready money will discharge a debt of 543*l.* 7*s.* due 4 months and 18 days hence, at 4$\frac{5}{8}$ per cent. per annum?    *Ans.* 533*l.* 18*s.* 1$\frac{1}{2}$*d.*

(6.) Bought a quantity of goods for 150*l.* ready money, and sold them again for 200*l.* payable $\frac{3}{4}$ of a year hence; what was the gain in ready money, supposing discount to be made at 5 per cent.?    *Ans.* 42*l.* 15*s.* 5*d.*

(7.) What is the present worth of 120*l.* payable as follows: viz. 50*l.* at 3 months, 50*l.* at 5 months, and the rest at 8 months, discounting at 6 per cent.?    *Ans.* 117*l.* 5*s.* 5*d.*

# Compound Interest.

COMPOUND INTEREST is that which arises from adding the interest, as it becomes due, to the principal, and then considering the sum that accrues, at the end of each stated time of payment, as a new principal.

———

some principal (called here the present worth) at a certain rate per cent. and for the given time, that amount must be in the same proportion, either to its principal or interest, as the amount of any other sum, at the same rate, and for the same time, is to its principal or interest.

*Note.* When goods are bought or sold, and discount is to be made for present payment, at any rate per cent., without regard to time, the interest of the sum, as calculated for a year, is the discount.

### RULE.*

Find the amount of the given principal, for the time of the first payment, by simple interest.

Then consider this amount as the principal for the second payment, the amount of which calculate as before, and so on through all the payments to the last, still accounting the last amount as the principal for the next payment.

### EXAMPLES.

(1.) What is the amount of 320*l*. 10*s*. for four years, at 5 per cent. per annum, compound interest?

$$
\begin{array}{lll}
\pounds & s. & d.
\end{array}
$$

$\frac{1}{20}$)320 . 10 . 0   *1st year's principal.*
  16 . 0 . 6   *1st year's interest.*

$\frac{1}{20}$)336 . 10 . 6   *2nd year's principal.*
  16 . 16 . 6$\frac{1}{4}$   *2nd year's interest.*

$\frac{1}{20}$)353 . 7 . 0$\frac{1}{4}$   *3rd year's principal.*
  17 . 13 . 4   *3rd year's interest.*

$\frac{1}{20}$)371 . 0 . 4$\frac{1}{4}$   *4th year's principal*
  18 . 11 . 0   *4th year's interest.*

£389 . 11 . 4$\frac{1}{4}$ *whole amount, or the answer required.*

(2.) What is the compound interest of 760*l*. 10*s*. forborne 4 years, at 4 per cent. ?     *Ans.* 129*l*. 3*s*. 6$\frac{1}{4}$*d*.

(3.) What is the amount of 15*l*. 10*s*. for 9 years, at 3$\frac{1}{2}$ per cent. per annum, compound interest?   *Ans.* 21*l*. 2*s*. 5$\frac{1}{2}$*d*.

(4.) What is the compound interest of 410*l*. forborne for 2$\frac{1}{2}$ years, at 4$\frac{1}{2}$ per cent. per annum; the interest payable half-yearly?     *Ans.* 48*l*. 4*s*. 11$\frac{1}{4}$*d*.

(5.) Find the several amounts of 50*l*. payable yearly, half-yearly, and quarterly, supposing it to have been forborne 5 years, at 5 per cent. per annum, compound interest.

*Ans.* 63*l*. 16*s*. 3$\frac{1}{4}$*d*. ; 64*l*. 0*s*. 1*d*. ; *and* 64*l*. 2*s*. 0$\frac{1}{4}$*d*.

---

* The reason of this rule is evident from the definition, and the principles of simple interest.

Money cannot lawfully be lent at compound interest; but in granting or purchasing annuities leases, or reversions. compound interest is allowed.

# Equation of Payments.

EQUATION OF PAYMENTS is the finding a time to pay, at once, several debts due at different times, so that no loss shall be sustained by either party.

### RULE.*

Multiply each payment by the time at which it is due; then divide the sum of the products by the sum of the payments, and the quotient will be the time required.

### EXAMPLES.

(1.) A. owes B. 190*l.* to be paid as follows, viz. 50*l.* in 6 months, 60*l.* in 7 months, and 80*l.* in 10 months; what is the equated time to pay the whole?

---

* This rule is founded upon a supposition, that the sum of the interests of the several debts which are payable before the equated time, from their several terms to that time, ought to be equal to the sum of the interests of the debts payable after the equated time, from that time to their terms; which some writers have defended, by observing that what is gained by keeping some of the debts after they are due is lost by paying others before they are due; but this is not the case; for though by keeping a debt unpaid after it is due, there is gained the interest of it for that time, yet by paying a debt before it is due, the payer does not lose the interest for that time, but the discount only, which is less than the interest; and therefore the rule is not true. In most questions, however, that occur in business, the error is so trifling, that it will always be made use of as the most eligible method.

That the rule is universally agreeable to the supposition may be thus demonstrated:

Let $\begin{cases} d = \text{first debt payable, and } t \text{ the distance of its term.} \\ \text{D} = \text{last debt payable, and T the distance of its term.} \\ x = \text{distance of the equated time.} \\ r = \text{rate of interest of } 1l. \text{ for one year.} \end{cases}$

Then, since $x$ lies between T and $t$, the distance of the time $t$ and $x$ is $= x - t$; and the distance of the time T and $x$ is $= \text{T} - x$.

But the interest of $d$ for the time $x - t$ is $dr(x-t)$; and the interest of D for the time $\text{T} - x$ is $\text{D}r(\text{T}-x)$: hence $dr(x-t) = \text{D}r(\text{T}-x)$ by the supposition; and consequently, from this equation, $x = \dfrac{\text{DT} + dt}{\text{D} + d}$, which is the rule; and the same may be shown of any number of payments.

The rule is given in equation of payments by decimals.

$$50 \times \quad 6 = 300$$
$$60 \times \quad 7 = 420$$
$$80 \times \quad 10 = 800$$

$$50 + 60 + 80 = 190)\overline{1520}(8$$
$$\phantom{50 + 60 + 80 = 190)}1520$$

*Answer,* 8 *months.*

(2.) A. owes B. 52*l.* 7*s.* 6*d.* to be paid in $4\frac{1}{2}$ months, 80*l.* 10*s.* to be paid in $3\frac{1}{2}$ months, and 76*l.* 2*s.* 6*d.* to be paid in 5 months ; what is the equated time to pay the whole ?
*Ans.* 4 *mo.* 8 *da.* 21 *h.*

(3.) A. owes B. 240*l.* to be paid in 6 months, but in 1 month and a half pays him 60*l.* and in $4\frac{1}{2}$ months 80*l.* more ; how much longer, therefore, than 6 months should B. in equity defer the rest ?
*Ans.* $3\frac{9}{10}$ *months.*

(4.) A debt is to be paid as follows : viz. $\frac{1}{4}$ at two months, $\frac{1}{8}$ at 3 months, $\frac{1}{6}$ at 4 months, $\frac{1}{8}$ at 5 months, and the rest at 7 months ; what is the equated time to pay the whole ?
*Ans.* 4 *mo.* 18 *da. and* 18 *h.*

(5.) A. owes B. 100*l.* to be paid in 9 months, and 500*l.* to be paid in a year and a half : from which it is required to find the equated time when the whole ought to be paid.
*Ans.* $16\frac{1}{2}$ *months.*

(6.) A debt of 1000*l.* is to be paid as follows : viz. $\frac{1}{2}$ at 8 months, $\frac{1}{3}$ at 12 months, and the rest in $1\frac{1}{2}$ year : from which it is required to find the equated time when the whole should be paid.
*Ans.* 11 *months.*

# Barter.

BARTER is the exchanging of one kind of commodity for another ; and directs merchants and tradesmen so to proportion the value of their goods that neither party may sustain loss.

## RULE.*

Find the value of that commodity whose quantity is given, then find what quantity of the other, at the rate proposed,

---

* .This rule is, evidently, only an application of the common Rule of Three, or of Compound Multiplication.

may be had for the same money, and the result will be the answer.

EXAMPLES.

(1.) How many dozens of candles, at 5s. per dozen, must be given in barter for 3 cwt. of tallow, at 1l. 17s. 4d. per cwt.?

```
              £   s.  d.
              1 . 17 . 4
                       3
                     ———————            doz.
        s.
        5  :  5 . 12 . 0  ::  1
              20
              ———————
              5)112
              ———————
        22 doz. 4⅘ lb. = the answer.
```

(2.) How much sugar, at 8d. per lb. must be given in barter for 20 cwt. of tobacco, at 3l. per cwt.?

*Ans.* 16 cwt. 0 qr. 8 lb.

(3.) How much tea, at 9s. per lb., can I have in barter for 4 cwt. 2 qrs. of chocolate, at 4s. per lb.? *Ans.* 2 cwt.

(4.) How many reams of paper, at 2s. 9½d. per ream, must be given in barter for 37 pieces of Irish cloth, at 1l. 12s. 4d. per piece? *Ans.* 428³⁶/₆₇.

(5.) A merchant has 1000 yards of canvas, at 9½d. per yard, which he barters for serge at 10¼d. per yard; how many yards must he receive? *Ans.* 926³⁴/₄₁.

(6.) A. delivered 3 hhds. of brandy, at 6s. 8d. per gallon, to B., for 126 yards of cloth; what was the cloth per yard?

*Ans.* 10s.

(7.) A. and B. barter; A. has 41 cwt. of hops, at 30s. per cwt., for which B. gives him 20l. in money, and the rest in prunes at 5d. per lb., what quantity of prunes must A. receive? *Ans.* 17 cwt. 3 qrs. 4 lb.

(8.) A. has a quantity of pepper, wt. 1600 lb. at 17d. per lb., which he barters with B. for two sorts of goods, the one at 5d. the other at 8d. per lb., and to have ⅓ in money, and of each sort of goods an equal quantity: how many lbs. of each must he receive, and how much in money?

*Ans.* 1394³⁴/₃₉ lb. and 37l. 15s. 6⅔d.

# Profit and Loss.

PROFIT AND LOSS is a rule that discovers what is gained or lost in the purchase or sale of goods; and instructs merchants and traders so to raise or lower the price of their commodities, as to gain or lose so much per cent. &c.

Questions in this rule are performed by the common Rule of Three, Practice, &c.

### EXAMPLES.

(1.) How must I sell tea per lb. that cost me 13s. 5d., to gain after the rate of 25 per cent.?

```
  £         £           s.  d.
 100  :   125   ::     13 . 5
          161          12
          ___          ___                    Or thus,
          125          161       25 per cent is ¼,
          750          ___                     s.  d.
          125                    Therefore ¼)13 . 5
          _____                                3 . 4¼
     1,00)201,25
                                 16s. 9¼d.=Ans.
     12)201 25/100                _____

       16s.  9¼d.=the answer.
```

(2.) At 1½d. in the shilling profit, how much per cent.?
             *Ans.* 12l. 10s.

(3.) At 3s. 6d. in the pound profit, how much per cent.?
             *Ans.* 17l. 10s.

(4.) If a lb. of tobacco cost 16d. and is sold for 20d., what is the gain per cent.?         *Ans.* 25l.

(5.) Bought goods at 4½d. per lb. and sold them at the rate of 2l. 7s. 4d. per cwt., what was the gain per cent.?
          *Ans.* 12l. 13s. 11½d.

(6.) Bought cloth at 7s. 6d. per yard, which not proving so good as I expected, it is required to find how I must sell it per yard, so as to lose only 17½ per cent.  *Ans.* 6s. 2¼d.

(7.) Bought goods at 2 guineas per cwt. and sold them again retail at 5¼d. per lb., what shall I gain per cent.?
          *Ans.* 16l. 13s. 4d.

(8.) If I buy $17\frac{1}{2}$ cwt. of sugar for 35 guineas, and retail it at $7\frac{1}{2}d$. per lb., what was the gain per cent.?

*Ans.* 66*l.* 13*s.* 4*d.*

(9.) If I buy tobacco at 10 guineas per cwt., at what rate must I retail it per lb., to gain 12 per cent.? *Ans.* 2*s.* 1$\frac{1}{4}$*d.*

(10.) If, when I sell cloth at 7*s.* per yard, I gain 10 per cent., what will be the gain per cent. when it is sold for 8*s.* 6*d.* per yard? *Ans.* 33*l.* 11*s.* 5$\frac{1}{7}$*d.*

(11.) If I buy 28 pieces of stuffs at 4*l.* per piece, and sell 10 of the pieces at 6*l.* and 8 at 5*l.* per piece, at what rate per piece must I sell the rest, to gain 20 per cent. by the whole?

*Ans.* 3*l.* 8*s.* 9$\frac{1}{2}$*d.* $\frac{2}{5}f.$

(12.) Bought 40 gallons of cider at 3*s.* per gall., but by accident 6 gallons of it were lost; at what rate must I sell the remainder per gallon, to gain upon the whole prime cost at the rate of 10 per cent.? *Ans.* 3*s.* 10$\frac{1}{2}$*d.* $\frac{6}{17}f.$

(13.) Bought hose in London at 4*s.* 3*d.* per pair, and sold them afterwards in Dublin at 6*s.* the pair ; now, taking the charge at an average to be 2*d.* the pair, and considering that I must lose 12 per cent. by remitting my money home again, what do I gain per cent. by this article of trade?

*Ans.* 19*l.* 10*s.* 11$\frac{1}{4}$*d.*

(14.) Sold a repeating watch for 50 guineas, and by so doing lost 17 per cent., whereas I ought in dealing to have cleared 20 per cent.: how much was it sold for under the just value? *Ans.* 23*l.* 8*s.* 0$\frac{3}{4}$*d.*

# Fellowship.

FELLOWSHIP is a rule, by which merchants, &c. trading in company with a joint stock, are enabled to ascertain each person's particular share of the gain or loss, in proportion to his share in the joint stock.

By this rule a bankrupt's estate may be divided amongst his creditors, as also legacies adjusted, when there is a deficiency of assets or effects.*

---

* By this rule, a given number or quantity may be divided into any number of parts which shall have an assigned ratio to each other; which is done by saying, as 1 + 2 + 3 &c. the number of parts : the given number :: each of these parts : the proportional parts required.

## Single Fellowship.

SINGLE FELLOWSHIP is when different stocks are employed for any certain equal time.

### RULE.*

As the whole stock is to the whole gain or loss, so is each man's particular stock to his particular share of the gain or loss.

### METHOD OF PROOF.

Add all the shares of gain or loss together, and the sum will be equal to the whole gain or loss, when the work is right.

### EXAMPLES.

(1.) Two persons trade together; A. put into stock 130*l.* and B. 220*l.*, and they gained 500*l.*: what is each person's share of the profit?

*Here* 130*l.* + 220*l.* = 350*l.* = *the whole stock.*
*Then* 350*l.* : 500*l.* :: 130*l.* : *x.*

*or, as* 7*l.* : 100*l.* :: 13*l.* : $\dfrac{13 \times 100}{7}l. = \dfrac{1300}{7}l. =$ 185*l.* 14*s.* $3\frac{1}{4}$*d.* $\frac{5}{7}f.$ = A's

*share* = 1*st Ans.*

*Again* 350*l.* : 500*l.* :: 220*l.* : *x.*

*or, as* 7*l.* : 100*l.* :: 22*l.* : $\dfrac{22 \times 100}{7}l. = \dfrac{2200}{7}l. =$ 314*l.* 5*s.* $8\frac{1}{2}$*d.* $\frac{2}{7}f.$ B's share

= 2*nd Ans.*

*The Proof* = 185*l.* 14*s.* $3\frac{1}{4}$*d.* $\frac{5}{7}f.$ + 314*l.* 5*s.* $8\frac{1}{2}$*d.* $\frac{2}{7}f.$ = 500*l.* 0*s.* 0*d.*

(2.) A. and B. have gained by trading 182*l.*; A. put into stock 300*l.* and B. 400*l.*; what is each person's share of the profit? 　　　　*Ans. A.* 78*l. and B.* 104*l.*

(3.) Divide 120*l.* between three persons, so that their shares shall be to each other as 1, 2, and 3, respectively.

*Ans.* 20*l.*, 40*l.*, *and* 60*l.*

---

* That the gain or loss in this rule is in proportion to the respective stocks is evident; for, as the times the stocks are in trade are equal, if I put in $\frac{1}{2}$ of the whole stock, I ought to have $\frac{1}{2}$ of the whole gain; if my part of the whole stock be $\frac{1}{3}$, my share of the whole gain or loss ought also to be $\frac{1}{3}$; and generally, if I put in $\dfrac{1}{n}$ of the stock, I ought to

have $\dfrac{1}{n}$ part of the whole gain or loss; that is, whatever ratio the whole stock has to the whole gain or loss, the same ratio must each person's particular stock have to his respective gain or loss.

(4.) Three persons make a joint stock : A. put in 184*l*. 10*s*., B. 96*l*. 15*s*., and C. 76*l*. 5*s*. : they trade and gain 220*l*. 12*s*.; what is each person's share of the profit?

*Ans.* A. 113*l*. 16$\frac{688}{715}$*s*., B. 59*l*. 14$\frac{12}{715}$*s*., C. 47*l*. 1$\frac{15}{715}$*s*.

(5.) Four persons in partnership, A., B., C., and D., put into stock 180*l*., 240*l*., 350*l*., and 430*l*. respectively, for 5 years certain, and at the end of that time they find they have gained 3600*l*. : what is each person's share of the profit?

*Ans.* A. 540*l*., B. 720*l*., C. 1050*l*., and D. 1290*l*.

(6.) Three merchants, A., B., and C., freight a ship with 340 tuns of wine; A. loaded 110 tuns, B. 97, and C. the rest. In a storm the seamen were obliged to throw 85 tuns over-board; how much must each sustain of the loss?

*Ans.* A. 27$\frac{1}{2}$, B. 24$\frac{1}{4}$, and C. 33$\frac{1}{4}$.

(7.) A ship worth 860*l*. being entirely lost, of which $\frac{1}{8}$ belonged to A., $\frac{1}{4}$ to B., and the rest to C., what loss will each sustain, supposing 500*l*. of her to have been insured?

*Ans.* A. 45*l*., B. 90*l*., and C. 225*l*.

(8.) A bankrupt is indebted to A. 275*l*. 14*s*., to B. 304*l*. 7*s*., to C. 152*l*., and to D. 104*l*. 6*s*., and his estate is worth only 675*l*. 15*s*., how must it be divided?

*Ans.* A. 222*l*. 15*s*. 2*d*., B. 245*l*. 18*s*. 1$\frac{1}{2}$*d*., C. 122*l*. 16*s*. 2$\frac{3}{4}$*d*., and D. 84*l*. 5*s*. 5*d*.

(9.) A. and B., venturing equal sums of money, clear by joint trade 154*l*. By agreement A. was to have 8 per cent. on account of the time he spent in the execution of the pro-ject, and B. was to have only 5 per cent.; what was A. allowed for his trouble? *Ans.* 35*l*. 10*s*. 9$\frac{2}{13}$*d*.

(10.) A person ordered 1000*l*. to be divided among his three sons, so that A. might have $\frac{1}{3}$ part, B. $\frac{1}{4}$, and C. $\frac{1}{5}$; what is the just share of each?

*Ans.* A. 425*l*. 10*s*. 7$\frac{1}{2}$*d*., B. 319*l*. 2*s*. 11$\frac{1}{2}$*d*., C. 255*l*. 6*s*. 4$\frac{1}{2}$*d*.

(11.) Three merchants, in partnership, A., B., and C., put into stock 2000*l*., 3500*l*., and 4550*l*. respectively, for 3 years certain, and at the end of that time find they have cleared 10000*l*., what is each person's share of the gain?

*Ans.* A. 1990*l*. 0*s*. 11$\frac{3}{4}$*d*., B. 3482*l*. 11*s*. 8$\frac{3}{4}$*d*., C. 4527*l*. 7*s*. 3*d*.

(12.) A detachment, consisting of 4 companies, being sent into a garrison, in which the duty requires 60 men a day, what number must each company furnish, in proportion to its strength, the 1st consisting of 42 men, the 2d of 49, the 3d of 56, and the 4th of 63?

*Ans.* 1st 12 *men*, 2nd 14, 3rd 16, 4th 18.

# Double Fellowship.

DOUBLE FELLOWSHIP is when equal or different stocks are employed for different times.

## RULE.*

Multiply each man's stock into the time of its continuance, then say:

As the sum of all the products is to the whole gain or loss, so is each man's particular product to his particular share of the gain or loss.

## EXAMPLES.

(1.) A. and B. hold a piece of ground in common, for which they are to pay 36*l.* A. put in 23 oxen for 27 days, and B. 21 oxen for 39 days; what ought each man to pay of the rent?

*Here* 23 × 27 = 621, *and* 21 × 39 = 819.

*Then* (621 + 819 = )1440 : 36*l.* :: 621 : *x.*

*or, as* 40 : 1*l.* :: 621 : $\frac{621}{40}$*l.* = 15*l.* 10*s.* 6*d.* = A.'s *share* = 1st *Ans.*

*Again, as* 40 : 1*l.* :: 819 : $\frac{819}{40}$*l.* = 20*l.* 9*s.* 6*d.* = B.'s *share* = 2nd *Ans.*

(2.) Two troops of horse rent a field, for which they are to pay 82*l.*; one of the troops sent 64 horses for 25 days, and the other 56 horses for 30 days: how much of the rent must each troop pay? *Ans.* 1st. *troop* 40*l.*; 2nd. 42*l.*

(3.) A., B., and C. hold a pasture in common, for which they pay 30*l.* per annum; A. put into it 7 oxen for 3 months,

---

* Several authors have given an analytical investigation of this rule; but the principle on which it is founded may be easily shown, as follows:—

When the times are equal, the shares of the gain or loss are evidently as the stocks, as in single fellowship; and when the stocks are equal, the shares are as the times; consequently, when neither of them are equal, the shares must be as their products.

B. 9 oxen for 5 months, and C. 4 for 12 months : what must each pay of the rent?

*Ans. A. 5l. 10s. 6¼d. ₁⁵₉f., B. 11l. 16s. 10d. ₁⁸₉f., and C. 12l. 12s. 7½d. ₁⁶₃f.*

(4.) Three graziers hired a piece of land for 60l. 10s.; A. put in 5 sheep for 4½ months, B. put in 8 for 5 months, and C. put in 9 for 6½ months : how much must each pay of the rent? *Ans. A. 11l. 5s., B. 20l., and C. 29l. 5s.*

(5.) Two merchants enter into partnership for 18 months ; A. put into stock at first 200l., and at 8 months' end he put in 100l. more ; B. put in at first 550l. and at 4 months' end took out 140l. Now at the expiration of the time they find they have gained 526l.; what is each man's just share?

*Ans. A. 192l. 19s. 0d. ₂¹¹₀²₉f.; B. 333l. 0s. 11¾d. ₂⁹₀⁷₉f.*

(6.) A. with a capital of 1000l. began trade January 1st, 1852, and, meeting with success in business, took in B. as a partner, with a capital of 1500l. on the 1st of March following. Three months after this they admit C. as a third partner, who brought into stock 2800l., and after trading together till the first of the next year, they find there has been gained, since A.'s commencing business, 1776l. 10s.; how must this be divided amongst the partners?

*Ans. A. 457l. 9s. 4¼d., B. 571l. 16s. 8¼d., C. 747l. 3s. 11¼d.*

(7.) A ship's company take a prize of 1000l., which is to be divided between them according to their pay, and the time they have been on board. Now the officers, who are 4 in number, and have each 40s. a month, and the midshipmen, who are 12 in number, and have each 30s. a month, have been on board 6 months; and the sailors, who are 110 in number, and have each 22s. a month, have been on board 3 months : what will be the share of each?

*Ans. Each officer 23l. 2s. 5d., each midshipman 17l. 6s. 9¾d., each seaman 6l. 7s. 2d.*

# Alligation.

ALLIGATION is the method of finding the value of any mixture or compound, that is formed of several ingredients ; the rule for which resolves itself into the following cases.

I 2

## CASE I.

*When the rates and quantities of the several ingredients are given, to find the value of the compound.*

### RULE.*

Multiply each quantity by its rate ; then divide the sum of the products by the sum of the quantities, or the whole composition, and the quotient will be the rate of the compound required.

### EXAMPLES.

(1.) Suppose 15 bushels of barley at 5s. per bushel, and 12 bushels of rye at 3s. 6d. per bushel, were mixed together : how must the compound be sold per bushel without loss or gain ?

$$5s.=60d. \qquad 3s.\ 6d.=42d. \qquad 15$$
$$15 \qquad\qquad 12 \qquad\qquad 12$$
$$\overline{900} \qquad\qquad \overline{504} \qquad\qquad \overline{27}\ \text{sum of the quantities.}$$
$$\qquad\qquad 900$$
$$\qquad\qquad \overline{\phantom{000}}$$
$$27)1404(52d.=4s.\ 4d.=the\ Ans.$$
$$135$$
$$\overline{\phantom{00}}$$
$$54$$
$$54$$
$$\overline{\phantom{00}}$$
$$\cdot\ \cdot$$

(2.) A composition being made of 5 lb. of tea at 7s. per lb., 9 lb. at 8s. 6d. per lb., and 14½ lb. at 5s. 10d. per lb., what is a lb. of it worth ?            *Ans.* 6s. 10½d.

(3.) Mixed 4 gallons of low wine at 4s. 10d. per gall. with 7

---

* The truth of this rule is too evident to need a demonstration.

*Note.* The 24*th* part of a pound of pure gold is called a carat; and if any mass of this metal be mixed with another of a baser kind, which is called the alloy, the mixture is said to be of so many carats fine, according to the proportion of pure gold contained in it; thus, if 22 carats of pure gold and 2 of alloy are mixed together, it is said to be 22 carats fine.

An ounce, or any other mass of silver, on the contrary, is said to be of so many pennyweights fine, according to the number of pennyweights of pure silver contained in it; and if, in either of these cases, any one of the simples should be of little or no value with respect to the rest, its rate is supposed to be nothing, as water mixed with wine, and alloy with gold or silver.

gallons at 5s. 3d. per gall., and 9¾ gallons at 5s. 8d. per gall.; what is a gallon of this composition worth? *Ans.* 5s. 4¼d.

(4.) A mealman would mix 3 bushels of coarse flour at 3s. 5d. per bushel, 4 bushels at 5s. 6d. per bushel, and 5 bushels at 4s. 8d. per bushel; what is the worth of a bushel of this mixture? *Ans.* 4s. 7½d.

(5.) A goldsmith melts 8 lb. 5½ oz. of gold bullion of 14 carats fine, with 12 lb. 8½ oz. of 18 carats fine: how many carats fine is this mixture? *Ans.* 16$\frac{5}{127}$ carats.

(6.) A refiner melts 10 lb. of gold of 20 carats fine, with 16 lb. of 18 carats fine; how much alloy must be put to it to make it 22 carats fine?

*Ans. It is not fine enough by* 3$\frac{3}{13}$ *carats, so that no alloy must be put to it, but more gold.*

### CASE II.

*To find what quantity of any number of ingredients, whose rates are given, will compose a mixture of a given rate.*

#### RULE.*

1. Write down the rates of the ingredients in a column directly under each other.

2. Connect by a curved line, the rate of each simple, which is less than that of the compound, with one or any number of those that are greater, and each greater rate with one or any number of those that are less.

3. Put the difference between the mixture rate, and that of each of the simples opposite the contrary rate with which it is linked.

4. Then if only one difference stand against any rate, it will be the quantity belonging to that rate; but if there be several, their sum will be the quantity.

#### EXAMPLES.

(1.) A merchant would mix wines at 17s., 18s. and 22s. per gallon, so as that the mixture may be worth 20s. the gallon; what quantity of each must be taken?

---

* *Demon.* By connecting the less rate with the greater, and placing the differences between them and the mean rate, alternately, the quantities resulting are such, that there is precisely as much gained by one quantity as is lost by the other, and therefore the gain and loss upon the

(6.) How much sugar at 4*d*., at 6*d*., and at 11*d*. per lb.

$$20 \begin{cases} 17 \\ 18 \\ \\ 22 \end{cases} \begin{cases} 2 \ at \ 17s. \\ 2 \ at \ 18s. \\ \\ 3+2=5 \ at \ 22s. \end{cases}$$

Obs. 22−20=2
22−20=2
$\left. \begin{array}{l} 20-17=3 \\ 20-18=2 \end{array} \right\} =5$

Ans. 2 *gallons at* 17*s*.; 2 *at* 18*s*.; *and* 5 *at* 22*s*.
Proof 2 *gals.*    *at* 17*s*.= 34*s*.
      2 *gals.*    *at* 18*s*.= 36*s*.
      5 *gals.*    *at* 22*s*.=110*s*.
      ‾9               9)‾180*s*.
*Value of the mixture* ‾20*s*.

(2.) How much low wine at 6*s*. per gallon, and at 4*s*. per gallon, must be mixed together, that the composition may be worth 5*s*. per gallon?       *Ans.* 1 *qt. or* 1 *gal. &c.*

(3.) How much British spirits, at 12*s*. and 15*s*. per gallon, must be mixed with home-made wine at 7*s*. per gallon, in order to produce a mixture worth 10*s*. a gallon?

*Ans.* 3 *at* 12*s*.; 3 *at* 15*s*.; *and* 7 *at* 7*s*.

(4.) A goldsmith has gold of 17, 18, 22, and 24 carats fine; how much must he take of each to make it 21 carats fine?

*Ans.* 3 *of* 17; 1 *of* 18; 3 *of* 22; *and* 4 *of* 24.

(5.) It is required to mix British spirits at 8*s*., low wine at 7*s*., cider at 1*s*., and water at 0 per gallon together, so that the mixture may be worth 5*s*. per gallon.

*Ans.* 5 *gals. of brandy,* 4 *of wine,* 2 *of cider, and* 3 *of water.*

---

whole must be equal, and is exactly the proposed rate; and the same will be true of any other two simples managed according to the rule.

In like manner, let the number of simples be what they may, and with how many soever every one is linked, since it is always a less with a greater than the mean price, there will be an equal balance of loss and gain between every two, and consequently an equal balance on the whole.

It is obvious, from the rule, that questions of this sort admit of a great variety of answers; for having found one answer, we may find as many others as we please, by only multiplying or dividing each of the quantities found by 2, 3, or 4, &c., the reason of which is evident; for if two quantities of two simples make a balance of loss and gain, with respect to the mean price, so must also the double or treble, the $\frac{1}{2}$ or $\frac{1}{3}$ part, of any other equimultiples or parts of these quantities.

These kinds of questions are called by algebraists *indeterminate* or *unlimited* problems, and by an analytical process formulæ may be obtained that will enable us to ascertain all the various answers of which they are susceptible.

must be mixed together, so that the composition formed by them may be worth 7d. per lb. ?

*Ans. 4 lbs. of each sort, cr 1 lb , or 1 stone, or 1 cwt., or any other equal quantity of each sort, would be worth 7d. per lb.*

### CASE III.

*When the whole composition is limited to a certain quantity.*

#### RULE.*

Find an answer as before by linking; then say, as the sum of the quantities, or differences thus determined, is to the given quantity, so is each ingredient found by linking, to the required quantity of each.

---

* A great number of questions might be here given relating to the specific gravities of metals, &c.; but as they are best performed by other means, I shall only give one of the most curious of them, and work out the example at large.

Hiero, king of Syracuse, gave orders for a crown to be made for him of pure gold; but suspecting the workman had debased it, by mixing it with silver or copper, he recommended the discovery of the fraud to the celebrated Archimedes; and desired to know the exact quantity of alloy in the crown.

Archimedes, in order to detect the imposition, procured two other masses, the one of pure gold, the other of silver or copper, and each of the same weight with the former; and by putting them separately into a vessel full of water, the quantity of water expelled by them determined their specific gravities; from which, and their given weights, the quantities of gold and alloy in the crown may be determined.

Suppose for instance the weight of each mass to be 10 *lb.*, and that the water expelled by the copper or silver was ·92 *lb.*, by the gold ·52 *lb.*, and by the compound crown ·64 *lb* , and that it was required to find the quantities of gold and alloy in the crown.

Here the rates of the simple are 92 and 52, and of the compound 64; therefore,

$$64 \begin{array}{|l} 92 \quad . \quad . \quad . \quad 12 \text{ of copper or silver.} \\ 52 \quad . \quad . \quad . \quad 28 \text{ of gold.} \end{array}$$

for 64 − 52 = 12; and 92 − 64 = 28.

But the sum of these is 12 + 28 = 40, which should have been but 10; whence, by the rule,

$$40 : 10 :: 12 : 3 \text{ } lb. \text{ of copper} \Big\} \text{ the answer.}$$
$$40 : 10 :: 28 : 7 \text{ } lb. \text{ of gold} \quad$$

This method of solving the question, however, though very ingenious, is now known to be inaccurate; as the specific gravity of a compound, of two or more metals, often differs considerably from the mean of the metals of which it is composed.

### EXAMPLES.

(1.) How much gold of 15, 17, 18, and 22 carats fine, must be mixed together to form a composition of 40 oz. of 20 carats fine?

*Here the differences between each of the quantities and the mean rate, as found by linking, are as below.*

$$20 \begin{cases} 15 & \text{-} \quad \text{-} \quad \text{-} \quad 2 \\ 17 & \text{-} \quad \text{-} \quad \text{-} \quad 2 \\ 18 & \text{-} \quad \text{-} \quad \text{-} \quad 2 \\ \\ 22 & \quad 5+3+2=10 \end{cases}$$

*And* $2+2+2+10=16$, *their sum.*

*Whence, by the other part of the rule,*

$$16 : 40 :: \begin{cases} 2 & : \dfrac{40 \times 2}{16} = \dfrac{80}{16} = 5 \\ \\ 10 & : \dfrac{40 \times 10}{16} = \dfrac{400}{16} = 25 \end{cases}$$

*Ans. 5 oz. of 15, 17, and 18 carats fine, and 25 oz. of 22 carats fine.*

(2.) A grocer has currants at 4*d*., 6*d*., 9*d*., and 11*d*. per lb., and would make a mixture of 240 lb., so that it may be sold at 8*d*. per lb., how much of each sort must he take?
*Ans.* 72 *lb. at* 4*d.*; 24 *at* 6*d.*; 48 *at* 9*d.*; *and* 96 *at* 11*d.*

(3.) How many gallons of British spirits, at 12*s*., 15*s*., and 18*s*. a gallon, must a rectifier of compounds take to make a mixture of 1000 gallons, that shall be worth 17*s*. a gallon?
*Ans.* 111⅑ *at* 12*s.*; 111⅑ *at* 15*s.*; *and* 777⅞ *at* 18*s.*

(4.) A druggist has two sorts of bark, worth 5*s*. 9*d*. and 10*s*. a pound; what portion of each must he take to make a mixture of 1½ cwt. that shall be worth 8*s*. 6*d*. a lb.?
*Ans.* 59$\frac{5}{17}$ *lb. at* 5*s.* 9*d., and* 108$\frac{12}{17}$ *at* 10*s.*

---

* In the same manner questions of this kind may be worked when several of the ingredients are limited to certain quantities, by finding first for one limit, and then for another.

The last two rules want no demonstration, as they evidently result from the first, the reason of which has been already explained.

## CASE IV.

*When one of the ingredients is limited to a certain quantity.*

### RULE.*

Take the difference between each price and the mean rate as before; then,

As the difference of that simple whose quantity is given is to the rest of the differences respectively, so is the quantity given to the several quantities required.

### EXAMPLES.

(1.) How much home-made wine at 5s., at 5s. 6d., and 6s. the gallon, must be mixed with 3 gallons at 4s. per gallon, so that the mixture may be worth 5s. 4d. per gallon?

$$64 \begin{cases} 48 \\ 60 \\ 66 \\ 72 \end{cases} \begin{matrix} 8+2=10 \\ 8+2=10 \\ 16+4=20 \\ 16+4=20 \end{matrix}$$

$$
\begin{matrix}
10 & : & 10 & :: & 3 & : & 3 \\
10 & : & 20 & :: & 3 & : & 6 \\
10 & : & 20 & :: & 3 & : & 6
\end{matrix}
$$

*Ans. 3 gallons at 5s.; 6 at 5s. 6d.; and 6 at 6s.*

(2.) A grocer would mix teas at 12s., 10s., and 6s. per lb. with 20 lb. at 4s. per lb., how much of each sort must he take to make the composition worth 8s. per lb.?

*Ans. 20 lb. at 4s.; 10 lb. at 6s.; 10 lb. at 10s.; and 20 lb. at 12s.*

(3.) How much gold of 15, of 17, and of 22 carats fine must be mixed with 5 oz. of 18 carats fine, so that the composition may be 20 carats fine?

*Ans. 5 oz. of 15 carats fine, 5 oz. of 17, and 25 of 22.*

(4.) A rectifier of compounds, who has 500 gallons of spirits, worth 13s. 4d. a gallon, means to mix them with three other kinds, worth 12s. 6d., 14s., and 16s. 6d. per gallon, in order to sell the whole at 15s. 4d.; how much of each must he take?

*Ans. 500 gals. at 13s. 4d.; 500 gals. at 12s. 6d.; 500 at 14s.; and 2642⁶⁄₇ at 16s. 6d.*

## 𝔖imple 𝔦nterest by 𝔇ecimals.

### RULE.*

Multiply the ratio, or rate of interest of 1*l.* for 1 year, by the time, and this product being again multiplied by the principal, will give the interest required: which interest, added to the principal, gives the amount.

THE RATIO, or rate at simple interest of 1*l.* for 1 year, from 3 to 5 per cent. is as follows:

| £ | | £ | £ | £ | | £ | | £ |
|---|---|---|---|---|---|---|---|---|
| 3 *per cent. is* ·03 | for 100 | : | 1 | :: | 3 | : | ·03 |
| 3½ —— ·035 | for 100 | : | 1 | :: | 3½ | : | ·035 |
| 4 —— ·04 | for 100 | : | 1 | :: | 4 | : | ·04 |
| 4½ —— ·045 | for 100 | : | 1 | :: | 4½ | : | ·045 |
| 5 —— ·05 | for 100 | : | 1 | :: | 5 | : | ·05 |

The interest of 1*l.* for *one* day is thus found.

*days*     £     *day*          £
As 365  :  ·05  ::  1  :  ·0001369863.

### EXAMPLES.

(1.) What is the interest of 945*l.* 10*s.* for 3 years, at 5 per cent. per annum?

*Theorem or rule.*
$prt=i$
$p=945.5l.$
$r=.05$
$t=3$

$$
\begin{aligned}
&£ \\
&945{\cdot}5 \quad =p \\
&\phantom{945{\cdot}}{\cdot}05 \quad =r \\
\hline
&47{\cdot}275 \quad =pr \\
&\phantom{47{\cdot}27}3 \quad =t \\
\hline
&141{\cdot}825 \quad =prt=i, \textit{ the interest.} \\
&\phantom{141{\cdot}8}20 \\
\hline
&16{\cdot}500 \quad \textit{Ans. } 141l.\ 16s.\ 6d. \\
&\phantom{16{\cdot}5}12 \\
\hline
&6{\cdot}000
\end{aligned}
$$

---

* The following theorems will show all the possible cases of simple interest; observing that $i$ = the interest, $p$ = principal, $t$ = time, $a$ = amount, and $r$ the ratio, or the rate of interest of £1 for a year.

1. $i = prt$.

2. $a = p(tr+1) = prt + p$.

3. $p = \dfrac{a}{tr+1}$.

4. $t = \dfrac{a-p}{pr}$.

5. $r = \dfrac{a-p}{pt}$.

(2.) What is the interest of 796*l.* 15*s.* for 5 years, at 4 per cent. per ann. ? *Ans.* 159*l.* 7*s.*

(3.) What is the simple interest of 880*l.* for 1¼ year, at 3½ per cent. per ann. ? *Ans.* 38*l.* 10*s.*

(4.) What is the interest of 537*l.* 15*s.* from November 11th, 1852, to June 5th, 1853, at 3⅝ per cent. ? *Ans.* 11*l.* 0*s.* 0¼*d.*

# Discount by Decimals at Simple Interest.

### RULE.*

As the amount of 1*l.* for the given time, and at the given rate per pound, is to 1*l.*, so is the interest of the debt for that time to the discount required: and if the discount be subtracted from the principal, the remainder will be the present worth.

*A TABLE showing the number of days from one day of any month to the same day of any other month.*

| To | Jan. | Feb. | Mar. | Apr. | May | June | July | Aug. | Sept. | Oct. | Nov. | Dec. |
|---|---|---|---|---|---|---|---|---|---|---|---|---|
| | | | | | *From any day of* | | | | | | | |
| Jan. | 365 | 334 | 306 | 275 | 245 | 214 | 184 | 153 | 122 | 92 | 61 | 31 |
| Feb. | 31 | 365 | 337 | 306 | 276 | 245 | 215 | 184 | 153 | 123 | 92 | 62 |
| Mar. | 59 | 28 | 365 | 334 | 304 | 273 | 243 | 212 | 181 | 151 | 120 | 90 |
| April | 90 | 59 | 31 | 365 | 335 | 304 | 274 | 243 | 212 | 182 | 151 | 121 |
| May | 120 | 89 | 61 | 30 | 365 | 334 | 304 | 273 | 242 | 212 | 181 | 151 |
| June | 151 | 120 | 92 | 61 | 31 | 365 | 335 | 304 | 273 | 243 | 212 | 182 |
| July | 181 | 150 | 122 | 91 | 61 | 30 | 365 | 334 | 303 | 273 | 242 | 212 |
| Aug. | 212 | 181 | 153 | 122 | 92 | 61 | 31 | 365 | 334 | 304 | 273 | 243 |
| Sept. | 243 | 212 | 184 | 153 | 123 | 92 | 62 | 31 | 365 | 335 | 304 | 274 |
| Oct. | 273 | 242 | 214 | 183 | 153 | 122 | 92 | 61 | 30 | 365 | 334 | 304 |
| Nov. | 304 | 273 | 245 | 214 | 184 | 153 | 123 | 92 | 61 | 31 | 365 | 335 |
| Dec. | 334 | 303 | 275 | 244 | 214 | 183 | 153 | 122 | 91 | 61 | 30 | 365 |

*Note.* In leap-year, if the end of the month of February be in the time one day must be added on that account.

---

* If *s* represent the sum due, or the sum to be discounted, *i* the in-

### EXAMPLES.

(1.) What is the discount, and also the present worth of 573*l*. 15*s*. due 3 years hence, at $4\frac{1}{2}$ per cent. per annum?

*Here* ·045 *rate of* 1*l. per annum*=*r*.

$$3=t$$

*The formula is* $d=\dfrac{srt}{1+rt}$

·135=*rt*=*int. of* 1*l. for* 3 *years*.

1·

1·135=1+*rt*=*amount of* 1*l. for* 3 *years*.

$s=573\cdot75l.$
$r=\cdot045$
$t=3$

$573\cdot75=s$
$\cdot045=r$

286875
229500

25·81875=*sr*
3=*t*

*i*=77·45625=*srt*=*int. of the debt for* 3 *years*.

Then $77\cdot45625\div1\cdot135=68\cdot243l.=\dfrac{srt}{1+rt}=d$, *the discount*.

*Or* 1·135*l*. : 1*l*. :: 77·45625*l*. : 68·24341*l*.= 68*l*. 4*s*. 10½*d. the discount, as before*.

*And* 573*l*. 15*s*. −68*l*. 4*s*. 10½*d*.=505*l*. 10*s*. 1½*d. the present worth. Or the present worth may be found by the formula* $p=\dfrac{srt}{1+rt}$. *Thus,* 573 75÷1·135=505·506=505*l*. 10*s*. 1½*d*.

---

terest, *p* the present worth, *t* the time, *d* the discount, and *r* the rate of 1*l*. per annum, we shall have the following theorems : —

Thus, $i=srt$; $d=\dfrac{srt}{1+rt}$; $p=\dfrac{s}{1+rt}$, *present worth*.

$s=p(1+rt)$; $t=\dfrac{s-p}{rp}$; $r=\dfrac{s-p}{tp}$, *the rate*.

And if the same letters be retained, except making *r* in this case the rate per cent. per annum, the following table will represent all the varieties that can happen, with respect to present worth and discount, for any number of years, months, or days, according as the nature of the question may require.

(2.) What is the discount of 725*l.* 16*s.* for 5 months, at 3$\frac{7}{8}$ per cent. per annum? *Ans.* 11*l.* 10*s.* 7$\frac{3}{4}$*d.*

(3.) What ready money will discharge a debt of 1377*l.* 13*s.* 4*d.* due 2 years, 3 quarters, and 25 days hence, discounting at 4$\frac{3}{8}$ per cent. per annum? *Ans.* 1226*l.* 8*s.* 2$\frac{3}{4}$*d.*

| The present worth of any sum *s* at simple interest. | | | |
|---|---|---|---|
| Rate *per cent.* | For *t* years. | *t* months. | *t* days. |
| *r* per cent. | $\dfrac{100s}{tr+100}$ | $\dfrac{1200s}{tr+1200}$ | $\dfrac{36500s}{tr+36500}$ |

| The discount of any sum *s*, paid before it is due. | | | |
|---|---|---|---|
| Rate *per cent.* | For *t* years. | *t* months. | *t* days. |
| *r* per cent. | $\dfrac{str}{tr+100}$ | $\dfrac{str}{tr+1200}$ | $\dfrac{str}{tr+36500}$ |

*Note.* To find a general expression for discount, let $p =$ the principal, $r =$ interest of 1*l.* for 1 year, and $t =$ time in years.

Then, since the person who advances the money loses no more than such a sum as, being placed out at interest for the time, will amount to the interest of the debt, this sum or loss is the proper discount, to find which we have

$$1+rt : 1 :: prt : \frac{prt}{1+rt} = discount\ required. \quad \text{Or,}$$

$$present\ worth : p :: 1 : 1+rt,$$

$$\therefore the\ present\ worth = \frac{p}{1+rt},$$

$$\text{and}\ p - \frac{p}{1+rt} = \frac{prt}{1+rt} = discount\ as\ before.$$

# Equation of Payments by Decimals.

HAVING two debts due at different times, to find the equated time to pay the whole at once.

### RULE.*

1. To the continued product of the first payment, the time between the payments, and the ratio or interest of 1*l*. for a year, add the sum of the payments, and call the result the first number.

---

* No rule in Arithmetic has been the occasion of more disputes than that of Equation of Payments. Almost every writer upon this subject has endeavoured to show the fallacy of the methods made use of by others, and to substitute a new one of his own. But the only true rule, as it appears to me, is that given by MALCOLM *in page* 621. *of his Arithmetic*, the principles of which are derived from the consideration of interest and discount.

I have therefore rendered the rule, given above, conformable to that of MALCOLM, except that it is not encumbered with the time before any payment is due, that being no necessary part of the operation.

*Demon. of the Rule.* Suppose a sum of money to be due immediately, and another sum at the expiration of a certain given time forward, and that it is proposed to find a time to pay the whole at once, so that neither party shall sustain loss.

In this case it is plain, that the equated time must fall between the two payments; and that what is got by keeping the first debt after it is due, should be equal to what is lost by paying the second debt before it is due.

But the gain arising from the keeping of a sum of money after it is due, is evidently equal to the interest of the debt for that time; and the loss which is sustained by the paying of a sum of money before it is due, is equal to the discount of the debt for that time.

It is therefore obvious, that the debtor must retain the sum immediately due, or the first payment, till its interest shall be equal to the discount of the second sum for the time it is paid before it is due; because, in that case, the gain and loss will be equal, and consequently neither party can be the loser.

Hence, to find such a time, let $a = $ 1st payment, $b = $ second, and $t = $ time between the payments; $r = $ ratio or interest of 1*l*. for 1 year, and $x = $ equated time after the first payment.

Then $arx = $ interest of $a$ for $x$ time; and $(btr - brx) \div (1 + tr - rx) = $ discount of $b$ for the time $t - x$. But $arx = (btr - brx) \div (1 + tr - rx)$ by the question; from which equation

$$x = \frac{1}{2ar}(a + b + art) \pm \frac{1}{2ar} \sqrt{\{(a + b + art)^2 - 4abrt\}}.$$

2. From the square of this number, take four times the continued product of the two payments, the ratio, and time, and extract the square root of the difference, which result call the second number.

3. Subtract the second number from the first; and the difference, divided by twice the product of the ratio and first payment, will give the equated time, after the first payment is due.

---

Or if, for the sake of greater simplicity, there be put $n = (a + b) \times \dfrac{1}{ar}$, and $m = bt \times \dfrac{1}{ar}$, the last-mentioned equation will become

$$x = \tfrac{1}{2}(t + n) \pm \tfrac{1}{2}\sqrt{\{(t + n)^2 - 4m\}}.$$

And since $\tfrac{1}{2}(t + n)$, or its equal $\tfrac{1}{2}\sqrt{\{(t + n)^2\}}$, is evidently greater than $\tfrac{1}{2}\sqrt{\{(t + n)^2 - 4m\}}$, it is plain that $x$ will have two affirmative values, the quantities $\tfrac{1}{2}(t + n) + \tfrac{1}{2}\sqrt{\{(t + n)^2 - 4m\}}$, and $\tfrac{1}{2}(t + n) - \tfrac{1}{2}\sqrt{\{(t + n)^2 - 4m\}}$, being both positive.

But it can be easily shown that only one of these values will agree with the conditions of the question; the true answer, in all cases, being

$$x = \tfrac{1}{2}(t + n) - \tfrac{1}{2}\sqrt{\{(t + n)^2 - 4m\}}.$$

For suppose the contrary, and let $x = \tfrac{1}{2}(t + n) + \tfrac{1}{2}\sqrt{\{(t + n)^2 - 4m\}}$. Then $t - x = t - \tfrac{1}{2}(t + n) - \tfrac{1}{2}\sqrt{\{(t + n)^2 - 4m\}}$; or, since $t - \tfrac{1}{2}(t + n) = \tfrac{1}{2}(t - n) = \tfrac{1}{2}\sqrt{\{(t - n)^2\}} = \tfrac{1}{2}\sqrt{\{(t + n)^2 - 4tn\}}$, we shall have $t - x = \tfrac{1}{2}\sqrt{\{(t + n)^2 - 4tn\}} - \tfrac{1}{2}\sqrt{\{(t + n)^2 - 4m\}}$.

But since $4tn = (at + bt) \times \dfrac{4}{ar}$, and $4m = bt \times \dfrac{4}{ar}$, it is evident that $\tfrac{1}{2}\sqrt{\{(t + n)^2 - 4m\}}$ must be greater than $\tfrac{1}{2}\sqrt{\{(t + n)^2 - 4tn\}}$; whence $\tfrac{1}{2}\sqrt{\{(t + n)^2 - 4tn\}} - \tfrac{1}{2}\sqrt{\{(t + n)^2 - 4m\}}$, or its equal $t - x$, will be a negative quantity; and, consequently, $x$ will be greater than $t$; that is, the equated time will fall beyond the second payment, which is absurd.

From this demonstration, therefore, it appears, that the double sign, made use of by MALCOLM, and every author since, who has given his method, cannot obtain, there being no ambiguity in the problem.

The equated time for any number of payments may also be readily found when the question is proposed in numbers; but it would not be easy to give algebraic theorems for these cases, on account of the variation of the debts and times, and the difficulty of finding between which of the payments the equated time would fall.

Also, supposing $r$ to be the amount of $1l.$ for 1 year, and the other letters as before, then $t + \dfrac{\log.(a + b) - \log.(art + b)}{\log. r}$ will be a general theorem for the equated time of any two payments, reckoning compound interest; which is found in the same manner as the former.

## EXAMPLES.

(1.) Supposing 100*l.* to be payable 1 year hence, and 105*l.* 3 years hence; what is the equated time to pay the whole, allowing simple interest at 5 per cent. per annum ?

```
100  1st payment.              215                     105
  2  time between              215                     100
     the payments.
  ───                          ────                   ─────
200                           1075                    10500
 ·05 rate                      215                      ·05
  ───                           430                   ─────
10·00                         ─────                   525·00
205 = 100 + 105 sum of the    46225 sq. 1st. No.          2
              payments.        4200                   ─────
  ───                         ─────                   1050·00
215 the 1st Number.          42025(205, the 2d No.         4
                                4                      ─────
                              ─────                    4200·00
                              405)2025
                                  2025
```

*

$$Then\ \frac{215-205}{2 \times ·05 \times 100} = \frac{10}{·1 \times 100} = \frac{10}{10} = 1 \text{ year, the equated}$$

time from the first payment; and consequently two years is the whole equated time.

(2.) Suppose 400*l.* is to be paid at the end of 2 years, and 2100*l.* at the end of 8 years: what is the equated time for one payment, reckoning 5 per cent. simple interest?
*Ans.* 7 *years.*

(3.) Suppose 300*l.* is to be paid at the end of one year, and 300*l.* more at the end of 1½ year; it is required to find the time to pay the whole in one payment, allowing 5 per cent. simple interest. *Ans.* 1·248437 *years.*

(4.) A hundred pounds is to be paid at the end of 2½ years, and another 100*l.* at the end of 3½ years: required the equated time to pay the whole, allowing 4½ per cent. simple interest. *Ans.* 2·9938 *years.*

# Compound Interest by Decimals.

## RULE.*

Find the amount of 1*l*. for a year at a given rate per cent., and involve it to such a power as is denoted by the number of years.

Then multiply this power by the principal or given sum, and the product will be the amount required.

---

* *Demon.* Let *r* = amount of 1*l*. for 1 year, and *p* = principal or given sum; then, since *r* is the amount of 1*l*. for 1 year, $r^2$ will be its amount for two years, $r^3$ for three years, and so on; for when the rate and time are the same, all principal sums are necessarily as their amounts; and consequently as *r* is the principal for the second year, it will be as $1 : r :: r : r^2 =$ amount for the second year, or principal for the third; and again, as $1 : r :: r^2 : r^3 =$ amount for the third year, or principal for the fourth, and so to any number of years.

Hence, if the number of years be denoted by *t*, the amount of 1*l*. for *t* years will be $r^t$: from which it is plain, that the amount of any other principal sum *p* for *t* years is $pr^t$, and the interest for that time, $pr^t - p$; which is the same as by the rule.

And if the rate of interest be for any other time than a year, as $\frac{1}{2}$, $\frac{1}{4}$, &c., the rule is the same, making *t* represent that time.

Let *r* = amount of 1*l*. for one year, at the given rate per cent.; *p* = principal or sum put out to interest; *i* = interest; *t* = time; and *a* = amount for the time *t*.

Then the following theorems will exhibit the solutions of all the cases in compound interest—

1. $a = pr^t =$ *the amount.*      3. $i = p(r^t - 1) =$ *the interest.*

2. $p = \dfrac{a}{r^t} =$ *the principal.*   4. $100(r-1) = 100\left(\dfrac{a}{p}\right)^{\frac{1}{t}} - 100 =$ *rate per cent.*

But the most convenient way of giving these theorems for the time, as well as for all the rest, is by logarithms, as follows:

1. $\log. a = t . \log. r + \log. p.$      3. $t = \dfrac{\log. a - \log. p}{\log. r}.$

2. $\log. p = \log. a - t . \log. r.$      4. $\log. r = \dfrac{\log. a - \log. p}{t}.$

And if *r* be made to represent the amount of 1*l*. for 1 time of payment, and *t* the number of times, the above theorems will be equally true for $\frac{1}{2}$, $\frac{1}{4}$, or any other part or multiple of a year.

It may here also be remarked, that from theorem 1, given above, and theorem 2, in single interest, it can be readily found that any sum of money, put out to compound interest, at five per cent., will double itself in about $14\frac{1}{4}$ years; and if it be put out to simple interest, at 5 per cent., it will double itself in twenty years.

And if the principal be subtracted from the amount, the remainder will be the interest.

When $p$, $r$, $t$ are given, to find $i$.

RULE. $pr^t - p = i$.

EXAMPLES.

(1.) What is the compound interest of 500*l.* for 4 years, at 5 per cent. per annum?

$$1\text{·}05 = \textit{the amount of } 1l. \textit{for 1 year at}$$
$$\underline{1\text{·}05 = r \qquad\qquad 5 \textit{ per cent.}}$$
$$525$$
$$\underline{1050}$$
$$1\text{·}1025 = r^2$$
$$\underline{1\text{·}1025 = r^2}$$
$$55125$$
$$22050$$
$$11025$$
$$\underline{11025}$$
$$1\text{·}21550625 = r^4 = \textit{4th power of } 1\text{·}05.$$
$$\underline{500 = p = \textit{principal.}}$$
$$607\text{·}75312500 = pr^t\textit{; that is, } pr^4 = \textit{amount.}$$
$$\underline{500\ \ldots\ldots = p = \textit{principal.}}$$
$$107\text{·}753125 \quad = pr^t - p = i = 107l.\ 15s.\ 0\tfrac{3}{4}d.,\ \textit{the}$$
$$\textit{interest required.}$$

(2.) What is the amount of 760*l.* 10*s.* for 4 years, at 4 per cent. per annum? *Ans.* 889*l.* 13*s.* 6½*d.*

(3.) What is the compound interest of 760*l.* 10*s.* for 4 years, at 4 per cent. per annum? *Ans.* 129*l.* 3*s.* 6½*d.*

(4.) What is the amount of 721*l.* for 21 years, at 4 per cent. per annum? *Ans.* 1642*l.* 19*s.* 9½*d.*

(5.) What is the amount of 217*l.* forborne 2¼ years, at 5 per cent. per annum, supposing the interest payable quarterly? *Ans.* 242*l.* 13*s.* 4½*d.*

# Annuities.

An ANNUITY is any periodical income, payable from time to time, either annually, or at other intervals.

They are usually divided into such as are in possession, and such as are in reversion; the former being those that have already commenced, and the latter such as will not commence till some particular event has happened, or some given period of time has elapsed.

When the debtor keeps the annuity in his own hands beyond the time of payment, it is said to be in *arrears*.

Also the sum of all the annuities, for the time they have been forborne, together with the interest due upon each, is called the *amount*.

And if an annuity is to be bought off, or paid all at once, at the beginning of the first year, the price which ought to be given for it is called its *present worth*.

### PROBLEM I.

*To find the amount of an annuity at simple interest.*

#### RULE.*

Find the sum of the natural series of numbers, 1, 2, 3, &c. to the number of years less one.

Then multiply this sum by one year's interest of the annuity, and the product will give the whole interest due.

---

* *Demon.* Whatever the time is, there is due upon the first year's annuity, as many years' interest, as the whole number of years, less one; and gradually one less upon every succeeding year to the last but one; upon which there is only one year's interest due, and none upon the last; therefore in the whole there is due as many years' interest of the annuity as is denoted by the sum of the series, 1, 2, 3, 4, &c., continued to the number of years less one. Consequently, one year's interest multiplied by this sum must be the whole interest due; to which if the product of the annuity and time be added, the sum will evidently be the amount.

Let $r$ be the annual rate of $1l$, $n$ the annuity, $t$ the time, and $a$ the amount; then will the following theorems give the solutions of all the different cases of this rule:

1. $a = \dfrac{nt}{2}\left\{2 + (t-1)\,r\right\}$.    3. $r = \dfrac{2(a-nt)}{nt(t-1)}$.

2. $n = \dfrac{2a}{t\left\{2 + (t-1)r\right\}}$.    4. $t = \dfrac{1}{2rn}\left\{n^2(2-r)^2 \times 8arn\right\}^{\frac{1}{2}} - \dfrac{2-r}{2r}$.

The last of which involves the solution of a quadratic equation.

These theorems are equally true when the annuity is payable half-yearly, quarterly, &c., provided $t$ be made to represent the number of half-yearly, quarterly, &c. payments, and $r$ be the interest of $1l$. for the time when the first half-yearly, quarterly, &c. payment becomes due.

And if the interest be added to the product of the annuity and time, it will give the amount sought.

### EXAMPLES.

(1.) What is the amount of an annuity of 50*l.* for 7 years, allowing simple interest at 5 per cent.?

*Or by the formula,*

$$a = \frac{nt}{2}\{2 + (t-1)r\}.$$

$$1 + 2 + 3 + 4 + 5 + 6 = 21 = 3 \times 7.$$

| £ s. | | £ | |
|---|---|---|---|
| 2 10 = 1 *year's interest of 50l.* | | 50 = *n* | 7 = *t* |
| 3 × 7 = 21 | | 7 = *t* | 1 |
| | | | — |
| 7 10 | | 2)350 = *nt* | 6 = *t* − 1 |
| 7 | | — | ·05 = *r* |

$$52 \; 10 = \text{the whole interest.}$$

$$350 \;\; 0 = 50l. \times 7$$

$$402l. \; 10 = \text{amount required.}$$

$$175 = \frac{nt}{2}$$

$$2·3 = 2 + (t-1)r$$

$$525$$
$$350$$

$$·30 = (t-1)r$$
$$2·$$
$$\overline{2·3 = 2 + (t-1)r}$$

$$£402·5 = \frac{nt}{2}\{2 + (t-1)r\} \; amount\, as\, before.$$

(2.) If a pension of 600*l.* per ann. be forborne 5 years, what will it amount to, allowing 4 per cent. simple interest?

*Ans.* 3240*l.*

(3.) What will an annuity of 250*l.* amount to in 7 years, to be paid by half-yearly payments, at 6 per cent. per annum, simple interest? *Ans.* 2091*l.* 5*s.*

(4.) What will an annuity of 100*l.* per annum, payable quarterly for 7 years, amount to at 4½ per cent. per annum, simple interest? *Ans.* 806*l.* 6*s.* 3*d.*

### PROBLEM II.

*To find the present worth of an annuity at simple interest.*

#### RULE.*

Find the present worth of each year by itself, discounting from the time it falls due, and the sum of all these will be the present worth required.

---

* The reason of this rule is manifest from the nature of discount, for all the annuities may be considered, separately, as so many single and independent debts, due after 1, 2, 3, &c. years ; so that the present

## EXAMPLES.

(1.) What is the present worth of an annuity of 100*l.* to continue 5 years, at 6 per cent. per ann. simple interest?

106 : 100 :: 100 : 94·3396 = *prt. worth 1st year.*
112 : 100 :: 100 : 89·2857 = . . . . *2nd year.*
118 : 100 :: 100 : 84·7457 = . . . . *3rd year.*
124 : 100 :: 100 : 80·6451 = . . . . *4th year.*
130 : 100 :: 100 : 76·9230 = . . . . *5th year.*

£425·9391 = 425*l.* 18*s.* 9¼*d.* =

*present worth of the annuity required.*

(2.) What is the present worth of an annuity, or pension, of 500*l.* to continue 4 years, at 5 per cent. per ann. simple interest? *Ans.* 1782*l.* 3*s.* 8¼*d.*

(3.) What is the present worth of an annuity of 50*l.* to continue 7½ years, at 4½ per cent. per ann. simple interest? *Ans.* 317*l.* 0*s.* 10¾*d.*

### PROBLEM III.

*To find the amount of an annuity at compound interest.*

#### RULE.*

Make 1 the first term of a geometrical progression, and the amount of 1*l.* for one year, at the given rate per cent., the ratio.

---

worth of each being found, their sum must be the present worth of the whole.

Some writers, however, have objected to this rule; but it would be needless to enter into the merits of the dispute, since the purchasing of annuities by simple interest is in the highest degree unjust and absurd; a single instance of which will be sufficient to show the truth of this assertion.

Thus the price of an annuity of 50*l.* to continue 40 years, discounting at 5 per cent. will, by either of the rules that have usually been given, amount to a sum of which one year's interest only exceeds the annuity. It would, therefore, be highly ridiculous to give, for an annuity to continue only 40 years, a sum which would yield a greater yearly interest for ever.

* *Demon.* It is plain, that upon the first year's annuity, there will be due as many years' compound interest, as is denoted by the given number of years less one, and gradually one year's interest less upon every succeeding year, to that preceding the last, which has but one year's interest due, and the last none.

Let $r$, therefore, = amount of 1*l.* for one year; then the series of amounts for 1*l.* annuity, for several years from the first to the last, is 1. $r$, $r^2$, $r^3$, &c. to $r^{t-1}$ : the sum of which series, according to the rule

Then find the sum of as many terms of the series as are equal to the number of years; and the result, multiplied by the given annuity, will give the amount sought.

## EXAMPLES.

(1.) What is the amount of an annuity of 40$l$. to continue 5 years, allowing 5 per cent. compound interest.

$$1 + 1{\cdot}05 + 1{\cdot}05^2 + 1{\cdot}05^3 + 1{\cdot}05^4 = 5{\cdot}52563125.$$

*Or by the formula,*

£5·52563125
 40
————————
£221·025250
 20
————————
0·505000
 12
————————
6·060000

$$a = \frac{n(r^t - 1)}{r - 1} \qquad \begin{array}{l} n = 40 \\ r = 1{\cdot}05 \\ t = 5 \end{array}$$

$$1{\cdot}05^5 = 1{\cdot}2762815 = r^t$$
$$1{\cdot}$$
$$\overline{\cdot 2762815} = r^t - 1$$
$$40 = n$$
$$r - 1 = {\cdot}05 \overline{)11{\cdot}0512600} = n(r^t - 1)$$
$$£221{\cdot}0252 = \frac{n(r^t - 1)}{r - 1} = a.$$

*Ans.* £221 0s. 6d.

———————————————————

in geometrical progression, will be $\dfrac{r^t - 1}{r - 1}$ = amount of 1$l$. annuity for $t$ years.

To find the sum of the series by geometrical progression.

Let 1, $r$, $r^2$, $r^3$, &c. to $r^{t-1} = a =$ *the amount.*
Multiplying by $r$; $r$, $r^2$. $r^3$, $r^4$, &c. . . . $r^t$ $= ar$
Subtracting eq. 1 from eq. 2 . . . . . . . . $r^t - 1 = ar - a$
Or $(r - 1)a = r^t - 1$

Whence the amount $a = \dfrac{r^t - 1}{r - 1}$.

And as all annuities are proportional to their amounts, we shall have

$1 : (r^t - 1) \div (r - 1) :: n : (r^t - 1) \times \dfrac{n}{r - 1}$ = amount of any given annuity $n$, as was to be proved.

Hence $a = \dfrac{n(r^t - 1)}{r - 1}$, and $n = \dfrac{a(r - 1)}{r^t - 1}$.

From which equations all the cases relating to annuities, or pensions, in arrears, may be conveniently exhibited in logarithmic terms, thus:

1. Log. $a =$ Log. $n +$ Log. $(r^t - 1) -$ Log. $(r - 1)$.
2. Log. $n =$ Log. $a +$ Log. $(r - 1) -$ Log. $(r^t - 1)$.
3. $t = \dfrac{\text{Log. } (n + ar - a) - \text{Log. } n}{\text{Log. } r}$.

The ratio cannot be found in a direct manner, but it may be obtained by the rule of Double Position, page 213.

(2.) If 50*l.* yearly rent, or annuity, be forborne 7 years, what will it amount to at 4 per cent. per ann. compound interest? *Ans.* 394*l.* 18*s.* 3½*d.*

(3.) If an annuity of 100*l.* be forborne 23 years, what will it amount to, reckoning 5 per cent. compound interest? *Ans.* 4143*l.* 0*s.* 1*d.*

(4.) If an annuity of 1212*l.* per annum be forborne 76 years, to what sum will it amount, at the rate of 4 per cent. per ann. compound interest? *Ans.* 566698*l.* 16*s.*

### PROBLEM IV.

*To find the present worth of an annuity at compound interest.*

#### RULE.*

Divide the annuity by the amount of 1*l.* for a year, and the quotient will be the present worth of one year's annuity.

Find, in like manner, the present worth for the 2nd, 3rd, 4th, &c. year by dividing the annuity by the square, cube,

---

* The reason of this rule is evident from the nature of the question, and what was said upon the same subject in the purchasing of annuities by simple interest.

And if $p$ be put = present worth of the annuity, and the other letters as before, we shall have

$$p = \frac{n(r^t - 1)}{r^t(r-1)} = \frac{n - \frac{n}{r^t}}{r - 1}, \text{ or, } \frac{n\left(1 - \frac{1}{r^t}\right)}{r - 1}.$$

If $n =$ *one pound*, then $p = \frac{r^t - 1}{r^t(r-1)}$; and $n = \frac{pr^t(r-1)}{r^t - 1}$, or $\frac{p(r-1)}{1 - \frac{1}{r^t}}$.

From which theorems all the cases, where the purchase of annuities is concerned, may be exhibited in logarithmic terms, as follows —

1. Log. $p =$ Log. $n +$ Log. $\left(1 - \frac{1}{r^t}\right) -$ Log. $(r - 1)$.

2. Log. $n =$ Log. $p +$ Log. $(r - 1) -$ Log. $\left(1 - \frac{1}{r}\right)$.

3. $t = \dfrac{\text{Log. } n - \text{Log. } (n + p - pr)}{\text{Log. } r}$.

Where the same observation may be applied to the logarithm of the ratio as at the bottom of the last page.

If $t$ be made to express the number of half-years, quarters, &c., $n$ the half-yearly, quarterly, &c. payment, and $r$ the sum of one pound and ½, ¼, or other given part, of a year's interest, then all the preceding rules are applicable to half-yearly, quarterly, &c. payments, the same as to whole years.

4th power, &c. of the amount of 1*l.* for a year, and the sum of all these will be the value of the annuity sought.

### EXAMPLES.

(1.) What is the present worth of an annuity of 40*l.* per ann. to continue 5 years, discounting at 5 per cent. per annum, compound interest?

$$\frac{40}{1 \cdot 05} = 38 \cdot 095 = present\ worth\ for\ 1\ year.$$

$$\frac{40}{1 \cdot 05^2} = 36 \cdot 281 = \quad \ldots \ldots \quad 2\ years.$$

$$\frac{40}{1 \cdot 05^3} = 34 \cdot 553 = \quad \ldots \ldots \quad 3\ years.$$

$$\frac{40}{1 \cdot 05^4} = 32 \cdot 908 = \quad \ldots \ldots \quad 4\ years.$$

$$\frac{40}{1 \cdot 05^5} = 31 \cdot 341 = \quad \ldots \ldots \quad 5\ years.$$

£173·178 = 173*l.* 3*s.* 6½*d.* = *whole present worth of the annuity required.*

*Or by the formula,*

$$p = \frac{n(r^t - 1)}{r^t(r - 1)} \qquad 1 \cdot 05^5 = 1 \cdot 276281 = r^t$$

$$\frac{}{\qquad} 1 \cdot$$

$$\cdot 276281 = r^t - 1$$

Here $n = 40$   $r^t = 1 \cdot 276281$          $40 = n$

$$r = 1 \cdot 05 \quad \frac{r - 1 = \quad \cdot 05}{\cdot 06381405)11 \cdot 051240(173 \cdot 178} = \frac{n(r^t - 1)}{r^t(r - 1)},$$

$t = 5\ years.$          6381405          *present worth as*
                                                      *before.*

46698350
44669835

20285150
19144215

11409350
6381405

50279450
44669835

56096150
51051240

4944910

(2.) What is the present worth of an annuity of $21l.$ $10s.$ $9\frac{1}{2}d.$ to continue 7 years, at 6 per cent. per annum, compound interest ? *Ans.* $120l.$ $4s.$ $10d.$

(3.) What is $70l.$ per annum, to continue 59 years, worth, in ready money, at the rate of 5 per cent. per annum ? *Ans.* $1321l.$ $6s.$ $0\frac{1}{2}d.$

(4.) If a lease of $55\frac{1}{4}$ years be purchased for $100l.$, what rent ought to be received in order that the purchaser may make $5\frac{1}{2}$ per cent. per annum for his money ? *Ans.* $5l.$ $16s.$

## PROBLEM V.

*To find the present worth of a freehold estate, or an annuity to continue for ever, usually called a perpetuity, at compound interest.*

### RULE.*

As the rate per cent. is to $100l.$ so is the yearly rent to the value required.

---

\* The reason of this rule is obvious; for since a year's interest of the price which is given for the annuity, is the annuity itself, there can neither more nor less be made of that price than of the annuity, whether it be employed at simple or compound interest.

The same thing may also be shown thus : The present worth of an annuity to continue for ever is $\frac{n}{r} + \frac{n}{r^2} + \frac{n}{r^3} + \frac{n}{r^4}$ &c. *ad infinitum*, as has been shown before ; but the sum of this series, by the rule given in geometrical progression, is $\frac{n}{r-1}$; therefore $r-1 : 1 :: n : \frac{n}{r-1}$, which, when the rate per cent. is substituted for $r$, is equivalent to the rule.

The following theorems show all the varieties of this rule :

1. $p = \frac{n}{r-1}$.     2. $n = (r-1) \times p$.     3. $r = \frac{n}{p} + 1$.

*Note.* The price of a freehold estate or annuity to continue for ever, reckoning simple interest, would be expressed by $\frac{1}{1+r} + \frac{1}{1+2r} + \frac{1}{1+3r} + \frac{1}{1+4r}$ &c. *ad infinitum;* but the sum of this series is infinite, or greater than any assignable number, which sufficiently shows the absurdity of using simple interest in these cases.

It may here also be observed, that freehold estates are generally valued at so many years' purchase; that is, at so many years' rent. Thus, if 30 years' purchase be given for an estate, it is equivalent to the making

K

## EXAMPLES.

(1.) A freehold estate brings in yearly 79*l.* 4*s.* : what would it sell for, allowing the purchaser 4½ per cent. compound interest for his money ?

$$£ \quad £ \quad £$$
$$4·5 : 100 :: 79·2 = n$$
$$100$$

4·5)7920·0(1760*l.* *Ans.*
  45
 ———
  342
  315
 ———
   270
   270
 ———
   · · ·

*Or by the formula,* $p = \dfrac{n}{r-1}$,

$$n = 79·2$$
$$r = 1·045.$$

*Hence* $1·045 - 1 = r - 1 = ·045.$

·045)79·2(1760*l.* $= \dfrac{n}{r-1}$.
  45
 ———   *Ans. as before.*
  342
  315
 ———
   270
   270
 ———
   · · ·

(2.) What is the price of a perpetual annuity of 40*l.*, discounting at 5 per cent. compound interest?          *Ans.* 800*l.*

(3.) What is a freehold estate of 75*l.* a year worth, allowing the buyer 6 per cent. compound interest for his money ?
                                                                   *Ans.* 1250*l.*

(4.) What is the difference between the value of a leasehold estate of 100*l.* per annum for 60 years to come, and a freehold, or perpetuity, of the same sum, reckoning compound interest at 5 per cent. per annum?          *Ans.* 107*l.* 1*s.* 5¼*d.*

## PROBLEM VI.

*To find the present worth of an annuity, or freehold estate in reversion at compound interest.*

---

a little more than 3¼ per cent. of the money laid out; if 25 years' purchase be given, it is 4 per cent.; and if 20 years' purchase, 5 per cent.

For example, a freehold estate which brings in to its owner 100*l.* a year is worth 2500*l.*, being 25 × 100, or 25 years' purchase, reckoning the compound interest of money at 4 per cent. per annum. And the same estate is only worth 2000*l.* if money be reckoned at 5 per cent per annum, compound interest.

### RULE.*

Find the present worth of the annuity, as if it were to be entered on immediately.

Then the present worth of the last present worth, discounting for the time between the purchase and commencement of the annuity, will be the answer required.

### EXAMPLES.

(1.) The reversion of a freehold estate of 79*l.* 4*s.* per annum, to commence 7 years hence, is to be sold : what is it worth in ready money, allowing the purchaser $4\frac{1}{2}$ per cent. for his money ?

$$\begin{array}{ccc} \pounds & \pounds & \pounds \\ \text{As } 4\cdot5 : & 100 :: & 79\cdot2 \\ & & 100 \end{array}$$

$$4\cdot5)7920\cdot0(1760l. = present\ worth,\ if\ entered\ on$$
$$45 \qquad\qquad\qquad\qquad immediately.$$

$$\begin{array}{c} 342 \\ 315 \\ \hline 270 \\ 270 \\ \hline \cdots \end{array}$$

*Hence* $(1\cdot045)^7 = 1\cdot360862$, the amount of 1*l.* for 7 years, at $4\frac{1}{2}$ per cent. and $\dfrac{1760}{1\cdot360862} = 1293\cdot297 = 1293l.\ 5s.\ 11\frac{1}{4} =$ *present worth of* 1760*l.* *to commence 7 years hence, or the whole present worth required.*

(2.) Suppose an estate is worth 20*l.* per annum, and that there is a fine of 100*l.* for a lease of 21 years : how much ought the rent to be increased, if the fine be dropped, allowing 5 per cent. compound interest? *Ans.* 7*l.* 16*s.*

---

* The reason of this rule is sufficiently obvious without a demonstration.

Those who wish to be acquainted with the manner of computing the value of annuities upon lives, may consult the writings of DEMOIVRE, SIMPSON, PRICE, MORGAN, MASERES, MILNE, BAILY, and DAVIES ; all of whom have treated this subject in a very skilful and masterly manner.

( 3 ) Which is most advantageous, a term of 15 years in an estate of 100*l.* per annum, or the reversion of such an estate for ever, after the expiration of the said 15 years, computing at the rate of 5 per cent. per ann. compound interest?

*Ans. The first term of 15 years is better than the reversion for ever afterwards by 75l. 18s. 7½d.*

(4.) Suppose I would add 5 years to a running lease of 15 years to come, the improved rent being 186*l.* 7*s.* 6*d.* per annum; what ought I to pay down for this favour, discounting at 4 per cent. per ann. compound interest?

*Ans.* 460*l.* 14*s.* 1¾*d.*

## Of Arithmetical Proportion and Progression.

ARITHMETICAL PROPORTION is the relation which quantities, of the same kind, have to each other with respect to their differences.

Hence, three quantities are said to be in arithmetical proportion, when the difference of the first and second is equal to the difference of the second and third. And four quantities are in arithmetical proportion, when the difference of the first and second is equal to the difference of the third and fourth.

Thus, 2, 4, 6, and 3, 7, 12, 16, are arithmetical proportionals.

Arithmetical Progression is when a series of quantities increase or decrease by the same common difference.

Thus, 1, 3, 5, 7, 9, 11, &c. is an increasing series in arithmetical progression, of which the common difference is 2.

And 18, 15, 12, 9, 6, &c. is a decreasing series in arithmetical progression, of which the common difference is 3.

The most useful parts of this doctrine, as far as it relates to common arithmetical purposes, are contained in the following theorems:

1. If three quantities be in arithmetical proportion, the sum of the two extremes will be double the mean; and if four quantities of this kind be proportional, the sum of the two extremes will be equal to the sum of the two means.

Thus, in the proportion, 3, 6, 9, we have $3+9=2\times6$; and in the proportion 2, 5, 7, 10, we have $2+10=5+7$.

2. Hence, also, an arithmetical mean between any two quantities is half the sum of those quantities.

Thus, an arithmetical mean between 3 and 5 is $\dfrac{3+5}{2}=4$.

3. In any continued arithmetical progression, the sum of the two extremes is equal to the sum of any two terms that are equally distant from them; or to double the middle term when the number of terms is odd.

Thus, in the series 2, 4, 6, 8, 10, &c. we have $2+10=4+8=2\times6=12$.

To this we may also add, that in all cases of arithmetical progression, any three of the five following terms being given, the rest may be found; *viz.* the *first* and *last* terms, commonly called the *extremes*, the *number of terms*, the *common difference*, and the *sum* of all the terms.*

### PROBLEM I.

*The two extremes, and the number of terms, being given, to find the common difference.*

### RULE.†

Divide the difference of the extremes by the number of terms less 1, and the quotient will be the common difference required.

---

* If $a$ = the first term, $l$ = last term, $n$ = number of terms, $d$ = common difference, and $s$ = sum of all the terms, then all the cases that can happen in arithmetical progression may be solved by means of the following theorems:

    1. $l=a\pm(n-1)d.$      2. $a=l\pm(n-1)d.$

    3. $s=\dfrac{n}{2}(a+l)$; or, $s=\dfrac{n}{2}\left\{2a\pm(n-1)d\right\}.$

    4. $d=\dfrac{l-a}{n-1}.$      5. $n=\dfrac{2s}{a+l}=1\pm\dfrac{a-l}{d}.$

In which formulæ, the upper sign is to be used, when it is an increasing series, and the lower sign when it is a decreasing series.

It may here also be further observed, that each of these expressions may be derived from the two values of *s*, given in the third.

† The difference of the first and last terms of the series, when it is an increasing one, evidently shows the increase of the first term, by all the subsequent additions that are made to it, till it becomes equal to the last; and as the number of those additions is one less than the number of terms, and the increase by every addition, is equal, it is plain

## EXAMPLES.

(1.) The extremes are 2 and 53, that is, the first term is 2 and last term 53, of an arithmetical progression, and the number of terms is 18; required the common difference.

*The theorem or formula is*

$$53=l \qquad 18=n$$
$$2=a \qquad 1$$

$$d=\frac{l-a}{n-1}$$

$$17)51(3=d=\frac{l-a}{n-1} \qquad 17=n-1$$
$$51$$

*Or*

$$d=\frac{l-a}{n-1}=\frac{53-2}{18-1}=\frac{51}{17}=3, \text{ the answer.}$$

(2.) If the extremes be 3 and 19, and the number of terms 9; what is the common difference?

*Ans. The difference is 2.*

(3.) A person having to travel from London to a certain place in 12 days, goes only 3 miles the first day, increasing every day by an equal excess, so that the last day's journey may be 58 miles; required the number of miles by which his journey is daily augmented. *Ans. Daily increase, 5 miles.*

### PROBLEM II.

*The two extremes, and the common difference being given, to find the number of terms.*

### RULE.

Divide the difference of the extremes by the common difference, and the quotient, increased by 1, will be the number of terms required.*

---

that the total increase, divided by the number of additions, must give the difference of each of them separately; and a similar mode of reasoning will hold when the series is a decreasing one ; whence the rule is manifest.

* Since the difference of the extremes divided by the number of terms less one, gives the common difference, according to the last problem, it follows that the same difference divided by the common difference, must give the number of terms less one ; whence this quotient, augmented by one, must be the number of terms, which is the same as the rule.

## EXAMPLES.

(1.) The extremes are 2 and 53, and the common differ-ence 3; what is the number of terms?

*The formula is*

$$n = \frac{l-a}{d} + 1$$

$$53 = l$$
$$2 = a$$

$$d = 3)\overline{51} = l - a$$

$$\overline{17} = \frac{l-a}{d}$$
$$1$$

*The number of terms* $\overline{18} = \dfrac{l-a}{d} + 1 = n.$

*Or* $n = \dfrac{l-a}{d} + 1 = \dfrac{53-2}{3} + 1 = 18,$ *the sum as before.*

(2.) The two extremes being 10 and 70, and the common difference 3, what is the number of terms?    *Ans.* 21.

(3.) If the first term of an arithmetical series be 1, the last term 10, and the common difference $\frac{1}{10}$; what will be the number of terms?    *Ans.* 91.

### PROBLEM III.

*The first term and the common difference being given, to find the last or any other assigned term.*

### RULE.*

Multiply the number of terms less one, by the common difference, and add this product to the first term, when the series is increasing; or subtract it from the first term, when it is decreasing, and the result will give the term required.

### EXAMPLES.

(1.) The first term of an increasing arithmetical series

---

* If there be taken any arithmetical series of the general form

$$a + (a \pm d) + (a \pm 2d) + (a \pm 3d) + (a \pm 4d) + \&c. ;$$

where $a$ denotes the first term, and $d$ the common difference, it is plain, that whatever number $n$ may be made to represent, that the

$$n\text{th term} = \{a \pm (n-1)d\} ;$$

which expression, for both the cases above-mentioned, agrees with the rule.

being 2, the common difference 3, and the number of terms 30; it is required to find the last term.

$$\textit{The formula is}$$
$$l = a \pm (n-1)d.$$

$$30 - 1 = 29 = n - 1$$
$$3 = d$$
$$\overline{\phantom{xxx}}$$
$$87 = (n-1)d$$
$$2 = a$$
$$\overline{\phantom{xxx}}$$

$$\textit{The last term } 89 = a + (n-1)d = l.$$

(2.) If the first term of a decreasing arithmetical series be 30, the common difference $1\frac{1}{2}$, and the number of terms 20, what is the last term?

$$20 - 1 = 19 = n - 1$$
$$1\frac{1}{2} = d$$
$$\overline{\phantom{xxx}}$$
$$19$$
$$9\frac{1}{2}$$
$$\overline{\phantom{xxx}}$$
$$28\frac{1}{2} = (n-1)d$$
$$30 = a$$
$$\overline{\phantom{xxx}}$$

$$\textit{The last term } 1\frac{1}{2} = a - (n-1)d.$$

(3.) If the first term of an increasing arithmetical series be $\frac{1}{4}$, the common difference $\frac{1}{2}$, and the number of terms 50, what is the last term? *Ans.* $24\frac{3}{4}$.

(4.) It is required to find the 100th term of an increasing arithmetical series, of which the first term is 1, and the common difference $1\frac{1}{2}$. *Ans.* $149\frac{1}{2}$.

(5.) It is required to find the 15th term of a decreasing arithmetical series, of which the first term is $6\frac{1}{2}$, and the common difference $\frac{1}{3}$. *Ans.* $1\frac{5}{6}$.

(6.) Supposing a debt can be discharged in a year, that is in 52 weeks, by paying 1*l.* the first week, 2*l.* the second, 3*l.* the third, and so on; what will be the last payment? *Ans.* 52*l.*

### PROBLEM IV.

*The two extremes, and the number of terms, being given, to find the sum of all the terms.*

### RULE.*

Multiply the sum of the extremes by half the number of terms, and the product will be the answer.

Or if, instead of the last term, the first term, the common difference, and the number of terms be given, the sum of the series may be found thus :

Multiply the number of terms less one by the common difference, and find the sum or difference of this product and twice the first term, according as the series is increasing or decreasing. Then, if this result be multiplied by half the number of terms, it will give the sum of the series.

---

* Let $a = 1$st term of the series, $d =$ common difference, $n =$ number of terms, and $s =$ sum of all the terms. Then, in any increasing arithmetical series of the form $a + (a+d) + (a+2d) + (a+3d)$ &c. to $a + (n-1)d$, we shall have

$$s = \frac{n}{2}\left\{2a + (n-1)d\right\}.$$

And if the series be decreasing, or of the form $a + (a-d) + (a-2d) + (a-3d)$ &c. to $a - (n-1)d$, we shall have

$$s = \frac{n}{2}\left\{2a - (n-1)d\right\}.$$

The truth of which formulæ may be shown thus :

Suppose the same series to be placed under the given one, in an inverse order.

Then will the sum of every two corresponding terms, from the beginning, be the same as that of the first and last.

Whence any one of those sums multiplied by the number of terms, must give the whole sum of the two series ; and consequently half that sum will be the sum of the given series : thus, in numbers,

Let 1, 2, 3, 4, 5, 6, 7, be the given series,

and 7, 6, 5, 4, 3, 2, 1, the same inverted,

then $8+8+8+8+8+8+8 = 8 \times 7 = 56$ ; and therefore

$$1+2+3+4+5+6+7 = \frac{56}{2} = 28 ;$$

which will hold in all cases, and is the same as by the rule.

*Note.* The sum of any number of terms $(n)$ of the series of natural numbers 1, 2, 3, 4, 5, 6, 7, &c. is $= \frac{1}{2}n(n+1)$.

Thus $1+2+3+4+5$, &c. continued to 100 terms is $= \frac{100 \times 101}{2} = 50 \times 101 = 5050$.

Also, the sum of any number of terms $(n)$ of the series of odd numbers, 1, 3, 5, 7, 9, 11, &c. is $= n^2$.

Thus $1+3+5+7$, &c. continued to 50 terms, is $= 50^2 = 2500$.

K 5

## EXAMPLES.

(1.) The first term of an arithmetical progression is 2, the last term 53, and the number of terms 18; required the sum of the series.

*Formula.*

$$s = (a+l)\frac{n}{2}$$

$$or \; s = \frac{(a+l)}{2} \times n.$$

$53 = l = last \; term.$

$2 = a = first \; term.$

$55 = a + l = sum \; of \; the \; extremes.$

$\frac{18}{2} = 9 = \frac{n}{2} = half \; num. \; of \; terms.$

*Sum of the series* $\overline{495} = \frac{n}{2}(a+l) = s.$

(2.) Given the first term 2, the common difference 3, and the number of terms 18, to find the sum of the series.

*Formula.*

$$s = \frac{n}{2}\{2a \pm (n-1)d\}$$

$18 - 1 = 17 = n - 1 = No. \; of \; terms \; less \; 1.$

$3 = d = common \; diff.$

$51 = (n-1)d$

$4 = 2a = twice \; first \; term.$

$55 = 2a + (n-1)d$

$\frac{18}{2} = 9 = \frac{n}{2} = half \; num. \; of \; terms.$

*Sum of the series* $\overline{495} = s = \frac{n}{2}\{2a + (n-1)d\}.$

(3.) The first term is 1, the last term 21, and the number of terms 11; required the sum of the series.   *Ans.* 121.·

(4.) How many strokes do the clocks of Venice, which go on to 24 o'clock, strike in the compass of a day?   *Ans.* 300.

(5.) The first term of an arithmetical series being 1, the common difference 3, and the number of terms 1001, what is the sum of the series?   *Ans.* 1502501.

(6.) Supposing a triangular battalion to consist of 20 ranks, the first rank being 1 man, the second 4, the third 7, the fourth 10, and so on; what is its number?   *Ans.* 590 *men.*

(7.) The first term of a decreasing arithmetical series is 10, the common difference $\frac{1}{3}$, and the number of terms 21; required the sum of the series?   *Ans.* 140.

(8.) If 100 stones be placed in a right line, exactly a yard asunder, and the first a yard from a basket, what length of ground must a person go who gathers them up singly, returning with them one by one to the basket?

*Ans.* 5 mi. and 1300 yds.

### PROBLEM V.

*To find one or more arithmetical mean proportionals, between any two given numbers.*

### RULE.*

For one proportional only, add the two terms together, and take half their sum for the arithmetical mean required.

But if two or more proportionals be required, subtract the less extreme from the greater, and this difference, divided by one more than the number of means, will give the common difference; which being added continually to the less term, or subtracted from the greater, will give the number of means sought.

### EXAMPLES.

(1.) Required the arithmetical mean between the numbers 6 and 15.

*The formula is*

$$m = \frac{a + nb}{n + 1}$$

$$a = 6$$
$$b = 15$$
$$n = 1$$

Here $6 = a$, and $n = 1$
$$15 = 1 \times 15 = nb$$

$$n + 1 = 2)21 = a + nb$$

$$\text{Ans. } 10\tfrac{1}{2} = \frac{a + nb}{n + 1}.$$

---

* The finding of any proposed number of arithmetical means between two given numbers, is the same as to interpose all the several terms of the series between two given extremes; which may be done thus:

Let $a$ = less extreme, $b$ = greater, and $n$ = number of means or terms that are to be interposed.

Then, since $n + 2$ = number of terms of the series, if this be substituted for $n$, in the formula given for the last or $n$th term of the series in note, p. 199., we shall have

$$a \pm (n + 1)d = b \text{ ; whence } d = \frac{b - a}{n + 1}.$$

Whence, by adding this value of the common difference continually to $a$, and all the following terms, there will arise

$$\frac{na + b}{n + 1}, \quad \frac{(n - 1)a + 2b}{n + 1}, \quad \frac{(n - 2)a + 3b}{n + 1}, \&c. \dots \text{ to } \frac{a + nb}{n + 1},$$

for any number ($n$) of arithmetical means, or interposed terms, between $a$ and $b$, as was required.

K 6

(2.) It is required to find two arithmetical means between the numbers 2 and 8.

$$d = \frac{b-a}{n+1}$$

Here $8 = b$
$2 = a$

$n+1 = 2+1 = 3) 6 = b-a$

Common difference $2 = \dfrac{b-a}{n+1}$

Then 2
  2
 —
  4 *one mean.*
  2
 —
  6 *the other mean.*

(3.) Required the arithmetical mean between the numbers 4 and 14. *Ans.* 9.

(4.) It is required to find 3 arithmetical means between 1 and 2. *Ans.* $1\frac{1}{4}$, $1\frac{1}{2}$, *and* $1\frac{3}{4}$.

(5.) It is required to find 5 arithmetical means between 2 and 14. *Ans.* 4, 6, 8, 10, 12.

## Of Geometrical Proportion and Progression.

GEOMETRICAL PROPORTION is that relation of two quantities of the same kind, which arises from considering what part or parts the one is of the other, or how often it is contained in it.

Hence three quantities are said to be in geometrical proportion, when the first is the same part or multiple of the second, as the second is of the third.

And four quantities are in geometrical proportion, when the first is the same part or multiple of the second, as the third is of the fourth.

Thus 3, 6, 12, and 2, 8, 3, 12, are geometrical proportionals.

Direct proportion is when the same relation subsists between the first of four quantities and the second, as between the third and fourth.

And inverse or reciprocal proportion is when the first and second of four quantities are directly proportional to the reciprocals of the third and fourth.

Thus 3, 6, 5, 10, are directly proportional; and 2, 6, 9, 3, are inversely proportional; because $2 : 6 :: \frac{1}{9} : \frac{1}{3}$.

Geometrical Progression is when a series of quantities increase by a common multiplier, or decrease by a common divisor; which multiplier, or divisor, is called the ratio.

Thus 2, 4, 8, 16, 32, &c., and 1, $\frac{1}{3}$, $\frac{1}{9}$, $\frac{1}{27}$, $\frac{1}{81}$, &c. are series in geometrical progression; the ratio of the first being 2, and that of the second $\frac{1}{3}$.

The most useful parts of this doctrine, as far as it relates to common arithmetical purposes, are contained in the following theorems:

If three quantities be in geometrical proportion, the product of the two extremes is equal to the square of the mean; and if four quantities be proportional, the product of the two extremes is equal to that of the two means.

Thus, if the proportionals be 2, 4, 8, and 3, 9, 5, 15, we shall have $2 \times 8 = 4^2$, and $3 \times 15 = 9 \times 5$.

Hence, also, a geometrical mean between any two quantities is equal to the square root of their product.

Thus, a geometrical mean between 4 and 9 is $\sqrt{36}$, or 6.

In any continued geometrical series, the product of the two extremes is equal to the product of any two terms that are equally distant from them, or to the square of the mean when the number of the terms is odd.

Thus, if the series be 2, 4, 8, 16, 32, we shall have $2 \times 32 = 4 \times 16 = 8^2 = 64$.

To this we may add, that in all cases of this kind, any three of the five following terms, being given, the rest may be found; viz. the *first* and *last* terms, commonly called the *extremes*, the *number* of terms, the *ratio*, and the *sum* of all the terms.*

---

* If $a$ = first term, $l$ = last term, $n$ = number of terms, $r$ = ratio, and $s$ = sum of all the terms; then all the various cases that can happen in geometrical progression, may be solved by means of the following theorems;

$$1. \ l = ar^{n-1}. \qquad\qquad 2. \ a = \frac{l}{r^{n-1}}.$$

$$3. \ s = a\left(\frac{r^n - 1}{r - 1}\right) = \frac{ar^n - a}{r - 1}; \ \text{or} \ s = \frac{rl - a}{r - 1}.$$

$$4. \ r = \left(\frac{l}{a}\right)^{\frac{1}{n-1}}. \qquad 5. \ n = 1 + \frac{\log. l - \log. a}{\log. r}.$$

Where it is to be observed, that each of these formulæ may be readily derived from the two values of $s$ given in the third.

## PROBLEM I.

*The first term, the ratio, and the number of terms being given, to find the last, or any other term assigned.*

### RULE.[*]

Find such a power of the ratio as is denoted by the number of terms less one, and the result multiplied by the first term will give the term required.

### EXAMPLES.

(1.) The first term of a geometrical series is 2, the ratio 2, and the number of terms 13; required the last term.

$$\begin{array}{ll}
\textit{Here by the 1st} & 2 \\
\textit{theorem,} & 2 \\
l = ar^{n-1} & \overline{\phantom{--}} \\
\textit{Or } l = 2 \times 2^{13-1} & 4 = \textit{2nd power.} \\
\textit{Or } l = 2 \times 2^{12} = 8192 & 4 \\
& \overline{\phantom{--}} \\
& 16 = \textit{4th power.} \\
& 16 \\
& \overline{\phantom{--}} \\
& 96 \\
& 16 \\
& \overline{\phantom{--}} \\
& 256 = \textit{8th power.} \\
& 16 \\
& \overline{\phantom{--}} \\
& 1536 \\
& 256 \\
& \overline{\phantom{--}} \\
& 4096 = \textit{12th power of 2.} \\
& 2 = \textit{first term.} \\
& \overline{\phantom{--}} \\
& 8192 \; \textit{which is the last term,} \\
& \overline{\phantom{--}} \qquad \textit{as required.}
\end{array}$$

But as $n$ only enters into these expressions as an exponent of $r$, its value cannot be commodiously exhibited in any other way than by logarithms.

[*] In order to show the truth of this problem, let $a =$ first term, $r =$ ratio, and $n =$ the number of terms; then it is evident, from the nature of geometrical progression, that the series will be of the form $a$, $ar$, $ar^2$, $ar^3$, &c. to $ar^{n-1}$, where the last term is the same expression as that which is required to be found by the rule.

(2.) Required the 12th term of a geometrical series, whose first term is 3, and ratio 2.  *Ans.* 6144.

(3.) The first term of a geometrical series is 1, the ratio 2, and the number of terms 23; required the last term.
  *Ans.* 4194304.

(4.) The first term of a geometrical series is $1\frac{1}{2}$, the ratio, or multiplier 3, and the number of terms 10; what is the last term?  *Ans.* $29524\frac{1}{2}$.

(5.) The first term of a decreasing geometrical series is 100, the ratio $\frac{1}{2}$, or divisor 2, and the number of terms 10; what is the last term?  *Ans.* $\frac{25}{128}$.

### PROBLEM II.

*Given the first term, the last term, and the ratio, to find the sum of the series.*

### RULE.*

Multiply the last term by the ratio, and divide the difference of this product and the first term by the difference between 1 and the ratio, and the quotient will be the sum required.

Or the sum of any series in geometrical progression may be found, by dividing the difference between 1 and such a power of the ratio as is denoted by the number of terms, by the difference between 1 and the ratio, and then multiplying the quotient by the first term.

### EXAMPLES.

(1.) The first term of a series in geometrical progression is 1, the last term is 2187, and the ratio 3: what is the sum of the series?

*Formula 3.*
$$s = \frac{lr - a}{r - 1}.$$

$2187 = l$, *the last term.*
$3 = r$, *the ratio.*

$6561 = lr$, *product.*
$1 = a$, *the first term*

$r - 1 = 3 - 1 = 2)6560 = lr - a$

$Answer = 3280 = \dfrac{lr - a}{r - 1} = s.$

---

* The demonstration of this rule may be given as follows:
It is plain, from the nature of geometrical progression, that the series will be
$$a + ar + ar^2 + ar^3 \ \&c. \cdots \text{to } ar^{n-1} = s.$$

Or, if the last term be omitted, and the number of terms 8 be taken instead of it, we shall have

$$s = \frac{ar^n - a}{r-1} = \frac{a(r^n - 1)}{(r-1)}$$

$$s = \frac{1 \times 3^8 - 1}{3 - 1} = 3280$$

Or thus, $3^8 = 6561 = r^n$ or $r^8$

$$r - 1 = 3 - 1 = 2)\overline{6560} = r^n - 1$$

$$3280 = \frac{r^n - 1}{r - 1}$$

$$1 = a$$

*The sum of the series, as before,* $= 3280 = \dfrac{a(r^n - 1)}{r - 1}$

(2.) The extremes of a geometrical progression are 1 and 65536, and the ratio 4; what is the sum of the series?
*Ans.* 87381.

(3.) The extremes of a geometrical series are 1024 and 59049, and the ratio is $1\frac{1}{2}$; what is the sum of the series?
*Ans.* 175099.

(4.) A person being asked to dispose of a fine horse, said he would sell him on condition of having one farthing for the first nail in his shoes, two farthings for the second, a penny for the third, and so on, doubling the price of every nail to 32, the number of nails in his four shoes; what would the horse be sold for at that rate? *Ans.* 447392*l.* 5*s.* 3¾*d.*

(5.) One Sessa, an Indian, having first discovered the game of chess, showed it to his prince Shehram, who was so

---

And if each side of this equation be multiplied by $r$, we shall have

$$ar + ar^2 + ar^3, \&c. \cdots \text{ to } ar^n = rs.$$

Hence, if the first of these equations be subtracted from the second, there will remain

$$-a + ar^n, \text{ or } ar^n - a = rs - s = s(r - 1).$$

And, consequently, by transposition and division, we shall have

$$s = \frac{ar^n - a}{r - 1} = a\left(\frac{r^n - 1}{r - 1}\right) \text{ or } \frac{a(r^n - 1)}{r - 1};$$

wh is the sum of the series when it is an increasing one.

And if $\dfrac{1}{r}$ be substituted for $r$, this last expression will become

$$s = \frac{(r^{\frac{1}{n}} - 1)}{\frac{1}{r} - 1} = a\left(\frac{1 - r^{\frac{1}{n}}}{1 - \frac{1}{r}}\right)$$

Which is the sum when the series is a decreasing one, agreeably to the rule.

delighted with the invention, that he bid him ask what he would as a reward for his ingenuity : upon which Sessa requested that he might be allowed one grain of wheat for the first square on the chess-board, two for the second, four for the third, and so on, doubling continually to 64, the whole number of squares : now, supposing a pint to contain 7680 of these grains, it is required to find what number of ships, each carrying 1000 tons burden, might be freighted with the produce, allowing 40 bushels to a ton?

*Ans.* 938249922 *ships.*

PROBLEM III.

*To find one or more geometrical mean proportionals between any two given numbers.*

RULE.*

1. If one geometrical mean only be required ; multiply the two numbers together, and the square root of the product will be the mean sought.

2. When two means are required ; divide the greater of the given numbers by the less, and the cube root of the quotient will be the common ratio of the terms ; which being

---

* To find any number of geometrical means between two given numbers is, as in arithmetical proportion, the same as to interpose all the several terms of the series between two given extremes ; which may be done thus :

Let $a$ = less extreme, $b$ = greater, and $n$ = number of means or terms that are to be interposed.

Then, since $n + 2$ = number of terms of the series, if this be substituted for $n$, in the formula given for the last term in the preceding note, we shall have

$$ar^{n+1} = b \; ; \; \text{or} \; r = \left(\frac{b}{a}\right)^{\frac{1}{n+1}}.$$

Whence, by multiplying $a$, and all the resulting terms, continually by this value of the ratio $r$, there will arise

$$\left(a^n b\right)^{\frac{1}{n+1}}, \; \left(a^{n-1} b^2\right)^{\frac{1}{n+1}}, \; \left(a^{n-2} b^3\right)^{\frac{1}{n+1}}, \; \&c. \; \ldots \ldots \; \text{to} \; \left(ab^n\right)^{\frac{1}{n+1}}.$$

For any number ($n$) of geometrical means, or interposed terms, between $a$ and $b$, as was required.

Note. The arithmetical mean $\frac{1}{2}(a + b)$ of any two unequal numbers, $a$, $b$, is always greater than the geometrical mean, $\sqrt{ab}$ ; the difference between them being less as the two given numbers, $a$, $b$, approach nearer to equality.

multiplied by the least of the given numbers, gives the first mean, and this multiplied by the ratio gives the second mean.

3. When any number of means are required; divide the greater number by the less, as before; then take such a root of the quotient as is denoted by the number of means, plus 1, and it will be the common ratio; with which multiply each term continually from the first term, and it will give the number of means sought.

## EXAMPLES.

(1.) Required a geometrical mean between the numbers 3 and 12.

$$
\begin{array}{r}
12 \\
3 \\
\hline
36(6 \text{ the mean required.} \\
36 \\
\hline
*
\end{array}
$$

Or $\sqrt{(3 \times 12)} = \sqrt{36} = 6$ *the mean required.*

(2.) It is required to find two geometrical means between 3 and 24.

Here $\frac{24}{3} = 8.$

And $\sqrt[3]{8} = 2$ *the ratio.*
Whence $3 \times 2 = 6$ *the 1st mean.*
And $6 \times 2 = 12$ *the 2nd mean.*

(3.) Required the geometrical mean between 10 and 20.
*Ans.* 14·1421356.

(4.) It is required to find two geometrical means between 10 and 100. *Ans.* 21·54435 *and* 46·415901.

(5.) It is required to find three geometrical means between 6 and 1536. *Ans.* 24, 96, *and* 384.

(6.) It is required to find four geometrical means between 3 and 96. *Ans.* 6, 12, 24, *and* 48.

# Position.

POSITION is a method of resolving certain questions that cannot be determined by the common direct rules of arithmetic; being so called because it makes use of assumed numbers to work with, as if they were the true ones; and by that means, discovers the numbers sought.

It is usually divided into two cases, called Single and Double Position.

## Single Position.

SINGLE POSITION is a method of resolving such questions as have their results proportional to their suppositions; being chiefly of use in determining such numbers, or quantities, as are increased or diminished by themselves, or any parts of themselves, a certain proposed number of times; or by the multiplication or division of the number sought by any proposed number.

### RULE.*

1. Take any number, and perform the same operations with it as would be required by the question to be performed by the true one.

2. Then say, As the result of this operation is to the number made use of, so is the result mentioned in the question to the number required.

### EXAMPLES.

(1.) A.'s age is double of B.'s, and B.'s is triple of C.'s, and the sum of all their ages is 140: what is each person's age?

---

* The reason of the method of resolving the kind of questions here mentioned, is founded upon the principle given in the rule, that the results are proportional to the suppositions; which is too obvious to require any formal demonstration.

$$\text{For } nx : x :: na : a \text{; or } \frac{x}{n} : x :: \frac{a}{n} : a.$$

$$\text{And } \frac{x}{n} + \frac{x}{m} \text{ &c. } : x :: \frac{a}{n} + \frac{a}{m} \text{ &c. } : a \text{; and so on.}$$

So that when the question involves the square or any higher power of the unknown quantity, this method of assumption cannot be applied.

*Suppose* A.'s *age to be* $=60$

*Then will* B.'s $=\dfrac{60}{2}=30$

*And* C.'s $=\dfrac{30}{3}=10$

_____

100 *sum.*

*Then* $100 : 60 :: 140 : \dfrac{140 \times 60}{100} = 84 = $ A.'s *age.*

*Consequently,* $\dfrac{84}{2} = 42 = $ B.'s.

*And* $\dfrac{42}{3} = 14 = $ C.'s.

*Whence* $84 + 42 + 14 = 140$, *the proof.*

(2.) A person, after spending $\frac{1}{3}$ and $\frac{1}{4}$ of his money, had 60*l.* left : what had he at first?  *Ans.* 144*l.*

(3.) What number is that which being increased by $\frac{1}{2}$, $\frac{1}{3}$, and $\frac{1}{4}$ of itself, the sum shall be 125? *Ans.* 60.

(4.) A general, after sending $\frac{1}{2}$ of his men a-foraging in one direction, and $\frac{1}{3}$ of them in another, had 700 remaining : what number had he in command?  *Ans.* 4200.

(5.) A shepherd being asked how many sheep he had in his flock, said, If I had as many more, half as many more, and seven sheep and a half, I should have just 1000 : how many had he?  *Ans.* 397.

(6.) A certain sum of money is to be divided between 4 persons, in such a manner, that the first shall have $\frac{1}{3}$ of it; the second $\frac{1}{4}$; the third $\frac{1}{6}$; and the fourth the remainder, which is 80*l.* : what was the sum?  *Ans.* 320*l.*

(7.) It is required to divide 108 into three such parts, that $\frac{1}{2}$ of the first, $\frac{1}{3}$ of the second, and $\frac{1}{4}$ of the third, shall be all equal to each other?  *Ans.* 24, 36, *and* 48.

(8.) A person bought a chaise, horse, and harness, for 60*l.*; the horse came to twice the price of the harness, and the chaise to twice the price of the horse and harness : what did he give for each?

*Ans.* 13*l.* 6*s.* 8*d. for the horse* ; 6*l.* 13*s.* 4*d. for the harness* ; *and* 40*l. for the chaise.*

# Double Position.

DOUBLE POSITION is a method of resolving certain questions in the higher parts of arithmetic, by making two suppositions of false numbers.

It is chiefly applicable to the determination of such numbers as have their parts or multiples increased or diminished by some number which is no known part of the number sought ; and in finding an approximate value of the unknown quantity in various abstruse algebraical expressions, some of which scarcely admit of any other mode of solution.

### RULE.*

Take any two convenient numbers, and proceed with them separately, according to the conditions of the question, noting the results obtained from each.

Then, as the difference of these results is to the difference of the supposed numbers, so is the difference between the true result and either of the former, to the correction of the number belonging to the result used ; which correction, being added to that number, when it is too little, or subtracted from it, when it is too great, will give the answer required.

*Note.* When the question is of such a kind, that the answer to it can only be obtained by approximation, the two supposed numbers should be each taken as near to the number sought as can be conveniently done ; and after the operation has been performed according to the rule, the number so obtained, and the nearest of the two former, may be taken as new suppositions ; and so on, till the answer is found to a sufficient degree of exactness.

---

* This method, like that in Single Position, is founded upon the supposition mentioned in the rule ; which is, that the differences between the true and supposed numbers are proportional to the differences between the true and erroneous results : being a similar assumption to that which has usually been given by most other writers on the subject ; but the new form of the rule here proposed, which is rendered as simple as could be wished, will, it is presumed, be found better adapted to practice, and more easy to be remembered than any other that has yet been devised.

## EXAMPLES.

(1.) What number is that, which being multiplied by 6, the product increased by 18, and the sum divided by 9, the quotient will be 20?

*Let the two supposed numbers be 18 and 30.*

| *Then* 18 | *And* 30 |
|:---:|:---:|
| 6 | 6 |
| 108 | 180 |
| 18 | 18 |
| 9)126 | 9)198 |
| 14 *the 1st result.* | 22 *the 2nd result.* |

*Then* 22—14 : 30—18 :: 20—14.

*Or* $8 : 12 :: 6 : \dfrac{6 \times 12}{8} = 9$ *the correction for the supposed number* 18; *and* $18 + 9 = 27 =$ *the answer.*

*Or* $8 : 12 :: 22 - 20 : \dfrac{12 \times 2}{8} = 3$ *the correction for the supposed number* 30.

*And* $30 - 3 = 27 =$ *the answer, as before.*

(2.) It is required to find such a number, that if the square of it be added to the number itself, the sum shall be 10.

*Here it is soon found that the number sought lies between* 2 *and* 3; *which let, therefore, be the supposed numbers.*

*Then* $(3 \times 3) + 3 = 12$ *the 1st result.*
*And* $(2 \times 2) + 2 = 6$ *the 2nd result.*

*Whence,*

$12 - 6 : 3 - 2 :: 12 - 10 : \dfrac{1 \times 2}{6} = \dfrac{1}{3}$ *the correction belonging to the 1st result.*

*And consequently,* $3 - \dfrac{1}{3} = \dfrac{8}{3} = 2\cdot6'666$ *&c. for the 1st approximation.*

*Again, let* 3 *and* $\frac{8}{3}$ *be the two supposed numbers.*

*Then,* $(3 \times 3) + 3 = 12$ *the 1st result.*

*And* $\left(\frac{8}{3} \times \frac{8}{3}\right) + \frac{8}{3} = \frac{64}{9} + \frac{24}{9} = \frac{88}{9}$ *the 2nd result.*

*Whence* $12 - \frac{88}{9} : 3 - \frac{8}{3} :: 10 - \frac{88}{9}.$

*Or* $\frac{20}{9} : \frac{1}{3} :: \frac{2}{9} : \frac{1}{3} \times \frac{2}{9} \times \frac{9}{20} = \frac{2}{3 \times 20} = \frac{1}{3 \times 10} = \frac{1}{30}$ *the cor-*
*rection.*

*And, consequently,* $\frac{8}{3} + \frac{1}{30} = \frac{81}{30} = \frac{27}{10} = 2 \cdot 7$ *the 2nd approxi-*
*mation.*

*Again, let* $\frac{27}{10}$ *and* $\frac{8}{3}$ *be the two supposed numbers.*

*Then,* $\left(\frac{27}{10} \times \frac{27}{10}\right) + \frac{27}{10} = \frac{729}{100} + \frac{270}{100} = \frac{999}{100}$ *the 1st result.*

*And* $\left(\frac{8}{3} \times \frac{8}{3}\right) + \frac{8}{3} = \frac{64}{9} + \frac{24}{9} = \frac{88}{9}$ *the 2nd result.*

*Whence* $\frac{999}{100} - \frac{88}{9} : \frac{27}{10} - \frac{8}{3} :: 10 - \frac{999}{100}.$

*Or* $\frac{191}{900} : \frac{1}{30} :: \frac{1}{100} : \frac{1}{30} \times \frac{1}{100} \times \frac{900}{191} = \frac{3}{10 \times 191} = \frac{3}{1910}$ *the*
*correction.*

*And, consequently,* $\frac{27}{10} + \frac{3}{1910} = \frac{5160}{1910} = 2 \cdot 70156$ *the 3rd ap-*
*proximation, or answer required; which is true to the last de-*
*cimal figure, inclusively.*

(3.) What number is that which, being divided by 7, and the quotient diminished by 10, three times the remainder shall be 24? *Ans.* 126.

(4.) What number is that which, being multiplied by 3, the product increased by 4, and that sum divided by 8, the quotient shall be 32? *Ans.* 84.

(5.) It is required to find the cube root of 17, to six places of decimals. *Ans.* 2·571282.

(6.) It is required to find a number which being added to its cube shall make 70. 　　　*Ans.* 4·040415.

(7.) What number is that which, being added to its square, and that sum again to its cube, shall make 100?
　　　　　　　　　　　　　　　　　*Ans.* 4·264 *nearly.*

(8.) It is required to find a number, that when multiplied by 16 times its cube root, and then added to 7 times the square root of the sum of that number and 55, the result shall be 110. 　　　*Ans.* 2·57 *nearly.*

# Permutations and Combinations.

PERMUTATION is the changing or varying the relative positions of a given number of things, so that no two parcels of them shall have the quantities they are composed of placed in the same order.

Thus, the three letters, *a*, *b*, *c*, may be permuted, or made to change their positions in six different ways; as *a b c*, *a c b*, *b a c*, *b c a*, *c a b*, and *c b a*.

COMBINATION, is the several ways that a less number of things can be taken out of a greater, and combined together without regarding their order, or the places in which they may stand.

Thus, the number of combinations of four letters, taken out of the five, *a b c d e*, are the five following: *a b c d*, *a b c e*, *a b d e*, *a c d e*, *b c d e*.

COMPOSITION, is the taking a given number of things, out of as many equal rows, or sets of different things, one out of each row, and combining them together.

### PROBLEM I.

*To find the number of permutations, or changes of position, that can be made of any given number of things that are all different from each other.*

### RULE.*

Multiply all the terms of the natural series of numbers

---

* The reason of the rule may be shown thus: Any one thing *a* is incapable of change, and therefore admits only of one position, as *a*.

from 1 up to the given number, continually together, and the last product will be the answer.

### EXAMPLES.

(1.) How many changes may be rung on 6 bells.

$$
\begin{array}{r}
1 \\
2 \\
\hline
2 \\
3 \\
\hline
6 \\
4 \\
\hline
24 \\
5 \\
\hline
120 \\
6 \\
\hline
720
\end{array}=\textit{the answer.}
$$

*Or* $1 \times 2 \times 3 \times 4 \times 5 \times 6 = 720$ *the answer.*

(2.) How many days can 5 persons be placed in a different position, round a table at dinner?  *Ans.* 120 days.

(3.) How many separate permutations, or changes, may

---

Any two things, as, $a$ and $b$, are only capable of two variations, or positions, as, $a\,b$, $b\,a$; the number of which is expressed by the product of $1 \times 2 = 2$.

If there be three things, $a$, $b$, and $c$; any two of them, leaving out the 3rd, will have $1 \times 2$ variations; and consequently, when the 3rd is taken in, there will be $1 \times 2 \times 3 = 6$ variations.

In the same manner, when there are four things, every three, leaving out the 4th, will have $1 \times 2 \times 3$ variations; consequently by taking in successively the one left out, there will be $1 \times 2 \times 3 \times 4$ variations; and so on for the following numbers.

It may here be remarked, as a thing useful to masons, paviors, &c. that if two equal square pieces of any substance be divided diagonally, and the four separate pieces be each stained with different colours, they may be arranged, or put together, in 64 different ways, so as to form as many kinds of chequer work.

And if four square pieces be divided diagonally, so as to make eight triangles, seven of which are stained with the primitive colours, red, orange, yellow, green, blue, indigo, and violet, and the 8th white, the number of different kinds of chequer-work squares which may be formed of them is 256.

L

be made of the letters in the words *Roma, Romani,* and *Romanis?*

*Ans. In Roma* 24, *in Romani* 720, *and in Romanis* 5040.

(4.) How many changes, or transpositions, can be made of the words in the following verse : *Tot tibi sunt dotes, virgo, quot sidera cœlo.*          *Ans.* 40320 *changes.*

(5.) How many changes may be rung on 12 bells, and what time would it require, supposing 10 changes to be rung in a minute, and the year to consist of 365¼ days?

*Ans.* 479001600 *changes*; 91 *years,* 26 *days,* 6 *hours.*


#### PROBLEM II.

*To find how many permutations, or changes of position, can be made out of any given number of things, of which there are several of one sort, and several of another, &c.*


#### RULE.*

1. Take the series $1 \times 2 \times 3 \times 4$, &c. up to the number of things given, and find the product of all the terms.

2. Take, also, the series $1 \times 2 \times 3 \times 4$, &c. up to the number of given things of the first sort ; and $1 \times 2 \times 3 \times 4$, &c. up to the number of given things of the second sort ; and so on for the third or fourth, if necessary.

3. Divide the product of all the terms of the first series by the joint product of all the terms of the remaining ones, and the quotient will be the answer.

---

* This rule is expressed in algebraic terms thus :

$$\frac{1 \times 2 \times 3 \times 4 \times 5, \&c. \text{ to } m}{1 \times 2 \times 3, \&c. \text{ to } p \times 1 \times 2 \times 3, \&c. \text{ to } q, \&c.} \&c.$$

where $m=$number of things given, $p=$number of things of the first sort, $q=$number of things of the second sort, &c. ; the demonstration of which may be shown as follows :

Any two different quantities, $a, b$, admit of two changes ; but if the quantities are the same, or $ab$ becomes $aa$, there will be only one, which may be expressed by $\frac{1 \times 2}{1 \times 2} = 1$.

Any three quantities, $abc$, all different from each other, afford 6 variations ; but if the quantities be all alike, or $abc$ becomes $aaa$, these variations will be reduced to one, which may be expressed by

$$\frac{1 \times 2 \times 3}{1 \times 2 \times 3} = 1.$$

## EXAMPLES.

(1.) How many variations can be made of the letters in the word *Bacchanalia?*

$$1 \times 2 \; (= number \; of \; c's) = 2$$
$$1 \times 2 \times 3 \times 4 \; (= number \; of \; a's) = 24$$
$$1 \times 2 \times 3 \times 4 \times 5 \times 6 \times 7 \times 8 \times 9 \times 10 \times 11$$
$$(= number \; of \; letters \; in \; the \; word) = 39916800$$

$$2 \times 24 = 48)39916800(831600 = the \; answer.$$
$$151$$
$$76$$
$$288$$
$$\overline{\phantom{288}}$$

(2.) How many different numbers can be made of the following figures, 1220005555?  *Ans.* 12600.

(3.) How many varieties will take place in the succession of the following musical notes, *fa, fa, fa, sol, sol, la, mi, fa?*
  *Ans.* 3360.

---

And if two of the quantities only are alike, or $abc$ becomes $aac$, then the six variations will be reduced to these three, $aac$, $aca$, and $caa$; which may be expressed by $\dfrac{1 \times 2 \times 3}{1 \times 2} = 3.$

Again, any four quantities, $abcd$, all different from each other, will admit of 24 variations; but if the quantities be the same, or $abcd$ become $aaaa$, the number of these variations will be reduced to one; which is $\dfrac{1 \times 2 \times 3 \times 4}{1 \times 2 \times 3 \times 4} = 1.$

And if three of the quantities only be the same, or $abcd$ becomes $aaab$, the number of variations will be reduced to the four following—$aaab$, $aaba$, $abaa$, and $baaa$; which are $\dfrac{1 \times 2 \times 3 \times 4}{1 \times 2 \times 3} = 4.$

In like manner, it may also be shown, that if two of them be alike, or the four quantities be $aabc$, the number of variations will be reduced to twelve; which may be expressed by $\dfrac{1 \times 2 \times 3 \times 4}{1 \times 2} = 12,$

And by reasoning in the same manner, it will appear that the number of changes which can be made of the quantities $abbccc$, is equal to 60; which may be expressed by $\dfrac{1 \times 2 \times 3 \times 4 \times 5 \times 6}{1 \times 2 \times 1 \times 2 \times 3} = 60$; and so on.

## PROBLEM III.

*To find how many permutations, or changes of position, can be made out of any given number of things, that are all different from each other, by taking a given number of them at a time.*

### RULE.\*

Take a series of numbers, beginning at the number of things given, and decreasing by 1, to as many terms as there

---

\* This rule, expressed in algebraic terms, is as follows :

$$m \times (m-1) \times (m-2) \times (m-3) \text{ &c. to } n \text{ terms ;}$$

where $m$ = number of things given, and $n$ = quantities to be taken at a time ; the demonstration of which may be readily obtained by means of the following lemma :

LEMMA. The number of changes of $m$ things taken $n$ at a time, is equal to $m$ changes of $m-1$ things taken $n-1$ at a time.

For suppose any five quantities $a\,b\,c\,d\,e$ to be given.

Then, leaving out $a$, let $v$ = number of all the changes, or variations, of every two, $b\,c$, $b\,d$, &c. that can be taken out of the four remaining quantities $b\,c\,d\,e$.

And, in like manner, if $b$, $c$, $d$, $e$, be successively left out, the number of variations of all the two's will still be = $v$ ; as before.

Also, if $a$ be now put before each of these, in the form $a\,b\,c$, $a\,b\,d$, &c. the number of changes will not be altered ; that is, $v$ will still be = number of variations of every three out of the five, $a\,b\,c\,d\,e$, when $a$ is first. And the same will evidently take place, when $b\,c\,d\,e$ are put first.

But these are all the variations that can happen of three things out of five, when $a$, $b$, $c$, $d$, $e$, are successively put first ; and therefore the sum of all these is the sum of all the changes of three things out of five.

But the sum of these is so many times $v$ as is equal to the number of things ; that is $5v$, or $m\,v$, = all the changes of three things out of five. And the same way of reasoning may be applied to any numbers whatever.

This being premised, the demonstration of the rule is as follows :—Let any seven things $a\,b\,c\,d\,e\,f\,g$ be given, and $m$ be the number of quantities to be taken ; in which case $m = 7$ and $n = 3$.

Then, it is evident, that the number of changes that can be made by taking one by one out of five things will be 5, which let = $v$.

Then, by the lemma, when $m = 6$ and $n = 2$, the number of changes will = $m\,v$ = $6 \times 5$ ; which let = $v$ a second time.

And, consequently, by the lemma, when $m = 7$ and $n = 3$, the number of changes will = $m\,v$ = $7 \times 6 \times 5$ ; that is, $m\,v$ = $m \times (m-1) \times (m-2)$, continued to three, or $n$ terms. And the same may be shown for any other numbers.

are quantities to be taken at a time; then the product of all the terms of this series will be the answer required.

EXAMPLES.

(1.) How many changes can be rung with 3 bells out of 8?

$$
\begin{array}{r}
8 \\
7 \\
\hline
56 \\
6 \\
\hline
336 = Answer.
\end{array}
$$

*Or* $8 \times (8-1) \times (8-2) = 8 \times 7 \times 6 = 336 = Ans.$

(2.) How many different numbers can be formed, by taking 5 digits out of the 10 that compose the common scale of notation? *Ans.* 30240.

(3.) How many different words can be made of 4 letters out of the 26 that compose the alphabet, admitting the consonants? *Ans.* 358800.

PROBLEM IV.

*To find the number of combinations of any given number of things, all different from each other, taking any given number at a time.*

RULE.*

Take the series 1, 2, 3, 4, &c. up to the number to be taken at a time, and find the product of all its terms.

Also, take a series of the same number of terms, decreasing

---

* This rule, expressed algebraically, as in the former instances, is,

$$\frac{m}{1} \times \frac{m-1}{2} \times \frac{m-2}{3} \times \frac{m-3}{4}, \text{ &c. to } n \text{ terms;}$$

where $m$ is the number of given quantities, and $n$ those to be taken at a time.

*Demon. of the Rule.* 1. Let the number of things to be taken at a time be *two*, and the things to be combined $= m$.

Then when $m$, or the number of things to be combined, is only two, as $a$ and $b$, it is evident that there can be but one combination, as $a\,b$, but if $m$ be increased by one, or the letters to be combined be three, as $a, b, c$, it is plain that the number of combinations will now be increased by 2, since with each of the former letters $a\,b$, the new letter $c$ may be joined;

L 3

by 1, from the given number, out of which the election is to be made, and find the product of all its terms.

Then divide the last product by the former, and the quotient will be the number sought.

### EXAMPLES.

(1.) How many combinations can be made of 6 letters out of 10?

---

thus making $ab$, $ac$, $bc$. In this case, therefore, it is evident, that the whole number of combinations will be truly expressed by $1 + 2 = 3$.

Again, if $m$ be increased by one letter more, or the whole number of letters be four, as $a$, $b$, $c$, $d$, it is evident that the whole number of combinations must be increased by 3, since with each of the preceding letters the new letter $d$ may be combined. Whence the combinations, in this case, will be truly expressed by $1 + 2 + 3$.

And in the same manner it may be shown, that the whole number of combinations of two in five things, will be $1 + 2 + 3 + 4$; or two in six things, $1 + 2 + 3 + 4 + 5$; and of two in seven, $1 + 2 + 3 + 4 + 5 + 6$, &c.; whence, universally, the number of combinations of $m$ things, taken two by two, is $= 1 + 2 + 3 + 4 + 5 + 6$ &c., to $(m-1)$ terms.

But the sum of this series is $= \frac{m}{1} \times \frac{m-1}{2}$; which agrees with the rule.

2. Let now the number of quantities in each combination be supposed to be three.

Then, it is plain, that, when $m = 3$, or the things to be combined are $a$, $b$, $c$, there can be only one combination; but if $m$ be increased by one, or the things to be combined are four, as $a$, $b$, $c$, $d$, the number of combinations will be increased by 3; since three is the number of combinations of two in all the preceding letters $a$, $b$, $c$, and with each two of these the new letter $d$ may be combined: whence the number of combinations, in this case, is $1 + 3$.

Again, if $m$ be increased by one more, or the number of letters be supposed to be five; then the former number of combinations will be increased by 6, that is, by all the combinations of two in the four preceding letters $a$, $b$, $c$, $d$; since, as before, with each two of these the new letter $e$ may be combined: and, therefore, in this case, the number of combinations is $1 + 3 + 6$.

Whence, universally, the number of combinations of $m$ things, taken three by three, is $1 + 3 + 6 + 10$ &c. to $m-2$ terms; the sum of which series is $= \frac{m}{1} \times \frac{m-1}{2} \times \frac{m-2}{3}$, agreeably to the rule.

And the same thing will hold, let the number of things to be taken at a time be what they may.

Therefore the number of combinations of $m$ things, taken $n$ at a time,

$= \frac{m}{1} \times \frac{m-1}{2} \times \frac{m-2}{3} \times \frac{m-3}{4}$, &c. to $n$ terms, as was to be shown.

$1 \times 2 \times 3 \times 4 \times 5 \times 6 (= \textit{the number to be taken at a time}) = 720.$

$10 \times 9 \times 8 \times 7 \times 6 \times 5 \ (\textit{same number from } 10) = 151200.$

$$720)151200(210 = \textit{the answer.}$$
1440
———
720
720
· ·

(2.) How many combinations can be made of 2 letters out of the 26 letters of the alphabet? *Ans.* 325.

(3.) How many different ways can 5 cards be taken out of 20, as in the game of piquet? *Ans.* 15504.

(4.) In how many ways can 4 persons be taken for sentinels, out of a company consisting of 100 men?
*Ans.* 3921225.

(5.) Required the number of combinations that can be made of 13 things out of 52; or how many deals a person may play at the game of whist without holding the same cards twice? *Ans.* 635013559600.

### PROBLEM V.

*To find the combinations that any given number of things, all different from each other, can be made to undergo, when taken by two's, three's, &c. up to the number of things given.*

### RULE.*

From such a power of 2, as is denoted by the number of given things, subtract the number of given things plus 1, and the remainder will be the whole number of combinations required.

---

* *Demon.* It appears by the former rule, that the combinations of $m$ things, taken two at a time, $= \frac{m}{1} \times \frac{m-1}{2}$; when taken three at a time $= \frac{m}{1} \times \frac{m-1}{2} \times \frac{m-2}{3}$; when taken four at a time, $= \frac{m}{1} \times \frac{m-1}{2} \times \frac{m-2}{3} \times \frac{m-3}{4}$; and so on to $n$ at a time; whence the sum of all these combinations is

### EXAMPLES.

(1.) It is required to find all the possible combinations that can be made of a common suit of 13 cards, taking them by two's, three's, &c. at a time, up to 13.

*Here* $2^{13}-(13+1)=8192-14=8178$ *the whole number of combinations required.*

(2.) Required the number of combinations, or conjunctions, that the 7 planets, Mercury, Venus, the Earth, Mars, Jupiter, Saturn, and the Georgium Sidus, can undergo, when reckoned two by two, three by three, &c. up to 7.  *Ans.* 120.

(3.) Required all the possible combinations, taken as in the last question, that the notes of the 12 registers, or rows of pipes in an organ, are susceptible of, and by which the sound is made to change from a soft and gentle one to others that are loud and solemn.  *Ans.* 4083.

### PROBLEM VI.

*To find all the possible permutations and combinations that any number of things can be made to undergo, when taken by two's, three's, &c. up to the whole number of things given.*

### RULE.*

Raise the number which is equal to the given number of things to such a power as is denoted by the number itself, and multiply the result, less 1, again by that number.

---

$$\frac{m}{1}\times\frac{m-1}{2}+\frac{m}{1}\times\frac{m-1}{2}\times\frac{m-2}{3}+\frac{m}{1}\times\frac{m-1}{2}\times\frac{m-2}{3}\times\frac{m-3}{4}+ \&c. \ldots \text{to}$$

$$\frac{m}{1}\times\frac{m-1}{2}\times\frac{m-2}{3}\times\frac{m-3}{4}, \&c. \ldots \times\frac{m-(n-1)}{n}.$$

But $2^m$ or its equal $(1+1)^m=1+m+\frac{m}{1}\times\frac{m-1}{2}+\frac{m}{1}\times\frac{m-1}{2}\times\frac{m-2}{3}+$

$\frac{m}{1}\times\frac{m-1}{2}\times\frac{m-2}{3}\times\frac{m-3}{4}+\&c.$ ; which is the same as the former series, when $n=m$, excepting the two first terms $1+m$.

Whence the number of combinations which $m$ things can be made to undergo, when taken by two's, three's, &c. up to the given number, will be expressed by $2^m-(1+m)$, agreeably to the rule.

* *Demon.* Any one thing $a$ admits of only one position, as $a$.

Any two things $a\,b$ may be permuted and combined $2^2$ or four ways, as, $a\,a,\ a\,b,\ b\,a,\ b\,b$.

Then this product, being divided by the same number less 1, will give the whole number of permutations and combinations required.

### EXAMPLES.

(1.) It is required to find the whole number of permutations and combinations that can be made of the four letters $a$, $b$, $c$, $d$, when they are taken by two's, three's, and by four's.

$$\text{Here } \frac{4^4-1}{3} \times 4 = \frac{256-1}{3} \times 4 = \frac{255}{3} \times 4 = \frac{1020}{3} = 340 = the$$

answer required.

(2.) Required the whole number of permutations and combinations that can be made of a suit of 13 cards, taking two by two's, three's, &c. at a time up to 13. *Ans.* 328114698808273.

(3.) How many permutations and combinations, in the form of words, can be made of the 26 letters of the alphabet, taking them by two's, three's, &c. up to 26?
      *Ans.* 6402364363415443603228541259936211926.

### PROBLEM VII.

*To find the compositions of any number, in any equal number of sets, the things themselves being all different.*

### RULE.*

Multiply the number of things in each set continually together, and the product will be the answer required.

---

Any three things, $a$, $b$, $c$, taken by two's, may be permuted and combined $3^2$ or 9 ways: as $aa$, $ab$, $ba$, $ac$, $bb$, $ca$, $bc$, $cb$, $cc$.

And, in general, $n$ things, taken by two's, may be permuted and combined $n^2$ different ways. In like manner, when they are taken by three's, the whole number of permutations and combinations will be $n^3$; when by four's, $n^4$: and universally, when they are taken $n$ at a time, they will be $n^n$. Hence, adding all these together, the whole number of permutations and combinations in $n$ things, taken by two's, three's, four's, &c. to $n$'s, will be the sum of the geometrical series $n + n^2 + n^3 + n^4$, &c. to $n^n$, which is $\dfrac{n^n-1}{n-1} \times n$, agreeably to the rule.

* *Demon.* Suppose there are only two sets; then it is plain, that, if every quantity of one set be combined with every quantity of the other, it will make all the compositions of two things in these two sets; and the number of these compositions is, evidently, the product of the number of quantities in one set by that in the other.

### EXAMPLES.

(1.) Suppose there are 4 companies, in each of which there are 9 men; it is required to find how many ways 9 men may be chosen, one out of each company.

$$
\begin{array}{r}
9 \\
9 \\
\hline
81 \\
9 \\
\hline
729 \\
9 \\
\hline
\end{array}
$$

*Or* $9 \times 9 \times 9 \times 9 = 6561 = Answer.$

(2.) Suppose there are four companies; in one of which there are 6 men, in another 8, and in each of the other two 9; what are the choices, by a composition of 4 men, one out of each company? *Ans.* 3888.

(3.) How many changes are there in throwing 5 dice? *Ans.* 7776.

## On Exchanges.

EXCHANGE is the method of finding what sum of the money of one country is equal to any given sum of the money of another, according to a certain given rate.*

*The real money* of any country is certain pieces of metal,

---

Again, suppose there are three sets; then the composition of two, in any two of the sets, when combined with every quantity of the third, will make all the compositions of three in the three sets. That is, the compositions of two, in any two of the sets, being multiplied by the number of quantities in the remaining set, will produce the compositions of three in the three sets; which is evidently the continual product of all the three numbers in three sets. And the same manner of reasoning will hold, let the number of sets be what it may.

The doctrine of permutations, combinations, &c. is of very extensive use in various branches of science; particularly in the calculation of annuities and chances. The subject might have been pursued to a much greater length; but what is here done will be found sufficient for most of the purposes to which things of this nature are applicable.

* Exchanges are carried on by the various merchants and bankers of Europe, by means of an instrument in writing, called a *bill of exchange,*

coined and made current by public authority; as sovereigns, shillings, &c. in England; francs, centimes, &c. in France.

*Imaginary money* is that which is chiefly used in keeping accounts; as pounds sterling used to be, for which there was formerly no coin of equivalent value.

*The par of exchange* is such a quantity of the money of one country, whether real or imaginary, as is intrinsically equal to a certain quantity of the money of another.

Thus, 100*l.* sterling is worth from 105*l.* to 115*l.* Irish, as the exchange may happen to be; and from 130*l.* to 140*l.* of the currency of the West Indies.

*The course of exchange* is such a variable or *uncertain* sum of the money of one place, as is proposed to be given for a *certain* or constant sum of that of another.*

Thus London gives 100*l.* sterling, which is a *certain* price, to Dublin for an *uncertain* number of pounds, shillings, and pence, Irish. And, on the contrary, Dublin gives an *uncertain* number of pounds, shillings, and pence, Irish, for a *certain* number of pounds sterling.

*Agio* is the difference, in Amsterdam and other places, between the money of exchange, or that issued from the bank, which is usually called *banco*, and the *currency*; the former being generally something finer than the latter.

*Usance* is a certain time allowed by the merchants of one country to those of another, for the payment of bills of exchange.

Thus, *usance*, when employed singly, means at one month after date; *double usance*, at two months after date, &c. And *half-usance* is 15 days, whatever may be the length of the month.†

*Days of grace* are a certain number of days that are

---

and are usually transacted on the Royal Exchange of London, the Royal Exchange of Dublin, the Exchange of Amsterdam, and of the other principal cities of the Continent and America.

* The fluctuation in the course of exchange is chiefly occasioned by what is usually called the *balance of trade*, which is the difference between the commercial exports and imports of one place with respect to those of another.

† The term of a bill varies according to the agreement of the parties, or the custom of different countries; some are drawn at sight, others at a certain number of days, or weeks, or months, after date. When the term of the bill is expressed in months, calendar months are understood. Thus, if a bill at one month be dated Jan. 1., the term

allowed for the payment of a bill after it becomes due; which varies according to the custom of different countries, or to the distance of places from each other.*

All the operations in exchange may be performed by the Rule of Three and by Practice.

## ENGLAND, WITH HOLLAND, FLANDERS, AND GERMANY.

Accounts are kept in these places in guilders, stivers, and pfennings; or in pounds, shillings, and pence, as in England.

The money of Holland and Flanders is distinguished by the name of *Flemish*, and they exchange by the pound sterling.

| 8 pfennings | | grote or penny Flemish. |
|---|---|---|
| 12 pfennings | | schilling. |
| 2 grotes | | stiver. |
| 6 stiver | make one | schilling. |
| 20 stivers | | florin, or guilder. |
| 2½ florins | | rix-dollar. |
| 6 florins | | pound Flemish. |

Exchange from 33s. 6d. to 36s. 6d. Flem. per pound sterling.

---

expires, Feb. 1.; and if the bill were dated Jan. 28, 29, 30, or 31., the month would expire on the last day of February.

* In England, all bills must be paid on the third day after their date is expired; and such as fall due on a Sunday must be paid on Saturday. For bills at sight or on demand, no days of grace are allowed.

It may here, also, be proper to remark, that when the holder of a bill disposes of it to another, he must indorse it, by writing his name on the back of it, which renders him a security for the payment.

When a bill is presented for acceptance, which should be done as early as possible, it is generally left till the next day; in which case the common method is for the person on whom it is drawn to write his name at the bottom of it, with the word *accepted*; but any other writing, by him or his clerk, which does not imply a refusal, is deemed a legal acceptance.

If a bill be refused acceptance, it must be put into the hands of a *Notary Public*, and noted for non-acceptance; if an accepted bill be refused payment, it must be noted or protested accordingly, and returned to the drawer; by which he or any of the indorsers are liable to pay the bill with all costs. But if the holder makes an unnecessary delay in returning it, he can only sue the acceptor.

A bill is not invalidated by bearing date on a Sunday, Christmas day, Good Friday, or any other holiday.

Agio from 3 to 6 per cent. for currency.

*Note.* Any kind of foreign money is reduced to English, by saying, As the given rate of exchange is to 1*l.* sterling, so is any given sum foreign to the sterling sought ; and sterling money is reduced to foreign by reversing the operation.

Also, banco is reduced to currency, by saying, As 100 added to the agio : 100 :: banco : currency ; and currency is changed into banco by the reverse statement.

### EXAMPLES.

(1.) In 96*l.* 6*s.* 11*d.* sterling how many florins, &c. ; exchange at 34*s.* 3*d.* Flemish per pound sterling ?

$$
\begin{array}{lll}
\text{At } 20s. & \textit{is once} & 96l. \ . \ 6s. \ . \ 11d. \\
10s. & \textit{is } \frac{1}{2} & 48 \ . \ 3 \ . \ 5\frac{1}{2} \\
3s. \ 4d. \ \textit{is } \frac{1}{3} & & 16 \ . \ 1 \ . \ 1\frac{3}{4} \\
10d. \ \textit{is } \frac{1}{4} & & 4 \ . \ 0 \ . \ 3\frac{1}{2} \\
1d. \ \textit{is } \frac{1}{10} & & 0 \ . \ 8 \ . \ 0\frac{1}{4} \\
\end{array}
$$

£164 . 19 . 10

6 *florins* = £1 *Flem.*

£989 . 19 . 0 *Ans.* 989 *flor.* 19 *st.*

(2.) In 612*l.* 14*s.* 9½*d.* sterling, how many Dutch rix-dollars ; exchange 35*s.* 4⅞*d.* Flem. per pound sterling ?
*Ans.* 2603 *rix-dol.* 18 *st.* 1 *gr.* 5 *pfen.*

(3.) In 3758 flor. 15 st. current, agio 5⅝ per cent., how many pounds sterling ; exchange at 35*s.* 11*d.* ?
*Ans.* 330*l.* 5*s.* 3*d.*

(4.) In 456*l.* 8*s.* sterling, how many rix-dollars current ; agio 4⅝, exchange at 36*s.* 1½*d.* ?
*Ans.* 2069 *rix-dol.* 2 *flor.* 10 *st.*

(5.) In 2714 guild. 15 stivers, how many pounds sterling ; exchange at 35*s.* 6*d.* Flemish per pound sterling ?
*Ans.* 254*l.* 18*s.* 1¼*d.*

(6.) In 290*l.* 11*s.* 10*d.* sterling, how many pounds Flemish ; exchange at 33*s.* 10*d.* Flemish per pound sterling, and agio at 4½ per cent. ?
*Ans.* 513*l.* 14*s.* 1¼*d.*

(7.) In 805*l.* 15*s.* Flemish, how many pounds sterling, the agio being 4 per cent. and exchange 34*s.* 6*d.* Flem. per pound sterling ?
*Ans.* 449*l.* 2*s.* 8½*d.*

(8.) The course of exchange between London and Amsterdam being 34*s.* 3*d.* at 2½ usance; what ought Amsterdam to give at sight, supposing the interest of money to be 4 per cent. ? *Ans.* 1*l.* 13*s.* 11¾*d.*

## HAMBURGH.

Accounts are kept at Hamburgh in marks and schillings, and the exchange is by the pound sterling, as in Holland.

6 phennings ⎫     ⎧ a grote, or penny ⎫
12 pence   ⎬ make ⎨ a schilling       ⎬ Flemish.
20 schillings ⎭     ⎩ a pound        ⎭

12 phennings ⎫     ⎧ a schilling       ⎫
16 schillings  ⎪     ⎪ a mark banco    ⎪ Hamburgh banco,
2 marks      ⎬ make ⎨ a dollar of exch. ⎬    and currency.
3 marks      ⎭     ⎩ a rix-dollar     ⎭

Hence a schilling banco is = 2 pence Flemish,
And a mark banco is = 32 pence Flemish.

Exchange from 33*s.* to 36*s.* Flem. per pound sterling.

The mark banco is worth about 17½*d.* sterling, making the par of exchange about 13 marks 10½ schillings per £ sterling.

Agio from 18 to 20 per cent. for currency, and from 30 to 35 per cent. for light coin.*

---

* The different moneys of Hamburgh are as follows:
1. *Bank money,* which is inscribed in the bank-books, and transferred in payment from one person to another.
2. *Specie,* or the hard rix-dollar, which is worth, when full weight, about ⅓ per cent. more than banco.
3. *The gold ducat,* which is about 1 per cent. better or worse than banco, according to the price of bullion.
4. *Light coin,* consisting chiefly of foreign moneys, which lose about 38 per cent. against banco.
5. *Currency,* which consists of various denominations of silver money coined at Hamburgh, since the year 1726.
Hamburgh money was formerly distinguished by the word *Lubs,* (from Lubec, the place of its coinage,) but the term, though still retained in most books of exchange, appears to be out of use among men of business, the word Hambro' being usually substituted in its place.
It may here, also, be proper to observe, that the *par* between Hamburgh banco and currency is reckoned at 23 per cent. agio, or 13 marks banco for 16 marks currency. And the *par* between English money and currency is 43*s.* Flemish for 1*l.* sterling; but there can be no permanent *par* with banco, on account of the agio being always fluctuating. If the agio

### EXAMPLES.

(1.) Reduce 2347 marks, 10 schillings, into pounds sterling; xchange at 34s. 6d. Flemish per pound sterling.

| Flem. | | Flem. | | ster. |
|-------|---|-------|----|-------|
| 34s. 6d. | : | 2347 mar. 10s. | :: | 1l. |
| 12 | | 16 | | |
| 414 | | 37562 | | |
| | | 2 | | |

414)75124(181$\frac{190}{414}$=181l. 9s. 2d.=Ans.
3372
604
190

(2.) Exchange 100l. sterling into marks, at 13 marks, 10 schillings per 1l. sterling.

| £ | | £ | | mar. sch. |
|---|---|-----|----|-----------|
| 1 | : | 100 | :: | 13 . 10 |

$$10 \times 10 = 100$$

136 . 4
10

*Marks* 1362 . 8 *sch.=Ans.*

(3.) In 536l. sterling how many marks; exchange at 36s. 4d. Flemish per pound sterling?  *Ans. 7303 marks.*

(4.) Reduce 300l. sterling into marks and schillings banco; exchange at 35s. 3d. Flemish per pound sterling.
*Ans. 3965 marks, 10 sch.*

(5.) Reduce 4500 marks current into pounds sterling; exchange at 35s. 6d. Flemish per pound sterling, and agio 20 per cent.  *Ans. 281l. 13s. 9½d.*

(6.) Reduce 8234 marks, 10 schillings, banco, into pounds sterling; exchange at 33s. 10d. Flem. per pound sterling.
*Ans. 649l. 0s. 8¼d.*

(7.) Reduce 8732 marks current into pounds sterling; exchange at 34s. 5d. Flemish per pound sterling, agio 20 per cent.  *Ans. 563l. 16s. 2¼d.*

---

be 23, 1l. sterling is equal to 34s. 11½d.; but, by the estimation of merchants, the *par* is from 34s. 7d. to 34s. 10d., varying according to the price of gold and silver, and the fluctuation of the agio.

## FRANCE.

Accounts were kept in France, before the Revolution, in livres, sols, and derniers; but, at present, they are kept in francs and centimes, and they exchange by the franc.*

The derniers and livres being now abolished, the exchanges are carried on through the medium of francs and centimes.

10 centimes        =2 sous  =1d. nearly English.

100 centimes      =1 franc=9·52d. or about 9½d. English.

25 fr. 21 centimes = £1 sterling English, and this is the par of exchange.


### EXAMPLES.

(1.) Reduce 125l. 10s. into francs and centimes; exchange at 25 francs, 6 centimes, per 1l. sterling.

```
 1l.    :   125l. 10s.   ::   25 fr. 6 cents.
 20          20                100
 __          __
 20         2510               2506
            2506
          _____                      £      £        fr.
           15060           Or 1 : 125·5  ::  25·06
          125500                       25·06
            5030                       _____
          _____                       7530
  2,0)629006,0                          6275
          _____                       2510
  1,00)3145,03                         _____
          _____                      3145·030 fr.
      3145 fr. 3 cents.                 _____
```

Ans. 3145 fr. 3 cents.

---

* Francs and livres were formerly synonymous; but by a coinage some years ago, the 5-franc pieces were, by some mismanagement in the Mint, made too heavy, being worth 101¼ sous instead of 100; in consequence of which the franc has been adapted to this accidental value, and is so estimated in all accounts, except in the small shop business, which is frequently settled in livres, as they still, in many cases, buy and sell by the old weights and measures.

(2.) Exchange 21420 francs, 75 centimes, into pounds sterling at 25·35 per £.

$$\begin{array}{ccccc}
fr. & & fr. & & £ \\
As \; 25·35 & : & 21420·75 & :: & 1 \\
& & 1 & &
\end{array}$$

$$25·35)21420·75(845l.=Ans.$$
$$20280$$

$$\begin{array}{c} 11407 \\ 10140 \end{array}$$

$$\begin{array}{c} 12675 \\ 12675 \end{array}$$

(3.) In 800*l.* sterling how many francs; exchange at 25·35 per 1*l.* sterling?      *Ans.* 20280 *francs.*

(4.) In 16914 francs, 19 cents. how many pounds sterling; exchange at 24 francs per pound?    *Ans.* 704*l.* 15*s.* 1¾*d.*

(5.) Reduce 96*l.* 10*s.* 6*d.* into francs; exchange at 25·55 per 1*l.* sterling.      *Ans.* 2466·2 *francs.*

(6.) Reduce 32576 francs, 47 centimes into pounds sterling; exchange at 25·21 per 1*l.* sterling.    *Ans.* 1292*l.* 4*s.* 1*d.*

## SPAIN.

Accounts are kept in Spain in pesos, or dollars, reales, and maravedis, and they exchange by the peso, or dollar of plate.

| | | |
|---|---|---|
| 2⅛ maravedis | = | 1 cuarto of exchange. |
| 4 maravedis | = | 1 cuarto of hard silver. |

---

The old-coined pieces of France, were
       24-livre pieces, called louis       ⎫
       48-livre pieces, called double-louis ⎬ in gold.
                 And,
       6-livre pieces, 3-livre pieces     ⎫
       24-sols, 12-sols, and 6-sols pieces ⎬ in silver.
The new-coined pieces of money of France, are
       40 francs, 20 francs, and 10 francs, in gold.
       5 francs, 2 francs, 1½ franc    ⎫
       1 franc, ½ franc, and ¼ franc ⎬ in silver.
       And copper sous, half-sous, and centimes.

$$34 \text{ maravedis or } 16 \text{ cuartos vellon, or } 8\tfrac{1}{2} \text{ cuartos, hard money} \Big\} = \Big\{ 1 \text{ real vellon *, or of exchange} = \text{about } 2\tfrac{1}{2}d. \text{ English.}$$

$$20 \text{ reales vellon, or } 680 \text{ maravedis vellon} \Big\} = \Big\{ 1 \text{ hard dollar, or peso duro, or peso fuerte} = 50d. \text{ to } 51d. \text{ English.}$$

$$15 \text{ reales, } 2 \text{ marvs. vellon, or } 512 \text{ marvs. vellon.} \Big\} = \Big\{ 1 \text{ peso of exchange, or dollar of plate} = \text{from } 37d. \text{ to } 41d.$$

8 reales of plate = .... ditto ... ditto ...

$10\tfrac{1}{2}$ reales of plate = 1 peso fuerte, or hard dol.

$$4 \text{ pesos or } 32 \text{ reales of exchange} \Big\} = 1 \text{ doblon of exchange.}$$

$$375 \text{ marvs. vellon, or } 11 \text{ reales } 1 \text{ marv. vellon.} \Big\} = 1 \text{ ducat of exchange.}$$

OBS. The *peso fuerte* or *hard dollar* = 680 maravedis, = from 50d. to 51d. Eng.; and the *peso of exchange* or *dollar of plate* = 512 maravedis = 36d. to 39d., depending on the course of exchange.

The *real of plate or silver* = $4\tfrac{3}{4}d.$ nearly of English money; but the *real vellon* is not quite $2\tfrac{1}{2}d.$

## EXAMPLES.

(1.) In 9764 reales of plate, how many pounds sterling; exchange at $41\tfrac{7}{8}d.$ per peso of exchange or dollar of plate?

8)9764 *reales plate.*

$40 = \tfrac{1}{6}$ *of a £* 1220  10

d.

Hence 40 *is* $\tfrac{1}{6}$    203 . 8 . 4

1 *is* $\tfrac{1}{40}$    5 . 1 . $8\tfrac{1}{2}$

$\tfrac{4}{8}$ *is* $\tfrac{1}{2}$    2 . 10 . $10\tfrac{1}{4}$

$\tfrac{2}{8}$ *is* $\tfrac{1}{2}$    1 . 5 . 5

$\tfrac{1}{8}$ *is* $\tfrac{1}{2}$    0 . 12 . $8\tfrac{1}{2}$

£212 . 19s. . $0\tfrac{1}{4}d.$ = *Ans.*

*Or thus,*

peso.    d.    *reales.*

1 : $41\tfrac{7}{8}$ :: 9764

8    $41\tfrac{7}{8}$

8 *reales*    9764

39056

$8543\tfrac{1}{2}$

8)$408867\tfrac{1}{2}$

12)$51108\tfrac{1}{4}$

2,0)425,9 . $0\tfrac{1}{4}$

£212.19.$0\tfrac{1}{4}$

---

* The *real vellon* is now only an imaginary money, used in exchanges, and in the public accounts.

The money of Spain is distinguished into *plate* and *vellon*, the former being to the latter as 32 to 17; that is 23 maravedis vellon = 17 maravedis

(2.) In 8756 reales vellon how many reales of plate?
*Ans.* 4651 *reales of plate,* 20 *mar.*

(3.) Reduce 7869 reales vellon, 19 mar. into pounds sterling; exchange at $41\frac{1}{2}d$. sterling per peso.
*Ans.* 90*l.* 7*s.* $3\frac{1}{4}d$.

(4.) In 89*l.* 2*s.* $11\frac{1}{2}d$. sterling how many reales of plate, &c.; exchange at $40\frac{1}{8}d$. per piece of eight, or peso of 8 reales?
*Ans.* 4265 *reales of plate,* $25\frac{1}{2}$ *mar.*

(5.) In 2375 pesos, 6 reales, 17 mar. how many pounds sterling; exchange at 34*d.* per peso of exchange?
*Ans.* 336*l.* 11*s.* $5\frac{1}{4}d$.

(6.) In 16144 pesos, 4 reales, 22 mar. vellon, how many pounds sterling; exchange at $34\frac{1}{2}d$. per peso or dollar of plate?
*Ans.* 1232*l.* 18*s.* $3\frac{3}{4}d$.

## PORTUGAL.

Accounts are kept in Portugal in reis and milreis, and the exchange is by the milreis.

$$\left.\begin{array}{l} \text{400 reis} \\ \text{1000 reis, or } 2\frac{1}{2} \text{ crusados} \end{array}\right\} \text{make one} \left\{\begin{array}{l} \text{crusado.} \\ \text{milreis.} \end{array}\right.$$

Exchange from 60*d.* to 67*d.* per milreis.

### EXAMPLES.

(1.) In 669 milreis 72 reis, how many pounds sterling; exchange at 5*s.* 7*d.* per milreis?

mil. d.  mil. reis.      *Or thus,*
1 : 67 :: 669 72         669 *milreis.*
1000        1000         ——
——          ——
1000 *reis*  669072 *reis*   5*s. is* $\frac{1}{4}$  167 . 5 . 0
——               67       6*d. is* $\frac{1}{10}$  16 . 14 . 6
             ———          1*d. is* $\frac{1}{6}$   2 . 15 . 9
             4683504      72 *reis =*  0 . 0 . $4\frac{3}{4}$
             4014432                   ——————
             ———                  £186 . 15*s.* . $7\frac{3}{4}d$. *Ans.*
    1,000)44827,824
       12)44827$\frac{3}{4}$
      2,0)373,5 . 7$\frac{3}{4}$
         £186 . 15 . 7$\frac{3}{4}$=*Ans.*

of plate. In exchange with England plate only is used, when the *dollar of plate,* or *peso of exchange,* is worth $37\frac{1}{4}d$. sterling English; then the *peso duro* or *peso fuerte,* or *hard dollar,* is worth 50*d.*

(2.) In 569*l.* 17*s.* 10*d.* sterling how many milreis; exchange at 5*s.* 6*d.* sterling per milreis?

*Ans.* 2072 *milreis,* 333⅓ *reis.*

(3.) In 754*l.* 18*s.* 6*d.* sterling how many crusados; exchange at 64¼ per milreis? *Ans.* 7022 *cru.* 223 *re.*

(4.) In 2729 crusados, 372 reis, how much sterling; exchange at 62*d.* per milreis? *Ans.* 282*l.* 1*s.* 10¼*d.*

(5.) Reduce 827 milreis, 160 reis, into pounds sterling; exchange at 63⅜*d.* per milreis. *Ans.* 218*l.* 8*s.* 5¼*d.*

## VENICE.

They keep their accounts at Venice in dollars, soldi, and denari, and exchange by the ducat and piastre.

| | | |
|---|---|---|
| 12 denari | make one | soldo. |
| 20 soldi | make one | lira, or piastre of Leghorn. |
| 6⅕ lira | make one | ducat current.* |

Exchange from 52*d.* to 54*d.* per ducat, and from 45*d.* to 54*d.* per piastre or lira.

Agio from 20 to 30 per cent.

*Note.*—Leghorn, Naples, Genoa†, and most other parts of Italy, keep their accounts in the same denominations.

### EXAMPLES.

(1.) In 7456 pias. 9 sol. 6 den. lira money, how many pounds sterling, exchange being at 49⅞*d.* per lira?

| *d.* | | *pias.* | *s.* | *d.* |
|---|---|---|---|---|
| | | 7456 | 9 | 6 |
| 40 | *is* ⅙ | 1242 | 14 | 11 |
| 8 | *is* ⅕ | 248 | 10 | 11¾ |
| 1 | *is* ⅛ | 31 | 1 | 4¼ |
| ⅘ | *is* ½ | 15 | 10 | 8 |
| ⅜ | *is* ½ | 7 | 15 | 4 |
| ⅛ | *is* ½ | 3 | 17 | 8 |

£1549 . 10*s.* 11*d.*=*the answer.*

---

* There are three sorts of money at Venice, viz. *bank money,* in which they keep their accounts; *current money,* which is the standard of their coin; and *picola,* used for the purchase and sale of merchandise.

† In Genoa and the Sardinian States they keep their accounts in *centisimi* and the *lira nuova,* which latter is equal in value to the French franc, or about 9½*d.* English; 100 centisimi = 1 lira nuova.

(2.) In 278*l*. 17*s*. 9*d*. sterling how many piastres of Leghorn ; exchange at 47⅜*d*. per piastre ?

*Ans.* 1412 *pias.* 16 *sol.* 8 *den.*

(3.) Reduce 1549 duc. 18 sol. 1 den. bank money of Venice into sterling money ; exchange at 47¾*d*. sterling per ducat. *Ans.* 308*l*. 4*s*. 3½*d*.

(4.) In 4789 duc. 19 sol. 3 den. current money how many pounds sterling ; exchange at 4*s*. 1*d*. per ducat banco, and agio 20 per cent. ? *Ans.* 814*l*. 16*s*. 5*d*.

(5.) In 415*l*. 17*s*. 4*d*. sterling how many ducats, &c. current ; agio 20 per cent., and exchange at 53*d*. per ducat ?

*Ans.* 2259 *duc.* 99 *soldi.*

(6.) In 100*l*. sterling how many piastres of Leghorn ; exchange at 52½*d*. per ducat ? *Ans.* 2834 *pias.* 5 *sol.* 8¼ *den.*

## RUSSIA.

They keep their accounts at Petersburgh in rubles and copecs, and exchange by the ruble.

50 copecs } make one { poltin.
2 poltins, or 100 copecs } make one { ruble.
2 rubles } make one { ducat.

Russia exchanges with London by way of Hamburgh or Amsterdam, at the rate of from 48 to 50 stivers per ruble ; and sometimes directly with London from 4*s*. to 5*s*. per ruble.

### EXAMPLES.

(1.) In 2634 rub. 58 cop. how many pounds sterling, exchange at 4*s*. 8*d*. sterling per ruble ?

2634 *rubles.*

| | | |
|---|---|---|
| 4*s*. 0*d*. *is* ⅕ | 526 . 16 . 0 | |
| 6*d*. *is* ⅛ | 65 . 17 . 0 | |
| 2*d*. *is* ⅓ | 21 . 19 . 0 | |
| 58 *cop.*= | 0 . 2 . 8¼ | |

614*l*. 14*s*. 8¼*d*.=*the answer.*

(2.) In 674*l*. 17*s*. 6*d*. sterling how many rubles ; exchange 49 stivers per ruble, and 33*s*. 9½*d*. Flemish per pound sterling ? *Ans.* 2792 *rub.* 46 *cop.*

(3.) A merchant at London remits to his correspondent at Petersburgh 471*l*. 17*s*. 4*d*. ster. ; exchange 34*s*. 9*d*. Flem. per pound ster. for Amsterdam, and the exchange from thence at 50 stivers per ruble; how many rubles must the correspondent receive?      *Ans.* 1967 *rub.* 68 *cop.*

(4.) Received from Archangel per bill of exchange 4675 rub. 46 cop.; exchange 122 copecs per rix-dollar of 50 stivers, and 34*s.* 7*d.* Flemish per pound sterling; how much sterling is the sum?      *Ans.* 923*l.* 9*s.* 2¼*d.*

(5.) In 4675 rub. 46 cop. how many pounds sterling; exchange 122 copecs per rix-dollar current, agio 3 per cent, and 34*s.* 7*d.* Flemish per pound sterling? *Ans.* 896*l.* 11*s.* 2¼*d.*

## POLAND AND PRUSSIA.

They keep their accounts at Dantzig in florins, groshen, and penins, and exchange by the grosh.

| | | |
|---|---|---|
| 18 penins | | grosh. |
| 18 groshen | | oort. |
| 30 groshen | make one | florin, or Polish guilder. |
| 3 florins, or 90 gr. | | rix-dollar. |
| 2 rix-dollars | | gold ducat. |

Exchange is made with Poland and Prussia by way of Holland, the exchange being from 240 to 295 groshen per pound Flemish.

### EXAMPLES.

(1.) In 478*l.* 14*s.* 9*d.* sterling how many Prussia florins, &c.; exchange 255 groshen per pound Flemish, and 33*s.* 6*d.* Flemish per pound sterling?

```
20s. 0d. is once   478l. 14s.   9d.
10s. 0d. is ½      239 .  7 .  4½
 3s. 4d. is ⅓       79 . 15 .  9½
      2d. is 1/20    3 . 19 .  9
                  ────────────────
                   801l. 17s.  8d.
                      8½=255 groshen.
                  ────────────────
                  6415 .  1 .  4
                   400 . 18 . 10
                  ────────────────
                  6816 florins = the answer.
```

(2.) In 6949 flor. 14 gros. 2 pen. Polish, how many pounds sterling; exchange 260½ Polish groshen per pound Flemish, and 34*s.* 8*d.* Flemish per pound sterling?

                     *Ans.* 461*l.* 14*s.* 5¾*d.*

(3.) In 875*l.* 14*s.* 8*d.* sterling, how many rix-dollars, &c.

Polish; exchange 290 groshen Polish per pound Flemish, and 34s. 4d. Flemish per pound sterling?

*Ans.* 4844 *rix-doll.* 9 *grosh.* 1 *pen.*

(4.) In 674*l.* 18*s.* 4*d.* sterling how many Polish guilders, &c.; exchange 274 Polish groshen per pound Flemish, and 35*s.* 6*d.* Flemish per pound sterling?

*Ans.* 10941 *guil.* 15 *grosh.* 12 *pen.*

(5.) In 546*l.* 17*s.* 8*d.* sterling how many gold ducats; exchange 295 groshen per pound Flemish, and 33*s.* 10*d.* Flemish per pound sterling? *Ans.* 1516 *gold duc.* 37 *grosh.* 10 *pen.*

## SWEDEN.

They keep their accounts at Stockholm in copper dollars and oorts, or in silver dollars, and exchange by the copper dollar.

| | | |
|---|---|---|
| 8 penins | | runstychen. |
| 3 runstychens | | stiver. |
| 8 stivers | make one | marc. |
| 32 runstychens | | copper dollar. |
| 96 runstychens | | silver dollar. |
| 24 marcs | | copper rix-dollar. |

The exchange here is subject to great variations, but is usually from 46 to 50 copper dollars per pound sterling.

### EXAMPLES.

(1.) In 146*l.* 17*s.* 6*d.* sterling how many copper dollars; exchange 48½ copper dollars per pound sterling?

$$146l. \quad 17s. \quad 6d.$$
$$6 \times 8 = 48$$
$$\overline{\phantom{00}881 \; . \; 5 \; . \; 0}$$
$$8$$
$$\overline{7050 \; . \; 0 \; . \; 0}$$
$$73 \; . \; 8 \; . \; 9 \; for \; \tfrac{1}{2}$$
$$\overline{7123 \; . \; 8 \; . \; 9}$$
$$8$$
$$\overline{5)70 \; . \; 0}$$
$$\overline{14 \; . \; 0}$$

*Ans.* 7123 *cop. doll.* 14 *runs.*

(2.) In 546*l.* 19*s.* 6½*d.* sterling how many silver dollars; exchange at 49½ copper dollars per pound sterling?

*Ans. 9025 silv. doll.* 11 *run.* 5 *pen.*

(3.) In 674*l.* 11*s.* 6*d.* sterling how many marcs, &c.; exchange 48 copper dollars per pound sterling?

*Ans.* 43172 *marcs,* 6 *st.* 9 *pen.*

(4.) In 11676 silver doll. 18 run. 7 pen. how many pounds sterling; exchange 49 copper dollars per pound sterling?

*Ans.* 714*l.* 17*s.* 4½*d.*

(5.) In 111*l.* 5*s.* 2½*d.* sterling how many Swedish rix-dollars; exchange 35*s.* 7*d.* Flemish per pound sterling, 106 Amsterdam rix-dollars current for 100 Swedish rix-dollars, and agio 3¾.

*Ans.* 465 *Swedish rix-doll.*

## IRELAND.

Accounts are kept in Ireland in pounds, shillings, and pence Irish, divided as in England.

The par of 1*s.* in English in 1*s.* 1*d.* Irish; and therefore 100*l.* English is 108*l.* 6*s.* 8*d.* Irish. But the course of exchange varies from 6 to 20 per cent.

### EXAMPLES.

(1.) London remits to Ireland 787*l.* 15*s.* sterling; how much Irish must London be credited, exchange at 10½ per cent.?

$$787l. \; 15s.$$
$$10 \times 11 + \tfrac{1}{2} = 110\tfrac{1}{2}$$

$$7877 . 10$$
$$11$$

$$86652 . 10$$
$$393 . 17 . 6$$

$$870.46 . \; 7 . 6$$
$$20$$

$$9.27$$
$$12$$

$$3.30$$
$$4$$

$$1.20 \qquad\qquad Ans. \; 870l. \; 9s. \; 3\tfrac{1}{4}d.$$

(2.) Ireland remits to London 879*l.* 6*s.* 6*d.* Irish; how much sterling must Ireland be credited for, exchange 11⅝ per cent.?                          *Ans.* 787*l.* 14*s.* 11¾*d.*

(3.) London remits to Ireland 540*l.* 10*s.* sterling; how much Irish must London be credited for, exchange 12 per cent.?                          *Ans.* 605*l.* 7*s.* 2¼*d.*

## AMERICA AND THE WEST INDIES.

In North America and the West Indies accounts are kept in pounds, shillings, and pence, as in England.

But as there are here but few coins, they are obliged to substitute a paper currency for carrying on their trade; which, being subject to many casualties, suffers a great discount in its negotiation.

### EXAMPLES.

(1.) Reduce 1575*l.* 14*s.* 9*d.* West India currency to pounds sterling; exchange being 35 per cent.

$$135l. \ : \ 100l. \ :: \ 1575l. \ 14s. \ 9d.$$
$$Or \ 27 \ : \ 20 \qquad 4 \times 5 = 20$$

$$6302 \ . \ 19 \ . \ 0$$
$$5$$

$$3 \times 9 = 27 \begin{cases} 3)31514 \ . \ 15 \ . \ 0 \\ 9)10504 \ . \ 18 \ . \ 4 \end{cases}$$

$$£1167 \ . \ 4s. \ . \ 3d. \ the \ answer.$$

### UNITED STATES.

100 cents = 1 dollar.
1 dollar = about 4*s.* 1½*d.* sterling.

But the fixed exchange value of the dollar at par is 4*s.* 6*d.* sterling or currency. Sterling often bears a premium upon this of about 10*l.* per cent., 100*l.* sterling being worth 110*l.* United States' money at 4*s.* 6*d.* per dollar.

M

(1.) Exchange 100*l.* sterling into United States' dollars at par, and also at 10*l.* per cent.

```
        s.  d.        £     dollar.
As    4   6  :  110  ::  1  :  488 dol. 88 cents.
      12          20
      ──          ──
      54        2200
                  12
                ─────
      54)26400(488 dollars, 88 cents. Ans.
         480
         480
          48
         100
         ───
      54)4800(88 cents.
```

(2.) A merchant in the West Indies is indebted to a merchant in London 575*l.* 19*s.* 6*d.* sterling ; with how much currency must he be credited in the West Indies, when the exchange is 33⅓ per cent. ? *Ans.* 767*l.* 19*s.* 4*d.*

(3.) A merchant of London consigns to the West Indies goods amounting to 578*l.* 19*s.* 6*d.*, which are sold for 847*l.* 15*s* 6*d.* currency ; what sterling ought the factor to remit, deducting 5 per cent. for commission and charges, and what does London gain per cent. upon the adventure, supposing the exchange at 30 per cent. ? *Ans.* 7*l.* 0*s.* 1*d.*

# Arbitration of Exchanges.

ARBITRATION OF EXCHANGE is a method of finding such a rate of exchange between any two places, as shall be in proportion with the rates assigned between each of them and a third place ; it being, by comparing the par of exchange, thus found, with the present course of exchange, that a person can judge which way to remit or draw his money to the most advantage, and what the advantage shall be.

All questions in this rule may be performed by one or more operations in the Rule of Three, or by Compound Proportion.

## EXAMPLES.

(1.) If the exchange between London and Amsterdam be
33*s*. 9*d*. per pound sterling, and the exchange between
London and Paris be 32*d*. per écu; what is the par of arbitration between Amsterdam and Paris?

$$240d. \quad : \quad 33s.\ 9d. \quad :: \quad 32d.$$

$$12$$

$$\overline{\phantom{xxx}}$$

$$405$$
$$32$$

$$\overline{\phantom{xxx}}$$

$$810$$
$$1215$$

$$\overline{\phantom{xxx}}$$

$$24,0)1296,0(54$$
$$120$$

$$\overline{\phantom{xxx}}$$

96   *Ans.* 54*d. Flem. per écu.*
96

$$\overline{\phantom{xxx}}$$

(2.) Amsterdam changes on London at 34*s*. 4*d*. per pound
sterling, and on Lisbon at 52*d*. Flemish for 400 reis; what
ought the exchange to be between London and Lisbon?

*Ans.* $75\frac{75}{103}d.$ *sterling per milreis.*

(3.) London exchanges on Amsterdam at 34*s*. 9*d*. per
pound sterling, and on Lisbon at 5*s*. $5\frac{5}{8}d.$ per milreis; what
is the arbitrated price between Amsterdam and Lisbon?

*Ans.* $45\frac{39}{84}$ *Flem. per crusado.*

(4.) London is indebted to Petersburgh 5000 rubles: now
the exchange between Petersburgh and England is at 50*d*.
per ruble; between Petersburgh and Holland 90*d*. per ruble;
and between Holland and England 36*s*. 4*d*.; which will be
the most advantageous method for London to be drawn upon?

*Ans. London will gain 9l. 11s.* $1\frac{3}{4}d.$ *by making payment
by way of Holland.*

(5.) Amsterdam has an order to remit a certain sum to
Cadiz: and at the time of this order been given Amsterdam
can remit to Cadiz at $94\frac{3}{4}d.$ per ducat of 375 maravedis, and
London can remit to Cadiz at 38*d*. per piastre of 272 maravedis; which then will be most advantageous, for Amsterdam

M 2

to remit directly to Cadiz, or by way of London, exchange being 35s. 10d. per pound sterling?

*Ans.* 18s. 8¼d. *per cent. in favour of London.*

(6.) A merchant of London has 6000 guilders in the Bank of Amsterdam, and was offered 22d. sterling a piece for them; but not liking the offer, he indorsed a bill for the whole to his factor in Paris, who brought the money to France, by exchanging at 55d. Flemish per crown; he allowed the factor ½ per cent. commission for his trouble, and then drew upon him for the whole exchange at 32d. per écu; how much was this better than the offer at 22d. per guilder? *Ans.* 28l. 18s. 2²⁄₁₁d.

## Miscellaneous Questions.

(1.) A. was born when B. was 18 years of age; how old will A. be when B. is 41, and what will be the age of B. when A. is 72? *Ans.* A. 23, B. 90.

(2.) How many bricks, 9 inches long and 4 inches broad, will floor a square room that is 20 feet on each side?

*Ans.* 1600.

(3.) What sum of money, at 3½ per cent., will clear 38l. 10s. in a year and a quarter's time? *Ans.* 880l.

(4.) If 2 acres of land will maintain 3 horses for 4 days, how long will 5 acres of the same pasture maintain six horses? *Ans.* 5 *days.*

(5.) If 3l. be taken off from every 17l. in assessing the rent of a farm, what will the landlord receive out of an estate of 140l. a year, reckoning the tax at 4s. in the pound?

*Ans.* 116l. 18s. 9¾d.

(6.) What annuity is sufficient to pay off a debt of 20000l. in 30 years, at 4 per cent. per annum, compound interest?

*Ans.* 1156l. 12s.

(7.) When will the hour and minute hand of a clock be perpendicular to each other next after 12 o'clock?

*Ans.* 16⁴⁄₁₁ *minutes past* 12 *o'clock.*

(8.) If by selling goods at 2s. 3d. per lb. I clear cent. per cent., what shall I clear per cent. by selling them for 9 guineas per cwt.? *Ans.* 50l. *per cent.*

(9.) Sold a piece of cloth, containing 1000 Flemish ells, for

850 guineas, and gained upon every yard $\frac{1}{8}$ of the prime cost of an English ell: what did the whole piece stand me in?

*Ans.* 771*l.* 17*s.* 10$\frac{2}{37}$ *d.*

(10.) Sold goods for 60 guineas, and by so doing lost 17*l.* per cent., whereas I ought, in dealing, to have cleared 20 per cent.: how much were they sold under their just value?

*Ans.* 28*l.* 1*s.* 8$\frac{20}{83}$*d.*

(11.) Laid out in a lot of muslin 500*l.*, but upon examination a third part of it proved to be damaged, so that I could make but 5*s.* per yard of it, and by so doing find I lost 50*l.*: at what rate per ell then must I sell the undamaged part, so that I may clear 50*l.* by the whole? *Ans.* 11*s.* 7$\frac{2}{7}$*d.*

(12.) How many oaken planks will floor a barn 60$\frac{1}{2}$ feet long, and 33$\frac{1}{2}$ feet wide, supposing the planks to be 15 feet long, and 15 inches wide? *Ans.* 108$\frac{7}{75}$.

(13.) A hare starts 40 yards before a greyhound, and is not perceived by him till she has been up 40 seconds; she scuds away at the rate of 10 miles an hour, and the dog, on view, makes after her at the rate of 18: how long will the course hold, and what ground will be run over, beginning with the outsetting of the dog?

*Ans.* 60$\frac{5}{22}$ *sec. the time, and* 530 *yds. run.*

(14.) An island is 73 miles in circumference, and 3 footmen all start together to travel the same way about it; A. goes 5 miles a day, B. 8, and C. 10: when will they all come together again? *Ans.* 73 *days.*

(15.) A., B., and C. are to share 100000*l.* in the proportion of $\frac{1}{3}$, $\frac{1}{4}$, and $\frac{1}{5}$ respectively; but C.'s part being lost by his death, it is required to divide the whole sum properly between the other two?

*Ans.* A.'s *part is* 57142$\frac{6}{7}$*l., and* B.'s 42857$\frac{1}{7}$*l.*

(16.) If 560 men are besieged in a garrison, and have provisions only for 3 months; how many men must leave the place, that the remainder may be supplied for 5 months?

*Ans.* 224.

(17.) The amount of a sum of money which had been put out to interest is 100*l.*, and the principal is just 7 times as much as the interest: what is the principal? *Ans.* 87*l.* 10*s.*

(18.) If a garrison of 1200 men have provisions for 12 months, but at the end of 3 months are reinforced with 500 men, and 2 months after with 400 more; how long will the provisions last, supposing no alteration to be made in the daily allowance of each man?

*Ans.* $8\frac{1}{2}\frac{1}{4}$ *months in the whole.*

(19.) If two men in three days can earn 15*s.*, how much can seven men earn in four days? *Ans.* 3*l.* 10*s.*

(20.) A pipe of 6 inches bore will run off a certain quantity of liquor in 3 hours, in what time will 4 pipes, each of 3 inches bore, discharge double the quantity? *Ans.* 6 *hours.*

(21.) If a barrel of beer be sufficient to last a family of 7 persons 12 days, how many barrels will be drunk by a family of 12 persons in a year? *Ans.* $52\frac{1}{7}$ *barrels.*

(22.) Suppose the population of a country has increased a tenth part every year, and that there were 14641 persons existing at the end of the first five years: how many must there have been at the beginning? *Ans.* 10000.

(23.) If I buy a certain commodity at 6*s.* per lb. troy weight, how must I sell the same per oz. avoirdupois, so as neither to gain nor lose by the bargain? *Ans.* 5·46*d.*

(24.) A general arranging a division of his army in the form of a solid square, found he had 44 men remaining; but increasing each side by another man, he wanted 49 to fill up the square; how many men had he? *Ans.* 2160.

(25.) A person dying worth 5460*l.* left his wife with child, to whom he bequeathed, if she had a son, $\frac{1}{3}$ of his estate, and the rest to his son; but if she had a daughter, $\frac{1}{3}$ to the daughter, and the rest to her mother. Now it happened that she had both a son and a daughter; how must the estate be divided, so as to answer the father's intention?

*Ans. The son's* 3120*l.*, *the mother's* 1560*l.*, *and the daughter's part is* 780*l.*

(26.) If 3 men or 4 women can do a piece of work in 56 days; how long will one man and one woman, working together, be in doing it? *Ans.* 96 *days.*

(27.) Supposing the circumference of the earth to be 25000 miles; what is the length of a degree, minute, and second, of that circle? *Ans.* 1 *degree*$=69\frac{4}{9}$ *miles,* 1 *minute*$=1\frac{17}{108}$ *mile, and* 1 *second*$=33\frac{77}{81}$ *yds.*

(28.) A lb. of gold, consisting of 11 oz. fine, and 1 oz. of alloy, used to be coined in the Mint of England into $44\frac{1}{2}$ guineas; what then is the value of a lb. of pure gold, supposing the alloy to be of no value? *Ans.* 50*l.* 19*s.* $5\frac{1}{2}d.$

(29.) A prize worth thirty thousand pounds is to be divided

among 1 colonel, 2 majors, 10 captains, 22 lieutenants, 10 ensigns, 50 sergeants, 20 corporals, and 1000 privates, in the following proportion : the colonel is to have one-eighth of the whole ; the majors one hundred shares each ; the captains 50 ; the lieutenants 25 ; the ensigns 20 ; the sergeants 5 ; the corporals 3 ; and the privates 1 : it is required to find the value of their respective shares ?

*Ans. Col. 3750l., majs. 951l. 1s. $8\frac{20}{23}d.$, capt. 475l. 10s. $10\frac{10}{23}d.$, lieuts. 237l. 15s. $5\frac{5}{23}d.$, ens. 190l. 4s. $4\frac{4}{23}d.$, serg. 47l. 11s. $1\frac{1}{23}d.$, corp. 28l. 10s. $7\frac{19}{23}d.$, priv. 9l. 10s. $2\frac{14}{23}d.$*

(30.) A merchant sold goods for 753l. more than he gave for them, and cleared by the bargain 15 per cent.; what sum did he buy them for ? *Ans. 5020l.*

(31.) A cistern, containing 60 gallons of water, has 3 unequal cocks for discharging it ; the greatest cock will empty it in 1 hour, the second in 2 hours, and the third in 3 hours; in what time will it be emptied if they all run together ?

*Ans. $32\frac{8}{11}$ minutes.*

(32.) If I buy goods for 600l. and sell them again immediately for 630l. giving 4 months' credit ; what do I gain by the bargain ? *Ans. 19l. 13s. $5\frac{1}{4}d.$*

(33.) If the scavengers' rate at $1\frac{1}{2}d.$ in the pound comes to 6s. $7\frac{1}{5}d.$ where they usually assess $\frac{4}{5}$ of the rent ; what will the tax for that house be at 4s. in the pound, rated at the full rent ? *Ans. 13l. 5s.*

(34.) If A. can do a piece of work alone in 10 days, and B. in 13 ; in what time will it be finished if they are both set about it together ? *Ans. $5\frac{15}{23}$ days.*

(35.) A. and B. together can build a boat in 18 days, and with the assistance of C. they can do it in 11 days; in what time then would C. do it by himself ? *Ans. $28\frac{2}{7}$ days.*

(36.) If A. can do a piece of work alone in 10 days, and A. and B. together in 7 days ; in what time can B. do it alone ? *Ans. $23\frac{1}{3}$ days.*

(37.) A., B., and C., together, can complete a piece of work in 12 days ; C. can do it alone in 24 days, and A. in 34 days; in what time would B. do it by himself ? *Ans. $81\frac{3}{5}$ days.*

(38.) A. can do a piece of work in 3 weeks ; B. can do thrice as much in 8 weeks, and C. 5 times as much in 12 weeks ; in what time can they finish it, if they are all employed at it together ? *Ans. 6 days, $5\frac{1}{5}$ hours.*

(39.) If a cardinal can pray a soul out of purgatory, by

himself, in an hour, a bishop in 3 hours, a priest in 5, and a friar in 7 ; in what time can they pray out 3 souls, all praying together?      *Ans.* 1 *h.* 47 *m.* $23\frac{2}{11}$ *sec.*

(40.) It is required to divide 1500*l.* between A., B., and C., so that B. may have 72*l.* more than A., and C. 112*l.* more than B.      *Ans. A's share is* $414\frac{2}{3}l.$, B.'s $486\frac{2}{3}l.$, C.'s $598\frac{2}{3}l.$,

(41.) Three merchants, A., B., and C., freight a ship with wine, A. had 284 tuns, B. 140, and C. 64; but the captain in a storm, was obliged to throw 100 tuns overboard ; what part of the loss did each sustain ?

     *Ans.* A. $58\frac{12}{61}$ *tuns,* B. $28\frac{42}{61}$ *tuns, and* C. $13\frac{7}{61}$ *tuns.*

(42.) A traveller left Exeter at 8 o'clock in the morning, and walked towards London at the rate of 3 miles an hour, without intermission ; while another set out from London at 4 o'clock the same evening, and walked towards Exeter at the rate of four miles an hour ; now, supposing the distance between these two cities to be 130 miles, whereabouts on the road will they meet?      *Ans.* $69\frac{3}{7}$ *miles from Exeter.*

(43.) A reservoir for water has two cocks to supply it ; by the first of which, alone, it may be filled in 40 minutes, and by the second in 50 minutes ; it has likewise a discharging cock, by which it can, when full, be emptied in 25 minutes ; now, if these three cocks are all left open when the water comes in, in what time would the cistern be filled, supposing the influx and efflux of the water to be always alike?

     *Ans.* 3 *ho.* 20 *min.*

(44.) If 231 solid inches make a gallon of wine old measure, and 282 a gallon of ale ; how many gallons of wine will a cask hold that was made to contain 38 gallons of ale ?

     *Ans.* 46·389 *gal.*

(45.) A person left by will one half of what he was worth to his son, a third to his daughter, and 10000*l.* which remained to his widow ; what were their respective shares ?

     *Ans. Son's* 30000*l. and daughter's* 20000*l.*

(46.) A court contains 40 square yards ; how many stones are necessary to pave it, each being 2 ft. by 1 ft. 6 in. ?

     *Ans.* 120.

(47.) A water-tub holds 147 gallons, and the pipe that supplies it usually brings in 14 gallons in 9 minutes, while the tap discharges at a medium 40 gallons in 31 minutes ; now, supposing these both to be carelessly left running for 3 hours before the tap is shut, it is required to find in what time the tub will be filled after this accident, in case the water continues flowing from the main?

*Ans.* 1 *h.* 3 *m.* 48$\frac{114}{217}$ *sec.*

(48.) A stationer sold quills at 11*s.* a thousand, by which he cleared $\frac{3}{8}$ of the money; but on their growing scarce he raised them to 13*s.* 6*d.* a thousand; what did he clear per cent. by the latter price?

*Ans.* 96$\frac{4}{11}$*l.* or 96*l.* 7*s.* 3$\frac{3}{11}$*d. per cent.*

(49.) It is required to find the number of fifteens that can be made out of a common pack of 52 cards, as in the game of cribbage? *Ans.* 17264.

(50.) Required the number of different sums that may be formed with a guinea, a half-guinea, a crown, a half-crown, a shilling, and a sixpence. *Ans.* 55986.

(51.) In what time will 100*l.* put out at four per cent. compound interest, amount to 1000*l.*? *Ans. in* 58·908 *years.*

(52.) If a company consisting of 30 men be drawn up in a column, with how many different fronts can this be done, supposing five men to be always in front? *Ans.* 142506.

(53.) Required the least number that can be divided by each of the nine digits, 1, 2, 3, 4, 5, 6, 7, 8, 9, without leaving a remainder? *Ans.* 2520.

(54.) How many palisades will surround a square fort, whose side is 150 yards, the centres of the palisades being 10 inches asunder? *Ans.* 2160.

(55.) Suppose a general lays a contribution of 2000*l.* on 4 towns, to be paid in proportion to the number of inhabitants in each; and that the 1st contains 1200, the 2nd 1400, the 3d 1600, and the 4th 1800; what part must each town pay?

*Ans.* 400*l.*, 466$\frac{2}{3}$*l.*, 533$\frac{1}{3}$*l.*, and 600*l.*

(56.) Suppose a farmer has a calf, which at the end of three years begins to breed, and afterwards brings a female calf every year; and that each calf begins to breed in like manner at the end of three years, bringing forth a cow-calf every year; and that these last breed in the same manner, &c.; it is required to determine the owner's whole stock at the end of 20 years? *Ans.* 1278.

# A CONCISE METHOD OF VERIFYING DATES IN ACCORDANCE WITH THE JULIAN AND GREGORIAN CALENDAR;

*Or a Perpetual Almanac of both Styles, from and to any Date, before and after the Christian Era, without Limitation. To which is subjoined Rules for finding Easter by New or Old Style in perpetuity, and determining the Moon's age at any given period.*

By Samuel Maynard, Editor of Keith's and Bonnycastle's Mathematical Works, &c. &c.

*Entered at Stationers' Hall, 1846,*

---

Directions for using the Table.— If the given date be old style, and less than 700 years, or new style and less than 400 years, it will be the tabular date for its respective style; but if the date be old style and 700 or more, divide by 700, or if new style and 400 or

**Remaining Years above Centuries after Christ.**

more, divide by 400, the remainder will be the tabular date, the *centuries* of this remainder or tabular date being given in the upper part of the middle portion of the table against their title, for new style (N. S.), and old style (O. S.), as well for before Christ (B.C.) as after Christ (A. C.); the remaining given years will be found on the right or left according as the given date is before Christ or after, then the Dominical letter of the given date will be found on the same horizontal line with these remaining years, in the same vertical column with their centuries.

**Centuries before and after Christ.**

Now the Dominical letter of the given year being known, take it on the same horizontal line with the given month, and directly under it (viz. the Dominical letter), on the same horizontal line with the given date of the month, will be found the day of the week as required. And note, all

**Remaining Years above Centuries before Christ.**

the years which are dotted are leap years except 100, 200, 300, N. S., A. C., and 100, 200, 301, N. S., B. C., which are common years, and for 100, 200, 300, N. S., B. C., take O for O, and in 101, 201, 301, N. S., B. C., take 1 for 1, and for Jan. and Feb. in leap years take Jan. or Feb. printed in Italics.

*Note.* A cycle of the Julian Calendar is 700 years, and that of the Gregorian Calendar 400 years; and on this principle the formulas of this Calendar are based.

*Examples for Practice on the preceding Table.*

(1.) Find the Dominical letter for 301, N. S. B. C. Under 3 centuries N. S. B. C.; and against **1** on the right under N. S. will be found C the Dominical letter.

(2.) Also for 1727 O. S. Here 1727 ÷ 700 leaves rem. 327, which gives A for Dominical letter after Christ, and E for the Sunday letter before Christ.

(3.) Required the day of the week 1*st* January, 1800, N. S. A. C., and 12*th February*, 1852, N. S. A. C.

Here 1800 is a common year, and 1800 ÷ 400 leaves 200 rem. for the tabular date, *viz.* 2 centuries, and no remaining years. Under 2 centuries N. S. A. C. and against 0., the remaining years above centuries after Christ, on the left, is E, the Sunday letter; under E in the line of Jan. and against 1*st*, the date of the month, is Wednesday, the day of the week required. For the year 1852 take the remainder 252, which gives C, and is a leap year, whence 12*th Feb.* is Thursday.

(4.) Required the days of the week corresponding to the dates of the following registrations:—Samuel was born on December 16*th*, 1789; Hannah on 14*th* July, 1791; Rebecca on 11*th* October, 1800; Ann on 25*th* December, 1813; Alfred on 23*rd* February, 1821; Augustus on 20*th* May, 1823; Sarah on 30*th* January, 1826; Newton on 6*th* December, 1832; and Mary Ann on 26*th* December, 1834?

*Ans.* Samuel on a Wednesday; Hannah on a Thursday; Rebecca on a Saturday; Ann on a Saturday; Alfred on a Friday; Augustus on a Tuesday; Sarah on a Monday; Newton on a Thursday; and Mary Ann on a Friday.

(5.) What day of the month did the last Friday in *January, February, August*, and December, fall on in the year 1844, N. S. A. C. ?

*Ans.* 26*th* of *January*, 23*rd* of *February*, 30*th* August, and 27*th* of December.

(6.) An elderly lady speaking of her age, says she was born in the year 1760, but does not know on what day of the month : she only recollects hearing her father say it was the second Wednesday in *February ;* required the day of the month she was born? *Ans.* 13*th*.

(7.) In what years of the 19*th* century, after Christ, new style, does 29*th* February fall on a Friday ?

Look in the table for 29*th* the given date of the month, and on the same horizontal line find the given day of the week, Friday, directly over which, on the same horizontal line with *Feb.* (since 29*th* indicates leap year) will be found E. the dominical letter for the required year.

For the 19*th* century find E, in the column for two centuries N. S. A. C. On the same horizontal line will be found the remaining years above centuries after Christ, viz. 0, 6, 17, 23, ·28, 34, 45, 51, ·56, 62, 73, 79, ·84, and 90, indicating 1800, 1806, &c.; the year 1800 is, however, excluded, since the 19*th* century does not begin before 1 Jan., 1801 ; moreover, for 29*th* February, leap years only are to be taken, whence the years required are 1828, 1856, and 1884.

(8.) On what years of the 19*th* century, New Style, does Midsummer-day (24*th* June) fall on a Sunday?

M 6

*Ans.* 1804, 1810, 1821, 1827, 1832, 1838, 1849, 1855, 1860, 1866, 1877, 1883, 1888, and 1894.

(9.) Required the *Dominical Letters* for leap years and common years, when the 1*st* of January and February fall on a Sunday?

*Ans.* In leap years only G and C for *January* and *February* respectively; and in common years A and D.

(10.) According to Mr. Baily an eclipse of the sun happened 30*th* September, 610, B. C. O. S. Required the day of the week.

In the column of 6 centuries B. C. O. S. (being the centuries of the given date, 610), and on the same horizontal line with 10 (the remaining years of the given date, 610), among the remaining years above centuries before Christ will be found the Sunday letter B. With which, as before, we find Friday, the day of the week required.

(11.) According to Archbishop Usher, the earth was created 23*rd* October, 4004, B. C. O. S. Required the day of the week.

*Ans.* Sunday.

(12.) On what days of the week, in the year 1724, Old Style, did 17*th* of *January*, leap year, and 16*th* of December fall? and in what other years of the 18*th* and 19*th* centuries will the same dates of the month fall on the same days of the week?

*Ans.* In the year 1724, O. S., 17*th January* happened on a Friday, and 16*th* December on a Wednesday. And the only other leap year, O. S., in the 18*th* century, which answers the question, is 1752; and the only leap year, N. S., which in the 18*th* century answers the question is 1772, therefore 17*th January* falls on a Friday. Similarly, in the 19*th* century, the years are ·1812, ·1840, ·1868, and ·1896, in which 17*th January* falls on a Friday.

With regard to 16*th* December, all years before 1752 are to be taken by Old Style; these years are 1702, 1713, 1719, 1724, 1730, 1741, and 1747, O. S.; the years after 1751 are to be taken by New Style, which, in the 18th century, are 1761, 1767, 1772, 1778, 1789, 1795. And, in the 19*th* century, 1801, 1807, 1812, 1818, 1829, 1835, 1840, 1846, 18 57, 1863, 1868, 1874, 1885, 1891, and 1896, in all which years 16*th* December happens on a Wednesday.

N. B. In England the year was commenced by the Church on the 25*th* of December, or Christmas-day, from the seventh to the twelfth century, and by civilians to the fourteenth century; from 1400 till 1752, the year began on the 25*th* of March; and from 1752 to the present time it began on the 1*st* of January: consequently, in some manuscripts, where the dates do not agree with the above calendar, between January 1*st* to the 25*th* of March, in any year from 1400 to 1752, one year should be added to the given year, before using either of the above Tables; also, from 700 to 1400, for dates between Christmas-day and the 1*st* of January, one year should be subtracted to give the correct date. But the whole of these particulars have been generally rectified in printed works on Chronology, &c. to agree with the historical year.

## TO FIND EASTER SUNDAY FOR ANY YEAR IN PERPE-TUITY BY NEW OR OLD STYLE.

*Easter Sunday* is that Sunday which happens next after the Paschal fourteenth of the moon.

*The paschal fourteenth of the moon* is that fourteenth day of the moon's age which happens on or next after the 21*st* March.

The paschal fourteenth of the moon depends on the moon's age on some specific day, (the choice of which is arbitrary).

*The epact of any year* is the moon's age on the last day of the preceding year.

The paschal fourteenth has therefore a dependence on the epact.

The epact depends on a cycle of 19 years; the nineteen numbers of this cycle are called *golden numbers*; in the Julian or Old style a lunar correction is in strictness required; in the Gregorian or new style there is a second correction required, which may be called the solar correction.

The lunar correction is a correction of 1 day every 312½ years, or of 8 days in 2500 years; its cycle is a passage through 4 lunations, or 15 × 2500 = 37500 years, or 375 centuries, because it is only varied from century to century.

The solar correction depends only on the change of style from the Julian to the Gregorian; the three days taken away by Pope Gregory XIII. every 400 years amounts to an entire lunation or 30 days in 4000 years, which is therefore the cycle of the solar correction.

In the process of determining Easter there are several divisions, in some of which the integral quotient only is to be taken, and others in which the remainder only is required.

When the letter $q$ is attached as an index to a formula of division, it denotes the integral quotient only is to be taken.

When the letter $r$ is attached as an index to a formula of division, it denotes that the remainder only is to be taken; thus in $\frac{116}{7} = 16$ the quotient and 4 the *remainder*; then $\left(\frac{116}{7}\right)_q = 16$, and $\left(\frac{116}{7}\right)_r = 4$.

### *To find Easter Sunday for any Year after Christ, New Style.*

*First.* Let the given date of the year be called . . . . . . $a$

*Second.* Let $\left(\frac{a}{100}\right)_q$, or the number of centuries contained in $a$, be called . . . . . . . . . . . . . . $b$

*Third.* Let $\left(\frac{b+8}{25}\right)_q = \left\{\frac{4 \times (b+8)}{100}\right\}_q$, or the number of centuries in $4 \times (b+8)$ . . . . . . . . . . . . $c$

*Fourth.* Let $\left\{ \dfrac{11 \times \left(\frac{a}{19}\right)_r + \left(\frac{b+1-c}{3}\right)_q + \left(\frac{b}{4}\right)_q + \left[38 - \left(\frac{b}{30}\right)_r\right]}{30} \right\}_r \ldots e$

If $e = 24$, change it always into 25. If $e = 25$, change it into 26, provided $\left(\dfrac{a}{19}\right)_r$ exceed 10 ; but not otherwise.

*Fifth.* Take $44 - e$, if $e$ be less than 24 ; but if $e$ exceed 24, take $74 - e$, and call the result $\hspace{4cm} p$

*Sixth.* Let $7 - \left\{ \dfrac{p + a + \left(\frac{a}{4}\right)_q + \left(\frac{b}{4}\right)_q + \left[9 - \left(\frac{b}{7}\right)_r\right]}{7} \right\}_r \ldots d$

*Seventh.* Then $p + d$, if $p + d$ does not exceed 31, is that day of March on which falls Easter Sunday.

And $p + d - 31$, if $p + d$ does exceed 31, is that day of April on which falls Easter Sunday.

In the above process $\left(\dfrac{a}{19}\right)_r$, which may be called $g$, is the golden number of the year preceding the given date $a$; its cycle is 19 years.

$\left(\dfrac{b+1-c}{3}\right)_q$ is the lunar correction (for which we may also take the remainder after dividing by 30).

$\left(\dfrac{b}{4}\right)_q + \left[30 - \left(\dfrac{b}{30}\right)_r\right]$ is the solar correction (for which we may also take the remainder after dividing by 30).

The sum of the above two corrections, $\left(\dfrac{b+1-c}{3}\right)_q + \left(\dfrac{b}{4}\right)_q + \left[30 - \left(\dfrac{b}{30}\right)_r\right]$, or the remainder after dividing it by 30, is the luni-solar correction ; its cycle is 300000 years, being the least common multiple of the two partial cycles of 37500 and 4000 years.

$e$ is the epact; its cycle is $19 \times 300000 = 5700000$ years, compounded of 19, the cycle of the Golden number, and 300000, the cycle of the luni-solar correction.

$p$ is the paschal term, or the number of days from the last day of the preceding February to the day of the paschal fourteenth ; its cycle is the same as that of the epact, *viz.* 5700000 years.

$\left(\dfrac{b}{4}\right)_q + \left[9 - \left(\dfrac{b}{7}\right)_r\right]$ is the week-day correction ; its cycle is 400 years.

$7 - d$ is the dominical number; it determines the day of the week upon which falls the paschal fourteenth for, as $7 - d$ is $= 0, 1, 2, 3, 4, 5,$ or 6, so does the paschal fourteenth fall upon Sunday, Monday, Tuesday, Wednesday, Thursday, Friday, or Saturday.

$d$ is the number of days by which Easter Sunday follows the paschal fourteenth.

## To find Easter Sunday for any Year after Christ, Old Style.

This determination is derived from New Style by making the luni-solar correction $\left(\frac{b+1-c}{3}\right)_q + \left(\frac{b}{4}\right)_q + \left[30 - \left(\frac{b}{30}\right)_r\right] = 0$, which reduces

the epact to $e = \left\{\dfrac{11 \times \left(\frac{a}{19}\right)_r + 8}{30}\right\}_r$ *; and the least value of $\left(\frac{a}{19}\right)_r$ which

makes $e = 24$, is $= 26$; hence $e$ is never $= 24$.

Also $\left(\frac{b}{4}\right)_q + \left[9 - \left(\frac{b}{7}\right)_r\right]$ the week-day correction $= 0$.

Whence the preceding process for the Gregorian or New style is for the Julian or Old style, reduced thus:

*First.* Let the given date be called   .   .   .   .   $a$

*Second.* Compute $e = \left\{\dfrac{11 \times \left(\frac{a}{19}\right)_r + 8}{30}\right\}_r$.

*Third.* Find $p$ as in *Fifth* of New Style.

*Fourth.* Compute $d = 7 - \left\{\dfrac{p + a + \left(\frac{a}{4}\right)_q}{7}\right\}_r$.

*Fifth.* Then $(p+d)$ of March, or $(p+d) - 31$ of April, as in *Seventh* of New Style, is Easter Sunday.

The cycle of $e$ is 19 years, that of $d$ is 28 years; the cycle of Easter Sundays is therefore $19 \times 28 = 532$ years.

*Note* 1. To find the remainder in dividing by 30, take the sum of all the digits except the last, which sum divide by 3; the remainder will be the tens' digits of the remainder, to which annex the unit's figure of the dividend.

### EXAMPLES.

(*Ex.* 1.) Required Easter Sunday for the year 1 after Christ.

For *New Style. First*, $a = 1$; *second*, $b = 0$; *third*, $\left(\frac{b+8}{25}\right)_q = \left(\frac{0+8}{25}\right)_q =$

---

* In strictness it should be $e = \left\{\dfrac{11 \times \left(\frac{a}{19}\right)_r + \left(\frac{b+1-c}{3}\right)_q + 6}{30}\right\}_r$;

and for dates before Christ instead of $g = \left(\frac{a}{19}\right)_r$ take $g = 20 - \left(\frac{a}{19}\right)_r$

which make $= 0$ when $\left(\frac{a}{19}\right)_r = 1$.

$$\left(\frac{8}{25}\right)_q = 0 = c \; ; \; 4th, \left\{\frac{11 \times \left(\frac{a}{19}\right)_r + \left(\frac{b+1-c}{3}\right)_q + \left(\frac{b}{4}\right)_q + \left[38 - \left(\frac{b}{30}\right)_r\right]}{30}\right\}$$

$$= \left\{\frac{11 \times \left(\frac{1}{19}\right)_r + \left(\frac{0+1-0}{3}\right)_q + \left(\frac{0}{4}\right)_q + \left[38 - \left(\frac{0}{30}\right)_r\right]}{30}\right\}_r$$

$$= \left\{\frac{11 \times 1 + \left(\frac{1}{3}\right)_q + 0 + 38}{30}\right\}_r = \left(\frac{11+0+0+38}{30}\right)_r = \left(\frac{49}{30}\right)_r = 19 = e \; ; \; fifth,$$

$$44 - e = 44 - 19 = 25 = p \; ; \; sixth, \; 7 - \left\{\frac{p + a + \left(\frac{a}{4}\right)_q + \left(\frac{b}{4}\right)_q + \left[9 - \left(\frac{b}{7}\right)_r\right]}{7}\right\}$$

$$= 7 - \left\{\frac{25 + 1 + \left(\frac{1}{4}\right)_q + \left(\frac{0}{4}\right)_q + \left[9 - \left(\frac{0}{7}\right)_r\right]}{7}\right\}_r = 7 - \left(\frac{25+1+0+0+9}{7}\right)_r$$

$$= 7 - \left(\frac{35}{7}\right)_r = 7 - 0 = 7 = d \; ; \; seventh, \; p + d - 31 = 25 + 7 - 31 = 1. \quad \text{There-}$$

fore, 1st April is Easter Sunday, *New Style.*

For *Old Style.* First, $a = 1$ ; second, $e = \left\{\frac{11 \times \left(\frac{1}{19}\right)_r + 8}{30}\right\}_r$

$$= \left(\frac{11 \times 1 + 8}{30}\right)_r = \left(\frac{19}{30}\right)_r = 19 \; ; \; third, \; p = 25, \text{ as before ; } fourth, \; d =$$

$$7 - \left\{\frac{25 + 1 + \left(\frac{1}{4}\right)_q}{7}\right\}_r = 7 - \left(\frac{25+1+0}{7}\right)_r = 7 - \left(\frac{26}{7}\right)_r = 7 - 5 = 2 \; ; \; fifth,$$

$p + d = 25 + 2 = 27$ ; whence 27th March is Easter Sunday, *Old Style.*

(*Ex.* 2.) Required Easter Sunday for the year 1852 after Christ.

For *New Style.* First, $a = 1852$ ; second, $\left(\frac{a}{100}\right)_q = \left(\frac{1852}{100}\right)_q = 18 = b$ ;

third, $\left(\frac{b+8}{25}\right)_q = \left(\frac{18+8}{25}\right)_q = \left(\frac{26}{25}\right)_q = 1 = c$ ;

fourth, $\left\{\frac{11 \times \left(\frac{a}{19}\right)_r + \left(\frac{b+1-c}{3}\right)_q + \left(\frac{b}{4}\right)_q + \left[38 - \left(\frac{b}{30}\right)_r\right]}{30}\right\}_r$

$$= \left\{\frac{11 \times \left(\frac{1852}{19}\right)_r + \left(\frac{18+1-1}{3}\right)_q + \left(\frac{18}{4}\right)_q + \left[38 - \left(\frac{18}{30}\right)_r\right]}{30}\right\}_r =$$

$$\left\{\frac{11 \times 9 + 6 + 4 + 20}{30}\right\}_r = \left(\frac{129}{30}\right)_r = 9 = e \; ; \; fifth, \; 44 - e = 44 - 9 = 35 = p \; ;$$

$$\text{sixth, } 7 - \left\{ \frac{p + a + \left(\frac{a}{4}\right)_q + \left(\frac{b}{4}\right)_q + \left[9 - \left(\frac{b}{7}\right)_r\right]}{7} \right\}_r$$

$$= 7 - \left\{ \frac{35 + 1852 + \left(\frac{1852}{4}\right)_q + \left(\frac{18}{4}\right)_q + \left[9 - \left(\frac{18}{7}\right)_r\right]}{7} \right\}_r$$

$$= 7 - \left(\frac{35 + 1852 + 463 + 4 + 5}{7}\right)_r = 7 - \left(\frac{2359}{7}\right)_r = 7 - 0 = 7 = d \quad \text{seventh,}$$

$p + d - 31 = 35 + 7 - 31 = 11$; whence 11*th* April is Easter Sunday, *New Style.*

For *Old Style.* First, $a = 1852$; second, $e = \left\{ \dfrac{11 \times \left(\frac{1852}{19}\right)_r + 8}{30} \right\}_r$

$$= \left(\frac{11 \times 9 + 8}{30}\right)_r = \left(\frac{107}{30}\right)_r = 17; \quad \text{third, } 44 - e = 44 - 17 = 27 = p; \quad \text{fourth,}$$

$$d = 7 - \left\{ \frac{p + a + \left(\frac{a}{4}\right)_q}{7} \right\}_r = 7 - \left\{ \frac{27 + 1852 + \left(\frac{1852}{4}\right)}{7} \right\}_r$$

$$= 7 - \left(\frac{27 + 1852 + 463}{7}\right)_r = 7 - \left(\frac{2342}{7}\right)_r = 7 - 4 = 3 = d; \quad \text{fifth, } p + d =$$

$27 + 3 = 30$; whence 30*th* March, is Easter Sunday, *Old Style.*

(*Ex.* 3.) Required Easter Sunday for the year 1234567890 after Christ.

For *New Style.* First, $a = 1234567890$; second, $b = 12345678$;

third, $\left(\dfrac{12345678 + 8}{25}\right)_q = \left(\dfrac{12345686}{25}\right)_q = \left(\dfrac{49382744}{100}\right)_q = 493827 = c$;

fourth, $\left\{ \dfrac{11 \times \left(\frac{a}{19}\right)_r + \left(\frac{b + 1 - c}{3}\right) + \left(\frac{b}{4}\right)_q + \left[38 - \left(\frac{b}{30}\right)_r\right]}{30} \right\}_r =$

$$\left\{ \frac{11 \times \left(\frac{1234567890}{19}\right)_r + \left(\frac{12345678 + 1 - 493827}{3}\right)_q + \left(\frac{12345678}{4}\right)_q + \left[38 - \left(\frac{12345678}{30}\right)_r\right]}{30} \right\}_r$$

$$= \left\{ \frac{11 \times 7 + \left(\frac{11851852}{3}\right)_q + 3086419 + (38 - 18)}{30} \right\}_r$$

$$= \left(\frac{77 + 3950617 + 3086419 + 20}{30}\right)_r = \left(\frac{7037133}{30}\right)_r, \text{ and by } \textit{Note } 1. \text{ p. 255.}$$

$$\left(\frac{7 + 0 + 3 + 7 + 1 + 3}{3}\right)_r = \left(\frac{21}{3}\right)_r = 0; \text{ whence } \left(\frac{7037133}{30}\right)_r = 03, \text{ or } 3 = e;$$

fifth, $44 - e = 44 - 3 = 41 = p$;

$$sixth, \quad 7 - \left\{\frac{p + a + \left(\frac{a}{4}\right)_q + \left(\frac{b}{4}\right)_q + \left[9 - \left(\frac{b}{7}\right)_r\right]}{7}\right\}_r =$$

$$7 - \left\{\frac{41 + 1234567890 + \left(\frac{1234567890}{4}\right)_q + \left(\frac{12345678}{4}\right)_q + \left[9 - \left(\frac{12345678}{7}\right)_r\right]}{7}\right\}_r$$

$$= 7 - \left(\frac{41 + 1234567890 + 308641972 + 3086419 + 7}{7}\right)_r =$$

$$7 - \left(\frac{1546296329}{7}\right)_r = 7 - 4 = 3 = d; \quad seventh, \quad p + d - 31 = 41 + 3 - 31 = 13,$$

whence 13th April is Easter Sunday, *New Style.*

For the *Julian Style. First,* $a = 1234567890$;

$$second, \quad e = \left\{\frac{11 \times \left(\frac{a}{19}\right)_r + 8}{30}\right\}_r = \left\{\frac{11 \times \left(\frac{1234567890}{19}\right)_r + 8}{30}\right\}_r$$

$$= \left\{\frac{11 \times 7 + 8}{30}\right\}_r = \left(\frac{85}{30}\right)_r = 25; \quad third, \quad p = 74 - 25 = 49;$$

$$fourth, \quad 7 - \left\{\frac{p + a + \left(\frac{a}{4}\right)_q}{7}\right\}_r = 7 - \left\{\frac{49 + 1234567890 + \left(\frac{1234567890}{4}\right)_q}{7}\right\}$$

$$= 7 - \left(\frac{49 + 1234567890 + 308641972}{7}\right)_r = 7 - \left(\frac{1543209911}{7}\right)_r = 7 - 5$$

$= 2 = d$; *fifth,* $p + d - 31 = 49 + 2 - 31 = 20$; whence 20th April is Easter Sunday, *Old Style.*

*Note* 2. Since the Easter Sundays recur again in the Gregorian style in a cycle of 5700000 years, we may, when the given date is above 5699999, divide by 5700000, and take the remainder for the given date; thus for the year 5700000 we may take $a = 0$; then $b = 0$; $c = 0$;

$$e = \left\{\frac{\left(\frac{0}{19}\right)_r + \left(\frac{0 + 1 - 0}{3}\right)_q + \left(\frac{0}{4}\right)_q + \left[38 - \left(\frac{0}{30}\right)_r\right]}{30}\right\}_r = 8; \quad p = 36;$$

$$d = 7 - \left\{\frac{36 + 0 + \left(\frac{0}{4}\right)_q + \left(\frac{0}{4}\right)_q + \left[9 - \left(\frac{0}{7}\right)_r\right]}{7}\right\} = 7 - \left(\frac{45}{7}\right)_r = 7 - 3$$

$= 4$; whence $36 + 4 - 31 = 9$ gives 9th April, for Easter Sunday, *New Style.*

*Again,* let the preceding example, 1234567890 be taken, then $\left(\frac{1234567890}{5700000}\right)_r = 3367890$. Hence, *first,* $3367890 = a$; *second,* $33678 = b$;

*third,* $c = 1347$; *fourth,* $e = 3$ as before; and *fifth,* $p = 41$ as before; *sixth,* $d = 3$ as before; whence the result is 13th April for Easter Sunday, *New Style,* as before.

*Note* 3. Since the Easter Sundays recur again in the Julian Style in a cycle of 532 years, we may, when the given date exceeds 531, divide by 532, and take the remainder for the given date.

Thus, taking the number 1234567890, we have $\left(\dfrac{1234567890}{532}\right)_r$

$=178$. Hence, *first*, $178=a$; *second*, $e=25$ as before; *third*, $p=49$ as before; *fourth*, $d=5$ as before; whence, *fifth*, 20th April is Easter Sunday, *Old Style*, as before.

*Note* 4. Aloysius Lilius, or Luigi Lilio Ghiraldi, a learned astronomer and physician of Naples, was the inventor of the Luni-Solar correction, and, according to his principles, a table of 3000 centuries, the Cycle, was inserted by Christopher Clavius in his great work on the Calendar printed in 1612, *folio*: each of these centuries is indicated by a letter (of which there are thirty) prefixed, those centuries requiring the same correction having the same letter, and those requiring a different correction having a different letter.

Now, if we take $\left(\dfrac{1234567890}{300000}\right)_r$ or $\left(\dfrac{3367890}{300000}\right)_r=67890$, of which the

number of centuries is 678; the same lunar correction 398 or 8, belongs equally to 1234567890, 3367890, and 67890, and to the centurial year in the Table of Clavius is prefixed the letter h. Now, there is another table in the same work of Clavius, containing the Epacts, &c. for the Gregorian Style, and the Golden Numbers, Sunday Letters, Paschal fourteenths, Easter Sundays, &c. both for New and Old Style, from the year 1600 to the year 5000, both inclusive, with which we compared our solutions; thus, in the first table commencing at *page* 112, we find the letter h prefixed to the centurial year 5000, which must, therefore, have the same lunar correction, 8, before found. Now, whenever *p* and *d* are the same, Easter Sunday is the same, or whenever *e*, the epact, and the Sunday letter are the same, Easter Sunday is the same; but *e* is always the same when the Golden Number and the luni-solar correction are the same. Next for the Sunday letter, if we divide 1234567890 or 3367890 by 400 and add 2000 years to the remainder, we shall find what year has the same Sunday letter as that proposed, and which year will be found in the second great table of Clavius, commencing at *page* 380; to find the year, it is sufficient to take the last four digits of

the given year; thus, $\left(\dfrac{7890}{400}\right)_r+2000=2290$, which, by the table of

Clavius, has the Sunday letter E; hence, every year in the table of Clavius, which has 3 for its epact and E for its Sunday letter, will have the same Easter Sunday, *New Style*, as the proposed year 1234567890, or 3367890; now, on referring to the table of Clavius, we find the year 1732 to have 3 for its epact and E for its Sunday letter; and the Easter Sunday, *New Style*, is there given 13th April, agreeing with the foregoing computed result. And we may, in like manner, compare any given year with the two tables of Clavius, of which two tables every error has been corrected. In the table of the cycle of 3000 centuries, only two errors were discovered; the year 57400, which has C, should have D; and the year 57700, which has D, should have C.

With regard to Old Style Easters, if we take $532 \times 3 + \left(\dfrac{a}{532}\right)_r$ for *a*, we have a corresponding year in the second table of Clavius; thus, for

$$a = 1234567890, \text{ we have } 532 \times 3 + \left(\frac{1234567890}{532}\right)_r = 1596 + 178 = 1774,$$

which in the table of Clavius has 20*th* April for Easter Sunday, *Old Style*, agreeing with our calculated result.

(*Ex.* 4.) Find Easter Sunday for the year 33 A.C. (year of the crucifixion), both for the New and Old Style.

*Ans.* 3 *April*, New Style; 5 *April*, Old Style.

(*Ex.* 5.) Find Easter Sunday for the year 100 A.C., both for New and Old Style.　　*Ans.* 18*th April* New, and 12*th April* Old Style.

(*Ex.* 6.) Find Easter Sunday for the year 325 A.C. (the year of the Council of Nice, which established the definition of Easter here given).

*Ans.* 19*th April* New Style; 18*th April* Old Style.

(*Ex.* 7.) Find Easter Sunday for the year 1583 (the first Easter observed according to the Gregorian or *New* Style).

*Ans.* 10*th April* New Style, and 31*st March* Old Style.

(*Ex.* 8.) Find Easter Sunday for 1600 (the first in the Table of Clavius).　　*Ans.* 2*nd April* New, and 23*rd March* Old Style.

(*Ex.* 9.) Find Easter Sunday for 1753 (the first observed in England according to New Style).

*Ans.* 22*nd April* New, and 11*th April* Old Style.

(*Ex.* 10.) Find Easter Sunday for 1693.

*Ans.* 22*nd March* New Style (*the earliest possible day*), and 16*th April* Old Style.

(*Ex.* 11.) Find Easter Sunday for 1734.

*Ans.* 25*th April* New Style (*the latest possible day*), and 14*th April* Old Style.

(*Ex.* 12.) Find Easter Sunday for 1954.

*Ans.* 18*th April* New Style, 12*th April* Old Style.

(*Ex.* 13.) Find Easter Sunday for 2060.

*Ans.* 18*th April* New Style, 12*th April* Old Style.

(*Ex.* 14.) Find Easter Sunday for the year 3909.

*Ans.* 18*th April* New Style, 4*th April* Old Style.

(*Ex.* 15.) Find Easter Sunday for the year 4763.

*Ans.* 7*th April* New Style, 15*th April* Old Style.

Gauss has taken this example, and by his formula also finds 7*th April* New Style, and 15*th April* Old Style.

N.B. The last six examples are taken from Delambre's Formulæ (see *Connaissance des Tems, Additions. Année* 1817, *page* 307.)

(*Ex.* 16.) Find Easter Sunday for the year 5000 (the last in the table of Clavius).　　*Ans.* 30*th March* New, and 5*th April* Old Style.

(*Ex.* 17.) Find Easter Sunday for the year 9876543210 both for New and Old Style, using the cycles of 5700000 and 532.

*Ans.* 11*th April* New Style, and 16*th April* Old Style.

The principal authority for the determination of Easter is Clavius, who carried out the principles of Aloysius Lilius, the inventor (*Encyc. Brit.*, Art. "Calendar," *p.* 10.). Gauss, also, in the *Monatliche Correspondenz von Baron von Zach*, Aug. 1800, has reduced the determination of Easter to an analytical formula, which Delambre says may fail after the year 4200, in consequence of omitting the term *c* in the lunar correction: his formula, applied to the year 9876543210, gives 18th April, *New Style*. This method of Gauss is given in the *Edin. Encyc.*, in the article "Chronology," together with two tables required; but it is not there shown how the tables are computed, but this Gauss himself has done. The formula of Gauss has been corrected by Ciccolini. Delambre, in his *Histoire de l'Astronomie Moderne*, vol. i. p. 25., has given a method of finding Easter, which, however, fails after 108 centuries, by requiring an impossible subtraction. He has given also a method in the Additions to the *Connaissance des Tems, Année* 1817, which, though not liable to this objection, is not so general as it might have been made; most of these formulæ are restricted to commence at a certain century. Those here given are unlimited, and they might even be carried back to years before Christ by means of the cycles of 5700000 and 532 years. Thus, let A be any date after Christ, c the number of years in a cycle; then

A and $\left(\dfrac{A}{c}\right)_r$ are equivalents; similarly, if A be any date before Christ,

then $c + 1 - \left(\dfrac{A}{c}\right)_r$ will be an equivalent date after Christ. The cycles

for the epacts are 300000 years, and 19 years.

The epacts $e$ here determined are annual epacts, if $m$ denote a monthly epact, $t$ the date of the month, then the moon's age for that day will be

$M = \left(\dfrac{e + m + t}{30}\right)_r$; the values of $m$ are given below.*

(*Ex.* 1.) For 30*th* September 610 B.C., Old Style. Here $A = 610$, $c =$

$300000$; $a = 300001 - \left(\dfrac{610}{300000}\right)_r = 300001 - 610 = 299391$; $b = 2993$;

*Next*, $c = 19$, then

$20 - \left(\dfrac{A}{19}\right)_r = 20 - \left(\dfrac{610}{19}\right)_r = 18$; $c = \left(\dfrac{2993 + 8}{25}\right)_q = \left(\dfrac{3001}{25}\right)_q = 120$; then,

by the foot note, *page* 255, $e = \left\{ \dfrac{11 \times 18 + \left(\dfrac{2993 + 1 - 120}{3}\right)_q + 6}{30} \right\}_r$

$= \left(\dfrac{198 + 958 + 6}{30}\right)_r = \left(\dfrac{1162}{30}\right)_r = 22$; $m = 7$; $t = 30$; whence, M, the Moon's

age, $= \left(\dfrac{22 + 7 + 30}{30}\right)_r = 29$ days.

---

\* MONTHLY NUMBERS OR VALUES OF $m$.

| Jan. | Feb. | Mar. | April. | May. | June. | July. | Aug. | Sept. | Oct. | Nov. | Dec. |
|------|------|------|--------|------|-------|-------|------|-------|------|------|------|
| 0 | 1 | 0 | 1 | 2 | 3 | 4 | 5 | 7 | 7 | 9 | 9 |

These numbers $m$ show the moon's age on the last day of the preceding month on the supposition that the annual epact = 0.

(*Ex.* 2.) Required the Moon's age 15*th* May 1852, New Style. Here *e* = 9, by *Example* 2 of Easter; *m* = 2; *t* = 15, then Moon's age =

$$\left(\frac{9+2+15}{30}\right)_r = 26 \text{ days.}$$

*Note* 5. When M = 0, it indicates New Moon; and when M = 15, it indicates full moon.

## A COLLECTION OF SOME OF THE MOST USEFUL PROPERTIES OF NUMBERS.

[EXTRACTED FROM EUCLID, AND OTHER WRITERS.]

### DEFINITIONS.

(1.) *A unit*, or *unity*, is that by which every thing, taken singly, or by itself, is considered as one.

(2.) *An integer*, or *whole number*, is that which is composed of one or more units, as 1, 2, 3, 4, &c.

(3.) *A multiple* of any number is some exact number of times that number.

Thus, 6 is a multiple of 2, or of 3, the former being taken three times, and the latter twice.

(4.) *A measure* or *aliquot part* of any number is the number by which it can be divided without leaving any remainder.

Thus, 2 and 3 are each measures, or aliquot parts of 6, being contained in it an exact number of times.

(5.) *A common measure* of two or more numbers is that number which will divide each of them without leaving a remainder; and if it be the greatest number that will divide them, it is called their greatest common measure.

Thus, 2 is a common measure of 8 and 12, being contained in the former of these numbers four times, and in the latter six; and 4 is their greatest common measure.

(6.) *An even number* is that which can be halved, or divided into two equal parts, as 2, 4, 8, 10, &c., each of which can be divided by 2.

(7.) *An odd number* is that which cannot be halved, or which differs from an even number by unity, as 1, 3, 5, 7, 9, &c., neither of which can be divided by 2, without a remainder.

(8.) *A prime* or *incomposite number* is that which cannot

be exactly divided by any other number, except by itself, or unity.

Thus, 2, 3, 5, 7, 11, 13, 17, &c. are primes, there being no number except 1, or themselves, by which they can be divided.

(9.) Two numbers are said to be *prime* to each other, when they cannot both be divided by any other number except unity.

Thus, 19 and 27 are prime to each other; for though 27 is divisible both by 3 and 9, yet 19 is not divisible by either of those numbers.

(10.) *Commensurable numbers* are such as have a common measure, or that can be each divided by some other number, without leaving a remainder.

Thus, 6 and 8 are commensurable numbers, being each divisible by 2: also $\frac{2}{3}$, or $\frac{3}{4}$, or $2\sqrt{2}$ and $3\sqrt{2}$ are commensurable, the two former being divisible by $\frac{1}{12}$, and the two latter by $\sqrt{2}$.*

(11.) *Incommensurable numbers* or *quantities* are such that no number, or quantity of the same kind, will measure or divide each of them without leaving a remainder.

Thus, the numbers 15 and 16 are incommensurable; because, though 15 can be divided by 3 and 5, and 16 by 2, 4, and 8, yet there is no single number whatever that will divide or measure both of them.

(12.) *A composite number* is that which can be divided by some number greater than unity; or which consists of two or more factors.

Thus, 12 is a composite number, formed by the product of the two factors 3 and 4, or 2 and 6; by each of which it is divisible.

(13.) *A perfect number* is that which is equal to the sum of all its divisors, or aliquot parts.

Thus, 6, which is the first perfect number, is equal to $1 + 2 + 3$, the sum of its aliquot parts; and the next perfect

---

* Any two fractions, when brought to the same denominator, have the reciprocal of that denominator for their common measure; so that, in this sense, all vulgar fractions may be said to be commensurable.

With respect to the next following definition, Euclid has demonstrated (Lib. x. Prop. 117.) that the side of a square and its diagonal are incommensurable to each other; which is also the case with the diameter and circumference of a circle, as well as many other quantities.

number, 28, is equal to $1+2+4+7+14$, which is the sum of all its aliquot parts.

(14.) *Amicable numbers* are such pairs of numbers as are each equal to the sum of all the divisors, or aliquot parts of the other.

Thus, the first, or least pair of amicable numbers, is 220 and 284; where $1+2+4+5+10+11+20+22+44+55+110$, the sum of the aliquot parts of 220, is equal to 284; and $1+2+4+71+142$, the sum of the aliquot parts of 284, is equal to 220.

*Axiom* 1. Any even number may be represented by $2n$, and any odd number by $2n+1$, or $2n-1$, $n$ being any whole number whatever.

Thus, if $n=7$, then $2n=2\times7=14$, an even number; and $2n+1=2\times7+1=15$, an odd number, or $2n-1=2\times7-1=13$, an odd number.

2. The sum, difference, or product, of any two whole numbers is a whole number; and any multiple of a whole number is a whole number.

## PROPOSITIONS.

(1.) The sum of any number of even numbers is an even number.

For, let $2a$, $2b$, $2c$, &c. be $=$ to any even numbers.
Then will $2a+2b+2c$, &c. be $=$ to their sum.
Which is, evidently, an even number, being divisible by 2. (*Def.* 6.)

*Cor.* Hence, an even number, taken any number of times, is an even number.

(2.) The sum of any even number of odd numbers is an even number.

For, let $2a+1$, $2b+1$, $2c+1$, $2d+1$, &c. be any odd numbers.
Then will $2a+2b+2c+2d$, &c. $+1+1+1+1$, &c. be $=$ to their sum.
And, since $2a+2b+2c+2d$, &c. is an even number, and any even number of units is also an even number, it is plain that the whole must be even.

*Cor.* An odd number, taken any even number of times, is an even number.

(3.) The sum of any odd number of odd numbers is an odd number.

For, let $2a + 1$, $2b + 1$, $2c + 1$, &c. be any odd numbers.

Then $2a + 2b + 2c + $ &c. $+ 1 + 1 + 1 + $ &c. $=$ their sum.

And, since $2a + 2b + 2c + $ &c. is an even number, and any odd number of units is an odd number, the whole must be odd.

*Cor.* An odd number, taken any odd number of times, is an odd number.

(4.) If an even number be taken from an even number, or an odd number from an odd number, the remainder will be even.

For, let $2a$ and $2b$ be any two even numbers, of which $2a$ is the greatest.

Then, since $2a - 2b$ is divisible by 2, it is evidently an even number.

And if $2a + 1$ and $2b + 1$ be any two odd numbers, of which $2a + 1$ is the greatest.

Then, since $(2a + 1) - (2b + 1)$, which is $= 2a - 2b$, is divisible by 2, it is evidently an even number.

(5.) If an even number be taken from an odd number, or an odd number from an even one, the remainder will be odd.

For, let $2a$, $2b$, be two even numbers, and $2c + 1$, $2d + 1$, be two odd numbers, of which $2c + 1$ is greater than $2a$, and $2d + 1$ less than $2b$.

Then, since $2c + 1 - 2a$, or $2c - 2a + 1$, and $2b - (2d + 1)$, or $2b - 2d - 1$, are not divisible by 2, they will evidently be odd numbers.

(6.) If an odd number be multiplied by an odd number, the product will be odd.

For, let $2a + 1$ and $2b + 1$ be any two odd numbers.

Then will $4ab + 2a + 2b + 1$, be $=$ to their product ; which is evidently an odd number, as it is not divisible by 2.

(7.) If an even number be multiplied by any number, either even or odd, the product will be even.

For, let $2a$, $2b$, be any even numbers, and $2c + 1$ an odd number.

Then will their products $2a \times 2b$, and $2a(2c + 1)$ be evidently even numbers, being each divisible by 2.

*Cor.* An odd number is not divisible by an even number.

(8.) If an odd number be divisible by an odd number, the quotient will be odd; and if an even number be divisible by an odd number, the quotient will be even.

For, let $\dfrac{2a + 1}{2b + 1} = q$ ; then will $2a + 1 = (2b + 1)q$.

N

And, because $2a + 1$ and $2b + 1$ are odd numbers, $q$ must also be an odd number. (Prop. 6.)

Again, let $\dfrac{2a}{2b + 1} = q$; then will $2a = (2b + 1) \times q$.

And, because $2b + 1$ is odd, and $2a$ is even, $q$ must also be even. (Prop. 7.)

(9.) If an odd number divides an even number, it will also divide the half of it.

For, let $\dfrac{2a}{2b + 1} = q$; then $\dfrac{a}{2b + 1} = \dfrac{q}{2}$.

And since $q$ is an even number (Prop. 8.), $\frac{1}{2}q$, or its equal $\dfrac{a}{2b + 1}$, must be a whole number. (Def. 6.)

(10.) If one number divides another, it will also divide any multiple of it.

For, let $n =$ be any number whatever, and put $\dfrac{a}{b} = q$; then, by multiplying each of the terms by $n$, the former expression will become $\dfrac{na}{b} = nq$:

And since $q$ is a whole number (by hyp.), $nq$, or its equal $\dfrac{na}{b}$, must also be a whole number. (Ax. 2.)

(11.) If a number divide the whole of any number, and a part of it, it will also divide the remaining part.

For, since $\dfrac{a + b}{c}$ and $\dfrac{a}{c}$ are each of them the whole numbers (by hyp.),

$\dfrac{a + b}{c} - \dfrac{a}{c} = \dfrac{b}{c}$ is also a whole number. (Ax. 2.)

(12.) If a number divide two other numbers, it will also divide their sum and difference.

For since $\dfrac{a}{c}$ and $\dfrac{b}{c}$ are each of them whole numbers (by hyp),

their sum and difference $\dfrac{a + b}{c}$ and $\dfrac{a - b}{c}$ must be also whole numbers. (Ax. 2.)

13.) The difference of the squares of any two numbers is divisible both by their sum and difference.

For $(a^2 - b^2) \div (a - b)$, or $\dfrac{a^2 - b^2}{a - b} = a + b$.

And $(a^2 - b^2) \div (a + b)$, or $\dfrac{a^2 - b^2}{a + b} = a - b$.

(14.) The sum of the cubes of any two numbers is divisible by the sum of these numbers; and the difference of their cubes is divisible by the difference of the numbers.*

For, $(a^3 + b^3) \div (a + b)$, or $\dfrac{a^3 + b^3}{a + b}, = a^2 - ab + b^2$.

And $(a^3 - b^3) \div (a - b)$, or $\dfrac{a^3 - b^3}{a - b}, = a^2 + ab + b^2$.

(15.) If a square number divide a square number, or a cube a cube, &c., the root will also divide the root.

For, $\dfrac{a^2}{b^2}, \dfrac{a^3}{b^3},$ and $\dfrac{a^n}{b^n}$, are each of them whole numbers (by hyp.);

Whence $\dfrac{a}{b}$ must also be a whole number, or otherwise whole

numbers, multiplied by whole numbers, would not produce whole numbers.

*Cor.* Since 10 is divisible by 2 and by 5; $10^n$ is divisible by $2^n$ and $5^n$.

(16.) The product of two square numbers is a square number, and the product of two cube numbers is a cube number, &c.

Thus, $a^2 \times a^2 = a^4$, the square root of which is $a^2$.
And $a^3 \times a^3 = a^6$, the cube root of which is $a^2$.
Also $a^n \times a^n = a^{2n}$, the $n$th root of which $a^2$.

*Cor.* Every power of a square number is a square number, and every power of a cube number is a cube, &c.

But the product of a square or a cube, by a number that is not a square, or a cube, can never be a square, or a cube, &c.

(17.) The sum of two numbers, differing by unity, is equal to the difference of their squares.

---

* $a^n + b^n$ is divisible by $a + b$, when $n$ is any odd number; and $a^n - b^n$ is divisible by $a + b$, when $n$ is an even number.

Also $a^n - b^n$ is divisible by $a - b$, when $n$ is any whole number whatever. Thus, $\dfrac{a^n - b^n}{a - b} = a^{n-1} + ba^{n-2} + b^2 a^{n-3} + b^3 a^{n-4} \cdots b^{n-2} a + b^{n-1}$.

Let $a$ and $a + 1$ be the two numbers.

Then $2a + 1 = $ sum; and $(a + 1)^2 - a = a^2 + 2a + 1 - a^2 = 2a + 1 - $ difference of their squares.

*Cor.* The differences of the squares, $0^2$, $1^2$, $2^2$, $3^2$, $4^2$, $5^2$, &c. are the odd numbers, 1, 3, 5, 7, 9, &c.

(18.) If an odd number ($a$) be prime to any other number ($b$), it will also be prime to the double of it ($2b$).

For no even number can divide $a$ (Cor. Prop. 7.); and any odd number that divides $a$ and $2b$ will also divide $a$ and $b$. (Prop. 9.)

In this case, therefore, $a$ and $b$ would not be prime to each other, which is contrary to the hypothesis.

(19.) If each of two numbers ($a$, $b$) be prime to a third, $c$, their product ($ab$) will also be prime to $c$.

For if not, let $d$ be a prime divisor of $ab$ and $c$, and put $\dfrac{ab}{d} = n$; in which case $\dfrac{a}{d} = \dfrac{n}{b}$.

Then, because $d$ cannot be a divisor of $a$ or $b$, since they are each prime to $c$, $\dfrac{a}{d}$ will be a fraction in its lowest terms.

And if $\dfrac{n}{b}$ is not so, let $d'$ be the greatest common divisor of $n$ and $b$.

Then, since $\dfrac{a}{d} = \dfrac{n}{b} = \dfrac{d'r}{d'r'} = \dfrac{r}{r'}$, the first and last of these fractions must be identical, as they are both irreducible.

Hence we have $a = r$, and $d = r'$; and $b = d'r = dd''$, or $\dfrac{b}{d} = d''$.

a whole number, which is absurd; since $d$ has been shown not to be a divisor of $b$.

Therefore, if $a$ and $b$ be each prime to $c$, $ab$ will also be prime to $c$.

(20.) If one number ($a$) be prime to another ($b$), its square ($a^2$), cube ($a^3$), or any other power, will also be prime to it.

For, since $a$ and $b$ have no common factor,

Neither $a \times a$ (or $a^2$), nor $b$, can have a common factor;

Consequently, they must be primes; and the same will hold for any other power.

(21.) If two numbers ($a$ and $b$) be prime to each other, their sum ($a + b$) will also be prime to either of them.

For, if not, let $d$ be the common divisor of $a$ and $a + b$; then it will also divide the remaining part $b$. (Prop. 11.)

Hence the number $a$ would not be prime to $b$; which is contrary to the hypothesis.

*Cor.* If a number $(a+b)$ be prime to one of its parts $(a)$, it will also be prime to the remaining part $(b)$.

(22.) If $n$ be made to represent any of the natural numbers, 1, 2, 3, 4, 5, &c., then will $6n-1$ and $6n+1$ constitute a series which contains all the prime numbers above 3.

> Thus, if 1, 2, 3, 5, 7, &c. be substituted for $n$, we shall have 5, 7, 11, 13, 17, 19, 29, 31, 41, 43, &c. prime numbers.
>
> But it must be observed, that neither $6n-1$ nor $6n+1$ are always prime numbers, nor has any general expression yet been found that answers this purpose.*

(23.) All the powers of any number ending in 5 will end in 5; and if a number end in 6, all its powers will end in 6.

> For $5 \times 5 = 25$; and $6 \times 6 = 36$, and so on.

(24.) Every square number ends with one of the figures, 1, 4, 5, 6, or 9; or with an even number of ciphers, preceded by one of these figures.

> This will appear by squaring all the natural numbers to 10.
>
> And from the same proposition it follows, that no number ending with 2, 3, 7, or 8, can be a square.

(25.) A cube number may end with any of the natural numbers, 1, 2, 3, 4, 5, 6, 7, 8, 9, or 0.

> This will, likewise, appear by cubing those numbers.

*Note.* There is no such thing as the exact square root of 2, 3, 5, 6, 7, 8, 10, &c., nor the exact cube root of 2, 3, 4, 5, 6, 7, 9, &c.; these being called surds, or irrational numbers.

(26.) Any even square number is divisible by 4, and any even cube number by 8.

> For, since the square and cube are both even (by hyp.), the root must be even. (Prop. 7.)
>
> Let, therefore, $2n$ be that root; then $4n^2$ is the square of it, and $8n^3$ its cube, which are evidently divisible by 4 and 8.

(27.) An odd square number, when divided by 4, will leave a remainder of 1.

> For, since the root of an odd square number is odd (Prop. 6.), let $2n+1$ be that root; then its square $4n^n + 4n + 1$, being divided by 4, leaves 1.†

---

* All prime numbers, except 2, are odd, and have 1, 3, 7, or 9, in the place of units, 2 and 5 is excepted.

The greatest prime number known at present is $2^{31} - 1$, or 2147483647, which was discovered by *Euler.*

† It may be here further remarked, that a square number cannot end with an odd number of ciphers.

N 3

(28.) All square numbers are of one of the forms $4n$, or $4n+1$; $n$ being any whole number whatever.

> For the roots of all even squares are of the form $2n$ (Prop. 7.), and consequently their squares are of the form $4n^2$, or $4n$;
>
> Also the roots of all odd squares are of the form $2n+1$ (Prop. 6.), and therefore their squares are of the form $4n^2 + 4n + 1$.
>
> And as this quantity, when divided by 4, leaves a remainder of 1, it is evident that all odd squares are of the form $4n+1$.

*Cor.* If any number, when divided by 4, leaves a remainder of 2 or 3, that number cannot be a square.

(29.) No square number can be contained under the form of any repeating digit.

> For, since it has been shown, in Prop. 24., that no square number can end in 2, 3, 7, or 8, therefore no repetend of these numbers can be a square.
>
> And because any number of 1's or 5's, divided by 4, leaves 3 for a remainder, a repetend of this kind cannot be a square.
>
> Also, because any number of 6's, when divided by 4, leaves 2 for a remainder, therefore neither can this be a square. (Prop. 28.)
>
> And since every repetend of 4 or 9 is equal to a repetend of units, multiplied by 4 or 9, every such number must be equal to the product of two factors, one of which is a square, and the other not; therefore in this case, also, the product cannot be a square.
>
> Hence no repetend of any digit is square.

(30.) If, then, last $n$ digits of any number be divisible by $2^n$, the number itself is divisible by $2^n$.

> For any number whatever may be expressed under the form $a \times 10^n +$ the number expressed by the last $n$ digits.
>
> Wherefore, since $10^n$ is divisible by $2^n$ (Cor. Prop. 15.), it is evident, that when the last $n$ digits are divisible by $2^n$, the number itself ($a + 10^n +$ the number expressed by the last $n$ digits) is also divisible by $2^n$.

*Cor.* Hence, if the last two digits of any number be divisible by 4, the number itself is divisible by 4; also if the last three digits be divisible by 8, the number itself is divisible by 8; and so on.

---

Also, if the last figure of a square number be an odd number, the last but one will be an even number; and if the last figure be an even number, the last but one will be odd, except when it is 4.

(31.) If the sum of the digits of any number be divisible by 3 or 9, the number itself will be divisible by 3 or 9.

This has been shown in the former part of the work; but it may be proved otherwise, thus:

Any number may be expressed by the form $a10^n + b10^{n-1} + c10^{n-2} + d10^{n-3} + \&c. \dots \dots + r10^{n-n}$, where $a, b, c, d, \&c.$ are the digits of which the number is composed.

And since every power of 10, when divided by 3 or 9, leaves 1 for a remainder, it is evident that the number itself, when so divided, will leave the same remainder as the sum of its digits $(a + b + c + d + \&c. \dots . + r)$.

(32.) A number is divisible by 11, when the sum of the 1st, 3rd, 5th, &c. digits is equal to the sum of the 2nd, 4th, 6th, &c. digits.

For, let $a, b, c, d, e, \&c.$ represent the digits of which any number is composed.

Then this number may be expressed by $a10^n + b10^{n-1} + c10^{n-2} + d10^{n-3} + e10^{n-4} + \&c.$

And since all even powers of 10, when divided by 11, leave $+1$ for a remainder, it is evident that the sum of all the even terms in the above form, when so divided, will leave the same remainder as the sum of the digits belonging to those terms.

Also, all odd powers of 10, when divided by 11, leave $-1$ for remainder; whence, the sum of the odd terms, in the above form, when so divided, will also leave the same remainder as the sum of the digits belonging to them.

But, as this latter remainder is negative, and the former positive, they will mutually destroy each other, when their sums are equal; that is, when the sum of the digits in the even places is equal to the sum of those in the odd places.

Consequently, the number itself, in that case, is divisible by 11.

(33.) If a number be not divisible by some number, which is either equal to or less than its square root, it is a prime number, or one that has no divisor.

For every number that is divisible by another must consist of two factors, one of which is the divisor and the other the quotient.

And as one of these must be equal to or less than the square root of the proposed number, and the other equal to or greater than that root, it is plain that if the number cannot be divided by the former of these, it cannot be divided by the latter.

To this we may add, that it will only be necessary to try the division by the several prime numbers, up to the square root of the given number; for if it be divisible by a composite number, it is evidently also divisible by the prime factors of that number.

*Cor.* Hence if a number N be not divisible by any of the

prime numbers that are equal to or less than $\sqrt{N}$, N is a prime number.

(34.) The number of factors, or divisors, of any given number, may be found as follows:

Divide the number, and the several quotients that arise, by 2, as often as can be done; then the last quotient by 3, in the same manner; and so on, in order, with the smallest prime numbers 5, 7, 11, &c. till the quotient is one; then will these numbers be all the prime divisors of the given number.

And if every two, every three, every four, &c. of the several figures made use of be multiplied together, the results will give the compound divisors; which, together with the former, will be all the divisors of the given number.

Thus, if it were required to find all the divisors of 360, we shall have, by the rule,

$$\frac{2}{360} \left| \frac{2}{180} \right| \frac{2}{90} \left| \frac{3}{45} \right| \frac{3}{15} \left| \frac{5}{5} \right| 1$$

when 2, 3, and 5 are the prime divisors of 360;

And if the products of every two, every three, &c. of the numbers 2, 2, 2, 3, 3, and 5, above used, be taken, we shall have, when they are united to the former,

1, 2, 3, 4, 5, 6, 8, 9, 10, 12, 15, 18, 20, 24, 30,
36, 40, 45, 60, 72, 90, 120, 180, and 360,

which are all the divisors of 360; being 24 in number.

*Note.* It is evident, from the above problem, that any number N may be expressed by the form $a^m$, $b^n$, $c^r$, $d^s$, &c.; where $a$, $b$, $c$, $d$, &c. are its prime factors.

And it can be shown that the number of its divisors is expressed by the formula,

$$(m+1)\ (n+1)\ (r+1)\ (s+1),\ \&c.$$

Also all the divisors of N may be determined from the formula, $(1 + a + a^2 + a^3 + \&c.\ \text{to}\ a^m)\ (1 + b + b^2 + \&c.\ \text{to}\ b^n)\ (1 + c + c^2 + \&c.\ \text{to}\ c^r)\ (1 + d + d^2 + \&c.\ \text{to}\ d^s)\ \&c.$ by multiplying them together, after the manner of compound multiplication in Algebra, and taking the several terms of the product.

(35.) The sum of any number of consecutive cubes, beginning with unity, is a square, the root of which is equal to the sum of the roots of the cubes.*

For the sum of the series $1^3 + 2^3 + 3^3 + \&c. \ldots + n^3$ is shown,

---

* It has been shown by EULER, LEGENDRE, and other writers on the Diophantine Algebra, that neither the sum nor the difference of two cubes can be a cube; nor the sum nor the difference of two biquadrates, a biquadrate.

by the writers on algebra, to be equal to $\dfrac{n^4 + 2n^3 + n^2}{4} = \left(\dfrac{n^2 + n}{2}\right)^2$,

and $\dfrac{n^2 + n}{2} = 1 + 2 + 3 + 4 + \&c.$ to $n$, as was to be proved.

(36.) If $n$ be made to denote any number whatever, then $(2^n - 1)2^{n-1}$ is a perfect number, whenever $2^n - 1$ is a prime number.

> The proof of this is easily deduced from Euclid's Elements, (B. IX. last Prop.) where it is shown, that if the geometrical series, 1, 2, 4, 8, 16, 32, &c. be continued to such a number of terms as that their sum shall be a prime number, then the product of this sum by the last term of the series will be a perfect number.
>
> That is, since $1 + 2 + 2^2 + 2^3 + 2^4 + 2^5 + \&c. \ldots$ to $2^{n-1}$ is $= 2^n - 1$, it follows that $(2^n - 1)2^{n-1}$ is a perfect number, whenever $2^n - 1$ is a prime number.

*Note.* The first eight perfect numbers, with their factors and products, are as below; being all that are known at present.

| | |
|---|---|
| 6 | $(2^2 - 1)2$ |
| 28 | $(2^3 - 1)2^2$ |
| 496 | $(2^5 - 1)2^4$ |
| 8128 | $(2^7 - 1)2^6$ |
| 33550336 | $(2^{13} - 1)2^{12}$ |
| 8589869056 | $(2^{17} - 1)2^{16}$ |
| 137438691328 | $(2^{19} - 1)2^{29}$ |
| 2305843008139952128 | $(2^{31} - 1)2^{30}$ |

(37.) If $a$ be put $= 2$, and $n$ be some integer number, such that $3a^n - 1$, $6a^n - 1$, and $18a^{2n} - 1$ are all prime numbers, then $(18a^{2n} - 1) \times 2a^n$ will be one of two amicable numbers, of which the sum of the aliquot parts of one will be equal to the other.

This property is demonstrated by SCHOOTEN, sect. 9. of his *Exercitationes Mathematicæ*, who also gave the three following pairs of these numbers :

220 and 284

17296 and 18416

9363584 and 9437056.

But EULER, whose attention was directed to almost every subject of an analytical investigation, has given a table of 63 pairs of amicable numbers, in a miscellaneous tract, pub-

lished in 1750 ; which may be all seen in the Appendix to
LEYBOURN's publication of the Mathematical Questions proposed in the *Ladies' Diary*.   (*See* vol. iv. p. 342.)

(38.) Every number is either a square, or the sum of two,
three, or four squares.

$$\text{Thus } 5 = 4 + 1, \; 30 = 25 + 4 + 1, \; 63 = 49 + 9 + 4 + 1,$$
$$\text{or, } 36 + 25 + 1 + 1.$$

This curious property has been demonstrated generally by
EULER, LAGRANGE, LEGENDRE, and others; and lately, in a
manner peculiar to himself, by GAUSS, a German analyst of
considerable reputation, in a work entitled *Disquisitiones
Arithmeticæ*; which has since been translated into French by
M. POULLET DELISLE.   The investigation, however, is of too
abstract a nature to be inserted in a work like the present.

# Arithmetical Recreations,

CONSISTING OF A SELECT COLLECTION OF SOME OF THE MOST
CURIOUS AND ENTERTAINING QUESTIONS RELATING TO
NUMBERS.

(1.) What is $\frac{1}{2}$ the quarter of ?                     *Ans.* 2.

(2.) If the third of 6 be 3, what must the fourth of 20 be ?
                                                *Ans.* $7\frac{1}{2}$.

(3.) If the half of 5 be 7, what part of 9 will be 11 ?
                                                *Ans.* $\frac{55}{126}$ of 9.

(4.) Place four 9's so that their sum shall be 100.
                                                *Ans.* $99\frac{9}{9} = 100$.

(5.) Place four 5's so that their sum shall be $6\frac{1}{2}$.
                                                *Ans.* $5 \cdot 5 + \frac{5}{5} = 6\frac{1}{2}$.

(6.) What part of threepence is a third part of twopence?
                                                *Ans.* $\frac{2}{9}$ of 3*d.*

(7.) If a herring and a half cost three halfpence, how many
can be had for a shilling ?                     *Ans.* 12.

(8.) John was born when Thomas was 18 years of age:
how old will Thomas be when John is 72 ?        *Ans.* 90.

(9.) If 12 apples be worth as much as 21 pears, and 3
pears cost a penny; what is the price of 100 apples?
                                                *Ans.* $58\frac{1}{3}d.$

(10.) Place the 9 digits in two different ways, so that, in
one case, their sum shall be 17, and in the other 31.
                                                *See the Key.*

(11.) Fifteen years ago I was three times as old as my eldest son, but am now only twice as old; what are our present ages? *Ans.* 60 *and* 30.

(12.) It is required to find such a number that 9 shall be two thirds of it. *Ans.* 13½.

(13.) What number is that, the third and fourth parts of which, taken together, is 24½? *Ans.* 42.

(14.) It is required to find four such weights as will weigh any number of pounds, from 1 lb. to 40 lbs.

*Ans.* 1*lb.*, 3*lb.*, 9*lb.*, 27*lb.*

(15.) Place the 9 digits so that the sum of the odd digits shall be equal to the sum of the even ones. *See the Key.*

(16.) A snail, in going up a maypole, 20 feet high, ascended 8 feet every day, and came down again 4 feet every night: how long would it be in getting to the top of the pole?

*Ans.* 4 *days.*

(17.) A Cheshire cheese, being put into one of the scales of a false balance, was found to weigh 16 lbs.; and when put into the other only 9 lbs; what was its true weight?

*Ans.* 12*lb.*

(18.) A company at a tavern spent 7*l.* 4*s.*, and each of them had as many shillings to pay as there were persons in company: how many persons were there? *Ans.* 12.

(19.) A hundred hurdles may be so placed as to enclose 200 sheep, and with two hurdles more the fold may be made to hold 400; how is this to be done? *See the Key.*

(20.) How must a board that is 16 inches long and 9 inches broad be cut into two such parts, that when they are joined together they shall form a square? *See the Key.*

(21.) A market-woman being asked how many eggs she had in her basket; said, If I had as many more, half as many more, and thirteen eggs and a half, I should have 136: how many had she? *Ans.* 49.

(22.) A person left 100*l.* to be distributed among three poor widows, desiring that the shares of the eldest, the middle-aged one, and the youngest, should be in the proportion of ½, ⅓, and ¼: how is this to be divided between them?

*Ans.* 46$\frac{2}{13}$*l.*, 30$\frac{10}{13}$*l.*, and 23$\frac{1}{13}$*l.*

(23.) An Indian gardener being desirous of presenting a basket of oranges, of a peculiar quality, to the Nawab, had seven gates to pass before he could reach the audience chamber; at the first of which he was obliged to give half the number he had to the porter, at the second half of what remained, and so on ; when, at length, coming into the presence of the prince, he found he had only one orange left: how many had he at first? *Ans.* 128.

(24.) A person having an 8-gallon bottle of choice wine, wishes to part it equally between two friends, but has nothing but a 5-gallon bottle and a 3-gallon bottle to measure it with ; now, with these 3 bottles only, how can this be done?

*See the Key.*

(25.) Seven out of 21 bottles being full of wine, 7 half full, and 7 empty, it is required to distribute them among 3 persons, so that each person shall have the same quantity of wine, and the same number of bottles. *See the Key.*

(26.) Supposing there are more persons in the world than any one of them has hairs upon his head, it then follows, as a necessary consequence, that some two of these, at least, must have exactly the same number of hairs on their heads, to a hair ; required the proof. *See the Key.*

(27.) Three persons bought a quantity of sugar, weighing 51 lbs., which they wish to part equally between them, but having only a 4 lb. weight and a 7 lb. weight, it is required to find how this can be done? *See the Key.*

(28.) A dishonest butler stole every day, from his master's cellar, a quart of wine from a particular cask, containing 42 gallons, and supplied its place each time with an equal quantity of water ; when at the end of 30 days the theft was discovered, and the butler discharged : what quantity of wine did he rob his master of, and how much remained in the cask?

*Ans.* 140·448 *quarts left, and* 27·522 *taken away.*

(29.) A gentleman left by will 11000*l.* between his widow, two sons, and three daughters, directing that the mother should have double the share of a son and a son double the share of a daughter : how is this to be divided?

*Ans. Mother's share* 4000*l.*, *each of the two son's shares* 2000*l.*, *and each daughter's share* 1000*l.*

(30.) A person being asked what o'clock it was, said, It is exactly between 8 and 9, and the hour and minute hands are together : what was the time? *Ans.* $43\frac{7}{11}$ *minutes after* 8.

(31.) How must the nine digits 1, 2, 3, 4, 5, 6, 7, 8, 9, be placed in the form of a square, so that when reckoned upwards, downwards, horizontally, and diagonally, the sum of each row shall be 15? *See the Key.*

(32.) I owe my friend a shilling, and as he has nothing about him but louis-d'ors, worth 17s. each, and I have nothing but guineas worth 21s. each, it is required to find how an exchange between us must be managed, so that I may just acquit myself of the debt? *Ans. I must give* 13 *guineas, and receive* 16 *louis-d'ors.*

(33.) The eldest of three sisters having 50 eggs to dispose of, the next 30, and the youngest 10, they so contrive it, that each of them sold their eggs at the same rate, and each got the same sum of money for them: how was this done?

*See the Key.*

(34.) Being desirous of planting 2000 elms in 15 rows, so that the trees in each row may be 20 feet asunder: I desire to know how long the grove will be? *Ans.* 2666⅔ *feet.*

(35.) Supposing 26 hurdles can be placed in a rectangular form, so as to enclose 40 square yards of ground, how can they be placed, when two of them are taken away, so as to enclose 120 square yards? *See the Key.*

(36.) A general, after a battle, found, upon reviewing his troops, that a third part of them had been killed, a fourth part taken prisoners, and a fifth part had run away; so that he had only 1300 men left: how many had he at first?

*Ans.* 6000.

(37.) Three men, having each an equal number of oranges, were met by nine women, who asked for some of them: upon which each man having given to each of the women the same number, it was found that both men and women had now equal shares: how many had the men at first? *See the Key.*

(38.) A gentleman gave to the first of three poor persons that he met half the number of shillings he had about him, and one shilling more; to the second half what remained and two shillings more; and to the third half what now remained and three shillings more, after which he found he had only one shilling left; how many of them had he at first?

*Ans.* 42.

(39.) A mule and an ass travelling together, the ass began to complain that her burden was too heavy. "Lazy animal," said the mule, "you have little reason to grumble; for if I take one of your bags, I shall have twice as many as you, and if I give you one of mine, we shall then have only an equal number;" with how many bags were each loaded?

*Ans. Mule* 7, *Ass* 5.

(40.) The sum of 212*l.* 14*s.* 7*d.* is to be divided among a captain, four men, and a boy; the captain is to have a share and a half, the men each a share, and the boy half a share: what ought each person to receive? *Ans. Captain,* 53*l.* 3*s.* 7¾*d.; men,* 141*l.* 16*s.* 4⅔*d.; boy,* 17*l.* 14*s.* 6$\frac{7}{12}$*d.*

(41.) A person has a fox, a goose, and a peck of oats, to carry over a river; but, on account of the smallness of the boat, he can only transport them one at a time: now how can this be done, so as not to leave the fox with the goose, nor the goose with the oats? *See the Key.*

(42.) A square convent has a cell in each of its sides, and one in each corner; in what manner may a number of nuns be disposed of in them, so that a blind abbess, who occupies a cell in the centre, shall always find, whenever she visits them, 9 in each row, and yet some of them may have gone out, or a certain number of women may have been introduced, so as to vary the number from 20 to 32? *See the Key.*

(43.) A party of soldiers, consisting of 40 men, having been quartered in a certain district, where they had rendered themselves odious by theft and outrageous conduct, the commanding officer was determined to have every tenth man shot, as a terror to the rest of the army; but knowing, from their general characters, which of them had been the ringleaders, desires to be informed how they may be placed in a circular manner, so that by taking every tenth of them in succession, the lot may fall upon the most culpable.

*See the Key.*

(44.) Three jealous husbands and their wives having to cross a river find a boat without its owner, which can only carry two persons at a time: in what manner, then, can these six persons transport themselves over, by pairs, so that none of the women shall be left in company with any of the men, except when her husband is present? *See the Key.*

(45.) A person having by accident broken a basket of eggs, offered to pay for them upon the spot, if the owner could tell how many he had; to which he replied, that he only knew there were between 50 and 100, and that when he counted them by 2's and 3's at a time none remained; but when he counted them by 5 at a time, there were 3 remaining: how many eggs had he? *Ans.* 78.

(46.) A poor woman carrying a basket of apples, was met by 3 boys, the first of whom bought half of what she had, and then gave her back 10; the second bought a third of what remained and gave her back 2; and the third bought half of what she had now left and returned her 1; after which she found she had 12 apples remaining: what number had she at first? *Ans.* 40.

(47.) A market-woman bought 120 apples at 2 a penny, and 120 more, of another sort, at 3 a penny; but not liking her bargain, she mixed them together, and sold them out again at 5 for two-pence, thinking she should get the same sum; but on counting her money, she found to her surprise, that she had lost four-pence: how did this happen?

*See the Key.*

(48.) A person bought 100 animals, consisting of calves, pigs, and geese, for 100*l.*; the calves cost him 5*l.* a piece, the pigs 1*l.* a piece, and the geese a crown a piece: how many of each sort did he buy? *See the Key.*

(49.) Two travellers, one of whom had with him five bottles of wine, and the other three, were joined by a third person, who, after the wine was drunk, left 8*s.* for his just share of it: how is this to be divided between the other two?

*Ans. The former must receive 7s. and the latter 1s.*

(50.) A person went out with a certain number of guineas about him, in order to purchase necessaries at different shops; at the first of these he expended half the number he had and half a guinea more; at the second half the remainder and half a guinea more; and so on at a third and fourth shop: at the last of which, having paid for his articles, he found he had laid out all his money: how much had he at first?

*Ans.* 15 *guineas.*

(51.) A rajah's audience chamber has eight doors, which can be opened one at a time, 2 at a time, 3 at a time, and so on, through the whole number, till they are all opened together; how many times can this be done? *Ans.* 19173960.

**THE END.**

LONDON:
Spottiswoodes and Shaw,
New-street-Square.

CPSIA information can be obtained at www.ICGtesting.com
Printed in the USA
LVOW03s0719161015

458484LV00007BA/68/P

9 781148 607184